Take Me to My Paradise

Take Me to My Paradise

TOURISM AND NATIONALISM IN THE BRITISH VIRGIN ISLANDS

COLLEEN BALLERINO COHEN

RUTGERS UNIVERSITY PRESS
New Brunswick, New Jersey, and London

Library of Congress Cataloging-in-Publication Data

Cohen, Colleen Ballerino.
    Take me to my paradise : tourism and nationalism in the British Virgin Islands /
Colleen Ballerino Cohen.
        p.   cm.
    Includes bibliographical references and index.
    ISBN 978–0–8135–4809–8 (hardcover : alk. paper) —
    ISBN 978–0–8135–4810–4 (pbk. : alk. paper)
        1. Tourism—British Virgin Islands. 2. Culture and tourism—British Virgin
Islands. 3. Nationalism—British Virgin Islands. 4. British Virgin Islands—Social life
and customs. I. Title.
    G155.B73C65 2010
    972.97'25—dc22
                                                    2009052304

A British Cataloging-in-Publication record for this book
is available from the British Library.

Visit our Web site: http://rutgerspress.rutgers.edu

Manufactured in the United States of America

Typesetting: Jack Donner, BookType

I dedicate this book to the memory
of Kenneth "Kenne" Renaldo Hodge (1953–2001).
Brother, friend, poet. And teacher without peer.

I dream, I dream, you understand,
Of a day when freedom
Won't be a contract of compromise
Negotiated among selfish men.
And I will make a reality
The ticketed pathway necessary,
To travel between this domiciled island
And the place where my ancestors came from.
Abyssinia! Ethiopia! Africa!
I've got my ticket
I'm on my way.

From "A Ticket Home," by Kenne Hodge, 1999

Contents

ILLUSTRATIONS

ACKNOWLEDGMENTS

THIS BOOK WOULD NOT HAVE BEEN POSSIBLE without the support of the people in the British Virgin Islands who taught me, schooled me, and invited me into their lives. I acknowledge as many of them as possible, and offer apologies to anyone I fail to mention. I also thank in advance my British Virgin Islands readers for their engagement with the ideas and analyses that I present here, especially knowing that a book about tourism can never convey the fullness, richness, and complexity of their lived experiences.

Several people played key roles from the earliest stages of my research until today and I am particularly indebted to them for their support, invigorating conversation, clear-eyed guidance, and enduring friendship: Dr. Charles Wheatley, Eileene Parsons, Dr. Michael O'Neal, and Elmore Stoutt. I thank Eugenie Todman-Smith for providing a home for my students and for educating me on the details of electoral reform; Janice Braithwaite-Edwards and Keith Dawson for their insights into the BVI Tourist Board (and Janice for her companionship during many rainy nights at Festival Village); Gil Trott for courage; and Eugenia O'Neal and Dr. Patricia Turnbull for their collegiality and encouragement, particularly on issues related to gender. For enabling my research on Festival and queen shows I thank Ivy O'Neal, Luce Hodge-Smith, Patsy Lake, Monica Allen, Lynette Harrigan, Claudette Francis, Zoe Walcott, Floyd Penn, Rita Kirketerp, and Ann Lennard; I also thank BJ, Joseph John, and the late Leslie De Castro for introducing me to pan; the moco jumbie crew of Kevin "Binghy" Barry, Skelly, Charlie, and Trevor for inviting me into the magic world of stilt dancing; George Lewis and calypsonian Vanclair "Benji V" Benjamin for teaching me what to listen for; Claudia Colli and Paul Backshall for enabling my work in *The BVI Welcome Guide* archive; and the entire VITV crew for our many years of Festival coverage together, especially Dave Douglas, Eno Soman, Robbie Soman, Floyd Sutton, Chris Stevens, and Ludwell Archer. I thank Lorna Smith and Beverly Hodge for their support in the early years of my research, and especially for aiding my work with the late Hon. H. Lavity Stoutt, to whom I am also indebted for his generosity in sharing with me his life story. Special thanks are due Jennie Wheatley, Dr. Patricia Turnbull, and Dr. Quincy Lettsome for their poetry (and Jennie Wheatley for her tarts and straw plaiting lessons); Dr. Karl Dawson, Emma Baker, Janice Dawson, Sauda Smith, Dr. Christine Dawson-Hodge, Judith Vanterpool, Eugenie Glasgow, Marietta Bodley, LuVerne Vanterpool Baptiste, Michael "Mitch" Kent, and Delight Charles at the H. Lavity Stoutt Community College for their help on various components of my research; and the students in my Cultural Tourism course at the H. Lavity Stoutt Community College— Abbarah Brown, Cara Christopher, Dwynel Davis, Enya Douglas, Olympia Fahie, and Sherene Liburd—for their insights and forthrightness. Edward Wheatley, Stanley Hodge, Linda Nibbs, Esther Walcott, Joseph Hodge, and Segrid Leslie shared their understanding of the BVI with me well before I started formal research. Cassandra Lanns, Quito Rymer, Elmore and Gera-nium Stoutt, Vivian and Christopher Morris, Ethlyn and Neville Burke, Patricia Turnbull, Charles and Jennie Wheatley, Lloyd Wheatley, Jacque-line Albright, Sauda, Joseph, and Esteban Smith, Cheryl Johnson, Carvin Malone, and Eldred Williams provide the friendship that nourishes the soul. Finally, I express special gratitude to the family that embraces me as a "child of the house": the late Irene Todman-Hodge and Henry Hodge; the Todman sisters and brothers Jennie, Gracie, Violet, Harris, Walter, and Cromwell and their families; Robert and Prudence Mathavious; Algernon and Agnes Mathavious; Vessilie Mathavious; Ray and Renee Barry; Allen Hodge; and David "Timba" Turnbull.

Four British Virgin Islanders contributed to this text in ways that deserve special mention. Dr. Michael O'Neal pioneered work on BVI tourism in his 1983 dissertation, and the transcripts from a symposium on tourism and social change that he convened in 1982 are of inestimable historic value. I draw from this transcript and from Dr. O'Neal's assessment of key moments in the early years of BVI tourism development in chapter 3. My discussion in chapter 8 of the contradictory positions of individuals who perform culture for a tourist and nationalist audience alike benefited from the insights of Dr. Patricia Turnbull's 2002 dissertation on the practice of tourism in the BVI as well as from discussions we had over the years. Dr. Charles Wheatley and I have been friends and colleagues since I first started research in the BVI, during which time we had countless discussions about BVI culture and politics. Dr. Wheatley and I co-wrote a paper on race and nationalism for presentation at an American Ethnological Society meeting in 1994, and this paper is the basis for the discussion of race, ethnicity, and categories of belonging in chapter 4. In 1994 I began a collaboration with British Virgin Islander Kenne Hodge, which resulted in the production of three ethnographic videos about the British Virgin Islands. Kenne Hodge and his many relatives also provided a family for me when I was in the

British Virgin Islands, and a home for my boxes of stored belongings when I was away. When Kenne Hodge died of cancer in 2001 he left me his papers, his poems, and a large extended British Virgin Islands family. His death also left me without one of my best friends. Kenne Hodge's contributions to this text are registered in field notes in which he appears as an interlocutor and a teacher, and in chapter 5, where I detail our collaboration on the first of our three videos. I dedicate this book to his memory.

I also benefited from the support and counsel of many people in the United States. Fran Mascia-Lees and Bill Maurer deserve special thanks for their companionship, collegiality, inspiration, and insights when they were in the BVI with me during various stages of my research. Fran Mascia-Lees and I also co-authored an article that is the basis of some of the discussion in chapter 3, and I always benefit from her sharp analytical mind. I thank Paul Stoller, Martha Kaplan, Barbara Page, Diane Harriford, Lucy Johnson, and John Kelly for their early encouragement of this work; Jeff Himpele and Rain Breaw for their encouragement and support of my video work; Joan Goodkind, Candice Lowe, Tom Porcello, Saul Mercado, Sauda Smith, and Tyrone Simpson for their feedback at various stages of this project; Meg Stewart for the map of the BVI that appears in the book and Karen Buckman for her wonderful cover photo; Terri Cronk for her conscientious and generous help with administrative details; Zoe Bachman and Sandra Carey for their work on the index; Margaret Case for her fine editorial eye and Marlie Wasserman for her patience and support of this project. I also thank the anonymous reviewers whose careful reading and incisive comments helped me sharpen the argument in this book. Portions of this book are extracted and revised from previously published articles and are reproduced with kind permission of *Social Analysis* and Berghahn Books (Cohen and Mascia Lees 1993), *The Annals of Tourism Research* (Cohen 1995), and the *American Ethnologist* and the *American Anthropological Association* (Cohen 1998).

My summer research in the BVI from 1990 to 2001 was supported by Vassar College Faculty Research Grants and Ford and Dana Fellowships for undergraduate research. I have been especially inspired by the good will and enthusiasm of the many Vassar students with whom I worked over the years, both in the BVI doing research and in the United States working with research materials. With apologies to anyone I might have overlooked, I thank Kathy Acosta, Dory Edwards, Jesse Green, Peter Hazen, Jubi Headly, Erica James, Naveeda Kahn, Chrissy Lewis, Rebecca Marcus, Katama Martelluci, MK McKeon, Maggie Negrete, Heather Rebmann, Liz Reilly, Paige Rozanski, Jeffrey Sabin-Matsumoto, Abra Sussman, Rosa Thomas, Rob Tonkin, Amanda Scott Vaccaro, Chris Vaccaro, Dave Warner, Traci Ann Wint, and Chrissy Yoo.

Finally, I thank my father, Richard Roberts, for introducing me to the BVI and for his incisive and helpful comments on an early draft of this manuscript; my mother, Gloria Ballerino, for her ear, her patience, and her insight during countless telephone readings of various parts of the manuscript; Robin Marcus for her constant support and for the doors she opened before I began formal research in the BVI; Catherine Sebastian for her companionship, good humor, inspiration, and beautiful photographs; and especially my husband, Jeffrey Cohen, and my sons Zachary Carey, Evan Cohen, and Gabriel Cohen for their patience and their unconditional support of all my work, including this project.

A Note on Notes and Names

Notes

THROUGHOUT THIS BOOK I incorporate field notes that I kept from 1990 to 2008 on my research and experiences in the British Virgin Islands. Ethnographic knowledge is always mediated and it is in our field notes that ethnographers engage in one of the first mediations of what we observe, participate in, and experience. Of course, what we observe, participate in, and experience are themselves mediations, and in this respect field notes can also reveal a process of coming to understanding. By incorporating my field notes into the text of this book, I underscore the partiality of my knowledge, but I also bring the reader into the process through which I came to see something the way I came to see it. Because field notes frequently convey the "immediate history" of the "on-the-ground realities captured in a moment in time" that is so much a part of the ethnographic experience (Waterston and Rylko-Baurer 2007, 41) they can also give access to a situation, a sentiment, or a sensibility whose immediacy is as much a factor of our understanding as it is reflection upon or analysis of it. Thus, I often use field notes in this book to provide a sense of a moment or an event, or to amplify what I am writing about in the text.

In many instances, my field notes record conversations that I had with people in the British Virgin Islands, and so field notes are also a way of bringing their voices into the text. Because I am interested in conveying what I have come to know about the British Virgin Islands from as many different perspectives as possible, on occasion I use my field notes to destabilize the text, to call into question a single interpretive voice. Finally, I use field notes in order to put myself into the text, and thereby to subject myself and my practice to scrutiny and critique. At times, I engage in this critique myself, reflecting upon what is going on in a field note entry; at other times I leave it to the reader to engage in the critique. In all these instances, but in this latter instance especially, I follow a practice in feminist and recent ethnographic scholarship that underscores the contingent and constructed nature of knowledge by identifying the contexts and conditions in which knowledge is produced, among them the subject position of the knowledge maker.

The field notes that I include here are unedited, except in the following circumstances. First and most obviously, after almost twenty years of formal research my field notes extend to hundreds of pages and simply by selecting some field notes and not others I engage in an act of editing. Second, my field notes on any given day run from a few paragraphs to fifteen pages or more and may detail a number of unrelated incidents or experiences, and so many of the notes that I include in this book are excerpts from longer notes. Within an excerpted note I sometimes omit material that might be used to identify an individual or a group or—in the interest of "'discretion,' rather than 'confession'" (Lovell 2003, cited in Leibing and McLean 2007, 13)—material that is not relevant either to the ethnographic context or to an understanding of the process of knowledge production. In cases where I eliminate sections from longer notes, the redacted materials are marked by ellipses or by brackets with a brief summary of what was redacted. Finally, if I think that a word in a field note may be unfamiliar to the reader, I put the gloss of the word in brackets; I do the same when I substitute a description of a general description of a person for the person's name.

The field notes are set in sans serif font so they are clearly distinguished from other text.

NAMES

In many instances in my field notes and in the text, I follow conventional ethnographic practice of maintaining the anonymity of people I describe, quote, or refer to. In field notes, in place of a person's name, I substitute an arbitrary capital initial—for example, "H. reported that...." If an individual is named in a field note, the name is an actual name, not a pseudonym, and I include it with the individual's permission. Likewise, in the text I refer to someone in general terms of status and occupation, for example, "a British Virgin Islander who manages a tourist hotel," or I use a pseudonym. When I use a pseudonym, I identify it as such. However, there are other instances in which I refer to individuals by name. When citing materials written by British Virgin Islanders, I use the author's actual name. Likewise, I use the actual names of individuals who are well known within and outside of the British Virgin Islands and about whom much has already been published; I also use the names of people whose job or position makes them publicly known. In chapter 8, I discuss four individuals who are central to the production of British Virgin Islands culture and whose lives and experiences illuminate the complicated positions of people who live in a country that is a major tourist destination. These individuals have made great efforts throughout their lives to have their voices and the voices of other British Virgin Islanders heard, and neither they nor I wanted what they said or experienced to be muted by pseudonyms or fictionalized life circumstances. Each individual who I discuss in chapter 8 read the chapter and, apart from a few corrections of specific dates or names, left it unedited.

The British Virgin Islands is a British Dependent Territory and is part of the larger Virgin Islands geographical group that includes the United States Virgin Islands of St. Thomas, St. John, and St. Croix. During my thirty-plus years visiting the British Virgin Islands, eighteen of them doing formal research, the terms that I heard used most frequently to refer to the islands constituting the territory were "British Virgin Islands" and "BVI." Likewise, natives of the British Virgin Islands were referred to and referred to themselves as "British Virgin Islanders" or "BVIslanders." These terms are relatively recent, coming into popular usage in the 1950s, after representative government was reestablished in the BVI after almost a century hiatus (Maurer 1997, 78). Thus, older British Virgin Islanders on occasion still refer to themselves as "Virgin Islanders." Beginning in the early 2000s, I started to hear the term "Virgin Islander" used more frequently among all segments of the population, and the BVI constitution of 2007 actually refers to the native population of this British Dependent Territory as "Virgin Islanders." A 2005 constitutional review report explained:

> By the purchase from Denmark in 1917 of the Danish West Indies (principally: St. Thomas, St. Croix and St. John), the United States of America established sovereignty over this group, which was renamed the Virgin Islands of the United States of America and soon became shortened to "The Virgin Islands." To avoid confusion in the day to day usage, the northerly group began to be called "British Virgin Islands." However, the official name of this Territory is the *Virgin Islands*. The Commission is of the view that every effort should be made, officially and otherwise, to reverse the trend towards the *de facto* surrender of the proper name of this Territory. (Report of Virgin Islands Constitutional Commissioners 2005: 1)

Throughout this book, I use the terms most commonly heard at the time of its writing: *British Virgin Islander* or *BVIslander* to refer to natives of the island group, and *British Virgin Islands* or *BVI* to refer to the island group itself. But given the symbolic import of a term that evokes a precolonial past and in consideration of an ongoing and strengthening interest in BVI independence, I suspect that were I to be writing this book ten years from now, *Virgin Islands* and *Virgin Islander* would be the preferred terms.

Take Me to My Paradise

Introduction

Take Me to My Paradise

Big ol' jet plane, wide-span, chrome-plated wings
Fly me to my island, fly me to that island in the sun.
Concrete jungle and that painted smile you put on me
Say I got to leave you, Yeah you know I got to leave you,
    now.
Come come come come take me, take me to my
    Paradise. . . .
I miss dancing to the reggae under island skies
I just got to be there, I miss my BVIs
Come come come come take me, take me to my
    Paradise. . . .
The cappuccino and caviar is not for me
Give me a salt fish patty and some co-co tea
Come come come come take me, take me to my
    Paradise. . . .

—Quito Rymer

The title of this book comes from the song "Paradise," written by Quito Rymer, a British Virgin Islands artist, songwriter, and musician who is known throughout the BVI and by his fans abroad simply as Quito. When I first heard Quito sing this song in his popular beach bar on Cane Garden Bay in the BVI, I was struck by how many different paradises it called forth. In "Paradise," Quito sings about being homesick while living away from the BVI. Contrasting the "concrete jungle" with his island home, he yearns to dance under the stars and to eat local food. The combined reggae and slow calypso rhythm of "Paradise" matches the sensual images of Quito's lyrics, and so tourists embrace as their own anthem this song that evokes the soft nights, swaying palms, and endless vacation of tourist brochures. When I am away from the BVI, I play the CD of "Paradise" and sing along to it, missing— but probably not in the same way that Quito does—"dancing to the

I

reggae under island skies" and feasting on "a salt fish patty, and some co-
co tea."

The various paradises that "Paradise" brings into being prompt two
related questions: Whose paradise is "my paradise"? And what is the difference between Quito's paradise, the tourist's paradise, and the anthropologist's
paradise? This last question in particular implies that the categories of
subjects that "Paradise" summons are mutually exclusive. However, as Mimi
Sheller points out in her work on the Caribbean as an object of consumption, images of paradise are ubiquitous, with a long history and "earlier
literary and visual representations of the 'Paradise Isles' have been mapped
into the collective tourist unconscious before they have even stepped foot
there. The real Caribbean is always a performance of the vivid Caribbean of
the imagination" (2004: 13). Although Sheller is referring here to the Caribbean paradise of tourist imaginings, the following field note suggests that our
positions as the subjects that these images call to are often blurred. The field
note is the end of a longer entry that details a night spent driving around
the island of Tortola with my BVI friend and colleague Kenne Hodge. As we
drove, we listened on the car radio to the Calypso Show that is one of the
events of the annual BVI festival that commemorates the 1834 emancipation
of slaves throughout the English-speaking Caribbean. The field note entry
begins just after a description of a calypso song about an encounter between
Kenne's elderly aunt and a bull that broke lose of its bounds.

[Field notes July 26, 1998]   [Hearing the song,] has Kenne promising himself
to call Aunt Jen in the morning and tell her she is in a calypso. The windows
are open to the night air, even though it blows warm. And the sea hits up
against the rocks, sending an occasional spray upon the windshield. The moon
has set and the clouds have passed, so the stars are bright and I can just see
the Southern Cross on the southwest horizon. By the time we finally make it
to Quito's it is already 12:20 a.m. We find a table right outside the bar, with
a perfect view of the band and the dance floor. Tonic is there with a loud
crowd of bareboat [charter yacht] tourists, and true to form is showing them
how to party. . . . After two songs, the band finishes. The sailing crowd and
Tonic are not in any mood to stop, though, and so they go behind the stage
and turn up the recorded dance music. For the next 45 minutes they prance
and dance and conga line around, their own self-contained party. Meanwhile,
Quito makes himself a drink and pulls up a chair to our table. And there we
sit, until 2:45 in the morning: Quito, Kenne, and me, talking about God, false
gods, love, music, men, women, death, and jumbies [ghosts]. Kenne shares
with Quito his ongoing argument with [a local radio talk show host] about how
God would never send his son into temptation, and Quito fairly pounds the

table in agreement: "that's right, that's right: take my son, just see if you can break him!!" The place gradually clears out and finally it is just the three of us at the table, all the shutters except the ones at which we sit, closed up for the night. The air is still warm, and there is no breeze or any sea movement to speak of. There is nothing happening anywhere else on the bay either, so the night is quiet. . . . At one point Quito mentions that, because of the Putamayo record, three of his songs are being picked up for the Sunset Beach soap opera: "Paradise," "Mix Up World," "Der Pon My Mind," and that "Paradise" might be used in the new Terry Macmillan flick. Meanwhile, I say that I am not too sure of the words in one verse of "Paradise." Quito tries for it but can't quite get it, because the recorded dance music is still playing. So he gets up and turns off the music, and sings the song through to the line I had missed, "your graceful movement so high," that refers to the airplane that he imagines bringing him home. For the most part, though, it is Kenne and Quito, talking back and forth and relishing the stimulation of each other's thoughts. As for me, I mostly sit quietly back, cherishing the time and feeling lucky to be here, this night, now. But, as Kenne says, we make our luck. As we left, Kenne turned to me and said, "that was a better night at Quito's than any night of music. Paradise."

Kenne's describing his evening at Quito's as "paradise" could as well have been voiced by the conga-line-dancing tourists, or by me, for that matter. For my sense of being part of Quito and Kenne's circle of sentiment was an anthropological paradise, even as the description with which I open the field note mirrors tourist-brochure descriptions of Caribbean paradise, and despite the fact that I have also on occasion experienced the paradise of dancing at Quito's. Likewise, although "Paradise" is a song that Quito Rymer wrote to express his love for the BVI, its use as background music for a soap opera also points to the circulation of paradise, "Paradise," and Quito Rymer as commodities in a global marketplace.

The tourist desire for paradise, the construction of the BVI as Caribbean paradise, Quito Rymer's construction of his country as his paradise home, and the paradise that emerges in my field notes through my thirty-year relationship with people in the BVI are all paradises that I contemplate in this book, as I look at the impact of tourism development on the BVI. As is the case of many other Caribbean islands, the BVI economy is based extensively upon tourism; in 2004, for example, close to half of the BVI Gross Domestic Product of $879 million (U.S.) came from tourism revenues. Likewise, visitors to the BVI seek what most Caribbean tourists do: the experience of an idealized tropical paradise (Kempadoo 1999, 2004; Pattullo 1996, 2005; Sheller 2003, 2004; Strachan 2002; Thompson 2006; Titley 2001). "It is the fortune, and the misfortune, of the Caribbean to conjure up the idea of 'heaven on earth' or 'a little bit of paradise' in the collective European imagination," Polly Pattullo claims, in her history of Caribbean tourism (1996: 141). Mimi Sheller's discussion of the Caribbean as an object of consumption makes the same observation but states it more bluntly: "The Caribbean has been repeatedly imagined and narrated as a tropical paradise in which the land, plants, resources, bodies, and cultures of its inhabitants are open to be invaded, occupied, bought, moved, used, viewed, and consumed in various ways" (2004: 13). In this book, I attend to tourists' desire for paradise, and particularly as this desire articulates with and is shaped by BVI tourism marketing campaigns, and is acted out in the places that BVI tourists visit. But I am even more concerned with the effects of tourism and tourist desire for paradise upon the people who live in the BVI. A good many of these people are occupied with servicing tourists and satisfying tourist expectations, but even the lives of BVI residents who do not engage directly with the visitors are shaped in multiple and complex ways by tourism.

The BVI is among the places frequently appearing on travel magazines' lists of Top Ten Vacation Paradises. Depending upon which travel magazine you are reading, the BVI is home to Little Dix Bay, Peter Island Yacht Club, Biras Creek Resort, the Moorings Yacht Charters, Foxy's Bar on "the barefoot island" of Jost Van Dyke, Bomba's Shack (famous for its full moon parties and mushroom tea), Stanley's Welcome Bar, Quito's Gazebo, and Necker Island (privately owned by Richard Branson of Virgin Airlines and a vacation spot for the rich and famous). The majority of overnight visitors to the BVI are white North Americans who charter yachts for a week or two of sailing in BVI waters or who stay for a week or two in rented private villas or at small boutique resorts, all forms of elite, rather than mass, tourism (Smith 1989a). Many of these tourists come as family groups or as groups of couples, although in recent years special programs bring groups of high school and college students from the United States for summer sailing camps, and groups of African American singles for summer sailing adventures. For all these tourists, the allure of the BVI resides in its "undeveloped" natural beauty. Since the early 1990s, BVI tourism has expanded to include regular visits by large cruise ships that service both North American and European markets. But even the masses of nonelite cruise passengers disembarking for a day's visit come to see the island paradise described in the 2008 *British Virgin Islands Welcome Cruise Ship Visitor Guide*, "The BVI is unique in its natural beauty and in the charm of its village communities. Breathtaking mountains rise from the sea and soft strips of white sand cling to its shore." Of course, Western imaginings of the Caribbean also tend to attribute to the people living in the region behaviors associated with tropical locales and, as Pattullo notes, "these images are crude: of happy, carefree, fun-loving men and women, colourful in behaviour, whose life is one of daytime indolence beneath the palms and a night-time of pleasure through music, dance, and sex" (Pattullo 1996: 142).

Such imaginings, paired with the practicalities of producing and main-taining a successful tourist destination, shape life in and constitute a major challenge for the BVI. For over fifty years, the people of the BVI have devel-oped and sold their country as a tourist destination. The success of the BVI tourist economy is the result of constant and conscientious work as well as the sort of legislative vigilance that ensures that the paradise to which visi-tors come is what marketing campaigns promise. In both respects, it is apt that the motto of the BVI is *Vigilate* (Be Vigilant!). This motto appears on the BVI flag, as well as on its premier tourist publication, *The British Virgin Islands Welcome Guide*. Since the mid 1980s, the BVI has also developed a strong financial services sector, the income from which matches or exceeds income from tourism. Both tourism and financial services implicate the BVI daily in a stream of information and people, not so much as a specific place, but as a nexus in a worldwide network of electronically transmitted data, and of consumer desire. The friction between consumer desire and the work that goes into providing the services and ambience that tourists expect under-scores the complexity of life in one of the world's leading paradise vacation spots. So, too, does the following field note, that reports an incident between a tourist on a charter yacht vacation and local residents.

[Field notes 4.8.1998]   M. has been going out to the outdoor church services every night, and recounts to me a story she was told by a woman in Cane Garden Bay about a yacht charterer who came ashore yesterday afternoon to complain about the noise of the loudspeakers the night before—the loud-speakers had been playing hymns and carrying the pastor's sermon to the outdoor crowds. M. recalled with indignation the story, and sucked her teeth at the misbehavior of tourists who have the nerve to come into someone's "home" and tell them not to be so noisy.

Materially, the complexity of life in the BVI is marked by an almost 400 per-cent increase in population from 1960 to 2007, and a greater than 400 percent increase in GDP over the same period; the 2008 BVI GDP was estimated to exceed one billion dollars (U.S.). Notably, most of the workers in the service sector of the BVI tourism economy are immigrants from other Caribbean islands, and these immigrants make up more than one-half of the present-day BVI population of over 23,000. During high season (December 15 to May 15), tourist visitors often outnumber the total resident population of the BVI.

The complexity of life in the BVI is also marked by social, economic, and political stratification based on race and nationality. For example, the woman in the above field note who expressed such indignation at the tourist coming into her "home" and telling her how to behave, is actually from Nevis and came to the BVI in the late 1980s to work in its tourist economy. While the prosperity of the BVI tourist economy depends on the labor of people like this woman, without BVI citizenship—a status marked erroneously by the term *belonger*—she cannot work without a permit and cannot freely buy land or hold a trade license.

The tension between *belongers* and *nonbelongers* is another key feature of life in the BVI. This tension is amplified by efforts on the part of BVIs-landers to consolidate for themselves a national identity, based on claims that the heterogeneous mix of the BVI population is against the norm and problematic, and that the nation, and the rights of citizenship in it and access to its bounty, are natural and God-given. Meanwhile, the experiences of the non-BVIslanders who have few legal claims to the rewards of their labor call into question representations of the BVI as national *or* tourist paradise. Looking at the "paradise" that is constructed and played out by belonger and nonbelonger alike enables a detailed account of the coming into being of the BVI nation, with its attendant problems and challenges.

Scholarship on nationalism and national identity points to the importance to the project of nation building of rhetorical strategies that "naturalize" membership in a nation by "turn[ing] a national history into a natural history" (Handler and Linnekin 1984: 278). Such strategies are played out frequently in the BVI when a history of cross-cutting and divergent social relationships and interdependencies is transformed into a story about shared blood and natural rights. Stories about the naturalness of BVI citizenship are abetted by tourism advertisements that posit the geography of the BVI as a natural rarity, and its people as naturally friendly and welcoming. The introduction to a 1983 booklet, *Preservation of Our Culture through Education*, in fact conflates tourist brochure and local claims to a "natural" BVI character: "Many visitors to our shores are thrilled with the natural beauty, the peace, and above all the friendliness of the people of the Territory. . . . Here one does not have to beg people to smile to welcome visitors, a smile or laugh is natural . . . friendliness is deep rooted in our culture, in our very upbringing and it is only *natural* for a British Virgin Islander to help his neighbour, to treat strangers well" (Ministry of Education 1983: 5; emphasis added). Yet while tourist brochures and local discourses make claims about a natural BVI fixed in place and time, the BVI's status as a commodity in the global tourism market, as a paradise in the Western imagination, and as a node in global flow of information and money makes the concept of a national border redundant. Thus, in the discussions that follow I find it useful to think of the BVI along lines Arif Dirlik proposes for considering the local—not as a fixed physical locale in opposition to or assaulted by global forces, but as "a very contemporary 'local' that serves as a site for the working out of the most fundamental contradictions of the age" (1996: 23).

In this book I combine ethnographic description and analysis with interviews and field notes to illuminate the linkages between the marketing of the BVI as a premodern paradise, the successful development of the BVI economy, and the making of a BVI nation. These linked processes inform how people in the BVI go about their activities, think about themselves, and interact with each other, and so the central question I consider in this book is how making a certain kind of tourist space—in this case, a space that fits Western ideals of what tropical Caribbean paradise is supposed to be— affects the people living in the place where this space is being constructed. This focus has particular relevance to tourism studies concerned with how tourist locales are made by the interactions and performances of people in them. But it is a focus equally pertinent to questions related to the space of the nation. In assessing the growth of BVI nationalism in the context of the commodification of the BVI as a tourist destination, I illuminate a sense of identity that is continually reshaped in response to the flows of money, tourists, and immigrants across BVI borders, even as it draws on enduring structures of sentiment and value to make distinctions among different classes of people residing and working in the BVI. This leads me to address critical questions about what forms of governmentality and citizenship materialize in places like the BVI that are configuring themselves as nations in the vortex of global economic forces and flows.

The book also contributes significant new ethnographic material to studies of tourism, nationalism, national identity, and globalization by providing a detailed account of the intricate ways that BVIslanders live and build lives that are geared toward satisfying tourist desire for a premodern and exotic paradise and are simultaneously committed to forging an identity for themselves and their country as modern, cosmopolitan, and independent. This entails looking at what tourists expect when they travel to a place like the BVI, how these expectations are constructed by the tourism industry, how they are met, and what happens when they are not met, for example. But it also entails clarifying and appreciating the complicated and contradictory positions that people occupy as residents of a place that is marketed and consumed as premodern paradise. Some of these complications and contradictions emerge on a daily basis, as in the example of Quito's song "Paradise," which was written by him about a very individual experience but is performed for and consumed by tourists who hear it differently. But they also have to do with questions of ownership and subjectivity more broadly cast. What, for example is, can, or should be the relation of the BVI to outsiders who invest in or want a piece of BVI prosperity? How is economic or political sovereignty expressed that acknowledges local and global interdependencies? What sorts of subjectivities emerge or are possible in a space that is marketed and produced as paradise?

This book is based on ethnographic research that I conducted in the BVI each summer and one to three weeks each fall and spring from 1990 to the present. So another of my objectives is to take account of my own position in relation to what I know, understand, and write about. During my time in the BVI, I worked as a camera person for the national television station, collaborated with a British Virgin Island poet to produce three ethnographic videos, danced with the BVI Heritage Dancers, fished and farmed with BVIslanders, spoke at the BVI Rotary Club, crewed on a chartered yacht, served on the Board of Governors of the H. Lavity Stoutt Community College, and attended house blessings, weddings, anniversary celebrations, funerals, and official government functions. Notwithstanding these multiple involvements, I am also on occasion affected by the same images that I so diligently critique. In this regard, as one of my BVI friends pointed out to me, I was also a tourist.

A field note that I wrote in the summer of 1998 gives a sense of the space within which I worked. The note is an excerpt from a longer field note that begins by detailing what I bought and cooked for dinner and ends by reflecting on land issues, which I will discuss at great length in subsequent chapters. The note describes the physical place that I lived in during most of my time in the BVI, and also conveys a sense of my relationship to the BVI. While the field note excerpt is long and detailed, its description of the quotidian draws attention to the fact that knowledge is always situated, constructed in the context of particular historical, political, cultural, and personal locations. Of course, descriptions of the details of life "in the field" also risk exoticizing the ethnographic enterprise; if so, this points to a tension that I frequently experienced as I worked, lived, and did research in one of tourism's premier paradise vacation destinations.

[Field notes 7.28.1998] I have spent almost my whole day here working (I had a 10 a.m. meeting/interview with Eileene Parsons, followed by a meeting with the acting Permanent Secretary of Communications and Public Works, then a quick trip to Scotia Bank for some money. But my morning started with Kenne coming by at 7:30 to work on his [bank] document, then Elmore stopping by at 8 a.m. (before going up to plant some corn and peas on his ground, and to weed)—when I returned from town, I wasn't here 15 minutes before Kenne showed up again to continue work—when he left at 3 p.m. I finished my own work in preparation for my meeting at the college. I realized, as I was straightening things up here upon my return from the college, that I call this place my house, and think of it as home while I am here. Indeed, I have a whole routine in place that makes it home within a few hours of my arrival. So I thought it would be good to describe it.

To the tourist who comes to stay here at Carrie's Island Comfort, the apartment in which I stay is quite probably a dream—each unit measures around 450 sq feet . . . [more room measurements]. . . . Both the bedroom and the living room have a ceiling fan; the bedroom has jalousied windows opening onto the outside corridor, the living room has a sliding door opening onto a balcony, measuring 8 x 10 and overlooking Cane Garden Bay. Each unit has a fully equipped kitchen, and a television with satellite reception. When I come, Stanley puts a phone in my room and Kenne brings me his VCR—these two items are crucial—the phone for making phone contact with people and vice versa, and the VCR for reviewing footage shot during the course of my day. As soon as I arrive in the BVI I begin to establish myself at home by first picking up the things that I keep stored at Kenne's house. These include a good linen suit and church hat, a good dress jacket, an iron, a hairdryer, a computer printer, a surge protector, a tape recorder with music tapes and blank tapes, office supplies, assorted necessities such as pantyhose, sunblock, bathing suit, extra hangers, and articles of clothing that I tend to wear only here, such as beach dresses, etc. I then make a trip to the Riteway, where I pick up the food that I will need, and bottled water. Then it is over the hill, with all the luggage and equipment that I have dragged with me from the States, my clothes on a hanger, my box of essentials, my printer in its case, my groceries and water. Kenne usually picks me up at the airport and as the time nears for the trip over the hill, he becomes increasingly miserable—for helping me to "move in" usually happens in the heat of the day and means our carrying a lot of heavy and bulky items.

I always seem to be carrying too many papers and books for my own use (but I never read them or use them), blank video and audio tapes, books, tapes, clothes, and toys to meet peoples' requests or to give as gifts. On some occasions I have carried a VCR, an 8-millimeter VCR, fresh lilacs, props for an Arabian Nights [Festival parade] troupe (2 dozen tambourines, 2 dozen pointy hats, and 10 scepters), computer hard drives and memory, a professional video tripod. I always carry my laptop and my video camera; on this trip I carried two video cameras—my new Canon XL-1 digital and my old Sony Hi eight. If Quito decides not to buy the Les Paul electric guitar that John Sebastian left for him to try, I will be carrying that back with me too. Needless to say, getting onto an airplane with these carry-ons, in these days of increasing regulations about such, is a real nightmare, and occupies my thoughts for days before my departure on either end.

As soon as I get to Cane Garden Bay, I begin to set up my space: the clothes that have been packed away in boxes are put out to air, and the clothes that I take out of my luggage are put on hangers. I am mortified when I take an inventory of my shoes—for I always forget what I have left here, and end up with far too many things, especially shoes . . . [a list of more items that I unpack]. . . . As soon as my clothes are unpacked, I move one of the bedside tables into the living room, where I set it up to serve as a small desk . . . [more furniture moving details]. . . . the large camera case for my new digital video camera sits against one wall and when it is closed it serves as an additional, albeit low, table. When I first arrived with the case it was shiny and un-dented—as impressive as the camera within. Now, after having been pulled quickly in and out of my car, maneuvered through tight spots, and even served for me to stand on in order to get a higher camera angle in a crowd, it is not so shiny and its top has scuffy dirt marks that I can't seem to wash out. It only serves occasionally as a piece of furniture when I have it back in the house. Usually, it stands open while I recharge batteries or while I use the camera to review tapes on the TV. Within a day or two of my arrival I frequently have posted a large calendar on which I enter the various festival events and appointments that I have to keep. Finally, to combat the mosquitoes, I light a mosquito coil—a big spiral of mosquito repelling incense that I try never to let burn out.

In all the years that I have been here, I have never lived in a village, per se, as anthropologists traditionally have. Rather, I have lived in various neighborhoods, or "parts" of Tortola, and my associations and interactions have developed as a consequence of my relation to certain people or families. If I associate myself with any part of Tortola, it is with the village of Cane Garden Bay. But for the most part I think of myself (and others think of me) as associated with particular families such as [list of four family names], and particular interests, such as education and culture. This doesn't seem to have been a hindrance, for a couple of reasons. First of all, with a primary focus on tourism, I end up needing to be where tourists are. Although for convenience sake, and especially around Festival time, I prefer living in Road Town [list of places I have stayed in Road Town], being in the Bay enables me quick and easy access to a major tourist site. The location of my apartment is such that I can make the trip to town in under 15 minutes, and when I get back here the view and the breeze and the quiet make it easy for me to wind down, and to concentrate on my notes. And as the years have passed, I have become involved in close relationships with many people living in the Bay—[list of seven families]—so that it feels more and more like coming "home." And there is the added advantage of being two minutes from Quito's—which means great music, and always someone to talk to. With the influx of people from outside, with enhanced mobility within the country, with BVIslanders who were away returning, the connection between a person and a village or place of origin is less strong. To be sure, a family name is still associated with a particular place, and when people return "home" for family reunions, the "home" to which they refer may very well be a cluster of houses in a very specific locale on Tortola or one of the other BVI. (Case in point: H. has many nieces, nephews, step-children, grandchildren arriving over the next few days, so the total of people coming back will be close to thirty. I asked if there would be many staying by her, and she responded no. Motioning up and behind her, toward [a region in the hills on Tortola's northwest coast], she explained that they all wanted to stay "up the hill" in Granny's house. Well, Granny's house is just a small wooden structure . . . around which other houses have been built over the years by other members of the family. . . . Presumably, the various nieces, nephews, grandchildren, and cousins will be scattered among these various households.) And when possible, BVIslanders still reside in the area with which their family is associated. But also residing there with them are people from other Caribbean countries—who join the community churches, become involved in community functions, become known for their skills, foibles, asso-ciations, etc. Increasingly, then, to be "known" in the BVI is more than to "be" from a certain place or to "belong" to a certain group of families associ-ated with that place . . . [examples of particular families]. . . . In the context of the diversity and the mobility of the resident BVI population, and in the context of a steady stream of tourists who return over and over again to the BVI, my not being associated with a place is not unusual; in this context as well, my association with a particular sphere of activity and with those people engaged in that activity works well—people can "locate" me within the local web of relationships. And the fact is, I am not from here. However much I may get to know the way things work, and behave accordingly, I will always be from away.

In the chapters that follow I detail what I have come to know and understand about how the BVI is affected by tourism culturally, economi-cally, socially, and politically. The first three chapters provide the historical context for the book; while most of the material in these chapters is original, some of it is drawn from previously published articles and book chapters (Cohen 2001, 1995; Cohen and Mascia-Lees 1993). In chapter 1, I give a historical sketch of the BVI, paying particular attention to the changing relationship of the BVI to Great Britain, from its political and economic insignificance throughout most of the colonial period to its current status as an economically independent British Dependent Territory. Notably, constitutional reform in the 1950s launched the BVI on a trajec-tory of increasing local control over its politics and economies, and since then the BVI has become increasingly involved in the global economies of tourism and financial services.

When the BVI turned to tourism as a source of revenue, it was able to exploit a fairly undeveloped natural environment and appeal to upscale tourists looking for something out of the way and different. In chapter 2, I trace the history of tourism development in the BVI, from the 1953 British Virgin Islands Hotels Aid Ordinance that provided tax incentives to investors in tourist-oriented enterprises and the 1964 construction of the Rockefeller-owned Little Dix Bay resort, to the present-day proposed development of five-star resort complexes on several of the islands of the BVI. From its inception, the BVI tourism economy depended on outside investment in the form of capital and labor, and so in this chapter I address the flows of capital and people into and through the BVI that to this day structure in profound and intricate ways BVIslanders' relation to each other, to the non-BVIslanders who make up half of the current population, and to the people who vacation in the BVI. I also discuss specific events and controversies that shed light on the politics of BVI tourist development and highlight factors in play as the BVI works to secure its position in a global tourism market while fortifying itself as a national community.

The processes of national identity formation and tourism marketing intersect in complex ways in the BVI. In chapter 3, I begin to explore these intersections by looking at BVI Tourist Board publications, travel magazines, travel guides, Web posts, and articles to track key themes in BVI tourist marketing strategies. Two themes predominate. Beginning with the earliest "Yes We Are Different" slogan that branded the BVI product, to the popular and ubiquitous "Discover Nature's Little Secrets" branding that persists to the present, the BVI is marketed as a natural and pristine paradise, and the people occupying the BVI are depicted as naturally friendly and accommodating. The emphasis upon nature, the untouched quality of the BVI, and the accommodating character of its people posits the BVI as outside the stream of time, a premodern paradise open for discovery and possession. The "Nature's Little Secret" slogan, when paired with the name *Virgin* Islands, also eroticizes and sexualizes the BVI. Representations of tropical paradise as outside of time, erotic, and female draw on longstanding conventions and associations, but in the BVI they also converge with a discourse about a natural BVI nation and people. While tourists visiting the BVI are enticed by an invitation to "Discover Nature's Little Secrets," claims to being a natural BVIslander are grounded in references to having "a piece of the Virgin," and are rooted in the construction of a timeless and pristine BVI motherland that is nation to some but certainly not all of its residents.

In chapters 4, 5, and 6, I take up at greater length several of the issues raised in chapter 3; in chapters 4 and 5, I also explore what it means to be producing ethnographic knowledge about the BVI. In chapter 4, I address the question of how colonial ideologies of racial difference ground conceptualizations of the BVI nation as a unified and homogeneous people. This question has profound relevance to the BVI, for in a short period of forty years its population increased by 400 percent, largely through immigration. Understandings of these newly arrived residents as *not* BVIslanders work together with legal, social, and cultural institutions to consolidate the diverse communities of the BVI into one entity, even as they establish the basis for differential access to the rewards of a prosperous tourist economy. But uncertainty about who can properly claim to belong to the BVI, and longstanding bonds with other island groups, confound the nation-building project.

In chapter 5, I provide a local perspective on the way that the BVI is depicted to and consumed by tourists, through a discussion of a video that I shot and produced with BVI poet Kenne Hodge (Cohen and Hodge 1995). The video contrasts images of the BVI that one sees in tourist brochures and videos with BVIslanders' efforts to control these images for themselves. Showcasing the cultural negotiations that went into this collaborative project, in this chapter I also address questions relevant to ethnographic practice: how what the ethnographer "knows" is shaped by her own gender-race-culture-class-bound understandings; the implications of speaking for other people; and the presumed difference between the anthropologist and the people she studies. The question of the presumed difference between the "us" and "them" of ethnographic inquiry is also relevant to the people of the BVI, whose lives are more like than unlike the lives of the tourists to whom they are marketed as exotic and Other.

In chapter 6, I look at tourists' interactions with objects, places, and people that evoke the premodern, exotic, and friendly BVI touted in tourist brochures. Stanley's Welcome Bar, Bomba's Surfside Shack, and Foxy's Tamarind Bar are among the most popular and well-known of BVI tourist locales, in no small part because of the opportunities they provide for visitors to get to know local people and to feel "at home." The allure of intimacy with an Other is related to a desire to discover an authentic Western self, and in this chapter I look at how tourists engage in this quest of discovery, as well as what happens when their quests fail. I also address challenges to subjectivity for people who live in a place where the quest for an authentic Western self is enacted.

Even as tourists to the BVI seek a sense of authenticity and interiority, BVIslanders are involved in a similar pursuit as they construct for themselves an identity as a national people. In chapters 7 and 8, I discuss the relationship between tourism and the creation of BVI culture. In chapter 7, I discuss the annual festival that commemorates the 1834 emancipation of slaves throughout the English-speaking Caribbean. Festival is an occasion for displaying BVI culture and pride as well as the focus of a good deal of public debate and political jockeying. My discussions in this chapter of band competitions, calypso contests, and beauty pageants that take place during Festival draw somewhat upon my earlier published work on BVI Festival (Cohen 1998, 1996). This work and the discussion in this chapter throw into relief the multiple identities and interests that are in contention and highlight some key dilemmas and contradictions facing the BVI.

My discussion of Festival as a site for performing, negotiating, and sometimes domesticating the complications of life in the BVI provides a framework for chapter 8. In chapter 8, I address the multiple and seemingly contradictory positions that people in the BVI occupy, by looking at the experiences of four individuals involved in making and performing culture for tourists *and* a national audience. This discussion also illustrates how tourist desire can and does engender a local preoccupation with culture and heritage, and in this respect how tourism in the BVI articulates with a nationalist project.

By way of conclusion, I return to the constructed and commodified context of the BVI experience to think about what is in store for the BVI as a tourism destination and as a major international financial services center. In this chapter I address the impact upon these two BVI industries of the global economic downturn that began in late 2008, and raise questions regarding the consequences for BVI sovereignty of its long involvement in global flows. In particular, the BVI sense of itself as a nation emerged as much through its existence as a commodity as through political development and constitutional reform, and this has radical implications for sovereignty, citizenship, and identity.

In all of these chapters, I interweave ethnographic analysis with narrative description, interviews, field notes, and materials from tourism brochures and Web posts, with the intention of creating what Faye Ginsburg, writing about ethnographic film, terms a "parallax effect" (1999). "Parallax effect" is used in physics to describe the phenomenon in which an object seems to move when the position of the observer moves. Applied to ethnographic representations, it is an approach that, putting different but related perspectives into play, "can offer a fuller comprehension of the complexity—the three-dimensionality, so to speak—of the social phenomenon we call culture" (Ginsburg 1999: 158). In this regard, all the descriptions and analyses in the chapters to follow are offered not as inert ethnographic entities but, much like the BVI itself, as sites of interaction and production of multiple meanings.

CHAPTER 1

Tourism's Paradise

HISTORICAL BACKGROUND

Big ol' jet plane, wide-span, chrome-plated wings
Fly me to my island, fly me to that island in the sun.
Concrete jungle and that painted smile you put on me
Say I got to leave you, Yeah you know I got to leave you,
    now.
Come come come come take me, take me to my Paradise.

—Quito Rymer

I BEGIN THIS CHAPTER looking at the first two lines of the song "Paradise," "Big ol' jet plane, wide-span, chrome-plated wings / Fly me to my island, fly me to that island in the sun." Where the chorus, "Take me to my paradise," calls forth images of a premodern Eden fixed in time, the first two lines reference modernity and mobility. The friction between a premodern paradise and modernity, between a place fixed in time and mobility characterizes the contemporary BVI experience. In this chapter I sketch a historical backdrop for the analysis of the modern and mobile lives of BVIsanders, lives that are also in many important respects shaped by the need to satisfy tourist desire for an untouched, premodern paradise. "Nature's Little Secrets," the slogan that brands the BVI as a tourist destination, targets this desire, and also conveys a sense of the particular character of BVI history. The uniqueness signaled by the "Nature's Little Secrets" slogan also reflects a sense on the part of BVIslanders that they and their native land have been specially blessed. This sense seems to be borne out by its contemporary circumstances.

The BVI is a British Overseas Territory located sixty miles east of Puerto Rico and just a few miles east of the U.S. Virgin Islands (USVI) island of St. Thomas, in the Lesser Antilles chain in the eastern Caribbean (figure 1.1) Throughout most of the three hundred years of its relationship to Great Britain, the BVI was, at best, economically dependent and politically marginal. Today, the BVI is financially self-sufficient, with a per capita income approaching $40,000 (U.S.). It also exercises great autonomy over its political, economic, and social development. A crown-appointed governor has executive authority over defense and the administration of the courts, but all other areas of governance, including internal legislation and statutory bodies, external relations, and consultation in the selection of the governor, are the purview of a locally elected premier, cabinet, and House of Assembly. The economic and political transformation of the BVI from an economic and political backwater to a prosperous semi-autonomous state has occurred so recently and so rapidly that most BVIsanders over fifty-five years of age still recall a pretourism BVI, when the mainstay of the economy was small-scale farming, fishing, goat raising, charcoal making, and the occasional rum smuggling. These memories were codified in a report, commissioned by government, "The British Virgin Islands MacroEconomy." "Before the 1950s, the BVI economy was primarily dependent on agriculture. With limited capacity to import, and the absence of investment, the populous [sic] depended on agriculture and fishing as a means for survival. During this period, the main means by

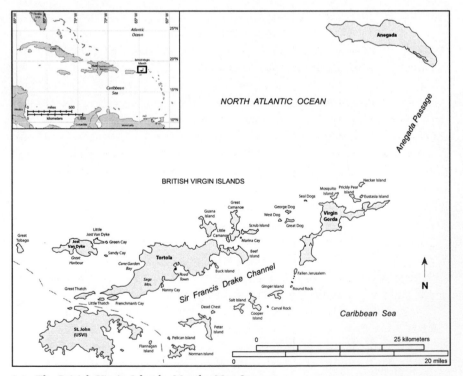

1.1. The British Virgin Islands. Map by Meg Stewart.

which goods were traded was the barter system—a system where people exchange one good directly for another. For example, people traded fish for provisions" (Smith n.d.).

Of the over fifty islands, rocks, and cays making up the BVI, sixteen are inhabited. At twenty-one square miles, Tortola is the largest and most densely populated of the islands, with an estimated 2007 population of close to 19,000 people; most of the remaining BVI residents live on Virgin Gorda to the east (with an estimated population of 3,500), Anegada to the northeast (with an estimated population of 225) and Jost Van Dyke to the northwest (with an estimated population of 200). With the exception of Anegada, which is a low-lying coral atoll, the islands of the BVI are hilly and dry, with rugged coastlines interrupted by coves, sandy beaches, and stands of palm trees and mangroves. Road Town, the capital of the BVI, is located on a natural harbor in the middle of the southern windward shore of Tortola. All the islands making up the BVI, with the exception of Anegada, are within sight of each other and can be reached in less than a half day of leisurely sailing. Approaching the BVI by sea—via regular ferry service from the USVI island of St. Thomas—one travels across turquoise water, cutting between several uninhabited cays before docking in a quiet and picturesque cove on the westernmost tip of Tortola, or in Road Town, across from a picturesque Main Street. Approaching the BVI by air, one sees the islands spread out below, with the channel between them dotted by sloops and catamarans in full sail; as a 2009 Caribbean travel writer put it, "flying over the BVI, your eyes brighten up slowly and start to turn as turquoise blue as the sea" (Escure 2009: 62). In either event, the particular nature of BVI geography enhances the sense that one has arrived in paradise.

Like all historical accounts, the following sketch is partial and constructed. It draws as much as possible upon histories written by BVIsanders; it also incorporates materials from BVI newspapers, government documents, tourism publications, and memoirs and stories written by BVIsanders. By way of introduction to this historical sketch, I refer to the first two stanzas of a poem, "Cherished Gems," written by self-proclaimed native poet Dr. Quincy Lettsome (1976). With their descriptions of the beauty of the geography and landscape, and references to homeland, home, heritage, and patronage, the lines are a fitting beginning to an account that stretches from the earliest occupation of the islands, through the development of the BVI from British colony to British Territory and from a subsistence agriculture to a tourism economy, to contemporary efforts to build an independent political entity and national homeland.

Fair graced Ursula's Islands,
Cherished gems, my homeland;
Isles of the blue;
Like thee I would be true; gems of the Caribbean
Jewels of the Ocean:
My home, sweet home.

Choice of Atlanta's rift:
Isles, rocks, cays coast and cliff;
Sea and white sands;
And shimmering waters
School of our mariners;
Uphold our heritage,
By patronage.

Beginning

The islands making up the Virgin Islands group were settled by Amerindian people from South America around 1000 B.C.E., and were inhabited by migrants from South American Taino groups when Columbus happened upon them on Saint Ursula's Day—October 22—in 1493. Upon sighting the several islands making up what is now the BVI, Columbus named them Las Once Mil Virgines, presumably because there were too many islands for him to name individually (Michael Kent, personal communication), although many accounts claim that the islands were named after the 11,000 martyred virgins of Saint Ursula. In any event, the British Virgin Islands flag evokes this moment of sighting: opposite the Union Jack, which takes up the upper left corner of the flag, is a rendition of Saint Ursula, holding an oil lamp in her hand and circled by eleven other lamps, each representing 1,000 virgins. By some accounts, Columbus gave the present-day island of Virgin Gorda the name of Santa Ursula (Harrigan and Varlack 1988), although other histories and most travel guides claim that the name Virgin Gorda was the original one given by Columbus, because he thought the island resembled a reclining woman with a large belly, or "La Gorda" (Colli 2006; Pickering 1987; Scott and Scott 1993). I detail these conflicting accounts because questions about names in the BVI continue to the present day, as newcomers give new names to bays and inlets, and even as many BVIslanders refer to themselves interchangeably as "Virgin Islanders," "British Virgin Islanders," or "BVIslanders." The field note below, reporting on a conversation that I had with BVIslander Kenne Hodge about research that I was doing in the archives of the national magazine published monthly for tourists, *The British Virgin Islands Welcome Guide*, provides a perspective on names and name changes.

[Field notes 4.7.1998] I tell Kenne that one of the more interesting things that I have found in going through the *Welcome Guide* are the changes in the maps included in the first three volumes (1971–1973). Specifically, I tell him about a map that first appears in Vol. 2, No. 1—an expanded rendition of the first Road Town map appearing in Vol. 1, No. 1, which just showed Main Street, with indications at either end, "to the east" and "to the west." This first map appears as an inset in the Vol. 2 map, which is expanded to include all of Road Town Harbor, and goes all the way from Duff's Bottom in the west to Baugher's Bay in the east. . . . What I first noted on the map (and this is in contrast to present-day renditions of the Road Town area appearing in more recent *Welcome Guides*) is that local place names like "Free Bottom," "Duff's Bottom," "Huntum's Ghut" are marked in large letters. I tell Kenne that I find this interesting, because it indicates a local sensibility still in operation—assuming that maps are meant to impart important knowledge that "makes sense" to their readers. Nowadays, although local people still use these place names as points of reference in giving directions or telling someone where they live, there is no map available with these names on it—I have spent many hours in conversation with people trying to get a sense of where certain "places" are. In talking to Kenne about this, I note it as an indication of the submission of the local system of meaning to the tourist system of meaning—what tourists want and need in a map is locations of direct relevance to their experiences and needs—shops, restaurants, hotels, etc. . . . Kenne's reading is somewhat different—he sees it as happening as a result of the filling in of spaces between what in the past had been "natural" boundaries with houses, roads, shops. More to the point, to his way of thinking, "is we who let it happen." "The building?" I ask. No, he explains, the leaving off of the place names, to the point that today no effort is made to educate the children not just about the place names here on Tortola, but even about the surrounding islands, to which many schoolchildren have never even traveled.

After Columbus's sighting of them in 1493, the islands making up the BVI were occupied by a number of European powers. Spain initially laid claim to the islands making up the BVI, and even established a copper mine on Virgin Gorda in the early 1500s. Following an edict by King Charles I in the mid-1500s declaring the indigenous inhabitants of the region enemies of Spain, the original inhabitants of the islands were exterminated or fled to the Windward Islands further south along the chain. Although the British took control of the islands in the mid-1600s, throughout the sixteenth and most of the seventeenth century the islands were for the most part uninhabited and unattended to, save as hideouts for pirates. Thatch Island, one of the westernmost islands of the BVI, was reportedly named after Edward "Black Beard" Teach; Dead Chest, off Peter Island, is said to be the Dead Chest of "Yo Ho Ho and a bottle of rum, ten men left on a Dead Man's Chest"; and Norman Island is said to have been the inspiration for Robert Louis Stevenson's *Treasure Island* (Colli 2006: 29; Lewisohn 1966). During this period, the BVI also served as a staging site for sorties against the Spanish by British privateer Sir Frances Drake (after whom the channel that runs between Tortola and Ginger, Cooper, Salt, Peter, and Norman Islands to the south is named), and as a base for Dutch buccaneers.

The Dutch established the first permanent European settlement on Tortola in 1602, but by 1666 they had been replaced by English planters, who initiated a plantation economy based first on cotton and later on sugar production. Despite this English presence, Great Britain expressed little or no interest in assuming governance of the island group. In fact, as a British Virgin Islands constitutional history pointed out, "Due to its geographical and geological characteristics, questions of the economic viability of the Virgin Islands as a socio-political unit have plagued this Territory from the 'get go'" (*Report of Virgin Islands Constitutional Commissioners* 2005: 3). In 1672, the islands making up the contemporary BVI were placed under the administrative umbrella of the government of the Leeward Islands, which was located in Antigua. It was not until 1773 that economic prosperity and a progressive governor of the Leeward Islands combined to convince King George III of England to grant the BVI a constitutional government, with a Legislative Council made up of nominated members and a House of Assembly made up of elected members. Only white male landowners were eligible to vote or to hold office (Harrigan and Varlack 1988: 19–21; O'Neal 2001: 2; *Report of Virgin Islands Constitutional Commissioners* 2005: 4–5).

The slave-based plantation economy characteristic of most of Caribbean development throughout the colonial period was successful in the BVI only for the twenty-seven years between 1756 and 1783, a period spoken of in most histories as the "golden era." Short-lived prosperity during this period was linked to increased trade with North American colonies during the American War for Independence, due to blockades of other larger and more agriculturally productive islands. Following the cessation of hostilities between Great Britain and the new United States of America, the BVI economy took a downward turn. A severe hurricane in 1819 destroyed what had become a marginal plantation economy, and by 1834, when all enslaved people in the English-speaking Caribbean were freed, the population stood at 477 whites and 6,338 blacks (Harrigan and Varlack 1988: 52).

With emancipation in 1834, much of the land in the BVI was left unattended, to be bought up or occupied by its freed slave population. The subsequent period saw the abandonment of estates, a radical reduction of land under cultivation, and a growing political and economic isolation of the BVI from Great Britain (Dookhan 1975; Harrigan and Varlack 1975; Varlack and Harrigan 1977). In 1871, when a single federal colony comprising all the Leeward Islands and Dominica was created by Great Britain, the economic insignificance of the BVI—and the absence of a white planter class—was reflected in the fact that the Virgin Islands was not represented by a single elected member. In 1902, the political decline of the BVI was marked by its colonial status being revoked altogether. Instead, it became a presidency within the larger Leeward Islands colony. And, as a British Virgin Islands constitutional history put it, "For the first thirty years of the twentieth century, constitutionally the Virgin Islands went to sleep" (*Report of Virgin Islands Constitutional Commissioners* 2005: 8).

From 1902, when the local BVI Legislature was abolished, to 1950 when it was reconstituted, the BVI experienced little in the way of direct governance by Great Britain. In the words of a 1907 British Virgin Islands government report, "The old Virgin Islands [planter] families abandoned their . . . estates to their former labourers, who raised degenerate stock and subsisted on fish and root crops, with the help of a certain amount of sugar and bad rum for local consumption. The Virgin Islands during these years were almost forgotten and no interest was taken in their inhabitants either in England or elsewhere" (quoted in Harrigan and Varlack 1988: 9). During the last two-thirds of the nineteenth century and the first half of the twentieth century, small-scale agriculture, livestock, fishing, charcoal production, and smuggling predominated as sources of support for the local population, with most of the produce being sent to neighboring St. Thomas on Tortola-based sloops. During the 1920s and 1930s, a good many BVI men also migrated off-island as workers in the still prosperous sugar economies of Cuba and Santo Domingo. In his memoir, BVIslander Joseph Reynold "J.R." O'Neal recalled that,

> the pattern of life [1920–1930] then was that young men, many of them fathers, or about to raise a family, would migrate in January, work in the sugar factories, and return home in late June or July. . . . The arrival of schooners such as the *Fancy Me* and the *Eagle* and the *Warsprite* of Anguilla registry coming from the Dominican Republic was the occasion

for great activity in Road Harbour. In fact, the arrival of more than 100
native sons in the course of one or two days was as important an event as
the arrival of the Queen, years later, in 1966. (O'Neal 2005: 31)

In the 1940s many BVIslanders went to their close neighbor St. Thomas on
twenty-nine-day contracts to work on the construction of U.S. naval bases
(twenty-nine days being the longest time one could stay in the United States
without a visa), and after World War II to work in St. Thomas's emerging
tourist economy.

Two folk songs, performed by BVIslander Elmore Stoutt for tourists
and BVI schoolchildren alike, evoke the sense of these times. One song,
"Ella Gift," tells the story of a large-bodied woman who was notorious for
her ability to smuggle rum into the U.S. Virgin Islands, a practice that U.S.
Prohibition made quite profitable. She did this by concealing the contra-
band bottles of rum in specially made pockets in her pantalettes, which
were quite roomy due to her large size. When a customs boat came across
the sloop carrying Ella and her rum, she was forced to remove her pantalettes and throw them "over the side, over the side, she threw she pantalettes
over the side." The second song tells the story of Louie, who was courting
a young woman from Brewer's Bay, on the north side of Tortola. Louie
made a living by going over to St. Thomas as a wage-laborer on a twenty-
nine-day contract. Upon one of his returns from St. Thomas he proceeded,
riding on his mule as usual, to the house of his betrothed. In the song he is
greeted at her door by her father, who lets him know that he is no longer
a suitor by refusing to allow him to tie up his mule by the door: "Louie
Louie loose yo mule / Louie Louie loose yo mule / Louie Louie loose yo
mule / Before he mess up in front the door."

The 1930s was a decade of political upheaval throughout the English-
speaking Caribbean. Although the politically marginal status of the BVI
meant that it experienced very little in the way of direct rule from the
United Kingdom, the people of the BVI were also growing restive, eager
for the reinstatement of legislative government. In 1947, the BVI sent a
representative to the Closer Union Conference in St. Kitts that was being
held to discuss the possibility of forming a Federation of the Windward and
Leeward Islands. The representative to this conference, Howard R. ("H. R.")
Penn, secured unanimous support for a resolution asking for an elected
Legislative Council for the BVI and for continued use of U.S. currency. But
by all accounts, it was the actions of a disgruntled fisherman from Anegada
that finally secured the reinstatement of representative government in the
BVI. As H. R. Penn recalls, the fisherman in question was quite upset that
his pregnant wife was unable to get proper medical care on Anegada, with
the result that he had to charter a seaplane to get his wife to the small

hospital on Tortola. Nightly, while his wife was in the hospital in Road Town, the fisherman went to the old market square and expressed his grievances to anyone who would listen.

> He was a drinking man, and began talking to the people by night in the old market square ... telling them how Anegada was neglected. . . . it seems that at this time many people had grievances. . . . They would chat about these grievances to [the fisherman] in the daytime, and at night [he] would get up in the market place and declare he had dreamed about whatever grievances he happened to have heard that day, and as our people love a commotion, each night more and more people would gather to hear the latest drama. (Penn 1990: 25)

A British Virgin Islands constitutional history tells the story somewhat differently: "Night after night he took to the rostrum in the market square in front of the administration building. He spoke to the issues that concerned him and the need for the people to have a say in the governance of the country. His public outcry resonated with the people as more and more persons gathered around to listen to his nightly lectures." In any event, the fisherman's "nightly lectures" resulted in a petition being drawn up demanding the reinstatement of representative government and, following "the largest demonstration in the history of the Territory" (*Report of Virgin Islands Constitutional Commissioners* 2005: 9,10), the Legislative Council was reconstituted in 1950.

The Legislative Council established in 1950 provided for four elected members out of a total of eight, with a Crown-appointed commissioner serving as its president. Constitutional reforms that followed in 1953 provided for even greater representation, with a Legislative Council made up of six elected members, "a small but important step on the road to ministerial responsibility" (*Report of Virgin Islands Constitutional Commissioners* 2005: 11). The market square where the notorious Anegadan fisherman gave his nightly "lectures" is still there, now named the Sir Olva Georges Plaza. And while the BVI today could hardly be described as a backwater, political or otherwise, much of today's politics are very local and face-to-face. People in the BVI still spend a lot of time and energy reviewing in great detail the latest set of grievances, and groups can be seen on any given day or night standing around discussing and arguing about local events and happenings. These arguments and discussions take place in a variety of venues—under tamarind trees, on the street, in rum shops, at fish fries, in the parking lot of the Rite Way market in Pasea—but a favored spot for discussing the news of the day is the taxi stand at the ferry dock that is directly across from Sir Olva Georges Plaza. My field notes report an encounter that Kenne Hodge had at this taxi stand early one morning in July 1998.

[**Field notes 7.25.1998**]   He had gone down to the taxi stand near the ferry dock, for he knew that on weekends the taxi men are there all night, watching TV and just hanging out. He had been limin' [hanging out] with a taxi man, S. and S.'s cousin R., who had failed to make the night ferry back to St. Thomas, and was trying to catch some sleep at the ferry dock before catching the 6 a.m. ferry back to St. Thomas and to work the next day. A white Englishman came up, someone who has been here for some time and who runs some wind surfing school. He started talking to Kenne about how he had organized the water sports activities for August Festival, and then claimed that it was the first time ever that there were to be water sports. Kenne set him straight on that right away, and then, after about 7 minutes of conversation, begged off from more talking, as he wanted to continue to watch the show he was watching. Apparently, the man didn't listen, and went on about how TV was ruining proper interaction and, moreover, about how the Tortolians who don't get on the program will find themselves locked out of their own country. This comment had followed the man's trying to get into a joking exchange between the taxi man and his cousin. S. had been riding R. about what a [mess] up he was, to have missed the ferry, and made mention of the fact that R. should just forget St. Thomas and come back home to reap the rewards of BVI progress. Apparently, it was to follow up on this jesting remark between two close relatives, that the white English guy made his comment. As Kenne tells it, he just kept quiet, trying to watch his TV show, but when the Englishman made his comment, Kenne couldn't stand it any longer, and lit into him, asking him did he know what the word *arrogance* meant. The man replied by protesting that he wasn't arrogant, that in fact when he had been in school in England he had helped many Nigerians, when everyone around him just put them down. Look brother, he said, to which Kenne replied, I'm not your brother, and I'm tired of you all coming into my country to tell us what we need to learn from you. Those Nigerians were in England going to school—could you go to Nigeria to go to school? No. So why did you think those Nigerians needed your help? Didn't it ever occur to you that you might have something to learn from them? It is the same here. The guy started to apologize by pointing out that he was, after all, drunk. No excuse, Kenne said, for it is said that people get drunk to be able to say what they can't say when they are sober. This being the case, he would appreciate it very much if the man would just shut his mouth and go home, so Kenne could continue to watch his show. As Kenne tells it, the man was quiet for a long time—maybe five minutes. As one minute passed into two and then three, the two friends of Kenne's started up a commentary about Kenne's power to make people stop talking. The Englishman endured the jokes at his expense a little longer, then turned and stumbled away to go home and sleep it off.

In addition to highlighting the importance of places like the taxi stand for public gathering and debate, this field note also signals the persistence of colonial relations and the cross-cutting personal histories of people who through economic happenstance occupy the same physical place. In the exchange between the two cousins about the relative merits of residence in the BVI and St. Thomas, the field note also points to the tenor of the relations between these neighboring island groups.

THE OTHER VIRGIN ISLANDS

Most accounts of British Virgin Islands history cite two dates as particularly relevant to the contemporary context. The first of these is 1950, when representative government was reestablished; the second is 1967, when the BVI achieved a ministerial form of government, with a Legislative Council of seven elected members and one nominated member, and a locally elected chief minister. I suspect that future histories will also cite 2007 as an important date, for this is when the most recent constitution was ratified. The constitution of 2007 replaced the office of chief minister with that of premier and grants the BVI greater political autonomy, paving the way for full independent political status; as BVI chief minister, Dr. Orlando Smith declared in his formal announcement of the ratification of the 2007 constitution, "the redistribution of power between the crown and our local Government in this Constitution says that we are a people ready to confidently assume the duties of self-determination" (Smith 2007a). What is noteworthy about all of these political watersheds is that they also coincide with significant economic trends as well as with key moments in the development of a BVI national consciousness. For example, the disaffection of the late 1940s that resulted in the reinstatement of representative government in the BVI was no doubt a factor of political events that were taking place throughout the region: labor unrest, independence movements, the weakening of colonial ties. But it was also a factor of more local economic circumstances, and in particular the migration of BVIslanders to other islands in search of wage labor. All of these circumstances also represented opportunities for BVIslanders to consider their relation not just to their family, home village, home island, or sister island, but to Great Britain and the rest of the Caribbean as well, and in particular to the USVI island of St. Thomas.

The largest and most heavily populated BVI island of Tortola is separated from St. Thomas by a narrow and easily traversed sea channel, and this physical proximity contributes to a long history of social and economic interaction and interdependence between residents of what are today two politically distinct island groups. In most historical accounts, the relationship between the two Virgin Islands groups is characterized in terms of a disparity between the urban USVI and the rural BVI (Dookhan 1975; Harrigan and Varlack 1975; Varlack and Harrigan 1977), with "the American island of St. Thomas . . . always . . . the axis around which the other orbited" (Bowen 1976: 68). In one account, the history of the British islands is characterized as "an almost continuous record of retrogression and decay," with the U.S. islands deemed to be "economically, socially, and politically more advanced than their British neighbors" (Varlack and Harrigan 1977: 3). While this account reveals a clear bias, it also under- scores complications and ambivalences in the relation between the two sets of Virgin Islands, for its authors are native-born BVIslanders. In a mid- nineteenth century BVI account, the USVI island of St. Thomas is described as "a point of easy daily resort" and the "grand ware-house" (in Dookhan 1975: 148); daily travel between the two islands was and continues to be easy and frequent.

Historically, Tortola provided St. Thomas with fish, charcoal, livestock, and agricultural produce in a relationship that BVIslanders today refer to proudly, pointing out, "we feed them." In contrast, as we have seen, in the middle decades of the twentieth century BVIslanders looked to St. Thomas for wage-employment. BVIslander Hugo Vanterpool recalls this period in his partly fictionalized account of life on Tortola and Virgin Gorda from the late 1930s to the mid-1950s.

> Times were hard in the British Virgin Islands, but the economy was beginning to look a little better now that large numbers of workers from the British Virgin Islands were going to the US Virgins to work. Soon they were sending back steady remittances to the BVI for the support and maintenance of their families, for improvements to their old homes or the construction of new ones. It was a time when new tourist facilities were being introduced for the first time on St. Thomas, and work flourished in construction. This was not only for the building of new hotels, but for private homes as well. A large range of job opportunities were also opening with St. Thomas' fast-developing tourist industry. (Vanterpool 1995: 127)

In addition to "passing through the window" to work on St. Thomas, many BVIslanders banked in St. Thomas banks (for there were none in the BVI), went to St. Thomas for medical care and consumer goods, and sent their chil- dren to live with St. Thomas relatives to complete their education. Even up to the present day, most BVI families have extensive branches in St. Thomas, and vice versa. Notices for reunions appear regularly at the ticket offices of the ferries that provide the primary means of transport between the two islands, and announcements on the BVI radio station of death condolences feature the deaths and condolences of St. Thomas residents as frequently as of BVI residents. Many people residing in the BVI today who claim to belong to the BVI through family name and land title were actually born on St. Thomas and hold U.S. passports.

The dependence of the predominately rural and agricultural BVI population upon the more urban St. Thomas was not without its problems. St. Thomians frequently used the demeaning terms "Tolas" and "29 dayers" to speak of the BVI workers who regularly crossed the channel to work on twenty-nine-day contracts. Many BVIslanders with whom I am acquainted recall being made to feel "backward" and "country" in relation to their more "urban" U.S. Virgin Islands relatives. For their part, BVIslanders point proudly to their history of agricultural self-sufficiency and land ownership, and particularly in contrast to what they see as an almost pathological economic dependence of St. Thomas upon the United States. In September 1995, Hurricane Marilyn struck the Virgin Islands, causing over a billion dollars of damages on St. Thomas, but leaving the BVI relatively unscathed. A November 1995 conversation between two BVIslanders about Marilyn and its aftermath that I recorded in my field notes illustrates the nature of the feelings that many in the BVI still hold about St. Thomas, the result of the particular nature of the historical relations between the two Virgin Islands groups. Both of the individuals in the field note are men; one is in his late fifties, the other is in his late forties. The older of these men has never traveled further from the BVI than St. Thomas or Puerto Rico, and the younger spent his high school years in St. Thomas and two years in the States at a Midwestern college. Both are natives of Tortola.

[Field notes 11.8.95] T. says God must vacation on Tortola, because there's no other reason Tortola got spared the wrath of Marilyn. Both R. and T. refer to Hugo as "a kiss" or "a joke" compared to Marilyn—a hurricane whose terror is measured in terms of the benign Louis who preceded her, the "ghuts and ghuts of water" she poured down in a few short hours, her winds and the fact that when she left St Croix she was still a class one, but when she arrived here she was a class four. In measuring the destruction on St. Thomas against the relatively mild damage on Tortola, both T. and R. make reference to the hurricane as a sign or a "God-hand"—punishing St. Thomas for its materiality and its people for their laziness, rewarding Tortola and Tortolians. At the very least, the behavior of St. Thomians after the hurricane seems to confirm [their] shared sense of people from St. Thomas as unable or unwilling to take care of themselves or their own, as people "with their hands out." They give many examples: In the 1940s and 1950s Tortolians going over to St. Thomas to sell charcoal, and being ridiculed for their cries of "coal" by St. Thomians saying, "Cold? I ain't cold"—and getting great pleasure out of St. Thomians walking the streets of Tortola now asking if there is anywhere they can buy charcoal. St. Thomians sending lists to their families of things they now need but making no effort to come here themselves to buy or convey the goods. Of boxes left sit on the dock in St. Thomas, to disappear when a back is turned, of a generator stolen, a lawnmower left in its place to confuse the hapless owner; of families who arrive in Tortola expecting their Tortola cousin or brother to take a day off to drive them around, and to strip their trees of fruits so they can carry them back to St. Thomas with them, but unwilling to even pick their Tortola relatives up at the ferry when they visit St. Thomas. Of a Tortola-born woman showing up after Marilyn to shop in Tortola and claiming it is her first visit in thirty years ("I ain't study [pay attention to] she after that"). And of people coming over to Tortola for a funeral, because the boat ride is free, feeding themselves and then returning, refusing to spend the night in Tortola because it's too dark. Both of them nod toward the darkening horizon where the outline of St. Thomas stands out sharply against the setting sun and T. says smugly, "it look like it's St. Thomas dark now" (referring to the still widespread lack of electric power over there). Considering the closeness of St. Thomas and the severity of the winds of Marilyn, the only thing they can think of to explain why St. Thomas was so damaged and Tortola was spared (T.: "I say to my aunt through that whole long night, 'I don't think we will live through the night, but if we do we will find Tortola completely destroyed'") was the general "depravity, selfishness and mean-mindedness" of St. Thomas people compared to Tortolians (who "wouldn't be waiting for government hand-outs, and wouldn't abide a curfew—they'd be out putting galvanized on their roofs as soon as the storm finished, curfew or no"). And, reiterates T., "these be family we speaking of, not strangers."

Such feelings notwithstanding, from the late 1940s to the early 1950s St. Thomas represented an important economic and social force, and particularly in the context of decades of neglect as a presidency of the Leeward Islands colony—"the colony's colony," as BVI historian Pearl Varlack puts it, "receiving only the crumbs that fell from the table at which the larger presidencies ate" (Varlack 1992: 4).

With the defederation of the Leeward Islands colony in 1956, the people of the BVI decided not to join the newly formed West Indies Federation. Upon this decision, the BVI was "elevated" from presidency to colony, "with greater legislative authority and a direct line to the Colonial Officer in the United Kingdom" (*Report of Virgin Islands Constitutional*

Commissioner 2005: 11). At the same time, the BVI also elected to retain the U.S. dollar as the Territory's sole legal tender. This move to retain the U.S. dollar as local currency signaled the power of St. Thomas's influence upon BVI life at the time; in strictly pragmatic terms. it addressed the predominant use of the U.S. dollar rather than the English pound as a unit of exchange. It also reflected a growing dissatisfaction with British rule as compared with the possibility of becoming a territory of the United States. In fact, from the late 1950s to the early 1960s the possibility of making the BVI a U.S. territory was even raised in discussions between Washington and London, but was rejected by the members of the British Virgin Islands Legislature, the peoples' disaffection notwithstanding (*Report of Virgin Islands Constitutional Commissioners* 2005: 11). The disaffection with the nature of its political relation to Great Britain was, however, the impetus for constitutional reform, initiated by Great Britain and resulting in 1967 in a new British Virgin Islands constitution.

The constitution of 1967 gave the BVI a ministerial form of government with a chief minister and two other ministers chosen from among the elected members of the Legislative Council. It also signaled a new attitude about the social and economic prospects of the BVI, sparked not only by an enhanced political standing vis-à-vis Great Britain but also by the prosperity heralded in an emerging tourist economy. In the foreword to a 1992 book commemorating twenty-five years of ministerial government, a prominent British Virgin Islander, McWelling Todman, recalled that "Ministerial Government brought with it a heightened sense of self-awareness, and a widening of horizons making it possible of government and people to see vistas hitherto unknown. Made suddenly aware that henceforth their fate would be largely in their own hands, all sectors of the community exhibited a burst of creative energy not only in economic and social development, but in the way people think, and feel, and, as a result, act" (Todman 1992: 5). Todman concludes his remarks by pointing to the fact that although "twenty-five years ago the BVI could hardly support at subsistence level a population of six or seven thousand," by 1992 the population had tripled, and the BVI enjoyed one of the highest standards of living in the Caribbean. Notably, in a veiled contrast between the BVI and St. Thomas, he attributes this transformation to self-sufficiency and the kind of moral superiority evinced in the conversation about the impact of Hurricane Marilyn; "economic development does not depend primarily on natural resources, but rather on people and the arrangements they make for the conduct and management of their affairs . . . men and women of good will . . . have collaborated in creating wealth, in capital formation, and in making the BVI a more congenial environment in which to live, and work, and rear one's children" (Todman 1992: 6).

THE VIRGIN ISLANDS' OTHER

Even considering the length and intensity of the relationship of the BVI and St. Thomas, the BVI historical experience diverges from that of the USVI in several important respects, but most notably, the BVI retained control over it most valuable resource—its land. Following emancipation in 1834, significant acreage was bought up or occupied by the BVI freed slave population, and the economic isolation of the BVI throughout the first two-thirds of the twentieth century effectively insulated the BVI and BVIslanders from the sort of land speculation and economic exploitation experienced by other British colonies such as Jamaica or Antigua. In 2008, almost 70 percent of BVI land still remained in BVI hands, and despite its status as a British colony, its economic and political unimportance throughout most of its history meant that the BVI experience has been one of independence and autonomy (McGlynn 1981; Harrigan and Varlack 1988). BVI historians Norwell Harrigan and Pearl Varlack summarize the distinctive circumstances of the BVI: "The former slaves quickly became small-holders owing allegiance neither to landlord nor employer. They were free in a sense and to a degree unknown in any other part of the British Caribbean" (1975: 175). We see allusions to this sense of freedom and autonomy in McWelling Todman's foreword to the booklet commemorating twenty-five years of ministerial government, quoted above. Even more explicit in this regard were remarks delivered by British Virgin Islander Pearl Varlack at the recognition ceremony held November 27, 1992, to celebrate the same twenty-fifth anniversary.

> Subsequent to our de jure freedom in 1834 our ancestors made sacrifices and endured hardships that can only barely be appreciated.... The Virgin Islander emerged from this crucible of hardship and sacrifice a rugged individualist, characterized by determination, pride, industry, and independence of spirit; these are virtues with which we are all familiar. He acquired, in spite of contrived hindrances, title to the land abandoned by the English when the going had got tough; he maintained his family in the face of laws designed to fleece him of virtually every penny he could earn; and he raised decent and respectable offspring steeped in the basic Christian values, whether or not they ever became wealthy. (Varlack 1992: 3)

As the legislative changes of 1950 and 1967 abetted BVI political autonomy and consolidation, improved transportation and communication between far-flung BVI islands and communities made possible such things as centralized education and banking. As McWelling Todman summarized them, these included "the roads we have built, the sea ports and harbours we have improved, the marine and telecommunications networks we have established" (1992: 5). Concurrently, BVI dependence on St. Thomas diminished. The establishment of a bank on Tortola in the late 1950s meant that BVIslanders no longer had to travel to St. Thomas to do their banking business or, importantly, to depend upon loans from U.S.-based banks to develop local resources. Simultaneously, the BVI government passed legislation encouraging the development of tourism, and this was followed by radical demographic and social change. From 1962, shortly after the BVI government targeted tourism as a primary economic development strategy, to 1965, BVI tourism was responsible for a 40 percent increase in the BVI Gross Domestic Product (GDP) from $2,251,000 to $3,157,000. By 1970, visitor expenditures and construction associated with tourism development had pushed the GDP of the BVI to $15,947,000 (O'Neal 1983: 113). By 1995, the BVI government was reporting a GDP of $396.7 million, of which $102.3 million, or 25.79 percent, came from tourism; in 2004 tourism revenues of $412.8 million constituted 46.97 percent of the total GDP of $879 million, and in 2005 an estimated 820,000 tourists, mainly from the United States, visited the BVI ("Tourism Summary").

Beginning in the early 1980s, the BVI began to develop the financial services sector of its economy. Between 1984, when the British Virgin Islands Legislative Council passed the International Business Company Act, and 1997, the BVI incorporated more than 210,000 companies (Cavaletti 1997). By 1994, revenues from financial services constituted 35 percent of BVI Gross Domestic Product, and in 2000 over 41 percent of all the offshore companies in the world were formed in the BVI ("The National Economy"). In 2008 there were close to one million offshore companies registered in the BVI, and the BVI was ranked second only to China as a destination for foreign direct investment (FDI) ("PRC Remains Most Attractive Destination" 2008). Also in 2008, the status of the BVI as an international financial center was recognized when the BVI was included, for the first time, in the Global Financial Centres Index of leading financial centers, just behind Zurich, Hong Kong, and the Isle of Man ("FAC Publishes Report" 2008). The estimated per capita income of the BVI for 2005 was $39,203 ("GDP Statistics"). By 2007, revenues from tourism and financial services combined to generate an estimated GDP of $1,143,254,000 (O'Neal 2008).

During this period of economic growth, the BVI experienced rapid population growth and demographic change. In 1960, when the BVI was on the brink of developing its tourism economy, the total population stood at 7,921. By 1970, the population had reached 9,672, and by 1990 "the total reached 10,985 followed by an accelerated growth of 46.6% reaching

16,108 by the 1991 census" (*National Population Report* 1994: 4.1.1). British Virgin Islands government figures from 2003 report a BVI population of 22,000, and estimates from the British Virgin Islands Government Development Planning Unit put the 2008 population at over 23,000. Some of this population growth can be attributed to the fact that BVIslanders were no longer leaving to seek work elsewhere in the numbers that they had in less prosperous economic times; likewise, some BVIslanders who were living abroad returned to work or to retire in the BVI. But most of this population growth is the result of immigration. According to the 1991 census, between 1981 and 1991 the BVI population grew by 61 percent, and over 80 percent of that growth was due to immigration. From 1992 to 1996, 55.2 percent of the growth of the BVI population was attributed to immigration, causing a report on the British Virgin Islands population situation to state, "'the table has now turned,' insomuch as population share is concerned, to favour immigrants" ("The Population Situation"). Today, more than half of the BVI population is made up of non-BVIslanders drawn to work in its tourist and financial services economies. Over 60 percent of the BVI labor force is made up of migrants. While immigrant laborers come to the BVI from throughout the Caribbean, according to the 1991 census, St. Kitts/Nevis, St. Vincent, Guyana, and the Dominican Republic predominate as countries of origin.

Enhanced political autonomy, economic development, and population growth went hand in hand with a growing sense of the BVI as a distinct national community, made up of people of "own kind" (Williams 1993: 153). We get a sense of a British Virgin Islands "own kind" in McWelling Todman's references to "government and people . . . seeing vistas hitherto unknown," and in Pearl Varlack's invocation of the "Virgin Islander" who emerges from the crucible of the slave and colonial experience. Even the discussion between the two BVIslanders about the aftermath of Hurricane Marilyn can be read as suggesting that the sparing of Tortola is an affirmation, by God and nature themselves, of a distinct BVI moral character. Certainly, the move to constitute BVIslanders as a single people is enhanced by constitutional reforms granting the BVI greater control over its governance; in this regard a sense of the BVI as a national community is a political artifact, "the relations between states and their subjects and between states and other states" (Verdery 1996: 226). Likewise, initiatives that began as early as the 1950s to promote a national culture muted long-standing distinctions between different communities of BVIslanders. The establishment in 1954 of a national beauty contest; in 1957 of Saint Ursula's Day as a national holiday; in 1979 of a national folk dance troupe; in 1982 of a culture officer; the publication in 1984 of a comprehensive collection of BVI folktales, songs, and recipes; and the opening in 1989 of a national college—all provided bases for the people inhabiting the BVI to think of themselves and their relations to each other in new ways. Rather than seeing themselves primarily in terms of connection to a certain family, or a specific community or island, BVIslanders began to see themselves as being from a single larger political, social, and cultural entity. In this regard, a sense of the BVI as a national community is symbolic and ideological, emerging "through discourse and political activity, as well as the sentiment that draws people into responding to this symbol's use" (Verdery 1996: 227).

While the restructuring of colonial relations, institutions, and networks laid the groundwork for conceptualizations of the BVI as a distinct and bounded entity, conflicts and concerns over membership in this entity, and claims to its resources, are related directly to recent economic prosperity and the demographic complexity ensuing from it. Indeed, claims to a natural BVI and BVIslander gain particular force in the context of a resident immigrant population that is greater in numbers than the population of "native" BVIslanders. The term that marks a "natural" BVIslander from the "others" in the BVI population is *belonger*. All non-BVIslanders are by default considered *nonbelongers*, while nationals from other Caribbean countries are also referred to as *down-islander, off-islander,* or *island man.*

Possessing and participating in a national culture may be a means by which a heterogeneous collection of people constitutes itself as a nation of "own kind," but it is also a means of excluding others from this collectivity (Foster 1991; Handler 1984, 1988; Williams 1989, 1991). Indeed, one of the reasons that identity assumes such importance and is so hotly contested is that what one can claim and legitimate as an identity has very much to do with what material and political resources one can also lay claim to; "identities," as Hanna Papanek has put it, "also represent entitlements" (1994: 42). Thus, the prosperity of the BVI tourist economy that is a source of pride to many BVI citizens is also a key factor in moves to consolidate historically disparate communities of BVIslanders, distinguishing them from communities of non-BVIslanders that swell the BVI population. In the same way, nationals from other parts of the Caribbean who are singled out as *down-islander* or *off-islander* in order to ground constructions of a distinctively BVI identity also represent a source of competing claims to the country's resources.

A population report compiled by the government of the BVI following the 1991 census concludes that in the decades between 1991 and 2021, "population will become one of the most critical factors in the development of the BVI." The same report distinguishes BVI "nationals" from a "large foreign born population" and notes that "with such a proportionately large foreign born population spread through all socio-economic groups of the country, nationals perceive that the country's resources are being drained through remittances of foreign workers, repatriation of profits by foreign owners and lost opportunity for up-and-coming nationals to enter the workforce and the ranks of entrepreneurship" (*National Population Report* 1994: 5.1). As early as 1969, a scant two years after the institution of ministerial government, the BVI had begun to institute means to protect BVI resources and rights from encroachment by the "foreigners" who were beginning to swell the ranks of the "national" population. In 1969, 1970, 1975, and 1977 the British Virgin Islands legislature passed laws and ordinances restricting the ability of non-BVIslanders to work, reside, and purchase land in the BVI. It was from a 1969 Passport Ordinance detailing who did and did not "belong" to the BVI and the Non-Belongers Ordinance, laying out employment restrictions, that the distinction between belonger and nonbelonger derives (Maurer 1997: 145–146). I discuss the history of the belonger/nonbelonger distinction and its misapplications and confusions at length in chapters 2 and 4. Of relevance to this discussion of the contemporary period of BVI history is the fact that the belonger/nonbelonger distinction emerged and was codified in the context of the influx of immigrant labor in the 1960s and 1970s, and is linked to local responses to the perceived threat of the immigrant population to the economic, social, and cultural welfare of "native" BVIslanders.

TOWARD INDEPENDENCE?

In her 1992 remarks on the occasion of the twenty-fifth anniversary of ministerial government in the BVI, Pearl Varlack warned of two challenges that BVIslanders would face in the years ahead. Calling upon a spirit of "solidarity and belongingness," and noting that "on land that belongs to foreigners our children can only be servants," Varlack urged her listeners to be mindful that "the first challenge is to preserve our heritage. Whether you prefer such terms as birthright, right, patrimony, or cultural inheritance, our heritage consists of the immovable property that has been passed on to us, primarily our land and culture." The second challenge, linked to the first, was to develop the institutional means and political will to "control of the political destiny of this country in the interests of the people who justifiably call them home" (1992: 3, 5). These remarks were remarkably prescient, for the most recent constitutional reform was designed precisely to secure greater control over the political direction of the BVI while clarifying who could and could not expect to govern the BVI and reap the rewards of its prosperity.

Ever since beginning research in the BVI in 1989, I have heard talk of the need for the BVI to prepare for independent political status. However, the status of the BVI as a country surfaced as the major issue in the national elections held in May 1999, during which debates addressed the question not whether there should be independence, but rather when and under whose leadership. The rise to power of a new political party in the 2003 elections reflected a growing consensus in favor of independence, and in a March 2006 address to the territory on the eve of the beginning of constitutional negotiations with the United Kingdom, BVI chief minister Dr. Orlando Smith (leader of the new party) emphasized the importance of proposed constitutional amendments for an independent BVI in the future.

> While we are clear that at this point in our history we do not seek independence, we acknowledge that this is a decision that future generations may wish to make. The revised Constitution will give BVIslanders in years to come the power and good standing to choose the way that is right for them. . . . let it also be perfectly clear that it is our firm resolve to stand strong in our determination to secure the legitimate rights of our people. We enter into these talks secure in the knowledge that we bring to the table a position that captures the hopes and aspirations of the people of the BVI. (Smith 2006a)

As was the case with earlier legislation that determined who properly belonged to the BVI, the move toward increased autonomy was abetted by the development of internal divisions within BVI society, in which people who lay claim to legitimate BVI heritage have greater access to the profits of the successful BVI economy than those who cannot establish such claim. The constitution of 2007 has gone further than any previous constitution with respect both to BVI political autonomy and to delineating which people can legally claim BVI citizenship and hence gain access to the rewards of BVI economic prosperity. In fact, the preamble to the 2007 constitution even claims a distinct BVI identity and essence, the result of the particular historical experience of the BVI: "Whereas the people of the territory of the Virgin Islands have over centuries evolved with a distinct cultural identity which is the essence of a Virgin Islander [and] recognizing that the people of the Virgin Islands have a free and independent spirit and have developed themselves and their country based on qualities of honesty, integrity, mutual respect, self-reliance and the ownership of the land engendering a strong sense of belonging to and kinship with those Islands" (*The Virgin Islands [British] Constitution Order 2007*: 5).

I treat the relationship between land ownership, kinship, and belonging at greater length in subsequent chapters. What is particularly notable about the preamble, however, is the extent to which it distills a very complicated social and political history into a natural history. While the 2007 constitution outlines the legal requirements for citizenship in BVI—noting the specifics of relations of birth, marriage, and so forth—the preamble naturalizes citizenship as an essence that has evolved. In this, the preamble mirrors tourist advertisements and tourist expectations, both of which posit a tropical essence to the BVI, the essence of an untouched paradise, outside of time.

CHAPTER 2

Making Paradise
as a Tourist Desti-Nation

THE PHYSICAL PLACE that tourists to the BVI visit is at once the historical place evoked in claims to a particular "essence"; the contemporary place that is the residence of people from the Caribbean, North America, and Europe and home to almost a million offshore companies; the popularized place of beach bars, resorts, and islands that are known throughout the world; and the idealized place of a premodern paradise. In order to understand what living in this BVI is like, I follow directions taken in recent scholarship and consider the BVI as a space that is always in the process of being shaped by the interactions of people, things, and ideas that move through it (Massey 2005; Sheller 2003; Sheller and Urry 2004). Development of the BVI tourism economy began in 1960, and in 2007 was generating close to one-half billion dollars in revenues annually. In my discussion of this development, I continue to illuminate the issues that affect life in a country that depends so heavily upon tourism, and that shape the contemporary BVI space.

The shape and sense of the contemporary BVI space can be conveyed through a comparison of two photos of the same landscape, separated in time by almost fifty years. A 1960 photo of the BVI capital of Road Town on Tortola (figure 2.1) shows a small seaside village around a perfect half-moon harbor, with two small cays in the middle and a large cay to the west. The green hillsides sloping down to the harbor appear to be divided into agricultural plots, and the fields surrounding a concentration of red-roofed single-story buildings close to the shore appear to be surrounded by lush palm groves. The harbor itself, Road Harbour, is empty of any sea traffic, as is the channel outside the harbor. The overall sense one gets when looking at the photo is of a sleepy town where nothing much is going on. A photo taken in 2008 from the same vantage point (figure 2.2) shows a vastly different landscape. In place of agricultural plots, houses and apartment houses dot the hillside running all the way from the harbor to the crest of the hills, and roads in different stages of construction crisscross the mountains that surround Road Town. To the west, the large cay has become part of the mainland, and is covered with buildings, the largest of which is four stories tall and houses the modern government administrative complex. At the tip of the reclaimed land on which the administrative complex sits is a large dock, with a cruise ship tied up. In the middle of the photo, where the two small cays were, there is what appears to be a forest of sailboat masts, and on the land across from this mast forest, every inch of space seems to be built on. The harbor itself is busy with sea traffic.

I do not make this comparison between the Road Town of 1960 and 2008 out of nostalgia, although Renato Rosaldo's notion of imperialist nostalgia—that is, Western nostalgia for that which we have had a hand in destroying—could certainly apply (Rosaldo 1989). Rather, I make it to suggest that regardless of one's occupation or one's age, regardless of whether you work in tourism or you live in a small village up on Great Mountain and raise goats, the landscape of the present-day BVI—the built environment, the tempo of life, the comings and goings of people—creates a space that emotionally, psychically, physically "speaks" the material conditions of a place on the move. And you cannot be in this space or pass

2.1. Road Town circa 1960. From collection of author.

through it without being affected by it. I begin my discussion of the development of BVI tourism with a field note that provides a picture of some of the complexities of life in the BVI.

[**Field notes 3.20.2004**] Every day since we have been here the beach has been swarming with cruise-ship tourists—on Friday, with three large and one small ship in town, the potential number of cruise tourists on Tortola was over 7,000! This on an island with a population of 17,000. Yesterday, though, there were no cruise ships in town, and the beach was relatively empty. It had rained all morning, so we didn't get to the beach until 1:30—exactly the time that our BVI friends [list of names] arrived. When we drove into the area behind Stanley's Welcome Bar we were surprised to find the place crowded with cars. After all, the beach had looked deserted when we had looked out at it from the verandah. When we drove in further we were able to see the reason for the crowded lot: Stanley's beach bar was hosting a post-funeral luncheon, and the cars belonged to the funeral-goers. In my bathing suit and cover-up I walked uncomfortably through the crowd of men in suits and women in fine dresses, high heels and hats. Just as I was about to settle on a chaise at

2.2. Road Town 2008. Photo by author.

the west end of Stanley's—where there were no funeral-goers—I was greeted by Allen Hodge, whose girlfriend Andrea had spotted me as I had made my way (invisibly I had hoped, but obviously not) to the beach. Allen and I made a date to meet at [his uncle] Henry's house Sunday after church, then he marched me through the crowd again, so I could say hello to Andrea. There may have been other people in the crowd whom I knew, but I kept my eyes averted the whole time, depending upon Allen to lead me to Andrea. I had been to enough funerals and knew enough about the local sense of propriety to be embarrassed about my informal dress. Once back on the beach and settled in with B. and company, I realized I wasn't the only one in a state of embarrassment. B. had taken the chair even further away from Stanley's than I. But to no avail. An elderly gentleman had spotted him, and had hailed him to come to talk. So B. slowly made his way to the front of Stanley's where he stood, in swim shorts and tee shirt, doing his social duty. When I made note of the fact that we were here in beach dress while all around us were the formally dressed funeral-goers, he muttered that this wasn't the worst of it—it was probably a funeral he should have attended. Shortly thereafter, B. disappeared to take a swim—one that lasted about two hours until all the funeral-goers had gone.

Around 4 p.m. D. called me to look over at Myette's restaurant, where a wedding party was getting its picture taken on the beach. The bride wore a full length gown with a train (that was getting completely ruined in the sand), her attendants (six of them) wore pastel tropical print sundresses, and the groomsmen wore khakis with blue blazers. D. swore it had to be people from abroad, as they were all white and she recognized no one in the wedding party. Because the wedding had taken over Myett's, Stanley's was becoming more crowded, as tourists seeking refreshments made their way in. . . . Among the "tourists" on the beach today were a wedding party from abroad, funeral-goers from St. Thomas, yacht charterers, villa guests, snow birds from North America, a British expatriate architect and his American wife, an anthropologist, the head of a leading BVI political party and his family, which included his brother-in-law and sister-in-law who live in Atlanta, one a surgeon and the other a doctor.

As this field note illustrates, the lives of tourists and the lives of BVI residents intertwine on a daily basis in the BVI, and the term *tourist* takes on multiple meanings. The field note is particularly good at conveying the places that are in play at a single beach bar on Cane Garden Bay, a beach bar that functions simultaneously as a post-funeral luncheon space; a leisure space for BVIslanders who came over to Cane Garden Bay from Road Town for a day at the beach; a different kind of leisure space for tourists for whom one beach bar is pretty much the same as any other; and a work space for its owners-operators who, as hosts, put on different faces for the funeral-goers, the locals, the tourists, and the anthropologist. What the field note does not adequately convey is that however intermingled the lives of tourists and the lives of BVI residents may be, for the most part they are experienced separately.

Generally, tourists engage in their activities paying little mind to the lives going on around them, except insofar as they fulfill expectations of what those lives are supposed to be like. BVI residents are certainly aware of the tourists in their midst and are friendly to them, but they generally don't pay much attention to them, unless the tourists are particularly offensive in their behavior or dress. For BVI residents who work in tourism, relationships with tourists range from the prescribed performances between host and guest (Smith 1989a) to more personal relationships that span multiple visits and may include sexual intimacy. This variety of engagement across lived experiences nonetheless takes place in a space that is indisputably shaped by fifty years of the BVI's being a premier Caribbean tourist destination. And while on a day-to-day basis BVI residents may not pay much attention to the individual tourists in their midst, tourists and tourism shape day-to-day experience in the BVI in varied and profound ways.

In contrast to the present day, when hundreds of thousands of visitors pass through the BVI yearly and thousands of individuals from other Caribbean countries move through its labor market, in the decades prior to the development of the BVI tourism economy, it was BVIslanders who were on the move. Periods of movement to and from the BVI for work figure importantly in the BVI collective memory. In a funeral eulogy in March 2006, a former chief minister of the BVI recalled the life of the deceased as a series of movements—to Virgin Gorda as an apprentice teacher, "through the window" to St. Thomas to seek work building a naval base, to Little Dix Bay to take a job as a charter yacht captain—and his recounting of each migratory event was greeted by a collective "yes" and "that's how it was" from the attendees. Movements of people, commodities, technologies, capital, and bodies have characterized the Caribbean experience for over five hundred years; indeed, as Mimi Sheller points out, "the modern Caribbean, defined by its turquoise-blue sea and loosely tied together by shipping routes, airline networks, and radio, cable, and satellite infrastructures, came into being out of these mobilities" (2004: 14). All of the people that I know in the BVI move around: they are from some other Caribbean island, to which they return periodically for visits home; they are from the BVI, and they travel periodically to San Juan, St. Thomas, Antigua, the States, Canada, for shopping, medical care, vacation, school, or to visit family; they are expatriates from Italy, France, the United Kingdom, the States, Canada; they are tourists.

A field note that I wrote during a four-day trip I took to the BVI for a meeting of the Board of Governors of the H. Lavity Stoutt Community College provides a good sense of the mobile space that is the contemporary BVI. This four-day trip was one of eight trips that I took to the BVI over a two-year period from 1995 through 1996, and so I imagine I was particularly conscious of my own and others' mobilities.

[**Field notes 5.6.1996**] I have just returned from driving from town all the way to the West to take my friend Kenne to the ferry dock. And on the radio on my return in to town, I heard an advertisement for an upcoming magic show in which the magician promised a great show on Wednesday, May 9: starting at the cruise-ship dock, and continuing all the way across Road Town harbor he will be driving a speed boat blind-folded! This same magician will be giving shows on May 12 and 13. Excitement is high, and comments ranging from the "I recognize him from TV" variety to the more surprising and intriguing "Oh yes, I went to school with him in the States." . . . A revival tent is set up on the Festival Village grounds and I could already see folks pulling chairs to the outside, the better both to catch a breeze and avoid the crowds. Of course, tonight the high school bands perform in the Cultural Center, so I imagine, as I drive by, a mini-exodus of sorts, 45 minutes hence, as parents in town for the revival make their way across this same highway outside my window, to the Cultural Center to hear the children play. The High School Band Concert is, by all accounts, a well-attended annual event, one of the only ones, according to W., that brings all the segments of the community together (black and white, as he amplified) . . . [meanwhile] at Governor's House, the Governor is commemorating VE Day with a reception, band, fireworks, and a ceremony focused on an assortment of World War II veterans patched together from the local community and the community of St. Thomas by an American expatriate who winters here at his retirement home on Cane Garden Bay. Aptly named Mr. Roberts, he is a pleasant fellow who never fails to wear to the beach his baseball cap with the name of the ship on which he served as a sailor in WWII emblazoned across the front. When I saw Mr. Roberts on the beach a few weeks ago, he mentioned to me that the Governor had asked him to organize this event, and that he had just discovered several vets on St. Thomas. He revealed this last fact to me with the astonishment of a latter-day Columbus at discovering a likeness among what he had taken to be an exotic other.

. . . When I arrived at the hotel on Thursday the first person I bumped into was D., a calypsonian I first met several years ago. Himself preparing for a trip to the States on the upcoming Wednesday, he asked if I had a copy of his performance from the last calypso show that he could use to put together a promotional video. A follow-up phone call from him today has me armed with a Brooklyn address and phone number to which I am to Fedex a video cassette by Wednesday. . . . And so it goes. One of the twenty-one framed photos of the H. Lavity Stoutt Community College that I had laboriously carried with me several trips back as a favor to the Chief Minister returned to the States today in the luggage of the daughter of a man with whom he served on Legislative Council over two decades ago. As I prepare to finish this entry, I hear the sounds of fireworks over by Governor's House and I worry that the noise will be disrupting the high school band concert.

Tourism scholars Mimi Sheller and John Urry urge us to think about tourist locales as "places in play," and to think about tourism principally in terms of the vectors of "people and objects, airplanes and suitcases, plants and animals, images and brands, data systems and satellites . . . memories and performances, gendered and racialized bodies, emotions and atmospheres" that converge in and shape these places in play (2004: 1). From this perspective, and regardless of whether or to what extent they pay attention to each other, the various categories of people who live in and move through the BVI are all operating in a space shaped and informed by the mobilities that pertain to the BVI context. A similar but more official characterization of the BVI can be found on the main page of a BVI government Web site. This characterization posits a BVI that emerges in the convergence of people, capital, and governance: "Being an export service oriented economy catering for the world's most sophisticated markets, human resources are the most critical component of our output. People are at the centre of our development and our changing population over the last decades is evidence of this phenomena . . . it is this combination of immigrants and BVIslanders, the people, who are responsible for the economic growth and development we see today" (*About Our Country*).

TOURISM DEVELOPMENT IN THE BVI:
MAKING A DESTI-NATION

The BVI was a relative latecomer to the Caribbean tourism industry. Tourism development in the BVI traces back to a 1953 Hotels Aid Ordinance that provided tax incentives to outside investors in tourist-oriented enterprises, and to a 1966 government-commissioned report that targeted tourism as the most viable development option for the BVI. In contrast, tourism in the Caribbean traces to the late nineteenth century, when wealthy Europeans first established winter residences there and wealthy Americans began to make it a regular stop on their winter yacht sojourns (Pattullo 1996). But it was not until after World War II that tourism became the major foreign exchange earner regionwide, with mass tourism—cruise-ship tourism, chain-hotel-based and tour-operated tourism—accounting for most of the growth (Pattullo 1996: 11). These days, tourism revenues constitute an important segment of the GDP of every country in the Caribbean; in 2000, tourism accounted for more than 50 percent of the national income of Anguilla (83.06 percent), St. Lucia (63.75 percent), Antigua and Barbuda (63.36 percent), and the U.S. Virgin Islands (56.74 percent) (Pattullo 2005: 18). This growth in Caribbean tourism is a direct result of factors and forces originating from outside the region: the introduction of nonstop international jet service, the investment of foreign capital in large-scale resorts and chain hotels like Hilton and Sheraton, the development of cruise-ship tourism. Thus, although tourism resulted in selected local infrastructural development in the form of new roads, airports, docks, and so forth, external interests control vast sectors of the industry.

The development of the BVI tourism industry was likewise made possible by foreign investment. But the impetus to the development of BVI tourism was the investment by foreign vacationers in a few small-scale boutique resorts for the use of themselves and their fellow elite travelers. A British Virgin Islands director of tourism recalled these beginnings in a booklet commemorating twenty-five years of ministerial government. Notably, he characterizes the early investors as "philanthropists."

> Tourism in the British Virgin Islands was significantly influenced by wealthy investors, *who may accurately be called philanthropists*, who visited the islands in the late fifties and early sixties, fell in love with the islands' beauty and people, and decided that the leisure business was a natural area for investment in these islands. As a result, tourism began with the construction of very upscale accommodations, directed at wealthy travelers with a conservative mindset. . . . Given the absence of any significant tourism history, such investments were perceived at the time as sound, and they indeed contributed to the development of the Territory and the industry. (Harrigan 1992: 79; emphasis added)

BVI government also played an early role shaping the nature of BVI tourism, and the relatively undeveloped state of the BVI physical and economic infrastructure post–World War II inhibited the development of the BVI as a mass-tourism destination. The adoption in 1959 of the U.S. dollar as legal tender assured a stable currency, and a 2008 per capita income of almost

$40,000 suggests that BVIslanders have on the whole benefited economically from tourist development.

Little Dix Bay and the Development of Elite Tourism

The opening in 1964 of the Little Dix Bay resort on the BVI island of Virgin Gorda marks the beginning of the BVI tourism industry (Bowen 1976; O'Neal 1983). The Little Dix Bay resort was built on 523 acres of land on Virgin Gorda that was purchased in the 1950s by Laurance Rockefeller. Following along the lines of his development of the Caneel Bay resort on the island of St. John in the USVI, Rockefeller built the Little Dix Bay resort as a retreat for "the world's most pampered guests," where "guests receive exceptional privacy, and [the] resort remains largely invisible from the outside" ("Laurance Rockefeller" 2007: 70–71). At the same time, Rockefeller also donated money to purchase additional tracts of land on Virgin Gorda and Tortola for environmental conservation; these donations were the basis for the formation in 1961 of the BVI National Parks Trust and reflect an emphasis even at this early stage of BVI tourism development upon safeguarding the natural resources upon which the tourism industry was to depend. A BVI government Web site acknowledges the importance to tourism of the BVI environment as well as of the institutions that are in place to protect it, declaring that "the successful BVI we see today was created with the use of the environment as a main component. The marine and land environments have been equally responsible for the expansion in tourist services, physical infrastructure developments and housing. The clear and pristine natural environment we enjoy today has been maintained as a result of deliberate policies and strategies of protection. . . . Even with the heavy flow of incomes from financial services today, the environment makes tourism the most dynamic sector in the economy" (*About Our Country*).

The Little Dix Bay project established a standard for the development of other small upscale resorts, and of the BVI as a destination for elite tourists. In the introduction to her ground-breaking collection of essays on tourism, *Hosts and Guests*, Valene Smith characterizes elite tourists as highly adaptive to the local culture, in contrast to mass tourists or charter tourists, who arrive en masse and demand Western amenities (1989b: 12–13). Other scholars also distinguish the elite tourist from the mass tourist on the basis of their experience as travelers, their interest in local culture, their willingness to spend money for a unique experience off the beaten track or in luxury accommodations (Crystal 1989; Graburn 1989; Greenwood 1989). These descriptions of elite tourists match a description that appears in a 1972 issue of *The British Virgin Islands Welcome Guide* that characterizes visitors to the BVI as travelers rather than tourists: "Fortunately, there are some travelers left in the world; and though the places where they can roam are becoming fewer, there is the occasional corner where it is still possible to be a 'traveler' in spirit, away from the rat-race of tourists. The British Virgin Islands is such an area. . . . Doctors, lawyers, professional people in general and the more affluent business men seem to form a high percentage of those who nose out the BVI" ("The BVI Scene").

The descriptions by tourism scholars of elite tourists are mirrored in the characterizations of the types of visitors to the BVI that appeared in a 1996 National Tourism Development Plan. This document divided U.S. tourists to the BVI into five groups: "estates and furs," "pools and patios," "nurseries and encyclopedias," "picket fences and heartland," and "Bingo and Baywatch." The latter two characterizations—"picket fences and heartland" and "Bingo and Baywatch"—were assigned, respectively, to white-collar residents of small towns with annual incomes of $45,000–$60,000 and to center city apartment dwellers with annual incomes of $35,000–$60,000; these groups combined made up only 9 percent of the total visitors to the BVI. In contrast, the first two groups of visitors were described as "established wealthy" and "upscale and well educated," respectively, and had annual incomes in excess of $100,000; these groups combined made up almost 40 percent of the total visitors to the BVI (*National Tourism Development Plan* 1996: Appendix 4).

At the time that the Little Dix project began, there were already a few tourist accommodations in the BVI, consisting of "an American private club on Guana Island, the Trellis Bay Club . . . on Beef Island, a guest house on Marina Cay, and the Fort Burt and Treasure Isle hotels on Tortola. A ferry, the *Youth of Tortola*, was also operating between Tortola and St. Thomas" (Encontre 1988: 29). Nevertheless, all accounts cite the construction of Little Dix Bay Hotel as the beginning of BVI tourism history. A prominent British Virgin Islander, H. R. Penn, devoted several pages of his seventy-page memoir to his recollections of the Little Dix Bay Hotel project. At the time that the Little Dix project began, he was the chairman of the BVI Tourist Board, and was called in to resolve a crisis related to the request on the part of Rockefeller to close a road that ran through the property, to secure the privacy of the hotel guests. The road in question led to a bay that was used by local sailors and fishermen at times when heavy surf made landing impossible at the bay they usually used, and local protests over its closure was threatening the entire project. Penn recalls a meeting at which two captains, one from Anegada and one from Virgin Gorda, were present.

[They] got up and spoke one after the other, showing the people of Virgin Gorda the great benefit they had already received from the Rockefeller work, and the still greater benefits both they and the people of the whole BVI would receive in the future if they would only co-operate with Mr. Rockefeller's request . . . the people of Virgin Gorda finally agreed. . . . Therefore, a special law was passed by the Legislative Council declaring that particular road to be closed as a public road, but reserving the right for the people of Virgin Gorda to land and pass through that road in times of emergency. (Penn 1990: 43)

Even thirty years after its inception, the Little Dix Bay Hotel development project figured centrally in stories told about how tourism came to the BVI, as in this introduction to a workshop on tourism awareness, organized by the BVI Tourist Board and convened in July 1992.

The British Virgin Islands forms an idyllic vacation destination, but it was not until the mid 60's with the Rockefeller development at Little Dix Bay that tourism really materialized. Prior to the Little Dix Bay Hotel development, the British Virgin Islands watched the rapid economic development of the neighboring United States Virgin Islands, while they did not have any economy save small-scale agriculture, fishing and charcoal. The British Virgin Islands exported almost everything to the prosperous U.S. Virgin Islands including its people, who sought various clandestine means of relocating to St. Thomas to work. The choice of tourism as an industry for economic progress was an easy one for the British Virgin Islands, given the benefits the U.S. Virgin Islands were realizing from it. (British Virgin Islands Tourist Board and Management Development Resources 1992: 1)

The construction of the Little Dix Bay resort initiated a boom in the construction of similarly upscale small resorts on Virgin Gorda, notably the Bitter End Yacht Club Hotel (1969), the Biras Creek Hotel (1973), Fisher's Cove Beach Hotel (1973), and Leverick Bay Resort (1980) (Encontre 1988: 37). Due to the inability of the Virgin Gorda labor force to meet all the construction and operating needs of Little Dix—and despite legislation that required the hiring of local labor whenever possible—the Little Dix and subsequent resort projects resulted in the influx of immigrant labor from other Caribbean countries. The 76.7 percent increase in the population of Virgin Gorda from 1970 to 1991 is a direct result of the development of these largely foreign-owned enterprises.

The major focus of BVI tourism is yacht charter tourism, small luxury beach resort tourism, and private villa rentals, all of which highlight and take full advantage of the BVI marine and coastal environments. In a book about the BVI put together by the BVI Chamber of Commerce, a British Virgin Islands author detailed the pleasures awaiting the BVI tourist: "From luxury resorts, small hotels and quaint inns to private villas and luxury yachts, your choices abound. Imagine spending your vacation in a secluded villa or on a yacht surrounded by tranquil breezes. Your experience could only be described as 'just beyond the imagination'" (Vanterpool 2004: 82). In addition to the beauty of the natural environment, another of the things contributing to an experience "just beyond the imagination" is the emphasis of BVI tourism upon small and exclusive rather than large and mass tourism. An advertisement on the back cover of the 2001 British Virgin Islands Tourism Directory highlights this. The advertisement pictures a small apricot-colored two-story guesthouse, trimmed in turquoise and nestled in a palm grove. Above the picture, but functioning as a caption, a headline reads, "Our Only High Rises Are the Palm Trees." Below the picture, in smaller text, the advertisement continues, "We do, however, have a whole raft of charming little places. Small hotels and historic inns that are extremely big on personality. Cottages tucked among the bougainvillea and mahogany trees. Apartments where you can see almost to forever." During the 2009 season (December 15–May 1) rates for efficiency rooms in guest houses ranged from $850 to $1,500 per week and for private villas from $1,400 to $31,000 per week.

Yacht Charter Tourism

Sail away. That probably should be the license plate motto on Tortola, the sailing center of the Caribbean's favorite cruising grounds, the British Virgin Islands. Whether you're an experienced sailor planning to "bareboat" your way from island to island, or look forward to hiring a skippered ("leave the driving to us") yacht, or just out for a day sail, the harbor at Road Town is the perfect place to start: the winds are usually steady, the sailing is easy, and there's always a buffet line of nearby islands to choose from. (http//www.islands.com)

While small resorts and private villas draw tens of thousands of tourists to the BVI annually, since the opening of the first yacht chartering—or bareboat—firm on Tortola in 1969, charter yacht tourism has been the mainstay of the BVI tourism economy. Yacht chartering is a specialized tourist industry in which crewed and un-crewed sailing yachts are rented out to tourists on a per-week basis. In the 2009 season, prices for chartering yachts ranged from $2,700 to $10,000 (U.S.) per week for monohulls and $7,000 to $11,000 (U.S.) per week for catamarans. The BVI is known as the premier bareboating area in the Caribbean, and its yacht chartering industry has the largest bareboat fleet in the world (Friel 2000: 1).

Most of the charter yachts in the BVI are privately owned, most of them by North Americans, but also by Canadians and Europeans. Conventionally, owners purchase their yachts directly from a yacht chartering company, which is able to secure discounted "fleet" prices from yacht manufacturers. The owners then lease their yachts back to the yacht chartering company for a period of four to five years, for rental to vacationers. The yacht chartering company maintains the yachts, and manages their rental, in much the same way that management companies oversee privately owned homes or time shares. In this arrangement, yacht chartering companies make money through the sale of yachts and management fees. Yacht owners can use their yachts (or similar yachts owned by the charter companies in locations throughout the world) three to six weeks per year, and use the rental income to pay off the mortgage on the yacht. They can also deduct vacation expenses and yacht depreciation from their annual income taxes. While the first of the BVI charter yacht companies were started by North American entrepreneurs, today the two biggest yacht charter companies in the BVI are owned by an international leisure travel conglomerate and have their management offices in Clearwater, Florida. Revenues related to the yacht chartering industry—import duties, cruising taxes, tonnage and trade license fees—are considerable, as is the money spent by bareboaters while in the BVI (O'Neal 1983: 117).

Typically, vacationers charter yachts in the BVI for one to two weeks and sail from island to island, staying overnight at marinas or in sheltered anchorages. In 1973, annual visitor expenditures in the BVI totaled $8,300,000, with 30.5 percent attributed to yacht charterers and the remaining 69.5 percent to hotel guests, reflecting the initial emphasis placed by BVI government on resort tourism. In 1981, annual visitor expenditures totaled $74,277,000 with 74.2 percent attributed to yacht charterers and only 25.8 percent to hotel guests (O'Neal 1983: 115–116). Statistics for the period 1977–1988 reveal that from 1979 through 1988 yacht charterers outspent land-based tourists, with the total visitor expenditures for 1988 amounting to $118.5 million (Encontre 1988: 88–89). Throughout most of the 1990s, expenditures by land-based tourists were slightly greater than expenditures by yacht charterers, but by 1998 this trend was reversed. BVI Tourist Board statistics show that from 1998 to 2003 yacht charter expenditures averaged almost twice the expenditures of land-based tourists, a trend that seems to relate both to the lengthening of the yacht charter season into the summer months and to the opening of several new marinas and yacht charter companies during the same period.

Cruise-Ship Tourism

Throughout the first thirty years of the development of the BVI tourism industry, cruise-ship tourists made up a very small portion of the visitors to the islands and cruise-ship tourism revenues contributed little to the increasing GDP of the BVI. The first recorded visit of a cruise ship to the BVI was on December 29, 1960, but despite predictions on the part of a local newspaper that the visit might "prove to be the most significant single event in the history of our economic development" (quoted in Encontre 1988: 29), tourism development during the subsequent three decades focused principally on small resort and charter yacht tourism. In consideration of a 1961 U.K. Trade Commission report finding the BVI underdeveloped with few passable roads and a poor water supply, but with "a glorious natural asset," in its beaches and waters (Encontre 1988: 28), this development focus seems appropriate.

Most BVI resorts are small and self-contained; many of the resorts located on islands other than Tortola are accessible only by sea, thus bypassing the need for roads. Most BVI resorts have their own cisterns for water and, up until the completion of an islandwide electrification project in the mid-1990s, most generated their own power. Charter yachts are also self-contained and function like a traveling resort, thus requiring far less in the way of infrastructural support than land-based accommodations. The completion of the BVI airport in 1968 facilitated travel to the BVI—although even today vacationers from the United States must take connecting flights from San Juan or St. Thomas—and the completion in the late 1960s of a coast road on Tortola's south shore enabled travel from east to west. These two developments further advanced the burgeoning charter yacht industry, and in 1991, charter yacht tourist arrivals outnumbered hotel and rented accommodation tourist arrivals 2:1 and all classes of overnight visitors outnumbered cruise-ship visitors 1.5:1 (*BVI Tourist Board Statistical Report* 2003). More important, in 1991 charter-yacht visitors and hotel and villa visitors outspent cruise-ship visitors 34:1 (Ministry of Finance 1992: 112).

Despite these radical differences in tourism subsector revenues, in the face of a global economic recession in the late 1980s, the BVI government took several steps to "enhance the destination's product" and retained a consulting firm to assess the cruise subsector (Harrigan 1992: 77). In 1991, the BVI Tourist Board published the first issue of a guide devoted exclusively to the cruise-ship tourist, and in November 1994, a new cruise-ship pier was completed off reclaimed land in Road Town. Since then, yacht charterers have continued to outnumber and to outspend other overnight visitors to the BVI, but cruise-ship visits have increased. In 1994, for example, 73 percent of the 333,035 visitors to the BVI were yacht charters and other overnight visitors and 20 percent were visitors off of cruise ships; the remaining 7 percent were day trippers from the U.S. Virgin Islands. In 1996, 59 percent of the 412,032 visitors to the BVI were yacht charters and other overnight visitors and 39 percent were visitors off of cruise ships. By

2003, cruise-ship visitors were outnumbering yacht charterers and other overnight visitors, making up 46 percent of the total 657,505 visitors to the BVI, compared to 44 percent for yacht charterers and overnight visitors. On the other hand, 2003 expenditures by yacht charterers and other overnight visitors constituted 80 percent of the total visitor expenditures of $377.85 million (50 percent and 30 percent, respectively), and expenditures by cruise-ship visitors constituted 7.5 percent (*BVI Tourist Board Statistical Report* 2003).

Cruise-ship tourism has been the subject of a good deal of debate in the BVI, beginning even before the cruise-ship dock was built in 1994. At issue is not just the impact of cruise-ship visitors upon the infrastructure, but the very nature of cruise-ship tourism itself. As the following field note suggests, cruise-ship tourism shapes the vacation space of the BVI in very particular ways.

[Field notes 3.22.2006] As is usually the case when we are here, we make our plans according to the cruise ship schedule that is published in the weekly paper. This schedule shows the arrival and departure times, the passenger count, and the location of dockage for all the cruise ships that are in the BVI on any given day. For example, on Thursday, March 16 the P&O cruise ship, *Ocean Village* (with a capacity of 1448) was docked at the Central Pier in Road Town from 8:10 am to 6:00 pm; there were three windjammer ships with a total of 388 passengers all day in Virgin Gorda and two windjammers at Jost Van Dyke all day with a total of 270 passengers. According to the figures in this week's *BVI Beacon* [weekly newspaper], for the twelve day period between March 18–30 there will be a total of 39,969 cruise passenger arrivals in the BVI—32,897 in Road Town alone. The arrivals in Road Town are more than twice the population of Tortola, and the total arrivals are almost twice the population of the whole territory.

For owners of local tourist-related businesses, the schedule of the arrival of cruise ships will determine how many shop assistants, waiters, cooks, they will have working for them on any given day, how much food they will have on hand. It also establishes a certain rhythm of life. . . . For local residents, the cruise ship schedule might determine what days they go shopping downtown, for when cruise ships are in town, the road traffic is horrible, the few narrow sidewalks are close to impassable, and the shops are crowded. . . . On the other hand, local department stores tend to be slow on cruise ship days, as local people avoid coming into town. And for land-based tourists, the cruise ship schedule will determine which beach they choose to go to or even whether one day is better than another for visiting the popular "Baths" in Virgin Gorda. . . .

On many occasions, I have heard BVIslanders complain that one of the things that is most irksome to them about the influx of cruise tourists is that "they don't know how to behave properly." In the most extreme cases this can refer to men walking down Main Street without shirts, or women walking down Main Street in a mini skirt and a skimpy bikini top. But it also refers to the fact that tourists walk in and out of shops without the graciousness of a "Good Day" and "Thank you."

At any rate, as we were looking through the racks of clothes [at a shop in town], I listened to the two shop clerks, who were engaged in a lively conversation about cruise tourists and tourism. One of the young women observed that as far as the cruise tourists were concerned, they could be in Jamaica or Trinidad. And not only did they have no idea that there were differences between Caribbean countries—"As far as them know, it's all Jamaica"—but they all acted as if the Caribbean was a savage and dangerous place. "It's like Africa," she exclaimed, accentuating the point by pushing her hand against her friend's chest. "All we ever know of Africa is lions and tigers. You think you go there, you get attack." Her friend hadn't really made the connection, so she continued, "Think on it. What you see of Africa? Natives dancin' with no proper clothes, and lions ready to eat we. It's all on the Discovery Channel, and National Geographic." When I heard this last part, I almost dropped the pair of linen pants I was holding up to test for size. "It's the same for here," she continued, and then, in a charitable tone, "You can't really blame them. It's all them know."

For a country whose tourism economy is based upon the elite tourism associated with villas, charter yachts, and small exclusive resorts, cruise-ship tourism can be particularly problematic. A report on tourism, part of the 1996 *National Integrated Development Strategy*, pointed out that cruise-ship tourism simply doesn't accord with the image being bought by BVI elite tourists, "Left uncontrolled, the islands might well be overrun by cruise passengers. Ultimately the quality of the visitor experience would decline, in turn impacting on the accommodations sector" ("Tourism Creates Both Positive and Negative Impacts"). In this same document, an owner of a major charter yacht company reported that "overall guest satisfaction with their vacation is lower when cruise passengers are on the playing field" ("Tourism Product and Infrastructure Strategy"). A 2001 report comparing cruise ship and yacht charter tourism also conveyed the sense of alarm with which many in the BVI greet the growth of cruise-ship tourism:

Typical mass tourism, such as large hotels or cruise ships, generally introduces crowds of visitors in relatively small areas. The impact is often substantial, and negative, for both natural and human environ-ments. Such large human concentrations, even when temporary, often result in environmental deterioration and conflict with the local popu-lation.... Local communities should never be overwhelmed by hordes of visitors.... Yachting, on the other hand, is very different.... Since yachting tourists are dispersed in time and space, they exhibit few of the objectionable characteristics of mass tourism. Yachting can provide the ideal combination of low impact on the environment, society and culture while making a substantial contribution to the economy. (Petro-vich and O'Neal 2001: 3–4)

Likewise, a 2008 guest editorial in the *BVI Beacon*, one of the leading BVI weekly newspapers, asked, "What about pollution and environmental dam-age? What about the resulting decline in high-end tourism, villa rentals, char-ter boats and other kinds of tourism that generate a huge spin-off revenue in the local economy? ... What about the additional congestion created in Road Town and on our roads? ... Anyone who must work, shop, pay bills, do business, banking, or simply attempt to pass through Road Town is well aware the we are already over-saturated with cruise ship passengers, taxis and safari buses" (Ball 2008: 2).

In contrast, while no one in the BVI is happy with the traffic on cruise-ship days, taxi drivers, small beach bar owners, and owners of small tee shirt stalls clearly benefit from the arrival of cruise ships. Taxi drivers are particularly vocal in their support of the cruise-ship trade. Having invested tens of thousands of dollars in safaris (flatbed trucks with benches and an awning) that carry visitors to and from beaches or on island tours, they would doubtless suffer were there to be a reduction in the number of cruise-ship visits to the BVI. In 2005, BVI government initiated a series of town meetings to discuss the cruise-ship issue, and BVI Tourist Board officials continue to seek a balance between an industry that benefits some sectors of the BVI population, but contributes minimally to overall tourism revenues, while challenging the BVI image as undiscovered para-dise. Complicating the issue is the fact that one of the main proponents of cruise-ship tourism was a BVIslander who acted as an agent for both the cruise ship lines and the taxi drivers. This popular and politically influential man was, until his death in 2007, a passionate advocate for the taxi drivers. Like the 2001 report that characterizes cruise-ship tourists as objection-able hordes, this man characterized the taxi drivers benefiting from the cruise-ship trade as small Afro-Caribbean entrepreneurs up against what he characterized as the big-time interests of a predominately white yacht chartering industry. However specious any of these characterizations may be, they nonetheless contribute to what is a deeply polarized debate.

In June 2008, the cruise-ship debate surfaced again in the context of an announcement by BVI government of plans to extend the existing cruise-ship dock. As in the past, arguments against the cruise-ship dock expansion cited too much traffic, not enough revenue to justify potential harm to other, more profitable, types of tourism, and so forth. But in the context of the higher airfares and cutbacks in scheduled flights to the Caribbean that resulted from the rising fuel prices in the spring and summer of 2008, these arguments carried less weight. As in the late 1980s, when the BVI turned to cruise-ship tourism as a hedge against a downturn in other sectors of the tourism economy, so in 2008 cruise-ship tourism was being cast as a solid fallback position. In the words of a 2008 guest editorial appearing in the *V.I. Standpoint*, a BVI weekly newspaper:

> with airfares rising and even talks of cutting some flights into the Caribbean, all of the Caribbean should be thankful for cruise ships. How much advertising dollars do you think we pay to get a ship with 2000 passengers to come here? . . . Our overnight visitors are not a dependable population, advertising alone costs thousands and factoring in other issues such as the American economy and election, passports, airfares, gas surcharges and exchange rates, we should be thankful for all the tourists we get, be they divers, sailors, residential or cruise. (Cullimore 2008: 11)

Of course, regardless of what position one takes in the debates about cruise-ship tourism, the fact is that the greatest influence over the future of this sector is wielded by the cruise lines themselves. As one BVI Tourist Board officer commented to me, while government may wish to limit the number and size of the ships calling on the BVI, the cruise lines hold all the cards. Should the BVI government seek to have only small ships come to the BVI, on a limited basis, the cruise lines could easily remove the BVI from the itineraries of all the ships in all the lines. In order to take "a more pro-active approach to cruise tourism," in 2008 BVI government formed a new committee to liaise with the Florida Caribbean Cruise Association, a not-for-profit trade organization composed of eleven cruise lines. In the first week of June 2008, members of the committee met with the Florida Caribbean Cruise Association to "discuss cruise tourism and its impact on the Virgin Islands." Although the president of the Florida Caribbean Cruise Association declared at that meeting the organization's intent "to be your partner and looked at as goodwill ambassadors together" ("Gov't Working with Cruise Lines"), it is unclear to what extent the BVI will be able to dictate the shape of its cruise-ship tourism sector.

THE POLITICS OF TOURISM IN THE BVI

The issues that surface around cruise-ship tourism in the BVI are at base about control: to what extent any single person in the BVI should have control over a segment of the tourist industry that has such a powerful impact upon other sectors of the industry as well as upon BVI daily life; to what extent the people of the BVI can exert control over a tourism economy that depends so heavily upon external investment. A 2001 report arguing for the continued development of charter yacht tourism pointed out that "traditional forms of coastal tourism development, such as large resorts and cruise ships, require large capital investments. Local governments and small communities usually must rely on outside investment. In exchange, governments must often relinquish control and enter into long-term agreements, possibly with unsatisfactory conditions. Along with the investment, outsiders frequently control key positions in the business. . . . Profits are controlled by the investors and rarely remain in the local community" (Petrovic and O'Neal 2001: 4). Even if it did not depend upon outside investment for the development of its tourism economy, the health of the BVI tourism economy is linked to the health of the economies from which tourists come. In a field note from August 2000, I make a link between public outrage over recurring power outages and concerns about the dependence of the BVI upon outside sources of support.

[Field notes 8.14.2000]   Since I arrived, the country has been plagued with power outages. It was particularly bad this past April, during a time when the country was waiting for a new power generator motor. But it doesn't seem to have improved since its installation. If anything, it is worse. At least in April the outages were scheduled, so you could plan your time around them. Now, they come and go at whim. For five days, VITV has been trying to duplicate some tapes for me, and have yet to get a solid two-hour run without the power going out. This wreaks havoc with their cable transmissions, of course. And E. can't count on getting her editing done without the power going off and screwing up her computer program. . . . Sunday's Queen show was slowed down (and made practically unbearable) by brownouts and finally a complete blackout that had one contestant finish modeling her evening gown under the light of hundreds of flashlights shined at her. I arrived at Stanley's several weeks ago to find a new concrete block shed at the top of the driveway—housing for a gleaming new diesel generator. Where Stanley used to spend his time in the laundry room or sitting in the shade of the bushes outside it, I am now most certain to find him in the generator house, sitting next to his new machine—same relaxed posture as under the bushes, same repartee, only now he and I talk across the pipes and gears of the generator that sits between us. In fact, as I write this, the power has just gone out. Fortunately, Stanley's generator kicked right in. But I still have the habit of taking my shower and doing my ironing when I have power, having been caught too many times with these essential tasks yet to do, and having no current when it is time to do them.

The country has also been plagued with a growing concern over its dependent economic status. More than ever before, I hear people talk gravely about the BVI dependency on offshore banking and tourism, and raise with alarm the dire consequences should "they pull the plug on us." The constant power outages and this concern with BVI dependency are surely related. "How high power can a country be," I have heard more than one person ask, "if we can't even keep the lights on?" The discussions I have heard about dependency also relate, I suspect, to a recent upheaval in St. Thomas over the proposal to sell the publicly held utility company to a consortium from Miami. One caller to a USVI talk show referred to the public utility as his birthright. BVIslanders understand this sort of claim, but are also quick to point out that after so many years of expecting the US to take care of them, it is little wonder that the folks in St. Thomas are in a position where they have no idea now how to safeguard and run this public utility. With the St. Thomas example right next door of what can happen if one becomes too dependent, it is no wonder that BVI confidence in its right to the prosperity it enjoys has been shaken. No matter how much they work to maintain a distinction between themselves as independent in contrast to St. Thomians with their history of dependence on US welfare, the big houses on the hillside and the fancy cars in the drive carry heavy mortgages. And as one BVIslander pointed out to me, "The money leave, you think the banks dem gonna worry for we?"

Questions about BVI economic dependency that I heard raised rhetorically in 2000 were being raised with a sense of urgency and alarm in the summer of 2008. With the price of oil in 2008 hitting record highs and the announcement of cutbacks in American Airline flights to the eastern Caribbean beginning in September 2008, people throughout all sectors of the economy in the BVI were wondering, as one BVIslander put it to me, "not if we gonna hurt, but how much" (field notes, June 9, 2008). This concern was even raised in the June 2008 Budget Address of the premier of the BVI, the Honorable Ralph T. O'Neal.

We must always without fail be vigilant, as this is a sine qua non, to our success and survivability. I would like to assure the people of this Territory that in fact we are paying very close attention to what is going on around us within the region and outside of it, knowing fully well that we will be buffeted by winds that originate in outer parts of the world. . . . We pay particular attention to the state of play in the US economy, as it is our largest trading partner, and our relationship is close enough that if in effect they sneeze, it would be logical to infer that we may catch a cold. (O'Neal 2008)

From its inception, the BVI tourism economy was fueled by outside investment. But as we saw in the recollections of H. R. Penn regarding the construction of the Little Dix Bay resort, BVI government made substantial efforts to accommodate developers such as Laurance Rockefeller, and Rockefeller's financial contributions paved the way for the formation of a BVI National Parks system. In like fashion, a cadastral survey of BVI lands in the 1960s transformed land that was held and used in common by members of extended families into fungible property. While this survey made land available for expatriate investment, it was also characterized as a stepping-stone to the development of an economy in which the BVIslander would be a "major shareholder," as a recent brief history recalls.

In the native consciousness, tourism to be financed by expatriate input, was the answer [to survive financially in a global capitalist economy]. This conscious decision was the starting point from which evolved much significance in Virgin Islands business development after 1950. First, it is critical to note that land had to be made available for the expatriate investor. This led to the British Government's rendering in the 1960s, for the first time in its possession of the Virgin Islands, the cadastral survey of lands. At that time, the native Virgin Islander was the major shareholder, and for him the economic benefit was the ready expatriate investor's sum for all or part of his land, the precise size of which he was learning for the first time after the cadastral survey. (Penn 2007: 35)

The growth of tourism in the BVI created internal divisions of the labor market and a related intensification of class stratification. Government legislation gives BVIslanders first preference in hiring, and as a result most higher-paid and higher-status public sector occupations are held by BVIslanders. Meanwhile, BVIslanders are underrepresented in the tourism workforce, and the low-status and low-paid service work in tourism is done instead by non- BVIslanders from other Caribbean countries. While the entry-to-middle level positions in the private sector are shared by BVIslanders and non-BVIslanders from other Caribbean countries, senior positions in the private sector are held principally by non-BVIslanders who are for the most part white British and Canadian expatriates. Likewise, most BVI resorts and yacht chartering companies are owned and managed by non-BVIslanders.

As we have seen, the 1964 construction of the Rockefeller resort on Virgin Gorda that marks the beginning of tourism development in the BVI was followed by construction of similar small upscale resorts throughout the BVI. Yet in 1979, locals owned only two of the fifteen major tourism establishments that were in operation (Turnbull 2002: 105), and only eight of fifty establishments listed in a 1988 BVI Tourist Board study were locally owned (Encontre 1988: 37). A 1996 report commissioned by British Virgin Islands government as part of a national tourism development strategy found that "the emergence of BVI's tourism economy was largely funded by offshore investment . . . [and] at the present time, the critical mass of the most visible land-based and sea-based tourism assets are foreign owned" (Coopers and Lybrand Consultants 1996: 7–7). A National Tourism Development Plan commissioned in the mid-1990s concurred that "the high visibility properties remain in foreign hands," but also pointed out that "there has been significant changes in the pattern of ownership in the industry in the past 10 years. Though no hard data is available, the anecdotal references indicate that the ancillary services are significantly occupied by the local population outside of the yachting sub-sector, there has been significant increases in the ownership of the Inns and Villas by BVIslanders, and in the tourist related retail sectors" ("The British Virgin Islands Today" 1996). To support the growth of local tourism-related businesses, in 2005 BVI government amended the Hotels Aid Ordinance so that smaller guesthouses would benefit from its tax advantages, and launched a program, "Jewels of the BVI," to market locally owned properties (Bakewell 2007a: 63).

Despite the historical reliance of the BVI tourism economy on outside financing, the BVI was singled out in 1989 as one of the few Caribbean microstates that had some success in exerting local control over tourism development (Wilkinson 1989). In some measure this success can be attributed to the unique circumstances of BVI early tourism development, in which individual members of BVI government worked with individual entrepreneurs to realize what were seen as mutually beneficial goals, as was the case of the construction of the Little Dix Bay resort. But it was legislation passed in the early 1960s and early 1970s impeding land speculation and prohibiting large-scale development that is in large part responsible for whatever success the BVI might have in exerting control over tourism development. The specific legislation impeding land speculation was passed by the Legislative Council in 1970. Entitled "The Restricted Persons (Commonwealth Citizens) Land Holding Regulation Ordinance," this legislation requires non-BVIslanders to apply for an Alien Landholder's License in order to buy land and also requires that all proposed development of the land be completed within a three-year period (Maurer 1997: 145, 155). In the decade before this ordinance was passed, BVIslanders had become increasingly wary of moves on the part of white British expatriates (who, as British citizens, had legitimate claim to the resources of this British Territory) to buy up and develop BVI land. A prominent BVI man recalled this during a 1982 symposium on the topic "Social Change: Implications for the British Virgin Islands."

> We had a number of Englishmen going around the countryside without cash, without money. They were, as all people who migrate, men on the make. But these men were going around the countryside to peasants who had never seen a thousand dollars at any one time in a lump sum . . . and these people were going around the hillside to Mr. X up in the mountains and saying, 'I would like to buy your land, I'll pay you five hundred dollars an acre if you sign a contract.' The man hasn't got five hundred dollars an acre to make a payment, but he would then get on the next plane to London, and he would sell it out to his colleagues over there, come back and make a good profit. And I can show you an article from the *Financial Times* where, in fact, one such person was boasting how he'd made a killing. (Quoted in O'Neal 1983: 125–126)

In 1967, a British developer, Ken Bates, secured from BVI government 199-year leases on four-fifths of the island of Anegada and all of Wickham's Cay in Road Harbor on Tortola. In the context of mounting concerns about the BVI being sold out from underneath BVIslanders, and when rumors began to circulate that "the only black people that would be allowed to go on Wickham's Cay were the maids" (O'Neal 2001: 76), things came to a head. A BVIslander recalls the incident in a 1992 book commemorating twenty-five years of ministerial government.

> The Wickham's Cay and Anegada agreements which were entered into during this period provided for the alienation of major portions of the reclaimed areas in Road Town and practically all of Anegada with attending benefits that were not available to BVIslanders elsewhere in the territory. The imposition of these Agreements seemed a denial of all the positive expectations. They were perceived as carting-off-birth-rights and future opportunities. . . . The death of Dr. Martin Luther King added a new dimension in that it took the fight to recover Wickham's Cay and Anegada to a higher and even more symbolic level. It now became a struggle against white dominance and black servitude. (Rhymer 1992: 44)

A march through Road Town in response to the April assassination of Dr.
Martin Luther King ended up at the Governor's House, where a group of
BVIslanders calling themselves the Postive Action Movement protested the
"sellout of the rights of the people" (quoted in O'Neal 2001: 76). More
marches followed, and in 1970, upon the presentation of findings of an offi-
cial commission of inquiry and with the aid of a $5.8 million loan from the
U.K., the BVI government bought back Ken Bates's interests in Anegada and
Wickham's Cay (Harrigan and Varlack 1975; O'Neal 1983; O'Neal 2001;
Turnbull 2002). That same year, the Restricted Persons (Commonwealth
Citizens) Land Holding Regulation Ordnance was passed.

One of the most significant consequences of this legislation was the
retention by BVIslanders of their land. Similarly, although the most profitable BVI charter yacht companies are foreign-owned, national legislation as
well as a government-supported community college provide structures for
local residents to secure an increased involvement at the managerial level of
these and other foreign-owned companies (Coopers and Lybrand Consultants 1996: 2–6). This legislation, and issues surrounding the involvement
of outsiders in BVI development, continue to have a profound effect on
the BVI, structuring the relation of BVIslanders to non-BVIslanders, and
influencing contemporary political debates and election outcomes. Today,
the reclaimed land around Wickham's Cay is the site on which the BVI
government administrative complex sits, along with the offices of most of
the trust companies that service the financial services sector. Construction of the Wickham's Cay complex enabled the development of a new
Road Town downtown, including a new coast road, as well as the pier that
made possible the development of BVI cruise-ship tourism. But perhaps
the most significant legacy of the Wickham's Cay affair is the role it plays
in BVI memory.

The Wickham's Cay affair continues to be invoked by BVIslanders as
a cautionary tale about the possibility of losing control over BVI resources
and the need to be vigilant about outsiders' greed. As recently as April 2006,
I heard a BVIslander refer to the Wickham's Cay affair in talking about the
sale of large tracts of land on Norman Island to an investment consortium
that, while including several BVIslanders, has as its principle investor a U.S.
billionaire. The Wickham's Cay affair also informed debate over a proposed
five-star resort development on Beef Island off the eastern tip of Tortola. In
fact, many in the BVI attribute the 2007 electoral defeat of the National
Democratic Party (NDP) by the Virgin Islands Party (VIP) to the support
by the NDP of the Beef Island project and widespread public opposition
to it. Meanwhile, as Bill Maurer correctly points out in his study of land,
law, and citizenship in the BVI, the legislation that was influenced by the
Wickham's Cay affair also confers differential access to the riches and spoils

of BVI's tourism economy: "Legislation designed to keep the English at bay served quite well to prevent immigrants from buying land and to keep them out of management positions and shunt them into service jobs and manual work" (1997: 145).

Tourism and Difference: Nationality, Race, and Gender

As this outline of the history of BVI tourism suggests, in the contemporary BVI, race and nationality figure crucially in determining individual opportunities for economic and social success. Less evident is the role that gender plays in determining such opportunities. Women's participation in tourism throughout the Caribbean is shaped in large measure by their roles in Caribbean society at large. Thus, where women have been involved traditionally in market activity or in crafts, they tend to become engaged in the tourist economy as vendors or producers of tourist craft goods. Throughout the region, the stereotypical association of women with the domestic sphere also results in women entering the tourism service sector as landladies running guesthouses or as owner-operators of small restaurants. Although advertisements for Caribbean tourism frequently feature pictures of women whose dress and demeanor suggest that they are sexually available and ready to serve, in fact, female prostitution directed toward tourists is less frequent in the Caribbean than is "beach boy" sex tourism directed toward women tourists. I address this aspect of BVI tourism in chapter 3. Rather, as a study of tourism and gender in the Caribbean by Janet Henshall Momsen suggests, "the main form of employment for women in the tourist industry is as maids in hotels" (1994: 112). Moreover, although more women are employed in tourism regionwide than men, men experience higher levels of training, advancement, and job security than women (Momsen 1994: 113).

Women have played an important role in the development of the BVI, including the development of its tourist economy, but few native BVI women actually work in the service sector of tourism. Rather, they contribute as educators, community leaders, and successful business owners (see O'Neal 2001 for a comprehensive history of women in the Virgin Islands). The first native-born director of the BVI Tourist Board was a woman, and several BVI women were centrally involved in the Positive Action Movement that culminated in the canceling of land leases in the Wickham's Cay affair. Nevertheless, it was not until 1995 that any woman was elected to public office. That year saw two BVI women elected to seats on the Legislative Council and one of them, Eileene Parsons, went on to serve as deputy chief minister and minister of culture and education in two separate administrations.

A population report put out by the British Virgin Islands Development-ment Planning Unit following the 1991 census reveals that women made up 48.7 percent of the total population, and 15 percent of these were immigrants who worked in the mid- to low-wage bracket. Women of all nationalities predominated in low-paying service sectors, although twice as many women as men were enrolled in tertiary educational insti-tutions, "including [preparing for] professions that were traditionally reserved for men." Notwithstanding advances being made by women in the professions, the greatest wage disparity was between uneducated men and uneducated women, "and the largest number of women falls in this category" (*National Population Report* 1994: 5.5.4). Although available census data do not provide a further breakdown by gender, anecdotal evidence and my own observations suggest that women's participation in BVI tourism follows a pattern similar to that throughout the region, with the exception that native British Virgin Islands women contribute to tourism through their positions in the public sector (as managers of Tourist Board depart-ments, as managers and middle managers in ministries of government, as educators) or in the private sector as managers of small hotels or villas, or as supervisors in service businesses such as car rental agencies, tourist-oriented shops, restaurants, hotels, and bars. The lower-paid, less secure, and largely unregulated positions of maids, cooks, waitresses, and street vendors are filled predominately by Afro-Caribbean women from other Caribbean islands.

From the inception of the BVI tourist industry, jobs in tourism in the BVI have exceeded the local labor supply (Coopers and Lybrand Consul-tants 1996), and so many of the Caribbean women who come to the British Virgin Islands seeking work in its tourism industry stay, setting up households and sometimes marrying, or having children with, BVI men. If a non–BVI woman marries a BVI man, she receives the full rights of citizenship accorded him. Although she will always be identified by her nation of birth (for example, as "from Anguilla" or "from Nevis"), her chil-dren will be reckoned as *belongers*, a term that is popularly held to stand for BVI citizenship, and that also conveys the cultural ascription of being of British Virgin Islands descent. However, within five years of divorce or her husband's death, the woman's rights to British Virgin Islands citizen-ship may be revoked. A child born to non-BVI parents or outside of a legal marriage union to a non-BVI woman and a BVI man is not automati-cally a citizen of the British Virgin Islands (see also Maurer 1997), but is deemed a citizen of the mother's country of origin. For such a child to be formally accorded *this* citizenship, however, requires that the birth be regis-tered in the mother's country of origin, and that proper citizenship papers be acquired. This is a lengthy and costly procedure, frequently requiring several trips off island, and there are residing in the British Virgin Islands today countless children who are "without papers," that is, without formal evidence of legal citizenship anywhere.

British Virgin Islanders fill almost all civil service positions, and BVIslanders are in a far better position than most non-BVIslanders to take advantage of legislative policies that limit alien land ownership and regulate the allocation of trade licenses by, for example, opening small tourist-oriented shops, restaurants, or guest houses. Nevertheless, while individuals from other Caribbean countries are most likely to work cleaning, waiting, and cooking at BVI upscale resorts where BVIslanders work as desk managers and white expatriate women keep the books, "to this day a significant mass of the Islands' high visibility tourism enterprises are in the private sector and owned by expatriates, many of whom live offshore" (Coopers and Lybrand Consultants 1996: 7–2). One BVI woman I know works Monday through Friday in a relatively high-status job as an associate in a real estate company that manages vacation rentals, and works weekends in a lower-status job as a clerk for a yacht-chartering company. Both of the companies for which the woman works are owned by white expatriates who live in the BVI. However, as a BVIslander, this woman is assured that her child will be educated through high school, and that he will receive government scholarship support to attend the national community college. A non-BVI woman from another Caribbean country who might have a similar occupational profile has no such assurances. Indeed, in response to the overcrowded conditions in all BVI primary schools and its two public high schools, British Virgin Islands government regularly warns individuals seeking entry to the BVI for work in its prosperous tourism economy that they cannot be assured that there will be a space for their school-age children in BVI schools.

In large measure, the disadvantaging of immigrants with respect to labor and educational opportunities is the result of a population policy that, beginning as early as the late 1960s, sought to control the social impact of what was cast as the necessary evil of imported labor. The BVI *National Population Report* prepared in 1994 summarized these measures, most of which were directed toward keeping immigrants from bringing their children with them or limiting the birthrate of "foreign nationals."

In order to ensure that development goals and economic growth targets were not severely hampered by conflicts between population, environment and development, Government's primary measures were the implementation of immigration laws and policies which gave the effect of reducing the number of persons being born in the BVI to foreign nationals. The Local Immigration Act of 1968 together with

the British Nationality Act of 1981 have the effect of substantially
controlling population growth by virtually eliminating the migration of
dependents of imported labour. To further influence the demographic
structure policy measures and implementation procedures institution-
alizing family planning and promoting reduced fertility were at the
centre of the strategy to avoid economic driven immigration creating
severe and unmeetable demands for social services in health, education
and welfare. (*National Population Report* 1994: 5.5)

Despite policies giving preference to BVIslanders in all hiring, land purchases,
and the awarding of trade licenses, only a small percentage of BVIslanders
work directly in tourism. The reasons for this are multiple and varied, but
seem to trace to several interconnected factors: an entrenched pattern of and
reliance on offshore investment in the BVI tourist industry; the long-term
practice of importing workers to fill high- and low-end jobs in tourism, a
reluctance on the part of BVIslanders to enter the tourism workforce at the
lower levels; and a lack of capital or credit necessary for investment in tourism, either through existing banking institutions or the British Virgin Islands
Development Bank established for that purpose.

These patterns of BVI involvement in tourism industry employment
are documented in a lengthy report, commissioned by the government
and completed by Coopers and Lybrand Consultants, entitled *National
Tourism Development Strategy 1996–2005.* The report is a remarkable combination of alarmism—stressing the dire consequences for BVIslanders if they
continue to import "foreign" labor to work in tourism—and condescension:
placing the blame for the low numbers of BVI owners and managers on the
shoulders of BVIslanders who, the report claims, "have made choices, and
often their choice largely was not to invest their money in the tourism
industry. This is probably due to the lack of training and knowledge of the
industry" (1996: 7–7). While chiding people native to the BVI for not taking
advantage of "the numerous post-secondary hotel management programs
and hospitality programs available" (1996: 7–11), another section of the
report points to what many BVIslanders consider common knowledge:
"The data seem to indicate that during the last three decades BVIslanders
have not had the pools of capital, nor sources of credit, at their disposal to
develop intermediate to large scale tourism products. The creation of the
Development Bank has not had an overall positive impact on this situation" (1996: 7–7). This finding echoes a sentiment I have heard expressed
by BVIslanders on many occasions, to the effect that the bank is happy to
give loans for cars, "but don't be asking them for money for a business."
As a BVI man, a teacher, explained to me, "the bank is always eager to
lend the local people *x* amount of money to finance a vehicle. They might

give you a hundred percent. Now what is needed is some gentle coercion to cause the banks to be willing to assist the indigenous Virgin Islander to get his first house or his first piece of land . . . or the first business" (field notes, July 29, 1993).

The case of one BVIslander is instructive here: The person in question, whom I give the pseudonym Robbie, is the owner of a small marina that has a small hotel, a restaurant, a marine supply store, and berths for sixteen boats. The marina is built on reclaimed land. When I first met Robbie in 1989, he was in the initial stages of reclaiming the land, a process that entailed dumping large boulders into the shallows of the bay across from his family's house. At the time, Robbie had been able to secure a bank loan only for the dump truck that he was using to haul rocks; the bank was unwilling to give him a small business loan, even though he was a native BVIslander. Robbie has worked in tourism almost his whole life, having been hired at the age of sixteen right out of high school to work at one of the BVI's first charter yacht company. Robbie's job at the charter yacht company consisted primarily of cleaning yachts when they came off charter, although eventually he worked up to the position of skipper. At the time, which was the late 1960s into the early 1970s, he made 75 cents an hour—$19 a week—and he recalls that if he was lucky, the departing charterers would leave unopened food behind—not just canned goods, but also frozen meat—that he would take home to his mother. When the charter company closed in 1987, a U.S. owner of one of the charter yachts asked Robbie to keep his yacht in service, managing it as a private chartered yacht. Robbie did this, and the man eventually added two more yachts to the fleet that Robbie managed. It was this same man who loaned Robbie the $250,000 that he needed to finish reclaiming the land and build the marina. It was only after the marina was built that Robbie was able to secure a loan from the bank, which he used to pay back his benefactor.

In all fairness, and by way of signaling discussions that will be taken up in subsequent chapters regarding the relationship between tourism development and the development of BVI national identity, the question of how and to what extent BVIslanders should invest their financial and human resources in a tourist economy is a long-standing one. Individually, BVIslanders tend to see work in tourism as less desirable than work in the civil service, in education, in the financial services sector, or—as in the case of Robbie—for themselves. Many BVIslanders point with pride to their long history of self-sufficiency as the foundation of their contemporary reluctance to work in tourist service. Even the exception to a pattern where most jobs in tourism are occupied by non-BVIslanders is illustrative of the attitude of BVIslanders toward work in the service sector of tourism. The exception here is taxi work.

For the most part it is non- BVIslanders who wait tables, cook in restaurants, clean rooms, sell tee-shirts and braid hair on the beach, clean and maintain charter yachts, and even greet visitors at the airport, but almost all taxi-drivers are native BVIslanders. Of these, almost all are men. One reason that I have been given for the exclusive participation of BVIslanders in taxi driving is that it is an activity that permits—or accords with—cultural practices long-standing among BVI men. As one BVIslander put it to me, "Going to the stand today is like going to the tamarind tree in the village long time [ago]. It could be two in the morning, but the men dem be there ponin' melé [gossiping]" (field notes, July 27, 1996). Another reason given for the preponderance of BVI taxi drivers is that the taxi drivers have a very strong professional association and as a result can dictate who can and cannot be a taxi driver. But by far the most common response to my question, "Why are all the taxi drivers BVIslanders?" is that BVIslanders are notoriously independent and entrepreneurial and taxi driving is an occupation that enables BVIslanders to work for themselves.

TOURISM DEVELOPMENT
AND NATIONAL DEVELOPMENT

From the initiation of the Little Dix Bay project in 1964, through debates in the mid 1980s about building a new cruise-ship dock, to the 2007 proposal to build a five-star resort on Beef Island off the eastern tip of Tortola, tourism development structures the way that BVIslanders think about their relation to each other, their community, and the larger world. Issues arising in the context of tourism development motivated the Ministry of Education in 1989 to make tourism part of the primary and secondary school curriculum, stimulated the founding in 1989 of the H. Lavity Stoutt Community College, and are the impetus to numerous training programs and workshops sponsored each year by the British Virgin Islands Tourist Board. Issues arising in the context of tourism development have made and toppled governments, and continue to shape BVI social, cultural, and political life. As recently as June 2007, an article in the first edition of *Business BVI* (which is subtitled "The Premier Business and Investment Publication of the British Virgin Islands") worried, "the B.V.I. is poised, ready to share some of 'nature's little secrets' on a much grander scale than ever before. But questions remain just how balanced the growth will be and whether the territory will be able to hold its head high in the global market with the quality of what is offered. Will the B.V.I. be able to maintain its global positioning as a unique upscale destination, which remains indelibly stamped with the pride of its people?" (Bakewell 2007a: 64).

This expression of concern mirrors the sort of critique that BVIslanders engage in on a regular basis, in the course of ordinary activities. This critique takes place everywhere from the editorial pages of BVI newspapers, to radio call-in shows, to government or business-sponsored workshops, to casual encounters on the street, and reveals the amount of time and thought that is devoted by BVIslanders to the analysis of the tourism industry. It also reveals the intricacies of the issues BVIslanders deal with in considering their particular place and role in a tourism economy. The following field note records a just such a critique, by the BVI owner of a small tourist hotel, upon his return from a vacation in Aruba.

Field notes 8.10.2000. T. was highly enthusiastic about the nice hotels in Aruba—as he talked to B. about them his eyes glowed. And as he talked on, going over the many times that government had been encouraged to do innovative projects to boost the BVI tourism product, only to do nothing, he sucked his teeth frequently in disgust—"They think the BVI so beautiful, so special, but I go to these other places and, man, they got nice shit happening. All that happening here the same thing been happening for years. Pretty soon the BVI not going to be so special, the BVI going down, man. How they think we going to make a living on four months of high season a year? They think I got money rolling in here, but it's only from maybe December through March that the big money come. After that, it's just scraps. And you can forget September altogether." . . . Apparently, T.'s real dream is to build a hotel down on the north, along Trunk Bay. I wonder aloud to them if the only way that will happen is if a big hotel chain comes in—would they really want that? This sets B. off: What do I think, that BVIslanders can't do for themselves—too stupid? I point out the history of Development Bank *not* supporting BVI projects, but he brushes that aside, continuing on about how tired he is of BVIslanders being thought of as good only for the small-time stuff.

While the issues that are the focus of public debate about tourism development may change—the closing of a public road one year, the building of a cruise-ship dock the next—the concerns and values that emerge in these debates have remained fairly consistent through the years. Consider, for example, the debate that took place during a 1982 symposium entitled "Social Change: Implications for the British Virgin Islands." The symposium was convened under the auspices of the BVI Mental Health Association by BVIslander Dr. Michael O'Neal, as part of his PhD research on tourism in the BVI (O'Neal 1983). The symposium brought together leading members of the BVI political, educational, and economic community, and the transcripts of this symposium, along with interviews conducted during O'Neal's dissertation research are invaluable, representing some of the only public documents of an important period in BVI contemporary history. What is particularly notable is that the concerns that participants in the 1982 symposium voiced about the impact of tourism development upon the BVI differ little from present-day concerns with BVI dependence upon an economy influenced by forces outside of local control, with the impact of economic prosperity on economic and political autonomy, and with the need for BVIslanders to play a larger role in the management of their own economic affairs.

Several participants in the 1982 symposium were wary of BVI government investing in an economic sector that was for the most part controlled by outside interests and that at any time and for any reason could "close their businesses down tomorrow ... [and] within a month the whole economy of this island would come to a dead stand-still. And those who talk about going back to plant sweet potato will suddenly discover what salt butter costs per pound" (quoted in O'Neal 1983: 130). Other participants in the symposium expressed a concern that the lure of quick money to be made from tourist development would undercut local autonomy: "If you want to have money to invest in big hotels, ships, sailing around the BVI, then you have to stop eating so much steak. You have to stop buying so many televisions, you've got to save money" (quoted in O'Neal 1983: 135–136). Still others expressed a concern about the need for BVIslanders to take charge of the tourism infrastructure: "There is more to tourism than watching the tourists come, and driving them around. You don't need very much training to be a good taxi driver, but you need a whole lot of training ... to be able to deal with the whole impact of tourism. And I'm not talking about training people to be waiters and this sort of thing" (quoted in O'Neal 1983: 134).

As the 1982 symposium on social change in the BVI illustrates, by the early 1980s it was clear that the future of the BVI was inextricably linked to its tourism economy, and the question of what this would mean for the BVI was entertained in public debate. In two decades the BVI economy had undergone radical transformation. While the demographic changes brought about by immigration stimulated BVIslanders to consider who they were in relation to the other Caribbean people living among them, likewise, involvement in a global tourism industry drew BVIslanders to consider themselves and their life circumstances in relation to a broader public. Thus, for example, in 1983 the BVI chief minister, H. Lavity Stoutt, concluded his Budget Address to the Legislative Council by comparing the BVI to other countries around the world. Beginning with a litany of problems in the Caribbean and abroad—"governments have come and gone; currencies have fluctuated ... delayed dept repayments ... world recession ... business failures ... unemployment at record levels"—the chief minister turned his attention to the BVI. Almost by way of a cautionary tale, he pointed out that "we have a nominal public debt because we live within our means; we contribute handsomely to our own development; we have no exchange controls; and there is a spirit of free enterprise in commerce and business, with the encouragement of a democratically elected government" (quoted in O'Neal 1983: 120).

At the time of the chief minister's address, the population of the BVI was 11,500 and visitor expenditures that year were $61,363,000. It was a time of unprecedented and rapid change in the BVI, characterized by one public figure as "just moving from a subsistence economy to a community which is a cash economy" (quoted in O'Neal 1983: 132). Also in 1983 the Ministry of Education published its first booklet commemorating Education Week, an annual event first organized in 1982 and devoted to the celebration of education in the BVI. Entitled *Preservation of Our Culture through Education*, this collection of essays, poems, reminiscences, recipes, and folk tales was seen as a first step in the critical task of "recapturing, restoring and preserving our cultural legacy" (Ministry of Education 1983: 8). As an introduction to the booklet by the minister of social services makes clear, this cultural project was linked directly to the sorts of changes that tourism development had fostered. Like voices being raised elsewhere, this project asked the question, "Will the British Virgin Islander become endangered?"

> Many visitors to our shores are thrilled with the natural beauty, the peace, and above all the friendliness of the people of the Territory and often times, we have been told to try and preserve these things. . . . It is therefore imperative that in our educational system, we learn how to manage the land properly, so that we could maximize the profits therefrom and not deprive ourselves of the heritage handed down to us. . . . As travel between the British Virgin Islands and the islands of the Eastern Caribbean became easier, people have come to live and work amongst us. As the Government sought to develop the Territory, investors, entrepreneurs and adventurers have also come. The question then may rightly be asked, will the British Virgin Islander become endangered. Will our culture be destroyed? Will the old values and traditions that meant so much to our parents and grandparents go out through the windows with the winds of change? (Ministry of Education 1983: 6)

If advertisements that market the BVI as a tourist destination were the only measure of the sorts of change that the minister of social services worried about, then his fears were unjustified. For over the fifty years of

BVI tourism development, advertisements continue to highlight a slow-paced, undeveloped destination, as in a *Caribbean Travel and Life* Web site that proclaimed "The BVIs are peaceful and harmonious. The people are reserved, the hotels refined, the beaches uncrowded and the sports noncompetitive. Development has been slow, helping to preserve the quintessential character of the islands" (http://www.caribbeantravelmag.com).

Yet twenty years after the 1982 symposium on social change, the BVI population had doubled, and over half of BVI residents were from other Caribbean islands; visitor expenditures had multiplied sixfold to $377,850,000; and for the first time, cruise-ship visitors outnumbered other visitors 56 percent to 44 percent (*BVI Tourist Board Statistical Report* 2003). To understand the contrast between the BVI represented in this description and the BVI represented by demographic and economic growth statistics, it is necessary to understand the relationship between the BVI space that is marketed to tourists and the BVI that is being constructed as a national space. I turn to this relationship in the next chapter.

CHAPTER 3

"Nature's Little Secrets"

MARKETING PARADISE AND MAKING NATION

WHEN I STARTED MY FORMAL RESEARCH in the BVI in 1990, I was guided by the question, "What is a British Virgin Islander?" As the discussions in chapters 1 and 2 suggest, this is a timely question. The BVI has a longstanding and complex relation to Great Britain as well as to the U.S. Virgin Islands and to other Caribbean countries. Likewise, when I began my research the BVI had only recently developed a stable economy and institutions that involve BVIslanders directly in their own governance. As the BVI population grows and diversifies. so that fewer than half of BVI residents are native BVIslanders, the question "What is a British Virgin Islander" is also one that BVIslanders ask themselves with increasing frequency. Indeed, as I suggested in chapter 1, the constitutional reforms that led to the 2007 ratification of a new BVI constitution were in no small part stimulated by just such a question.

In this chapter, I begin to address the question, "What is a British Virgin Islander?" through an analysis of the ways that the BVI is depicted in tourism representations. Following directions taken in postcolonial studies, I consider images and narratives that originate in the West about non-Western locales and people as constructions embedded in very particular histories and power relations and supporting Western superiority and hegemony (Bhabha 1990; Said 1994; Spivak 1987). However, as Krista A. Thompson (2006) points out in her study of photography and tourism in colonial Jamaica and the Bahamas, analyses of the ideological underpinnings of representations tend to reveal more about the West than about the people and places being represented. Thus, I am also interested in looking at the ways that images and narratives that are used to market the BVI as a tourist destination are also used locally, and particularly in the project to constitute a BVI national identity. Thompson undertakes a related project, exploring how tourism's representations of Jamaica and the Bahamas were given concrete form in the physical environments of those islands, shaping "the physical contours of the very 'social spaces' that they 'imagined'" (2006:

11). As we saw in the previous chapter, idealized images of the BVI can affect considerations of the physical look and feel of the BVI, particularly with regard to the perceived impact of cruise-ship tourism upon the elite tourism market. In this chapter, I also consider how narratives and images that are used to sell the BVI as a tourist destination intertwine with images and discourses that ground assertions of a natural BVI motherland.

I first visited Tortola in December 1977. I was a tourist, in the BVI with my boyfriend (now my husband) for a five-day learn-to-cruise course, followed by a week of bareboating. I don't remember much about that first trip. But a field note that I wrote in 2001 about the sounds that I heard from the apartment where I was living references that first visit, and suggests that I, like most tourists, was captivated by what I took to be true paradise.

[Field notes 8.6.2001]   The apartment I stay in when I am here is on a hillside overlooking Cane Garden Bay. Two nights ago, the Saturday of Bomba's Full Moon Party, I counted 75 boats in the turquoise waters of the perfect half moon shaped bay below. I first sailed into Cane Garden Bay in 1977, and the night we dropped anchor ours was the only boat in the bay. My most distinct memory from that night is of music. We sat on the deck of the sailboat and listened as steel band music carried across the water from Stanley's Welcome Bar. It was "Yellow Bird." The stars were bright, the music, combined with the lapping of water against the hull and the occasional clank of the halyard against the mast, made it a perfect paradise memory.

The music that drifted across the water to us then was steel pan. The music I hear at night from my verandah far up the hillside is more likely to be reggae from Quito's or the bass-heavy soca beat from Myette's a bit further down the beach. I have been in homes much further up the hill from where I am situated and have been struck by how well the sound carries—indeed, the "noise" from the beach bands has driven away a few North American retirees who built houses here in the late seventies. I wonder if they would have been so quick to sell their houses in paradise if the music they heard so distinctly from their verandahs was steel pan instead of soca. . . . Last night, I awoke to these noises: the neighbors in the apartment below, here for one of the numerous family reunions that are held during Festival, laughing and reminiscing, then leaving for town for *jouvert* [a predawn street dance that opens Festival]. The neighbors next door leaving a short while later for *jouvert*. . . . The neighbors returning from *jouvert*. Stanley's generator going on when the electric current went out. Early mornings, when it is not a Festival holiday, I am likely to awake to the sound of a backhoe moving slowly up or down the hill on its squeaky metal tracks, of a truck shifing gears.

With its references to people in town for family reunions, the comings and goings of neighbors, of backhoes and trucks driving up hills, even of the departures of disgruntled North American retirees, the above field note evokes a very active and mobile BVI. In contrast, my sense of the place I was visiting in 1977 was of emptiness, solitude, quiet; a sense not unlike that conveyed in the 2000/2001 *BVI Tourism Directory*: "Awaiting your pleasure just 50 miles east of Puerto Rico—but light years away in setting and style—are sixty-odd islands, islets and cays of virtually untouched splendour. . . . Nature's little secrets . . . provide an uncomplicated and grati-fying escape from the stresses of modern life." The images evoked in this 2000/2001 description of the BVI are consonant with images to be found in other advertisements and descriptions of the BVI, from the earliest days of its involvement in tourism to the present day. In short, the BVI are splendid, untouched, natural, uncomplicated, outside of time, awaiting your pleasure, *not* Puerto Rico (or other built-up and stressful locales), all of which is encompassed by the slogan that brands the BVI product "Nature's Little Secrets."

In what follows, I look at the images used to market the BVI from when I first started my research in the BVI in 1990 to 2008, when this book was being completed. I conclude with a discussion of the very first slogan to brand the BVI product, "Yes We Are Different!" and of a recent slogan, "Blue Is the BVI." This discussion moves more deeply into the development of BVI nationalism, in the context of BVI tourism development.

"Nature's Little Secrets"

BVI tourism advertisements have changed little since I first started my fieldwork there in 1990. In large measure, they play upon the slogan "Discover Nature's Little Secrets" and emphasize that "in today's bustling and over-stressed world, the [BVI] offers an enviable lifestyle, one that is slower paced and a little more gracious" (Colli 2006). The *Fodor's U.S. and British Virgin Islands* 2005 edition describes the BVI as "serene, seductive, spectacularly beautiful and still remarkably laid back . . . with the quali-ties of yesteryear's Caribbean" (163). This description differs little from a 1993 *Fodor's* description that also characterized the BVI as "serene, seduc-tive, and spectacularly beautiful even by Caribbean standards" (1993: 159). The phrase in the 1993 description, "even by Caribbean standards" works like the phrase "a little more gracious" to set the BVI apart from other Caribbean destinations and to tell the tourist that a BVI vacation is some-thing special. An ad in the November 2006 issue of *Condé Nast Traveler* evokes the sort of breathless BVI experience that my memory of my first visit thirty years ago conjures up. This full-page ad pictures a table set with linen and silver, on a deserted beach. A white man bends over the white woman seated at the table, his lips to her ear. A yacht standard bearing the "Nature's Little Secrets" slogan is in the left-hand corner of the ad and a heading above the picture reads, "Discover a secret world where silence is the only sound on earth." As a caption to the picture, the narrative continues, "'My breath is lost for words . . . whisper again how we're alone and all of this is ours,' she asked with a coy smile. Here fairy tales come true, often hidden among warm cozy beaches, expressed softly by the winds, forever surrounded by crystal clear waters. You've arrived at one of Nature's Little Secrets. Come, find them all."

The *Conde Nast Traveler* advertisement's emphasis on silence and solitude is in sharp contrast to the noisiness and busyness that my field note documents. It also masks the challenges the BVI confronts in its effort to maintain its position in the competitive global tourism market. From the 1953 BVI Hotel Aids Ordinance that provided tax incentives to investors in tourist-oriented enterprises to 2008 debates over the development of a five-star resort on Beef Island, BVI tourism has changed considerably. What the tourism industry characterized in 1989 as "virgin holiday territory" it now "characterizes as a 'market-worn' destination" (Bakewell 2007a: 63). In 2007, the BVI government was scrambling to regain the BVI's competitive edge in the Caribbean tourism market, and even the 2007 edition of

3.1. Panorama of Cane Garden Bay, Tortola. Photo by author.

Fodor's U.S and British Virgin Islands noted "the explosive growth in the territory's tourism" with a description that began, "Once a collection of about 50 sleepy islands and cays, the British Virgin Islands (BVI) are in the midst of transition. The main island of Tortola now sees huge cruise ships crowding its dock outside Road Town. Shoppers clog the downtown area on busy cruise-ship days, and traffic occasionally comes to a standstill" (2007: 134–135).

The "Nature's Little Secrets" campaign was developed by a U.K. consulting company, and was officially launched in 1989. With an initial budget of $800,000, the campaign was designed to market the BVI as "'virgin holiday territory,' one of the few remaining outposts of the old British Empire" (FCB/InterMarketing 1989). In drawing upon the concept "virgin," this BVI tourism campaign constituted a Caribbean of singular natural beauty, of pure white sands and crystal-clear water. At the same time, its reference to Empire constituted this Caribbean anew as a site of discovery. Even a press release announcing the launch of the "Nature's Little Secrets" campaign was subtitled, "Waiting to be Discovered" (FCB/InterMarketing 1989). Early ads from this campaign typically picture a deserted beach and/or a deserted anchorage, with the "Nature's Little Secrets" slogan prominently displayed. Most ads invite tourists to "Discover Nature's Little Secrets," while one ad invites tourists to consummate the relationship and *experience* "Nature's Little Secrets." In a popular ad that was run throughout the 1990s we see a white couple on a deserted white sand beach, looking for seashells in its turquoise blue shallows. A title running along the top of the picture reads, "What less could you want?" The caption running below it answers, "Glitz. Zero. Unspoiled tranquility, everything."

In some measure, the "Nature's Little Secrets" ad campaign reflected the state of BVI tourism industry at the time that it was launched, when the BVI was just beginning to make its mark in the global tourism market and was virgin territory for marketers and tourists alike. However, a visit in 2007 to the BVI Tourist Board Web site reveals that the notion of the BVI as pristine territory open for exploration is still a central component of the BVI tourism marketing strategy: "Welcome to the official site of the British Virgin Islands (BVI). Discover 'Nature's Little Secrets'—over 60 pristine Caribbean islands that comprise the BVI. Our unspoilt, idyllic islands are as beautiful as our people and culture. Come explore our white sand beaches, turquoise waters and vibrant lifestyle" (http://www.bvitourism. com). Advertisements appearing in 2006 and 2007 in *Travel and Leisure*, *Sailing World*, *Condé Nast Traveler*, and even *Bride Guide* and *Men's Journal* also highlight the "soft breezes, warm inviting waters and hidden sandy beaches" of "Nature's Little Secrets," and invite tourists to "Come, find them all." An ad in a May 2007 *Travel Agent* urges readers to "give your clients and civilization a rest . . . it'll be our little secret." Even an article in *Business BVI*—a magazine whose existence alludes to a BVI very much involved in a commercial world—points to the persistence of the images behind the Nature's Little Secrets brand that was first launched in 1989: "The BVI has earned a reputation in the Caribbean and the wider world for its 'less-is-more' attitude. The people who travel here are looking for beautiful surroundings, low-key but high-quality services, and a lot of peace and quiet. For these travelers, what is not there is just as important as what is" (Raas 2007: 69).

Discovering Nature's Little Secrets

Given the importance of yacht chartering tourism in the BVI, it is hardly surprising that many of the "Nature's Little Secrets" ads also play to the Western desire for adventure and discovery, while assuaging any fear of risk associated with sailing the open seas. A British Virgin Islands Tourist Board *Guide for Crewed Charter Yachts* that was available throughout the 1990s stressed that "the crystal clear waters provide protected cruising, and exhilarating sailing, always in the sight of land, with sheltered anchorages around every corner." An ad in the March 2007 issue of *Sailing World* proclaims, "It's impossible to get lost here," while the Web site of the Moorings, the leading BVI yacht chartering firm, assures potential clients with words like *trust*, *easy*, *consistent*, and *protected*:

> Stunning beauty, relaxed sailing and endless activities surround you in the BVI. Trust the trade winds to carry you to whatever you're looking for. Crystal clear waters, boulder-formed caves and picture-perfect beaches combine with oceanfront resorts and restaurants to provide sailors with a colorful wealth of welcomes. Easy deep-water island-hops, consistent breezes, line-of-sight navigation in protected waters and numerous anchorages for evenings ashore make this the ideal island paradise for less experienced sailors or those who simply want a more relaxed vacation. And you can island hop throughout the BVI without the hassles of customs clearance. (www.moorings.com/ Destinations.aspx?Destination=Tortola)

Other tourism materials suggest that the combination of safety and adventure marketed to BVI tourists is to be found not just on the BVI's world-famous sailing grounds but also in interactions with BVI people themselves. For example, the Union Jack and the BVI national motto *Vigilate* appear regularly in Tourist Board publications along side claims that "local residents are friendly and hospitable, and the territory is virtually crime free" (*British Virgin Islands: A Guide to Crewed Charter Yachts* 1989). Scenes from a BVI promotional video produced in the early 1990s show white tourists being greeted by smiling locals. This video that promises Western visitors an experience of the Other free of the stress and fear that may characterize racial relations at home also assuages tourist fears by suggesting that the friendliness, lawfulness, and dignity of BVIslanders are as "natural" as the landscape in which they live. For example, a voiceover in the video promises that "the majestic and relatively untouched panorama of land, sea and sky—and the gentle and nurturing quality of the people— can work their magic on the soul without interruption. This allows you to discover those enlightening (and rare) moments when man and the environment are in perfect harmony" (*The British Virgin Islands: Nature's Little Secrets* 1994). Of course, to the extent that the harmony promised in the video draws upon Western notions of a colonial stability, of compliant locals and social structures predictable in their rigidity, it also assures the tourist that in this adventure all will be well.

The marketing of colonial stability is nowhere more evident than at Pusser's Landing. Located at Soper's Hole, a sheltered anchorage on the extreme west end of Tortola, Pusser's Landing is a featured stop on cruise-ship land tours and a popular day stop for the bareboater. The Pusser's concept was developed in 1979 by American expatriate Charles Tobias, an early BVI "branding entrepreneur" (Bakewell 2007b: 13) who developed and marketed the Pusser's brand of rum, based on the original British Royal Navy recipe. Pusser's Landing is a restaurant and set of stores that, drawing on the BVI colonial past, is constructed as the Great House, surrounded by colorful vernacular Caribbean cottages. With its world-famous rum wrapped in a Union Jack, British navy paraphernalia, and line of adventure clothing, Pusser's also recreates the British club that so insulated colonials from their native subjects. There are five Pusser's restaurants and stores located throughout the BVI, and Pusser's establishments have even been opened in cities in the United States and Europe. Pusser's is perhaps most famous for the "Painkiller," a drink that embodies in liquid form the sort of reality-insulation that Pusser's seems to want to evoke.

Paradoxically, even as tourists are invited to consume literally and figuratively a very specific colonial past, the "Nature's Little Secrets" campaign sells them a BVI untouched even by time and history, as in a *Discover Nature's Little Secrets* brochure that flattens a history of conquest, enslavement, and colonization into a parade of "all 'visitors' through the centuries [for whom] the islands have . . . held a certain time-less fascination. . . . The very first visitors to the BVI were Arawak and Carib Indians—followed in turn by early English adventurers, Dutch, French and Spanish explorers, marauding pirates, plantation owners,

Quakers and other settlers. Today, visitors come by plane rather than boat, with relaxation on their minds." In conflating the contemporary BVI tourist experience with that of other Western visitors (among them Sir Francis Drake, whose visit to the BVI "enroute to conquering Hispaniola" is resuscitated in the same brochure as "personal whim as much as strategy"), this narrative obscures a history of domination by romanticizing it, illustrating the point that images of the Other in representations by or for the West work powerfully to conceal actual historical relations of power (Sheller 2003; Williamson 1986). A 2007 article explaining the ins and outs of buying property in the BVI operates similarly, exclaiming that, "Ever since Columbus came across the Virgin Islands on his second voyage to the New World in 1493, intrepid explorers have been discovering our islands by sea. But these days fewer pirates stop by!" (Chris Smith 2007: 87). And a yacht charterer's musings characterize discovery and plunder as "reverie."

> Savoring a freshly brewed mug of coffee, I sat on the front deck of our chartered 43-foot catamaran and watched the morning show. Laser-like rays of sunlight streamed through a cottony cloudbank, bringing life to the emerald islands and turquoise seas surrounding our anchorage. My mind drifted back several centuries. What would it have been like to sail with Columbus and chart these waters for the first time? How would it feel to cast about the deserted beaches for the perfect place to bury plundered treasure? The aroma of freshly made banana pancakes roused me from my reverie. (*Fodor's U.S. and British Virgin Islands* 2007: 197)

These narratives that collapse the history of the BVI into a parade of "visitors" also racialize the tourist to whom they are addressed, suggesting that the latter-day discoverers of nature's little secrets will, like discoverers before them, be Western, white, and male. That nature's little secrets are intended for discovery only by certain tourists became apparent when a colleague of mine, an African American sociologist, came down to visit me during one of my research trips:

[**Field notes 7.25.1996**]   Diane arrived today, and I could tell by the way that she walked off the plane that she had a story to tell. She hardly acknowledged that she had arrived before launching into her story/analysis. She reported being the only black person on the small plane from San Juan to Tortola, and that her seat mate—a white North American flying in for a two-week charter yacht vacation—assumed that this meant she was a British Virgin Islander. "Going home?" he asked her, by way of striking up a conversation. When she answered "no," he responded, "Oh, then you're visiting family." She told me that when she corrected him, telling him that she was going to the BVI for a vacation, he was completely mystified. "Like black people aren't in on the secret." She was going strong. "That's it. Nature's Little Secrets [she has read my articles] aren't for colored folk. We are either natives or with housekeeping."

Making "Nature's Little Secrets" Work

The BVI is able to exploit images of pristine and untouched tropical isles in a way that makes sense to local residents and tourists alike in part because of the historical circumstances that left it ignored by the United Kingdom—and the rest of the world for that matter—until its constant trade winds and safe waters made it an ideal location for the development of marine and yacht tourism. In the present day, the nature of the tourist traffic in the BVI helps to mask the busyness of the life of many BVIslanders as well as the business behind a successful tourist destination.

Accommodations for land-based tourists are for the most part provided by upscale resorts located on isolated islands with their own beaches or by secluded luxury villas with their own swimming pools. Yacht charterers who go ashore at select anchorages seldom venture beyond the laid-back beach bars and beach-side restaurants that have been established to serve them. Even individuals coming to do business in the BVI's growing offshore financial sector seem to have difficulty moving outside of the "Nature's Little Secrets" conceptual frame, as illustrated by a narrative appearing in *International Money Marketing* declaring that "On the surface, it is hard to believe that there is a substantial amount of business activity in Road Town, the sleepy metropolis of the Caribbean island of Tortola, largest of the BVI. Certainly, as a visiting businessman, you can't help feeling slightly incongruous in your shirt and tie as you step over chickens on the sidewalk. This is the deceptively laid-back face of a fast-growing offshore financial community" (Newell 1996: 3). In any case, BVI-bound tourists seldom even see Road Town—which is the center of government, banking, and industry—or the cruise-ship shoppers and traffic congestion to which the 2007 *Fodor's* description refers. Rather, tourists seek "the beaches where you can walk for miles all alone, and others sprinkled with quaint bars and restaurants where you can enjoy rum drinks, feast on local seafood and dance the night away" ("Beauty and the Beaches" 2007).

In his analysis of the economics of the tourist industry, John Urry stresses that the quality of the social interaction between the provider of a given service in a tourist locale and the tourist is an essential component of the product being purchased by the tourist. The tourist's assessments of both the locale and the quality of this interaction will, of course, depend on their consonance with the preconceptions that the tourist brings to them. In both respects, while producers of services are fixed spatially, service is being marketed globally. Therefore a tourist economy's strategies for marketing and delivery must be quite well conceived and organized (Urry 1990: 40–43). This need for savvy in marketing and delivery belies another BVI tourist brochure claim that "we are not a hive of busy social activity" and undermines images of British Virgin Island residents as passive or laid back. So too does the cosmopolitan experience of the many BVI citizens who travel throughout the islands and beyond, who participate actively in regional and international organizations and committees, who are engaged in global financial services activities, and who run the government and the economy.

The tension between images of natural ease and the actual demands of labor required to market it is evident in the line from an advertisement in a 1991 *Condé Nast Traveler* magazine: "Precious few hideaways remain where nature's innate drama and beauty successfully defy 'development's' insistent hand. But here in the 60-plus BVI, unmatched natural splendour allows the majesty of land and sea to work its magic on the soul without interruption. Man's major imprint in the BVI is to create better ways for you to discover nature's little secrets." The last line in this advertisement, "man's major imprint . . ." subtly acknowledges and obscures the purposive activity needed to ensure that the tourist will discover what nature already holds. The song "Welcome to the BVI" was written by British Virgin Islander Elmore Stoutt and serves the double function of representing the BVI at regional cultural festivals and entertaining tourists. This song also subverts what it promotes, luring tourists with images of relaxation and pristine beauty, while demonstrating an awareness of global politics and a keen knowledge of the psychology of Western tourists: "Welcome to the Virgin Isles / Throw out your frown and put on a smile. / Forget Hussein in the Arab land / And try to enjoy my virgin sand." Likewise, in contrast to the tourism brochures and advertisements that promote the BVI as untouched, available for discovery, just waiting for the opportunity to satisfy tourist desire, the song's welcome also reminds tourists that this is "my virgin sand."

EROTIC GEOGRAPHY

The Caribbean occupies a special place in the Western imagination, as a highly sexualized exotic paradise (Kempadoo 2004, 1999; Pattullo 1996; Sheller 2003; Strachan 2002; Thompson 2006). With its long history of slavery and colonialism, the Caribbean of the Western imagination also emerges as a site for playing out fantasies of conquest and control. An article appearing in a 1972 issue of *The Welcome Guide* brings both of these tropes together as it considers the potential impact upon the BVI of an emerging tourism economy: "At this moment in their history the BVI face the future of any young girl about to go out into the big wide world. Will she make a decent marriage to Good Development and Adequate Wealth? Will she be snapped up by some Rich Bounder who will, as likely as not, leave her in the lurch sometime? Or—Lard' a' Mercy—will she be raped and ruined forever by gamblers, junkies and profiteers?" ("The BVI Scene").

As the "Nature's Little Secrets" campaign demonstrates, BVI marketing strategies draw effectively upon fantasies of conquest and control; of course, the invitation to *discover* or even *experience* "Nature's Little Secrets" is also sexually suggestive. Where early ads in the "Nature's Little Secrets" campaign piqued tourist desire by drawing upon conventional associations with virginity, more recent advertisements use even more suggestive visuals and language. The visuals in an advertisement in the November 2006 issue of *Travel and Leisure*, for example, are at first glance fairly typical of advertisements that span the last eighteen years. A lone sailboat is anchored in a quiet cove of turquoise blue water; white clouds float in a bright blue sky and islands are silhouetted in the distance. But the focus of this advertisement is not the boat and the pristine landscape; these simply form the backdrop for a white man who is wading in the shallows of the cove, carrying a white woman in his arms. The narrative that captions the visuals reads, "off in the distance you see it, 'There! There! Take Me There!' A quick turn of the wheel and she comes about . . . a secret island cove is yours. Where crystal clear waters greet a pristine sandy beach embraced by a warm inviting breeze. You've arrived at one of Nature's Little Secrets. Come, find them all." The ambiguity of the visual image of this ad (is this a carrying-the-bride-across-the-threshold pose or does it allude to ravishing pirates?), the double entendre, "Take Me There!," and the confusion of the pronoun "she" point to the sexual undertones of the invitation, "Come, find them all."

"The Not So Virgin Islands"

The BVI that is eroticized for Western consumption was showcased in the 1999 *Sports Illustrated* swimsuit issue. Shot on location in the BVI, the 1999 *Sports Illustrated* swimsuit issue announced its content with a cover subcaption replete with sexual innuendo: "The Not So Virgin Islands." Apart from this insalubrious description, the only other references to the BVI appear in articles that make the BVI seem outside of time, with no local social or political history. Like the women displayed lounging on its beaches, the BVI appearing on the pages of this magazine is portrayed as existing solely for pleasure or consumption. For example, one of the articles on the BVI, entitled "Dissipation Row," features Bomba, a BVIslander, and his "Shack," a beach bar on the BVI island of Tortola, that is famous for its full moon parties and psychedelic mushroom tea. I discuss Bomba's

Shack at greater length in chapter 6, but what is notable with regard to this discussion of an eroticized BVI is that "Dissipation Row" describes Bomba as simultaneously "wild and . . . filled with an old old knowledge" (Lidz 1999: 130), the classic "primitive" (Torgovnick 1990). Similarly, although the article refers to Bomba's place of birth and residence on Tortola, it characterizes Bomba himself as "blissfully forgetful" of the particulars of his personal history—"time and me's one big ball"—who lives only to oversee the "Dionysian rapture" of the Shack (Lidz 1999: 130, 132). And Tortola, the center of one of the region's most successful tourism and financial services economies? The article attributes its allure to "its Sartrean sense of nothingness" (Lidz 1999: 134), thus replicating tourism ads that promote the BVIs as pristine and empty.

The construction in the 1999 *Sports Illustrated* swimsuit issue of a BVI outside of time and existing solely for the pleasure of Western consumers goes hand in hand with the eroticization of the women for whose bodies the BVI provide a picturesque backdrop. In one photo essay entitled "Island of Plenty," model Rebecca Romijn is sprawled on what looks like a food platter surrounded by tropical fruits; a subtitle/caption suggests that this main dish is "the most delectable fruit" (Winter 1999). This same model is referred to in the introduction to the *Sports Illustrated* 1999 special issue as an "exemplary specimen" who is "on our cover but 'off the market'" as she was at the time married to sitcom star John Stamos. A two-page advertisement that appears in the middle of the magazine also makes explicit the way in which deserted tropical islands, standing in for women, are used to pique consumer desire. The first page of this advertisement shows a deserted tropical beach, turquoise waves breaking gently on white sand. The caption running across the top of this picture reads, "Of all the curvaceous, sexy frames in this magazine . . ."; upon turning the page, we see the same tropical beach, but now there is a mountain bike on its sands. The caption on this page completes the caption from the previous page ". . . here's one you can actually get your hands on."

The marketing strategy that sells a mountain bike by piquing sexual desire works because it draws upon a convention that associates lush tropical islands with erotic pleasure. Of course, the mountain bike advertisement also works because in addition to piquing desire, it holds forth the possibility of possession, "here's one you can actually get your hands on." "Islands as Aphrodisiacs" is the title of a 1994 *Condé Nast Traveler* article that begins, "Islands are sexy. By nature they are" (1994: 106); more pointedly, Krista Thompson's study of the iconography of Jamaican postcards demonstrates how traveler's accounts of palm trees—"the quintessential image of the tropics"—gender and sexualize tropical nature (2006: 108). A 1993 article in *Outside* magazine describes explicitly the imagined connection between the tropics and sex that eroticizes objects as dissimilar as mountain bikes and palm trees. Referring to the tropics as "those latitudes synonymous with passion," the article asserts that "everything is ripe, tumescent, sticky, and all sensory information seems deliberately lascivious: the phallic fruits and the labial blossoms; the skunky, primal ooze of the mangrove swamps; the steamy jungle . . ." (Shacochis 1993: 74).

Allusions to the sexiness of tropical locales like the BVI characteristically center male libidinal desire and position women as objects of that desire. But in an interesting reversal, in the BVI it is the white Western woman tourist who is disparaged for her impropriety, for wearing clothes that are too skimpy, sexy, and revealing. For example, until 2005, the *BVI Tourist Guide* admonished the woman traveler to "wear proper attire . . . no bare midriffs, please," and *Fodor's* 2007 edition warns, "Cover up when you're not at the beach; Virgin Islanders are modest folks" (2007: 213). Meanwhile, local talk reveals a view of visiting women as sexually promiscuous, lending credence to Ian Strachan's observation that associations of the Caribbean with sexual licentiousness converts all women, even tourists, into objects of desire.

> The Caribbean . . . is a whore paid to play the virgin, in the sense that its virginity and deflowering is re-created and reenacted in advertisement after advertisement, for the benefit of a male consumer who is invited to be the first to take her maidenhead, on land or under water. The female tourist, in turn, is invited to play the role of the exotic, the licentious virgin. She is summoned to become the object of desire. She is invited to be as wild and unrepressed, as sensual and mysterious as the land itself. (Strachan 2002: 89)

Notwithstanding the literal sexualization that Strachan refers to, the sort of sex tourism that has come to be associated with Jamaica and the Dominican Republic (Campbell et al. 1999; Gregory 2006; Kempadoo 2004, 1999; Pattullo 1997; Pruitt and LaFont 1995) or that is the focus of the film, *Heading South* (Cantet 2006), is neither as prevalent nor as visible in the BVI, whose emphasis on yacht chartering and long-term stays at elite resorts or rented villas tends to draw more families and couples than single women. Surely, the possibility of a sexual encounter with a local man is one of the attractions of Bomba's Full Moon Party, and the regularity of such encounters is sufficient to draw occasional letters of protest or outrage to the local newspapers. Such an encounter even inspired a poem by a local poet, "your island is indeed a paradise; / what girl from a mill town in New / Hampshire would not fall / prey to playing mermaid, / earth child and sun goddess / all at once?" (Turnbull 1992).

Most BVIslanders with whom I have spoken disdain these sexual encounters, finding them not just morally repugnant but also mystifying, as conventional wisdom has it that the men that women tourists become involved with are poorer and less well educated than their tourist partners. BVIslanders who take a more benign view of these encounters tend to speak of them as just one of the many edifying experiences that a BVI vacation offers. In this, they mirror the rhetoric of tourist ads that cast the BVI as a special place with special experiences in store. This local assessment also corresponds with scholarly analyses of women's sex tourism in the Caribbean. These analyses argue that the association of the Caribbean with a colonized and raced other and the marketing of its island nations as places whose residents are experts at catering to Western desire eroticize the power differential between white Western tourists and the locals with whom they mingle (Davidson and Taylor 1999; Kempadoo 2004; Pattullo 1996).

Erotic pleasure and the will to possess are linked in the Western imagination. Likewise, the desire to know another place is conflated in the touristic imagination with women "as the quintessence of the exotic . . . something to be experienced" (Enloe 1990: 28), and as anthropologist Erve Chambers points out, "the traveler's 'eye' is an extension of a masculine will to conquer and control . . . one needs only to scan a handful of tourist brochures from almost any part of the world, but especially from 'hot and sexy' places like the tropics, to discover that there are merits to this interpretation" (2000: 60). But the sexualized representations of tropical destinations such as the BVI work so well not solely because of their appeal to a desire for possession, conquest, and control. They are effective also because they are predicated upon the notion that sexual difference and racial inequality are natural and given, making white Western male superiority natural and given as well. Pattullo makes a similar argument, when she attributes tourist fantasies about the Caribbean as an Edenic paradise "of daytime indolence beneath the palms and a night-time of pleasure through music, dance and sex" to long-standing and deeply entrenched racial stereotypes that secure Western hegemony (Pattullo 1996: 142). In either case, raced and sexed bodies emerge as key sites for naturalizing difference, and for normalizing Western power and Western subjectivity as white and male.

Sexualizing Nation and Naturalizing Identity

Constructions of national identity likewise depend upon the idea of natural sexual difference to signal the "natural" difference of people making up national communities from people who are not members of those communities. Andrew Parker, Mary Russo, Doris Sommer, and Patricia

Yaeger point out in their introduction to *Nationalisms and Sexualities*, that "in the same way that 'man' and 'woman' define themselves reciprocally (though never symmetrically), national identity is determined not on the basis of its own intrinsic properties but as a function of what it (presumably) is not" (1992: 5). Moreover, while gender differences in power and access to resources characterize the institutional structures of nations, gender difference also operates ideologically to ground conceptualizations of the nation as a unified whole and to sanction internal difference. As Anne McClintock notes in her study of Afrikaner nationalism, "gender difference between women and men serves to symbolically define the limits of national difference and power between men" (1993: 62). This overlap in the operation of precepts of sexual difference has particular relevance for the BVI, where tourism development fosters radical demographic and social change and goes hand in hand with a growing sense of the BVI as a distinct national community. While tourists visiting the BVI may be enticed by the sexual innuendoes in the invitation to "Discover Nature's Little Secrets," the discourse of naturalized heterosexual desire that eroticizes BVI geography as a commodity for Western consumption also animates notions of the BVI nation and citizenship in it as natural facts.

There is, for example, a strong historical connection between being a BVIslander and owning BVI land, a consequence of the unique historical circumstances of the BVI. Even following the cadastral survey and subsequent development of tourism in the 1960s, government legislation limited land speculation, to ensure that BVIslanders would have rights of first refusal on any property that went up for sale. The link between being a BVIslander and land ownership remains so strong that in 2005 BVI government launched a program to buy up large tracts of land in order to subdivide it into building lots for purchase by BVIslanders who had no land themselves. In the cultural arena, a sense of natural BVI citizenship through connection to the land is established through claims to having "a piece of the Virgin," and I have witnessed highly placed government officials point out to visiting dignitaries that their visit should be particularly memorable because "anything virginal is special and unique."

One of the most explicit instances of the conflation of sexuality and "natural" BVI citizenship that I witnessed occurred during the ceremonies opening a 1990 event hosted by the BVI government for ministerial officers from the English-speaking Caribbean. The first four BVI officials to address the assembled participants sprinkled their opening remarks with a running repartee with each other about their relative sexual skills. Drawing upon the symbolism of Saint Ursula and her 11,000 virgins, after whom the Virgin Islands were presumably named, the exchange was aimed at determining which political party had the most accurate count of the number of virgins in the country. This public flaunting of normative heterosexuality points to an important intersection of BVI and Western concepts of sexual intimacy, as they relate to structures of power. Surely, in the context of a meeting of officials representing Eastern Caribbean states, the public allusion to sexual prowess may work, much as Carolyn Cooper has argued for the sexual "slackness" of Jamaican dancehall culture, to turn the historically sexualized black body to the service of a politics of subversion, "a metaphorical revolt against the law and order" of colonial authority (1993: 141).

Meanwhile, allusions to sexual discovery and intimacy that are the cornerstone of the BVI tourism marketing strategy also reflect the state's desire for a heterosexual citizenry. In her study of the link between heterosexuality, tourism, and the nation-state in the Bahamas, M. Jacqui Alexander points out that "the significance of tourism, lies in its ability to draw together powerful processes of (sexual) commodification and (sexual) citizenship.... The state actively socializes loyal heterosexual citizens into tourism, its primary strategy of economic modernization by sexualizing them and positioning them as commodities" (1996: 67–69). In like fashion, the invitation in *Welcome to the BVI* to "enjoy my virgin sand" that targets tourist heterosexual desire also points to a sense of natural citizenship through a fundamental claim to the land. This claim itself is based upon the "natural" criterion of birth to a BVI woman or to a BVI man who legally acknowledges paternity. Both the idealized space that tourists visit and the national space of natural BVIslanders are also frequently grounded on the notion of the BVI as timeless and untouched, special and distinct. And this notion is bolstered in some measure by a gendering of the BVI as female. Thus, even as tourism's representations of the BVI as a pristine paradise open for possession appeal to a Western desire for power and control, local practices and knowledges link citizenship with a connection to an originary BVI motherland. For tourists, the BVI is a virginal space open for exploration and enjoyment. For BVIslanders the BVI is a motherland in need of protection and preservation.

"I CAME BACK TO BE WITH YOU": "NATURE'S LITTLE SECRETS" AS MOTHERLAND

Oh, Tortola, oh how you blew my mind. Oh, Tortola, with your gay
    sunshine.
Oh, Tortola, I couldn't get you off my mind.
So I came back to be with you for a long, long time.
So I came back to stay with you for a long, long time.

                  —Quito Rymer

The above is the chorus of the ballad-like song, "Tortola," written by the same Quito Rymer who wrote "Paradise." A love song to an island, "Tortola" is a much-requested favorite at Quito's Gazebo, Quito Rymer's beach bar/restaurant on Cane Garden Bay. Cane Garden Bay is a popular anchorage for yacht charterers, so most of the people in the Quito's Gazebo (or simply "Quito's") on any given night are tourists who have come ashore from their charter yachts. Quito frequently uses "Tortola" to introduce his twice-a-week performances at the bar. Even when he plays "Tortola" midway through his performance, he uses it as an opportunity to greet first-time visitors to the BVI and to welcome returning visitors "back home." For these returning visitors especially, the bridge to the song—"and oh what a happy day / when I got back to Cane Garden Bay"—has special resonance. Not surprisingly, the best selling of the many Quito Rymer CDs that are available in the small shop adjacent to his beach bar is the CD that features "Tortola" on it (Quito Rymer, personal communication).

Quito Rymer was featured performing "Tortola" in a 1994 video promoting the BVI as a tourist destination. The jacket of the VHS case for this video promises "An Intimate look at one of the world's last great hide-aways—where unmatched splendour of land, sea and sky work their magic on your soul" (*The British Virgin Islands: Nature's Little Secrets* 1994). In the opening scenes of this video, a male voiceover invites potential visitors to the BVI to give themselves over to a yearning similar to that expressed in the chorus of "Tortola": "Surviving intact through centuries of man's excess, the islands look now much as they did when the first visitors arrived. Today's visitors say this pristine beauty calls them back again and again. Will the British Virgin Islands cast their spell on you? Take a closer look." This narrative and the chorus of "Tortola" combine in the promotional video to romanticize and particularize otherwise generic visuals of dramatic Carib-bean sunsets, empty white-sand Caribbean beaches, crystal-clear Caribbean waters. Along with other scenes of BVI environs and people, these visuals are offered as enticements to "come to the BVI. It's time you discovered nature's little secrets for yourself." The yacht chartering tourists who hear in "Tortola" a sentimental anthem to their own personal voyages of discovery are realizing the promise held out in the "Nature's Little Secrets" promo-tional video that the "unmatched splendour of land sea and sky" will "work their magic" on their souls.

As is the case of the images appearing in BVI tourist brochures, the representations in the promotional video are self-conscious and targeted constructions. Originating in a U.K. advertising agency, they are represen-tative enough of what is being marketed to ensure consumer satisfaction upon purchase, while sufficiently idealized to attract and even to construct a particular tourist gaze (MacCannell 1976, 1992; Urry 1990: 66–67). But "Tortola" was not constructed in a U.K. advertising agency; rather, the song was written by a native BVIslander upon returning to his home island of Tortola in the early 1980s, after years spent working and living abroad. In a 1995 video interview, Quito Rymer recalled the night that he wrote the song:

> I lived away for a while. For about five years I was gone from Tortola. Lived in the U.S.Virgin Islands, some parts of the States, and I returned back to Tortola in '81. And it was the second night that I spent here after I decided, "this is it, I'm back to stay." And I look at the sunset and I just marvel, "how could I, how could I in my right mind ever leave this?" And that's where it started. I just—I sat there on the rocks, and the words just came to me: Oh Tortola, oh how you blew my mind, with your gay sunshine. I came back to stay with you for a long, long time. (Cohen and Hodge 1995)

The imagery of "Tortola" draws upon conventionalized notions of Caribbean paradise, even notions that circulate in BVI tourist brochures and promotional video. But the song also observes the BVI from a perspective familiar to many BVIslanders who, throughout the first two-thirds of the twentieth century, had to migrate to other countries for wage labor. The main verse of "Tortola" recounts this experience.

> Packed up and I roamed, searching for a new home.
> Now I sit and wonder leaving you: How could I ever?
> But the grass always look greener on the other side.
> Oh me oh my eyes took me for a ride.

With its reference to "the other side" and its acknowledgment of the foolishness of the search for a "new home," this verse from "Tortola" is like narratives that idealize the BVI as a place of pristine beauty in contrast to civilization's blight. A similar contrast is implied in another verse in which the singer actually sets both his country and himself apart from the more jaded existence on "the other side": "your snow white sand and blue green sea / is good enough for me." "That City" is a song that Quito Rymer wrote around the same time as he wrote "Tortola." In it, he makes a similar, but more explicit, contrast between "the bright lights of the city" and "my hometown."

> I've seen the bright lights of the city, the neon flashing lights
> Pusher with his needle, purse-snatcher with his knife.
> I've seen the coke man make his pick up, junkies all around

That whole downtown is crazy. Everybody's got a gun.
So I ain't going back to that city, I ain't going back to that town
I ain't going back to that city, I ain't leaving my home town

The songs "Tortola" and "That City" both make clear that Quito Rymer's experience living in the USVI and in the continental United States gave him a new perspective on the island home that he had left behind. Crucially, although these songs may romanticize the BVI as a land of "snow white sand and clear blue seas," what they personify and eroticize is not the unknown tropical isle awaiting discovery but Quito Rymer's "hometown" to which he has returned. In this respect, the same "Tortola" that is an anthem to tourists' personal voyages of discovery of "Nature's Little Secrets" is also an anthem, if not a love song, to Quito's motherland. Quito Rymer returned to Tortola in 1981, a time when tourism, and particularly charter yacht tourism, was beginning to have a powerful impact upon the BVI economy. Read in the context of this economic impact, the song "Tortola" also documents a historical moment when BVIslanders were beginning to see their home country in a new light. On the one hand, the BVI was enjoying an unparalleled prosperity and native BVIslanders were the primary beneficiaries of the rewards of the heated-up economy. On the other hand, BVIslanders were growing concerned to protect that which made the BVI unique to residents and visitors alike. This notion of the uniqueness of the BVI was encapsulated in the first slogan developed by the British Virgin Islands Tourist Board to brand the locale as a tourism product, "Yes We Are Different!"

YES WE ARE DIFFERENT!

Given the West's tendency to see all peoples of the Caribbean as similar, one of the challenges for the nascent BVI tourism industry was to differentiate the BVI in order to compete for tourist dollars, when the exotic paradise that the West wants is marketed by islands throughout the region. The first slogan developed by the British Virgin Islands Tourist Board to brand the BVI product, "Yes We Are Different!," addressed this challenge unambiguously. Combined with the prominent display of the Union Jack and the BVI national slogan, *Vigilate*, the slogan alluded to a BVI that was unspoiled, uncomplicated, and crime-free. Even local histories written at the time proclaimed, "*Yes we are different* . . . the reserved, conservative approach to politics, society, business and life in general makes the British Virgin Islands quite *different* from many other islands of the region" (Pickering 1987: 94; emphasis added). Tourism publications also stressed BVI difference. For example, a 1990 *Travel Host Magazine* featuring the BVI declared that its "intent is to tell potential guests that, although these islands may be located near the U.S. territory of St. Thomas, there is little in common save the name 'Virgin' in the names of both island groups."

The notion of the BVI being different, and particularly from its close neighbor, St. Thomas, was also a central feature in public discourse at the time, much of which was devoted to thinking about the emergence of the BVI as a major tourist destination. For example, an article appearing in the December 1978–January 1979 issue of the *British Virgin Islands Welcome Guide* submitted that "Tortola is what the Caribbean was—a virgin, verdant, comparatively undeveloped island in the BVI. . . . To imagine what Tortola is, think of a small town near you. You know the kind—a few thousand people, a few stores, a couple of restaurants. People know each other and wave or say hello when they meet—people who love, cherish and take care of their small town, their home. . . . That's Tortola—small town Caribbean" (Perlmutter 1978–1979: 4). A decade after this article appeared, two ten-year-old BVI students who contributed to a special Department of Education publication on the topic "Tourism Awareness through Education" wrote, "The BVI are quiet and peaceful, with not as much killing as in some other islands" (Department of Education and Culture 1989: 36). Finally, in a 1989 special supplement of *Euromoney* entitled, "British Virgin Islands: A New Force Emerges," BVI Chief Minister H. Lavity Stoutt made clear that although the BVI uses the U.S. dollar as sole legal tender and was beginning to develop a strong financial services sector, "we want no part of shady dealings whatsoever. . . . There's no future in it here. We must maintain a good image at all times. . . . There's no shady business, no game playing here. You want to play games, go elsewhere" (*Euromoney* 1989: 3)

As I pointed out in chapter 1, the connection between the U.S. Virgin Islands and the BVI is long-standing and complex. In the context of the BVI being seen as the more backward and rural of the Virgin Islands group, the declaration, "Yes We Are Different!" was more than a catchy slogan. It was also a declaration of independence from economic and social dependence upon the more urbanized USVI—and particularly St. Thomas—and an early sign of a growing sense of national pride. The islands making up the BVI are referred to by St. Thomians and BVIslanders alike as the more parochial of the Virgin Islands. Yet the success of the BVI as a destination for elite tourists focused BVI attention and knowledge beyond the eastern Caribbean toward a global tourism market, as its development as a financial services center implicated it in the world of multinational corporations and international trade. As these two pillars of the BVI economy grew, concerns about the impact of this growth were cast in terms of difference between the BVI and St. Thomas. As an elderly BVIslands man from a prominent Road Town family explained to me, "With all the money to be made, and with the legislation giving preference to belongers, people will be working two jobs, and it won't be like it used to be, or even now. You and I have stopped here on the street corner to talk. And I will stop to talk to a friend on the corner. But with everyone working so hard, no one will have the time to do this one simple thing that makes our lives so good. We will be just like in St Thomas and St Croix. Too busy to stop to talk to a friend" (field notes, July 23, 1990).

As we have seen, the prosperity of the BVI tourism economy is based on a development strategy of controlled growth, with an emphasis on the development of BVI marine resources over the development of mass land-based or cruise-ship tourism. This strategy was highlighted in advertising campaigns that stressed the "freshness" of the BVI as a major promotional asset (PKF Consultants 1992: II–19) and that represented the BVI as a natural and political rarity untouched by forces that defiled other Caribbean nations. A full-page advertisement developed by the British Virgin Islands Tourist Board for a 1996 special supplement of *Offshore Finance Annual* also marketed the BVI by stressing its difference from other Caribbean vacation spots. But unlike tourist brochure descriptions that emphasize the special qualities of the BVI as one among many choices the Caribbean tourist might make, this particular ad emphasizes the BVI as occupied by people who are both aware of the special "gifts" of their home, and actively involved in protecting them: "YACHTS, NOT SLOTS. No high rollers. No high rises. No singles bars, no topless beaches. Which is exactly the way we like it here, thank you very much. Nature has been generous to us in the British Virgin Islands. And we take our role as the keepers of her gifts very seriously." The conception of the BVI as a "natural" homeland to a people with a shared commitment as "keepers" of this gift from nature has gone hand in hand with the growth of its tourism economy. In conjunction with increasing BVI political autonomy and a declining economic dependence on Great Britain, the turn to nation is also a response to the demographic changes ensuing from economic growth and the perceived "impurity" introduced by immigration of laborers from other Caribbean nations. In this sense, "Yes We Are Different" can also be read as a claim of difference from the other Caribbean islanders coming to the BVI to work in its tourism industry.

The findings of a Territory-wide survey conducted in 1993 as part of a process of constitutional reform underscore the importance of claims of BVI difference to a sense of the BVI as a nation. The report found "widespread fear that the influx of persons from abroad if not adequately monitored could lead to the indigenous population being outnumbered to the detriment of the preservation of the local heritage and culture" (Secretary of State for Foreign and Commonwealth Affairs 1994: 21). In pointing to the possible "detriment of the preservation of the local heritage and culture," this finding of the constitutional review survey establishes an opposition between "persons from abroad" and possessors of BVI heritage and tradition, based on an opposition between impurity and purity. In this, the sentiment codified in the constitutional review document is like tourist-brochure narratives that construct the BVI as a Caribbean destination of special allure, an allure related to its serenity, seductiveness, and natural beauty in opposition to civilization's blight. However, where the pristine BVI of tourism's constructions invites discovery and possession by stimulating desire for an eroticized and sexualized Other, the BVI of local accounts is constituted as a motherland whose respectability, framed in terms of cultural integrity, must be safeguarded against outside influence. The transformation into a nation of what were historically diverse and widespread communities and islands of the BVI is also accomplished through notions of the BVI as a pristine and timeless space, like the BVI that is marketed to tourists.

As people of BVI heritage make their lives in the "serene and seductive" space of tourist ads, they do so as one BVI people, conceived as members of a nation with autochthonous origins. The preamble to the 2007 constitution endorses a natural origin for both the BVI and its people in an opening phrase that claims a distinct BVI identity and essence: "We, the people of the territory of the Virgin Islands have evolved with a distinct cultural identity which is the essence of a Virgin Islander." The opening phrase mirrors the rhetoric of materials that market the BVI as a tourist destination, which also assert a natural national BVI character. For example, one BVI tourist brochure turns a narrative about skill in teaching water sports into a narrative about natural ability and natural citizenship when it enthuses that "learning water sports takes on a new dimension, and not just for unmatched scenery. . . . Instructors make the big difference. *Typical BVI citizens*, they care a lot. Teaching you to enjoy the water is not just what they do, *it's what they are*" (emphasis added). And a 2005 British Virgin Islands Tourist Board publication naturalizes a shared BVI history when it invites tourists to "walk the streets of Road Town and read the rich history in friendly faces."

BLUE IS THE BVI

Representations of the BVI as natural and timeless, and of its people as having little agency apart from the desire to make visitors happy, have been central components of narratives appearing in Tourist Board publications since the inception of the BVI tourism industry. In the same way, the concept of a natural BVI character and citizenship that is key to a sense of national identity posits a natural BVI with little reference to the details of a complicated past. However, while the notion of an autochthonous BVI identity is codified in the 2007 preamble to the constitution, the constitution is also a reflection of a growing national will to address the BVI future as a nation in its own right. In this regard, the 2007 constitution points to a shifting national subjectivity, a shift that can be noted in both the cultural arena and in the approach being taken to marketing the BVI as a tourist destination. I address BVI national identity and the cultural arena in later chapters. But first, I turn to a recent and somewhat different approach to marketing the BVI as a tourist destination. This is an approach encapsulated in the slogan, "Blue Is the BVI."

When I arrived in the BVI in 1977, the plane landed at a small airstrip, and I proceeded through customs and immigration in a small hip-roofed building, with wooden jalousie windows and tiled floors. No signage or brochures greeted me; I could have been in any tropical paradise. In 2007, visitors to the BVI who arrive by air land at an airport with an extended runway, built to accommodate small private and commercial jets. A new airport terminal houses small shops, a cafeteria, an internet cafe, an air conditioned departure lounge, and desks representing six different airlines. Glass insets on the airport doors read "Nature's Little Secrets," and the BVI national seal with the motto *Vigilate* adorns the door leading from customs to the outside. Upon passing through customs, one encounters a large information kiosk brimming with *Business BVI*, the ubiquitous *Welcome Guide*, brochures advertising day sails, dive shops, spas, hotels, and restaurants, as well as numerous brochures on national points of interest: "Exploring the Past: A Guide to Heritage Sites on Tortola," "Sage Mountain," "Mt. Healthy," "BVI Eco Tours," "Guide to Road Town," "St. Philip's Anglican Church Ruins: 'The Church of the Africans.'"

As the numerous national-heritage and points-of-interest brochures in particular indicate, the BVI that greets the tourist in 2007 is a mapped and historical locale. Unlike the singular, pristine, and undiscovered BVI of the "Nature's Little Secrets" campaign, this BVI boasts multiple places of geographical interest and a rich selection of historical sites. While the "Nature's Little Secrets" logo still greets visitors, the points of interest brochures subvert any inclination to think of the BVI as virgin territory. A 2007 tourism publication likewise subverts the meaning ascribed to the BVI by the original "Nature's Little Secrets" campaign, with a table of contents listing articles such as "A Glimpse into the Past," "Arts and Culture," "Adventures in Shopping," and "Offshore Finance," and an introductory article that declares, "Today, the British Virgin Islands has one of the best standards of living in the Caribbean, with a thriving and robust economy. With friendly people, a warm climate and pristine islands in a tropical sea, the success story looks set to continue" (Putley 2007: 17).

In the same month that the 2007 constitution was ratified, the British Virgin Islands Tourist Board began to explore a new advertising campaign, developed around the concept *Blue* and with slogans such as "Blue Surrounds You" and "Blue Is the BVI." The "Nature's Little Secrets" slogan is still prominently displayed on British Virgin Islands Tourist Board publications and on the masthead of the BVI Tourist Board Web site, where visitors are still invited to "experience the BVI," and are enticed with statements like "the BVI has a secret to share" (http://www.bvitourism.com). But just as the numerous points-of-interest brochures at the airport point to a lived-in and historical BVI space, the Blue campaign showcases an active BVI that serves as a *constant traveling companion* and *a guide*, as the following statement from the BVI Tourist Board Web site illustrates.

> Everywhere you go in the British Virgin Islands, Blue goes with you. It is an ocean of adventures to experience, and your constant traveling companion. Whether you're throwing out your jib sail and crisscrossing the Sir Francis Drake channel, descending the depths to explore a century-old shipwreck, hooking into a world-class marlin or simply soaking in the radiant sun and wide skies, the BVI has a secret to share. Here, you'll discover white sand beaches, turquoise waters and friendly, warm-hearted people throughout sixty idyllic islands—and Blue is your guide to each and every one. (http://www. bvitourism.com)

A slide show that accompanies this statement intersperses photographs of white people with what I assume are meant to be BVIslanders. The white people are shown sailing on yachts, snorkeling in clear waters, wading in shallows, and staring across the water to distant islands. Among the photographs of BVIslanders is a smiling woman in a business suit and hat, three smiling young Girl Guides, a couple sitting on rocks and staring across the water to distant islands, and three young boys running into the sea. These BVIslanders are clearly involved in their own life activities, and many of them are doing what tourists in the BVI conventionally do—sightseeing and going to the beach. The slide show can be read in many ways. On the one hand, the smiling BVIslanders can be read as embodying the friendly and warm-hearted people characterized in tourist promotions and national sentiments alike; on the other hand, the photos of BVIslanders enjoying the sea and scenery distinguish these individuals from the non-BVIslanders who make up the major portion of the tourism workforce. But particularly in comparison to earlier marketing campaigns that showcased nature, emptiness, and solitude, the dominant message of the slide show is that BVIslanders are actively engaged in the world, including the world that the tourists are being invited to explore.

Mock-ups of ads by the firm that created the Blue campaign (a firm whose clients include Papa John's Pizza, Nissan, Skandia Vodka, the Miami Dolphins, and Longs Drugs) are similarly polysemic. One ad exhibits a notable degree of agency, claiming "Blue wants to catch your bouquet." This statement is in large block letters in the texture and color of the sea and runs over a sepia-toned picture of a white bride, running along a beach. The sepia picture and lettering are set above a color picture of a classic BVI scene of a yacht moored in a crystal blue cove. As is the case with the "Blue wants to catch your bouquet" phrase, the narrative that captions this picture uses phrases like "plans to" and "knows how to" to allude to an active, knowing BVI subject behind the tourist's BVI experience: "It's the most meaningful day of your life and Blue plans to make it lavishly unique. . . . Blue knows how to make it unforgettably special."

The chief minister's letter that opens a 2007 BVI Chamber of Commerce and Hotel Association visitor's book likewise asserts an active, knowing, and modern BVI subject and a consciously constructed BVI environment: "My government continues to grow our economy and strengthen the social infrastructure to create the perfect environment for your holiday. We have made substantial improvements to beaches at Cane Garden Bay, Josiah's Bay, Brandywine Bay and Savannah's Bay on Virgin Gorda. A Tourism Industry Services Standard programme is helping to train our people, from customs to the check-out desk." The chief minister concludes his letter by inviting visitors to "Discover 'Nature's Little Secrets,'" but also urges them to discover "our people, our food and our sites" (Smith 2007b: 2). This qualifying phrase articulates a sense of national ownership and pride, and mirrors a sensibility that is also articulated in the opening paragraph of the *2007 British Virgin Islands Tourism Directory*:

> When you think of the British Virgin Islands, your mind may drift to a scene of a picture-perfect beach with aquamarine waters and majestic palms gently swaying in the warm breeze. It's true that you'll find that this fantasy is a reality in the BVI, but the even better news is that

there's a whole lot more to discover in these stunning islands, free of the glitter, glamour and crowds one might find elsewhere in the Caribbean. In fact, these magical isles are steeped in rich history and culture just waiting to be discovered.

British Virgin Islands history and culture and the national pride attaching to them constitute the third pillar of BVI government's vision for the future of the BVI. The then BVI chief minister Dr. Hon. Orlando Smith stressed the importance of culture and national pride in his 2006 State of the Territory Address: "Increasing our national pride here in the BVI is truly the Third Pillar of this Government's vision for our Territory.... This pride ... is about knowing our history and honouring the sacrifices of our ancestors. It is about valuing our unique culture and preserving it in the modern world. It is about cherishing our sacred traditions and passing them on to our children" (2006b: 14). Likewise, the most notable aspect of the Blue campaign is its emphasis on BVI history and culture. Where the "Nature's Little Secrets" campaign tended either to flatten BVI history into a parade of explorers or to freeze the BVI in a colonial past, two mock-ups of ads for the Blue campaign assert, "Blue has a colorful past." These words are in large block letters in the texture and color of the sea and run over sepia-toned pictures that depict culture. One ad features an elaborately costumed festival troupe member, the other is a tableau of Miss BVI in formal dress, on the beach with three white children, with costumed stilt dancers (*moco jumbies*) and a sign for a local arts center in the background. The bottom half of each ad features a full-color picture of a single boat under sail with the narrative: "Calypso sights and sounds drift carelessly on soft breezes. The colorful and brilliant costumes of the Emancipation Festival parades surround you. This is just a small portion of the rich history and diverse culture of the British Virgin Islands. And whether you're seeing it all for the first time or a regular visitor, you'll always see Blue as an exhilarating mix of storied tradition and warm, friendly people."

The first sentence of this narrative, "calypso sights and sounds drift carelessly on soft breezes," is remarkably like my own narrative of my 1977 visit to the BVI, when I recall the steel pan music drifting across the water; likewise, the advertisement's visuals present a stereotyped image of a Caribbean carnival. But in speaking of the *Emancipation* Festival parade, the ad positions both the BVI and the tourists to whom it is being marketed unambiguously within a history of the plantation economy and slavery. As significantly, it signals that this history is an important component of "the rich history and diverse culture of the British Virgin Islands."

An article in a book published in 2007 by the BVI Chamber of Commerce and Hotel Association also highlights the Emancipation Festival, noting that "slavery . . . was largely responsible for the big profits made from exported items like sugar, molasses, rum and cotton which, instead of benefiting the islanders, enriched those in Liverpool, Bristol and London" (Putley 2007: 16). No "parade of visitors" narrative here. Instead the article continues, "today there are many ruined sugar works and rum distilleries around the island, and names like Cane Garden Bay, Brewer's Bay and Cooper Island are evocative of this bygone era" (Putley 2007: 16), thereby adding a history of oppression and exploitation to the BVI that tourists visit.

The Cane Garden Bay that is constructed in this 2007 article on BVI history is vastly different from the Cane Garden Bay constructed in my 1977 memory, in 1980s and 1990s tourist brochure descriptions of undiscovered paradise, in Quito Rymer's celebration of its "snow white sand and blue green sea." Notably, it is even different from the Cane Garden Bay that is described elsewhere in the same book as "the best-known and most popular beach in all the BVI" with "a gorgeous, soft sand beach that stretches its entire length" ("Beauty and the Beaches," 2007: 42). Rather, the Cane Garden Bay of 2007 advertisements and articles summons up a historical Cane Garden Bay of sugar plantations and slavery. Whether or not tourists engage with *this* Cane Garden Bay is less crucial to my analysis than is the fact of its appearance in tourist publication narratives at all. For it represents an important departure from the narrative of untouched islands open for discovery, and highlights the centrality of BVI culture and history to the contemporary BVI experience.

The possession of a national culture and history is key to contemporary notions of BVI subjectivity, as is the notion of birthright and essence codified in the 2007 constitution. But as geographer Kathleen Kirby points out, while identification with a particular place can provide a sense of origins, identity, and even agency as a political subject, the different spaces people occupy as physical bodies also determine subjectivity, and "each of these spaces shapes the subject's 'substance' according to different logics" (1996: 15). Representations of the BVI that are used to market it as a tourist destination shape the spaces in which people in the BVI live and interact as much as do the money, people, and ideas that flow continually in and out of the actual place. These representations address and activate tourist desire, and this desire informs the way that tourists engage the places in the BVI that they visit and the people in the BVI they encounter; satisfying this desire is crucial to the success of BVI tourist economy. Many of these marketing representations are also compatible with a sense of the BVI as a unique national space, and they thus fortify local imaginings of the BVI as a "natural" homeland to "natural" BVIslanders. But the BVI homeland that grounds assertions of a natural national identity also materializes through the interactions of BVIslanders and non-BVIslanders with each other. This BVI is constituted as a space of distinctions rooted in colonial ideologies about race and difference, and calculated in terms of one's physical connection to the historical place of the BVI, through land and family. I turn to this space of BVI subjectivity in the next chapter.

CHAPTER 4

Cultural Negotiations

RACE, IDENTITY, AND CITIZENSHIP

You know, Colleen, twenty, thirty, fifty, even a hundred years ago, people had a spiritual bond to the land. They took care of it, wouldn't have weeds growing on it. They manicured it, like you manicure your body. The land was like your body. Maybe because it nourished your body, you thought of it as an extension of you. This is changed, now. We need to bring some of this back, get people back to this connection with the things that nourish them.

(Field notes, March 16, 1994)

Recognizing that the people of the Virgin Islands have a free and independent spirit, and have developed themselves and their country based on qualities of honesty, integrity, mutual respect, self-reliance and the ownership of the land engendering a strong sense of belonging to and kinship with those islands . . .

Preamble, *The Virgin Islands*
(British) Constitution Order, 2007

THE BVI THAT IS MARKETED TO TOURISTS and the BVI that is constituted as motherland are both imagined spaces, constructed on the basis of idealized images of what we want them to be. The image of the pristine tropical beach that awaits discovery and the image of an island home made up of people of one's own kind both address a desire for something timeless and pure. Moreover, as we have seen in the case of BVI tourist desire and BVI nationalist desire alike, the idealized object of perfection is often constituted in terms of what it is not, the meaning with which it is imbued emerging in the context of relations of difference (Hall 1990). In chapter 3, I illustrated how representations of the BVI as a tourist destination gained special force through reference to the perfection and purity evoked by virginity and in contrast to more overbuilt, overcrowded locales. In this chapter, I look at distinctions that are made within the BVI itself, among British Virgin Islanders and between British Virgin Islanders and non–British Virgin Islanders, which are based upon socially constructed categories of race, kinship, and nationality.

The two quotes with which I begin point to a strong association between these categories of race, kinship, and nationality and BVI land, such that belonging to the BVI and kinship with the BVI are connected with land ownership. In respect to this, it is noteworthy that speeches given or essays written that memorialize or laud British Virgin Islanders conventionally refer to them as sons or daughters of the soil. In contrast, the apprehension expressed in the quote about the land becoming overgrown signals a concern with the disposition of the land that is the embodiment of spiritual and cultural citizenship. In its reference to things being different long ago and its stress on the need "to get people back to this connection with the things that nourish them," the quote, which is taken from an interview with a BVI man in his mid-sixties, infers an indigenous people linked to the land. Meanwhile, in the context of a resident population composed of over 50 percent non–British Virgin Islanders, the reference to "weeds" can be read as alluding to social disorder and infestation. A similar concern with disorder was expressed in less metaphorical terms in a 1996 National Integrated Development Strategy that warns "the BVIslander is precariously close to being a minority in his own country" and suggests that immigration "has implications for social harmony."

> The dynamics of population grown in the 1970 to 1980 period, when there was a net outflow of BVIslanders in search of employment was counteracted a decade later when there was a net inflow of labour to the BVI. Though some BVIslanders returned, the inflow was mainly non–BVIslanders. The result is that the BVIslander is precariously close to being a minority in his own country. . . . If the [tourism] sector continues to expand, then the importation of labour will have the direct impact of further reducing the number of BVIslanders relative to the total population. This has implications for social harmony. ("The Present Situation Has Implications for Tourism Development")

In looking at the categories of race, kinship, and nationality that ground distinctions made among the people residing in the BVI, I draw from a paper that I wrote together with BVI educator Dr. Charles Wheatley for the 1994 American Ethnological Society meeting on "Rethinking Race and Racism: Anthropological Contributions for the 21st Century" (Cohen and Wheatley 1994). Dr. Wheatley began his career as a teacher in Virgin Gorda, and his lengthy career in education includes service as the British

Virgin Islands chief educational officer and president of the H. Lavity Stoutt Community College. At the time of this writing, he is chairman of the Board of Governors of the H. Lavity Stoutt Community College. Our paper grew out of a series of conversations that Dr. Wheatley and I had about race and nationality, many of which were taped. We continue these conversations to this day, seeking through collaboration something akin to what Faye Ginsburg hopes for in collaborations between ethnographic and indigenous film makers, that is, "new discursive possibilities . . . [that] self-consciously reject notions of 'authenticity' and 'pure culture' as ways of understanding contemporary identities" (Ginsburg 1995: 260). While this chapter explores the connections among race, identity, and citizenship in the BVI, it also deals more generally with the ethnographic endeavor itself, and especially as it is affected by race. This exploration of ethnography, collaboration, and difference continues in chapter 5, where I explore in detail questions about the production of ethnographic knowledge about the BVI.

WHITENESS AND ETHNOGRAPHIC MOBILITY

When I first started my formal ethnographic research in the BVI in 1990, I had very little idea of what my focus would be. I knew that the BVI was undergoing a lot of change, related to its successful tourism industry and its growing financial services sector. As we have seen, after almost one hundred years of being the poor country cousin to St. Thomas, the BVI was developing as an economic and socially autonomous entity. So it made sense to me to focus my initial research around the general question, "What is a British Virgin Islander?" Apart from asking people to complete the blank, "A British Virgin Islander is _____ ," the best way to proceed was the classic ethnographic method of participant observation. I was fortunate to be in the BVI during Festival season, during which issues pertinent to the BVI experience are aired. In the summer of 1990, I was joined by Bill Maurer, who was beginning the PhD field work that was to be the basis of his book *Recharting the Caribbean: Land, Law, and Citizenship in the British Virgin Islands* (1997). I regularly cite Bill Maurer's cultural mapping method as an example of inspired fieldwork: he went through the phone book, with a map of the BVI at his side, and mapped the location of the family names appearing in the book. His "discovery" that certain family names were lumped in certain specific locales was the first inkling we had of the association between people, place, and affinity in the BVI. Of course, this association is at the base of how British Virgin Islanders understand themselves and relate to each other and to others living in the BVI. But as is the case with the basics of any culture, it is not immediately discernable to outsiders.

Through my first four summers of research, I employed fairly classic ethnographic techniques. I was an avid reader of the local newspapers, and always tuned into the local radio station, and particularly its talk shows. I observed, I participated in, and I interviewed people about the BVI tourism industry as well as about the events of Festival, which commemorates the August 1, 1834, emancipation of slaves in the English-speaking Caribbean. In fact, because so many of Festival events are used to display cultural pride and express political concern, Festival ended up becoming a major focus of my research. Beginning in 1991 and continuing through 1997, my friend Catherine Sebastian also spent two to three weeks in Tortola with me. An old friend whose children grew up with my children, Catherine is a gifted photographer with a background in photography for record albums and CDs. Through her work with rock-and-roll musicians, Catherine became adept at getting good photographs on the fly, as unobtrusively as possible, and this proved to be excellent training for the photo-ethnographic work that Catherine did with me during the weeks of Festival. Catherine also convinced me to start using video as another way of documenting Festival events, and by the summer of 1994 the two of us were regulars at Festival events and worked closely with Festival Committee, and later with the local television network, Virgin Islands Television (VITV) photographing and videotaping the Queen Show, the Calypso Show, and the Parade. I discuss my work with VITV in chapter 5, and I discuss Festival and its relationship to tourism and national identity in chapter 7.

I like to think that Catherine Sebastian and I were asked by Festival Committee to do so much video and photographic work because we were the only ones free enough, in both senses of the word, to do it. No doubt, the fact that Catherine and I were willing to do the work without compensation was a major draw. As well, considering my eagerness to learn about Festival and my enthusiasm for BVI culture, to say nothing of the fact that I had no visible job, I could be counted on to show up and do anything I was asked. Ivy O'Neal was my first entrée into Festival Committee. In addition to being an officer of the Queen Show Committee, Ivy O'Neal worked as the office manager of Tourist Board, and took both of her jobs very seriously. In some measure, Ms. O'Neal's eagerness to make us feel welcome and part of things was also responsible for Catherine and me being asked to work with the committee. But as an outsider, I also enjoyed mobility across social hierarchies that few other members of BVI society did. I carried no BVI name, with its historical associations of affiliation or ability. In addition to my social neutrality and possibly most important, I was a white American woman, and so my interest in Festival and my work videotaping Festival events reflected well on Festival and the committee. This had nothing to do with my abilities or expertise; in fact I was arguably the least knowledgeable person involved with Festival. It was, rather, a matter of my being white. As was pointed out to me on many occasions by many different people, and to paraphrase, "We will hear something from a Caribbean person, and pay it no attention. But if it comes out of the mouth of a white person, we wake up."

This holdover from colonialism of a racialist ideology is characteristic of life throughout the Caribbean, and the subject of the writing of many Caribbean intellectuals. George Lamming, for example, submits that "race is the persistent legacy of the Admiral of the Ocean Sea. No one born and nurtured in this soil has escaped its scars, and although the contemporary Caribbean cannot be accurately described as a racist society, everyone—whatever their ancestral origin—is endowed with an acute racial consciousness" (1995: 39). The "acute racial consciousness" of which Lamming writes is a factor of and overlays the colonial experience that even today shapes the way that people in the Caribbean see and operate in the world. As Caribbean scholar Michel-Rolph Trouillot points out, "Caribbean societies are inherently colonial. It is not only that all Caribbean territories have been conquered by one or another Western power. It is not only that they are the oldest colonies of the West and that their very colonization was part of the material and symbolic process that gave rise to the West as we know it. Rather, their social and cultural characteristics—and, some would say, individual idiosyncrasies of their inhabitants—cannot be accounted for, or even described, without reference to colonialism" (1992: 22). The contemporary conjunction of racial consciousness with colonialism is evident in the way that people locate themselves and others in the cultural and social universe of the BVI.

BLOODLINES: RACIALIST IDEOLOGY
AND LOCAL KNOWLEDGES

The telephone rings at 5:00 a.m. one morning early last November, and it is Charles. He wonders if I have received his fax:

Dear Colleen,
    The abstract sounds alright to me except I would use the verb "examine" where you use "explore," but that is a small matter. I would add "bloodlines" to the title.
    Title: Transforming Affiliations: Decolonization, Nationality, Bloodlines, Ethnicity, and Color.
    Sounds exciting. Best wishes.

In particular, he wants to know what I think of the title. I hedge, buying some time, but Charles jumps right in.

"It's bloodlines, I know."

"Yes, Charles," I reply, "it's so . . ."

I struggle for an adjective, but again Charles jumps in, "Blasphemous." (Cohen and Wheatley 1994: 1)

Bloodlines, as Charles Wheatley wrote it in his fax, refers to the notion that people can be grouped according to behavioral characteristics carried "in the blood" and transmitted from generation to generation such that, for example, some BVI families are "known" for their mathematical abilities, others for their agricultural abilities. It is a notion that historically informed a rigid system of stratification of British Virgin Islanders by skin color. It is a system that is manifested today, as individuals are assessed in terms of who they belong to, to determine what family a person comes from and by implication what rights and status the person holds vis-à-vis the BVI nation-state. Meanwhile, *bloodlines*, as a contested term, is blasphemous not just to a scholarship that eschews essentializing discourse, but also to a people who, in constituting themselves as a nation, hold strongly to an ideology of meritocracy and democracy. As we have seen, one of the main components of contemporary British Virgin Islanders' understanding of themselves, be it as a tourist destination or as a nation, is in terms of their difference from St. Thomas, and also from the other Caribbean people who make up more than half of the contemporary population. This sense of identity through reference to distinctiveness is itself grounded on practices in which British Virgin Islanders historically reckoned difference among themselves.

By all accounts, stereotypes that emphasized race-based characteristics, and a color-based socioeconomic hierarchy are long-standing in the BVI, as they are throughout the English-speaking Caribbean historically (Mintz 1989; Olwig 1993; Segal 1991, 1993; Williams 1991). For example, there existed in the BVI historically a strong association between skin color and morality or civility, such that, as one BVIslander put it to me facetiously, "the redder the skin, the closer to God" (field notes, July 28, 1992). Similarly, lighter-skinned individuals were assumed to have a greater predilection for mental tasks and educational pursuits, darker-skinned individuals for physical labor and agricultural pursuits. Of course, such associations were grounded both in broader assumptions about human nature and difference and in practices that established these assumptions as truth. Thus, a generation of older BVIslanders associates a certain kind of fancywork (a term referring to needlepoint and lacework) only with lighter-skinned women and, substantiating the link between skill and skin color, reports never having seen dark-skinned women doing it. In fact, local women learned this style of fancy work from two Englishwomen, who taught it in their homes only to the lighter-skinned individuals whom they deemed fit for it. In the context of a small, widely dispersed population and with travel and communication between communities difficult, such categorizations by skin color tended over time to be associated as well with family name, locale, and occupational specialization. As Charles Wheatley recalled,

> Traditionally we are familiar with a number of names, surnames. And each surname has some special significance in the context of BVI history. Whether it is Hodge, it is Wheatley, it is Penn, it is Frett. A name is not just a passing noun. It connotes something in many cases to us. Because if you say Thomas [pronounced *Tomá*], Thomas conjures up a history: location, and then a history of agricultural people, you know, a history of people of a certain physical size, who came from a special tribe in Africa and who were famous for their physical prowess. They could work beyond the imagination of anybody else. So you know, a name conjures up a number of things for us. . . . the moment you hear Flax you think Virgin Gorda, you wouldn't think of it as Tortola at all. So again, these are the kinds of things that come to mind when you hear names. (Cohen and Wheatley 1994: 3–4)

In the case of Tortola, the largest and most densely populated island of the BVI, distinctions were made between families from the southeastern and southwestern tips of Tortola who were engaged in sailing, sloop building, and sea trading, and were presumed to bear the cosmopolitan outlook and entrepreneurial drive with which such activities were associated, and agriculturalist families who lived along the rugged north coast of Tortola, east to west, and from the inland hills. Likewise, families in the east, on the southern coast, were divided between lighter-skinned families known for sailing, sloop building, and sea trading, and darker-skinned families who were agriculturalists (McGlynn 1981). These families were also set apart by historical circumstances that resulted in differential access to education. As a BVIslander from Tortola's East End recalled, "They were the mulattos, and the slave owner bought his children their freedom, and educated them. Here [pointing to the East End village where we are sitting] lots of people could read, too, too many to count. There [pointing toward Long Look] maybe you could find two" (field notes, October 24, 1996). Families along the northern coast, in the center of the island, were associated with subsistence agriculture, some cash crop production, rum making, fishing, and smuggling, and in the west with subsistence agriculture, some livestock production, and fishing. Charles Wheatley remembered "very distinctly at the eastern end of the island we referred to anyone coming from across the hills as the country people. They were the country people and they were the vendors of vegetables and that kind of thing. That's how they were perceived." He elaborated, "By the time you say 'country people' a number of things come in your mind. Patterns of speech and a whole set of things: where you live. And color, less educated. Because opportunities, although they were there, they were not able to take because of the employment, and the distance of the schools, and the lack of transportation" (Cohen and Wheatley 1994: 4).

The BVI capital of Road Town, in the center of Tortola on its southern shore, was where most of the BVI lighter-skinned elite resided. The center of mercantile exchange and local and colonial politics, Road Town and its families were associated with modernity, education, proper speech, and power. Notably, such associations conflate the "backwardness" signaled by dark skin in a racialist ideology with the stigma attached to the geographical isolation and agricultural labor associated with certain families; the education and civility signaled by light skin with the high status attached to the mobility and nonagricultural labor of other families. In some instances, the occupation and status of families of a particular community even came to stand for the whole surrounding area. For example, it was said of a particularly isolated agriculturalist community on Tortola's north shore that, "if you have sore foot, go to [village name]" (field notes, July 28, 1992). Marking the lower status of this village by reference to the assumed physical pathology of its residents, this statement exemplifies the link between racial stereotypes and physical pathology noted by Sander Gilman (1991, 1985) in nineteenth-century racial discourse. This association of a particular region with the people occupying it has special significance in the contemporary context, where we see ideologies of belonging that ground a very local group identity—what Brackette Williams in her study of the emergence of Guyanese nationalism terms "intrinsic racism"—being transformed into ideological grounding for conceptualizations of "the nation of own kind," or "extrinsic racism" (1993: 153).

TRANSFORMING AFFILIATIONS

By law, only BVI citizens have unrestricted rights to buy BVI land, and BVI citizens are given preference in all hiring and in the awarding of trade licenses, college scholarships, and low-interest development bank loans. In conventional practice and discourse, BVI citizenship is equated with *belonger* as opposed to *nonbelonger* status. However, the question of who legitimately belongs to the BVI and who can legitimately lay claim to the benefits accruing to BVI citizenship is complicated by the fact that from its inception the term *belonger* has been erroneously equated with BVI citizenship such that, as Bill Maurer points out in his study of British Virgin Islands citizenship law, "people in the BVI have recast the meaning of the identity categories *belonger* and *nonbelonger* to correspond with the meanings of citizenship. . . . *Belonger* as a category of identity has come to mean 'citizen'; *nonbelonger* has come to mean 'noncitizen'" (1997: 148). According to Maurer, the term *belonger* first appears in the 1969 Non-Belongers Ordinance, which established guidelines for entrance to and residence in the BVI by non-BVIslanders. According to this ordinance, the term *belonger* applies to anyone born in the BVI, anyone whose mother was born in the BVI, or anyone whose BVI father acknowledges paternity. However, under the terms of the British Nationality Act of 1981, children born in the BVI of immigrant parents are *not* BVI citizens, even though they may legally claim belonger status under the terms of the 1969 Non-Belongers Ordinance (Maurer 1997: 146). A major impetus to the drafting of the 2007 constitution was the need to clarify the link between belonger status and BVI citizenship; however, what constitutes BVI nativeness remains one of the most seriously contested issues in the BVI. In a field note from July 12, 1995, I note the conundrum faced by a BVI woman who gave birth in St. Thomas to a child fathered by a man from Antigua.

[Field notes 7.12.1995] At lunch today, L. noted that her son "still ain't got no papers," and that she is thinking of sending him to St. Thomas to school, as he hasn't got a chance of getting a BVI scholarship. "But he was born to you and carries your name," I argued. "I thought that a child born of a BVI woman would automatically be a belonger, regardless of who his father is or even if he signs papers for him." "Not if he not born here," L. replied, "and it don't seem fair, neither, because his daddy [from Antigua] not sign papers. But because he born St. Thomas and not here, he not eligible for a government scholarship."

Further complicating questions of citizenship and belonging is the fact that belonging to the BVI is as much a matter of being locatable in a system of local practices and knowledges that classify and locate individuals by family name, land, and blood, as it is a matter of constitutions and legislative ordinances. In this cultural and symbolic system, a belonger is marked by who one "belongs to": by what family and what part of the BVI one comes from, and even by one's physical, and frequently behavioral, characteristics. This link is expressed in the commonly asked question, "Who do you belong to?" referring to a person's family affiliations through mother's and/or father's side. Such affiliations are themselves widely understood to

be an indication of what part of the BVI one comes from, and by association what one looks and behaves like. Thus, for example, I observed a
schoolteacher guess correctly children's parentage and their place of origin
in the BVI on the basis of their facial characteristics alone. This conflation
of place and face, presumably based on the historical genetic insularity of
BVI communities, alludes to the sense that all that is required for *natural*
citizenship is a BVI family name and the connection to the land that this
implies, and not actual BVI birth.

Belonging in this sense also means being locatable in a local system
of knowledge such that, as Charles Wheatley put it, "If you saw a light-
skinned, mathematically oriented (surname) from East End out brawling,
you wouldn't even understand it; it would make no sense." In response to
this assertion, I asked Charles about a mutual acquaintance who, contrary
to what one would expect given his surname, was known to be belligerent
and argumentative. Without a moment's hesitation, Charles responded to
my question by giving me the name of a village on the northern shore
of Tortola, from which the mother of this individual mother came, the
implication being that it was her family's behavioral characteristics that
were being manifested (field notes, October 24, 1993). As my notes of an
interview with a former school administrator illustrate, belonging in the
cultural sense also means being locatable in a local system of vigilance
over behavior.

[**Field notes 10.23.1996**] Two students were sent to her for an infraction.
They were both late for class and the one who went in first with a note offering
a formal excuse passed the note out to the other. They were both caught in
the act, but she told the one who had received the note to go back to class.
After going over with the first one the issue in question, and before sending
him back to class, she asked him, "Who do you belong to?" When he replied
that he was John Smith, she asked him, "For Robert Smith of [community
name]?" When he replied "yes" she asked him, "And who is your grandfather?"
When he supplied his grandfather's name, and his village of origin, the principal let him go. Her comment on this was, "He will think on this, and I don't
think I will see him sent to me again." When I asked her why this would be,
she replied, "Because I know who he is."

In its most generic sense, belonging means being connected to the BVI
through association with a BVI place. This association with a particular BVI
place is so strong that individuals born on St. Thomas in the USVI, but of
BVI parentage, will use "I from here" or "I belong here" to mark their sense

that they belong to the BVI, through family name and the connection to a particular BVI place that is presumed to follow from this.

CHARLES: So now when you hear a name like Pemberton, you do not have any characteristics in your mind for it, you have no placement, no location, no locale. So in that sense, it stands to be not belonging. You get what I mean?

COLLEEN: I do.

CHARLES: This is in the mind.

COLLEEN: So say you hear the name Pemberton. How do you locate that person?

CHARLES: I locate it in Nevis. (Cohen and Wheatley 1994: 7)

In the terms set up in these discursive and cultural practices, the non-BVIslanders currently residing in the BVI have no means of belonging to the BVI, legal ability to make such a claim notwithstanding. Apart from the fact that there is no direct association that can be made between a non-BVI name and other "known" characteristics, few of the non-BVI citizens residing in the BVI actually own land. Even Santo Domingo–born individuals who migrate to the BVI carrying with them their BVI names frequently find that they don't really belong (Maurer 1997: 146). For example, on numerous occasions BVIslanders pointed people from Santo Domingo out to me, on the basis of what they deemed to be their provocative dress or rude behavior. While their use of Spanish certainly serves to single out Santo Domingo–born individuals, their BVI surname aside, they are also frequently held responsible for everything from litter on the roadside to the spread of HIV-AIDS. Most immigrants from Santo Domingo come to the BVI for the purpose of securing better jobs and a better lifestyle, and expect that they will receive help in this enterprise from the BVIslanders whose surname they share. However, a study of BVI Dominican residents conducted by Caribbean scholar Marcia Potter suggests that "on arrival, many have faced discrimination and resentment . . . even though they are related to people there" (2006: 60).

While children born in St. Thomas but carrying a BVI name might say "I belong here" to mark their sense of a connection to the BVI, children born in the BVI of non-BVI parents as frequently signal their sense of equality with their BVI peers by claiming, "I born here." As we have seen, this assertion that all births upon BVI soil are equal—or in the words of a St. Kitts–born BVI calypso king, "where we born is where we from"—has some legal merit, at least in terms of belonger status. But given the claims to belong to the BVI by citizens of the U.S. Virgin Islands or Santo Domingo, the use of the term "I born here" by children of non-BVI citizens also points up contradictions in claims to cultural citizenship, where a person of BVI parentage may not necessarily be a BVIslander. Complicating this situation, BVIslanders will use the phrase "I born here" to distinguish themselves from the "off-islanders" in their midst, regardless of where they were born. A post to a 2009 article in an online newspaper about the number of undocumented children in the BVI ("Lawmakers Worried about Undocumented Children") encapsulated the confusion signaled by different "born here claims" when it noted, "Ahh—so when someone says 'ah barn'ere' [I born here] it actually means 'ah barn in St Thomas.' And when someone says 'i dun [don't] have BVI passport' it means they were barn at Peebles [hospital in BVI]. Clear as mud."

"Born here" can also be used in a pejorative sense, referring to BVIslanders who take for granted their right to jobs, trade licenses, and the like, as in the following conversation that I reported in a field note from March 1993. The conversation took place between me and a BVI man, age fifty-six, at his home on Tortola.

[Field note 3.18.1993]. I'm keeping T. company on a slow afternoon and raise the subject of "born here." In contrast to M.'s understanding of "born here" as a category that does not necessarily refer to nativity—that is, it can be applied to someone born in St. Thomas (although not Santo Domingo, because the connections are too stretched out)—T. asserts that anyone born here can say "I born here," although because he is a British Virgin Islander, T. saying "I born here" would mean something different from a child born of two Nevisians saying "I born here." The bottom line for T., though, seems to be who uses it. According to T., the only ones who really use it are "lazy BVIslanders who no wanna work—they want somethin' for nothin'." These sorts, according to T., are called BH, or are said to have BhD's—Born Here Degrees. According to T., the first he heard the use of the term BH was from a doctor, in referring to lazy so and so's as "Dey just BH."

Although many BVIslanders might dispute the characterization in this field note, few would deny that the sense of entitlement that it alludes to poses a real problem, and particularly with respect to employment in the tourism sector. This is borne out by statistics that reveal that more than 50 percent of the jobs in tourism are held by non-BVIslanders and that overall unemployment rates for "native-born" men are higher than for men born in other Caribbean countries. It is also pointed to as a problem in a British Virgin Islands government document assessing the tourism industry,

The National Tourism Development Plan (1996). Citing interviews conducted with BVIslanders throughout the territory, this document reports a real antipathy toward employment in tourism on the part of BVIslanders. In short,

> We have been repeatedly told by BV Islanders that:
> - "We are owners, not employees."
> - "BV Islanders own land, they do not have to work as servants."
> - "The fact that some of us have a BH (Born Here) degree means no employer, be they a Belonger or an expatriate, wants to put up with the attitude that comes with the degree."
> - "Many parents born in the Territory place a much higher value on their children finding employment in other sectors of the economy. The suggestion is that they equate employment in a service role with servitude."
> - "The values, assumptions and beliefs the people in the educational establishment hold with respect to the tourism industry do not make them strong advocates for the industry. In their view, employment in other sectors of the BVI economy would be more suitable for their graduates."
>
> ("Cultural Factors and Attitudes Play a Part")

In point of fact, the competing claims to the rewards of a successful BVI economy that are framed in terms of "I born here" are cross-cut by compelling and complicated historical connections between BVIslanders and BVI residents from other Caribbean nations, many of whom are related through family ties, most of whom shared recent common citizenship as members of the British colonial administrative unit, the Leeward Islands colony. Further, given BVIslanders' own quite recent experience as the derogated migrant laborers to other islands, internal distinctions between belonger and nonbelonger, "born here" and "off islander" may, in the words of one BVI woman, "be turning around on others what has for so many years been done to us" (field notes, November 10, 1995). Indeed, considered in this comparative context, the confusions over how to determine who "belongs" to the BVI and competing meanings of the phrase "I born here" call forth the larger historical fact of the continuous movement of labor across borders that has characterized the Caribbean experience, the shared powerlessness of BVIslanders, Dominicans, St. Thomians, and Kittitians alike in the face of shifts in capital, investment, and power. These sorts of complications to the project of constituting identities prevail throughout the Caribbean where, Stuart Hall notes, "difference . . . persists—in and

alongside continuity," in a way that, for example, "positions Martiniquans
and Jamaicans as *both* the same *and* different" (1992: 225–226, author's
emphasis).

SPILT BLOOD: FROM INTERNAL DIFFERENCE
TO NATIONAL COMMUNITY

Decolonization and economic growth associated with tourism undercut,
or at least challenge, an ideology linking skin color, ability, and status.
This is the case in particular of the status of Road Town's elite families.
The reestablishment in 1950 of representative government and the establishment in 1967 of a ministerial system of government opened access to
seats of power to people in communities throughout the BVI. In fact, the
first chief minister of the British Virgin Islands under the 1967 constitution, H. Lavity Stoutt, came from a northwest coast agricultural family.
H. Lavity Stoutt and his Virgin Islands Party predominated in BVI politics
to Stoutt's death in 1995, and his influence and importance are reflected in
the fact that his birthday is celebrated as a national holiday. Likewise, the
historically higher status of Road Town's families must now be measured
against, for example, the economic success of families from north shore
communities, whose isolated pristine beaches are favored tourist destinations, as I note in field notes from 1992.

[Field notes 7.18.1992] I am chatting with N. and mention the name of
one of the brothers from a Road Town family, assuming that, because they
are the same age, they probably knew each other from school. In response
he says, "I never speak to them people—they never speak to me." He then
counts off on his fingers the names of [four prominent Road Town] families . . . and reflects "You know, they always were sending their children off
for good schooling—to Antigua, the States, the U.K.—and they come back
and they hardly have anything, some of them are even renting their houses."
Of course, this is being spoken as he sits with me in his successful business,
so the contrast between the old families and the new entrepreneurs is even
more tangible.

Simultaneous with these local shifts in political power and economic
standing, the Black Power movement of the 1960s and 1970s and more
recent African cultural movements complicate assessments people make
based upon skin color. Thus, at the very least, commonplace aspersions
against an individual by reference to dark skin can be, and frequently are,

rebuffed by reference to the African purity dark skin signifies, or to the "in-authenticity" of "mixed blood." A middle-aged BVI man from a village on Tortola's northwest coast recalled this change in an interview.

[Field notes, 7.29.1993] The thing is, after the 60s where people started to realize black was beautiful, it all didn't start in New York, you know. It hit also the Caribbean. And people began to develop more self-esteem and more love for themselves, and see that you couldn't have black parents and have straight hair, you couldn't have black parents and have a high nose, you couldn't have black parents and end up having thin lips, you couldn't have black parents and end up having a flat bottom. You know, it went along with the color. So people began to become aware that, um, you are what you are because of your heredity.

In other instances, race and racialist discourse is used in even more self-consciously political ways, as when a popular song claiming that "this is my father's land" warns against white incursion into BVI economic life asserting, "being the boss is in their blood." The entire verse of "Father's Land," by BVIslander Quito Rymer, reads,

> Come on down they say, come on down, we can take island in the
> sun.
> Oh, it makes their poor hearts bleed, when they find out they can't
> lead.
> Tears inside, like a raging flood, being the boss is in their blood.
> But they don't seem to understand.
> This is my father's land. This is my father's land.

As this verse suggests, "Father's Land" is concerned with the question of who can legitimately lay claim to the BVI. In fact, as Quito Rymer recalled to me in a 1993 interview, it was this question that inspired him to write the song.

> During the time when I wrote that song, I would sit in my own
> Gazebo and I would hear people criticize the BVI, the way things
> were done, the way people lived, people were, and what *should* be done
> and how it *should* be done and who should make the decisions, and
> I thought that we had a right, we had a right based on the fact that
> our ancestors' you know, sweat blood and tears had given us that right.

That had given us that right to call this our home, to make decisions, you know. I thought that that song needed to be sung, to pass on to people how we felt about that type of attitude. (Interview with Quito Rymer, August 4, 1993)

In stating that "this is my father's land," the song draws upon historic associations between bloodline and place. Yet it also challenges long-standing practices of distinguishing among BVIslanders by skin color or abilities "carried in the blood" in favor of a "father's land" that belongs to all BVIslanders. Similarly, in everyday interactions BVIslanders might still trace their family to a particular place on Tortola or to a particular BVI island, but they do so in the context of public discourse and cultural practices that attend increasingly to larger questions of national character: not "What is someone from the East End like?" "What is a Smith?" but "What is a British Virgin Islander?"

The question "What is a British Virgin Islander?" certainly makes sense, given the legislative policies of the 1960s that changed considerably the status of the BVI vis-à-vis the U.K., as well as the economic growth and the development of roads and communication systems that made possible the consolidation of the disparate communities and islands making up the BVI. But the question, "What is a British Virgin Islander?" seems to take on a special urgency in the context of the sort of demographic change heralded in a local newspaper headline, "B.V. Islanders Outnumbered: Socio-economic Horizon Cloudy" (1993) or in the context of the 1996 national tourism report that saw the growth of the non-BVI population as having "implications for social harmony." Even the preamble to the 2007 constitution that claims "a free and independent spirit" developed "on qualities of honesty, integrity, mutual respect, self-reliance and the ownership of the land" alludes to an Other who does not have such qualities.

In light of these sentiments, the answer to the question, "What is a British Virgin Islander?" is that a British Virgin Islander is someone who is not a *non*-British Virgin Islander. This category may be marked by racial difference, as tends to be the case for Canadian, English, and U.S. nationals residing in the BVI (and who are, for the most part, white); by ethnic difference, as tends to be the case for Guyanese individuals; by language difference, as tends to be the case for individuals from Santo Domingo; or by national difference, as tends to be the case for individuals carrying names like Pemberton that are readily associated with one of the many Caribbean countries from which immigrants to the BVI come. Nevertheless, as a group, non-BVIslanders are associated, as the 1993 newspaper article intimates, with social disharmony. Bill Maurer makes a related point, claiming that stereotypes that circulate in the BVI about Guyanese immigrants of South Asian descent function to differentiate "good citizens" from "bad citizens":

British Virgin Islanders stereotype Guyanese immigrants of Indian descent as "greedy," "clannish," and "crafty" . . . the idea that BVIslanders act out of "generous" motives while Guyanese act from "greed" supports liberal understandings of what it means to be a "good citizen" and a "good person." "Good citizens" are conceptualized as a group of normative "individuals" who are defined as similars and equals. "Bad citizens," different and unequal, are cast as unable to contribute to the social good. Hence, their actions, which may be identical to those of 'good citizens," are attributed to self-interested, greedy, or clannish motives. (Maurer 1997: 101)

The degree to which the association between the BVI immigrant population and social disharmony make an explicit link to traits carried in the blood varies. As in the "Father's Land" claim about white expatriates that "being the boss is in their blood," on multiple occasions I have heard the upswing in criminal activity in the BVI attributed to the "violent nature" of one or another immigrant group. Meanwhile, non-BVIslanders complain that the media play up crimes committed by immigrants, but pay scant attention to crimes committed by BVIslanders. Of course, these distinctions are always subject to being undercut by reference to shared African or Caribbean heritage, to mixed blood or diluted bloodline, and by political strategies making differential use of racial discourses, as well as by reference to principals of democracy and egalitarianism. But while the principals of democracy may forestall the rendering of absolute judgments about individuals based upon physiognomic variation or traits carried "in the blood," neither egalitarian ideology nor the BVI civic associations that foster pan-familial, pan-religious, pan-racial, pan-national affiliations fully address the challenge of constituting a more inclusive conceptualization of the national community.

In one respect, this is because this is a community that now constitutes itself as much in terms of a particular history of blood spilt as in terms of bloodline. Thus, "blood" in the song, "Father's Land" is also used to mark a sense of belonging to and ownership of the BVI based upon shared hardship and suffering, as when the song claims "Sweat and tears, blood sweat and tears, that's the price they paid / So I won't be leaving, I won't be running away." In reference to this verse, Quito Rymer reflected, "I think anybody who is an indigenous person of that area has a right to—even if I am the person coming in there, it don't matter—that person has a right to say 'I want to make my own decision, shape my own destiny'" (interview, August 4, 1993). In this sense, the spilt blood of BVI ancestors is constituted in "Father's Land" as providing a spiritual link between their descendants and the land. The 1923 sinking of the sloop *The Fancy Me* and the deaths of 56 BVIslanders returning to the BVI from work in the cane fields of Santo Domingo may be viewed as another such link, for it is an event that drew all BVIslanders into a shared circle of grief. Likewise, when heralding the adoption of the 2007 constitution, the BVI chief minister Dr. Orlando Smith rendered a pan-Caribbean heritage of slavery, oppression, and exploitation a heritage belonging to "natural" BVIslanders alone when he proclaimed, "Nobody gave us this Constitution. It was not a handout. It was not a gift. It was not an act of charity. This Constitution was born from the sweat of the brows of BVIslanders of every generation past. This Constitution belongs to the first Africans brought over to these islands in chains. This Constitution belongs to the ancestors who struggled for freedom and emancipation. This Constitution belongs to the great grandparents who hacked their survival out of the rocks and out of the seas" (Smith 2007a).

Unlike the spiritual rebirth that Daniel Segal claims accompanies U.S. naturalization and that is constituted through "a closure on past disassociation rather than a claim to primordiality" (1994: 3–4), naturalization to the BVI is thought to be superseded by loyalty to one's "primordial" national origins. One BVI man expressed this to me in terms of "born again" versus "not born again," claiming that in the case of individuals from other Caribbean countries who actually attain BVI citizenship, "they still have the . . . presence here, as like a tourist orientation. They get BVI status, they become British Virgin Islanders. But they are not born again British Virgin Islanders" (field notes, March 16, 1994).

SPLIT BLOOD: MAKING
BRITISH VIRGIN ISLANDERS

In the present-day context of economic prosperity, immigration, and residential, social, and genetic mobility, local distinctions between different types of British Virgin Islanders that are based upon historic associations of name, place, physical appearance, and behavior are blurring. By way of demonstrating this, a BVI educator was fond of testing the knowledge of other BVIslanders, using my Vassar student research assistant, a woman of mixed Afro-American/Afro-Caribbean heritage, but with no links to the BVI. Pointing to her, he would ask, "Who does she belong to?" In all instances, when his respondents replied, on the basis of her facial characteristics, that she was a Penn, from the East End of Tortola, he would laugh at the joke he had played, exclaiming, "correct, exactly correct." As people of BVI parentage return to the BVI after a one or two generation absence, and as BVIslanders and non-BVIslanders intermarry, one "knows" with less reliability who someone with a BVI name is. Recalling, of course that what one ever "knows" with certainty is always constituted within and not outside structures of power, and notwithstanding the ever-present potential for manipulating the system through the practice of tracing an individuals' heritage through four sides, there is in the BVI today a sense that native bloodlines are being diluted.

This sense that bloodlines are being diluted was expressed by a BVIslander in terms that referenced the historic insularity of BVI communities. "One of the problems in the BVI today," this woman claimed, "is that people aren't staying in place" (field notes, October 24, 1996). The concern that "people aren't staying in place" conveys a sense that one can no longer expect to find people living where they are supposed to be living. But it also conveys a sense that people aren't living with whom they used to be living. This is certainly the sentiment underlying a BVI government report, based on 1991 census data, on the impact of immigration to the BVI. Claiming that "just as the economic gains (for the host country) from migration are considered, so must be the social tensions that may result due to the unfavourable social atmosphere that might be created," the report implies that immigration is responsible for the diluted BVI bloodline. Of particular note, in this regard, was a statistic demonstrating that "almost 80% of all nuclear family households contained at least one immigrant" ("Social Issues: Immigration" 1996).

In the context of the movement of people and bloodlines, many BVIslanders are also concerned that the cultural features that "make" a BVIslander are being lost. A concern with the loss of a BVI essence was the subject of a conversation that I had in 2008 with BVIslander Eileene Parsons. Having devoted her adult life to BVI culture, she was worried that "our little traditions," were being overwhelmed by the traditions of people from other islands.

[Field notes 6.13.2008] In talking generally about culture, Ms. P. bemoaned "the deterioration of what is uniquely ours: manners, respect for ourselves" and cited as a prime example the use of food terms from other cultures to talk about British Virgin Islands food. She elaborated: "I hear people talking about jerk pork, which is from Jamaica, and I say 'what about our dove pork?' And the children talk about a 'bake' when what they are asking for is our fried Johnny Cake. We don't have 'bake,' that's a Jamaica thing. And salt fish and ackee; what the hell do we know about salt fish and ackee? And when we raise goats and use their head or foot for soup, we call it goat head soup, goat foot soup. Not goat water. Goat water is what they have in Montserrat, and it is different. Goat water from Montserrat is good, make no mistake. But it isn't goat head or goat foot soup. Just constantly, our little traditions are being eroded. Of course, there are so few of us here, and we are not strong enough to defend our traditions." I note to her the preamble of the new Constitution, which claims a unique BVI essence, and she says that this is so, "but we need to fight to find and maintain it."

One of the ways that BVIslanders are fighting "to find and maintain" a unique BVI essence is through events such as Festival, which is seen increasingly as a national cultural product, and through "recovering" BVI music and dance traditions and teaching them in the curriculum of the elementary and high schools. Likewise, a Virgin Islands Studies Program begun in 1999 at the H. Lavity Stoutt Community College spearheaded the study of BVI culture and history at the college level and promotes the excavation and restoration of historical sites. I discuss these efforts at cultural recovery and key individuals involved in them, including Eileene Parsons, in chapter 8.

In early 2008, the BVI government established a policy whereby individuals wishing to become naturalized British Virgin Islands citizens—characterized as "new belongers"—would be required to take and pass a course on the history and culture of the BVI. As the permanent secretary to the minister of education and culture explained in an online newspaper article, "The information to be learnt in the course will ensure that we are all saying the same things about the Virgin Islands. It will also go a long way to ensuring that we all appreciate where we live. Granted some of our own also need to participate in the course and so there is no intent to cast aspersions on non–Virgin Islanders, *but our culture must be preserved and prominent in our society*" (quoted in "New Belongers Must Take Local History and Culture Course"; emphasis added). The response to this announcement on the newspaper's blog was swift and intense. Most individuals who identified themselves as native BVIslanders supported the move, with posts such as one that said, "I think a history and culture course could be of benefit to non-belongers seeking belongership status. They MIGHT learn a thing or two about our culture and perhaps even a few things about our history." Pointing to his own experience as a naturalized U.S. citizen, another BVIslander argued, "If these are the requirements, you meet them or leave them. I am a BVIslander by birth and a U.S. citizen through naturalization. I took a test. I wanted something and simply did what the country required of me to get it. BVIslanders knowing or not knowing the history is not the issue here. The rights of the country was inherited by birth. Go to the class and pass—what's the big deal. If it is important to you do it—if it is not, then just live here and pay for a work permit every year."

In contrast, people posting responses to this article who identified

themselves as non–BVIslanders saw the history course requirement as indic-
ative of unequal treatment of the BVI immigrant population. One post
argued that the new requirement was an instance of BVIslanders pushing
work in tourism off on people from other islands, "we down and side
Caribbean people work at every inch of this country and have to know
about it in the first place when we get here, to deal with ur Tourist and
ur rude fellow citizen. u dont even know the half of it cause u are not
in our shoes." Along similar lines, another post questioned how an older
immigrant could be expected to take such a course, and at the same time
evoked "born here" to make a claim to equal rights.

> You gonna send a 50 years man who don't know A to Z and live here
> 28 years to [college]? When he knows where every water well used to
> be and where the fish lives and . . . where the roads used to pass and
> what was on Main Street. . . . I am not dissing BVI history, [I] am saying
> they themselves don't even know it. [The minister] should also send
> those of you who sold your rights to be US citizen back to STT [St.
> Thomas] 'cause the modern day BVIslander born their children in the
> US and you give us trouble to get passport for our children who born
> here. BVI laws are unfair to us and the table will turn soon.

Notions of racial purity and shared blood that are central to conceptualizations of the nation as a natural entity (Handler 1984, 1988; Segal
1991; Segal and Handler 1992; Williams 1989, 1993) are clearly operant
in the BVI. As we have seen, the sense of national unity that is heralded
in everything from national holidays and native foods to a constitutional
preamble that pronounces a BVI "essence" derive their legitimacy from
claims to a shared history on BVI land. Meanwhile, the concept of a BVI
bloodline that operated historically to mark difference in a rigid social
hierarchy and was upheld by racialist discourse was transposed to accommodate modern notions of unity as a "people of own kind." This turn
to the nation as a coherent and homogeneous grouping of people is in
many respects a response to the perceived impurity introduced by immigration. And this perception and response accord with our understanding
of nationalist ideologies as necessarily concerned with racial purity and
homogeneity. As Deborah Thomas puts it in her study of national cultural
identity in Jamaica, "nationalism's universalizing aspects have been dependent on simultaneous projects of exclusion" (2002: 512). In asserting rights
to the rewards of a BVI nation by reference to a shared heritage, however,
a discourse linking belonging and blood also signals a certain ambivalence,
as if this turn to a nation of "shared blood" were a sort of fall-back position, a site of natural identity/affiliation, by default.

One sees this sense of ambivalence in responses by BVIslanders to a 2008 online newspaper commentary by a British Virgin Islander discussing discrimination in the BVI. Contrasting the contributions made to the prosperous BVI economy by the immigrant population with what he characterized as a "social divide" in employment, education, and media treatment of criminal offenses, the writer claimed, "It's the colonial system being repeated again on different levels" (Uhuru 2008). Response to this editorial was mixed, with BVIslanders and non-BVIslanders weighing in fairly equally on both sides of the issue. The contemporary social situation in the BVI is far more complicated than can be treated in a single newspaper commentary, or even in a chapter in a book on tourism. But of particular relevance to this discussion of race, identity, and citizenship in the BVI were posts to this commentary by two self-identified BVIslanders, below.

I love Caribbean people and it is my deep wish that we BVIslanders as we go out each day continue the traditions of hospitality and equality that very much make up the true Virgin Islander. To expatriates, we have been harsh, we have been wrong at times, but it is a common reaction for people who feel like your presence and our sometimes mis-matched cultures threaten our own. I hope we can find a happy medium because BVIslanders are great and proud people, we just come off bad sometimes in ways we don't intend when we feel that the way we feel should have just as much a place as the way you are made to feel.

While many British Virgin Islanders express the desire to retain BVI resources and land for British Virgin Islanders (what is wrong with protecting what you own for your own, after all how much SQUARE miles are we?), they also recognize the need to acknowledge the contributions of non-British Virgin Islanders to the economy and society, and to provide for their inclusion in BVI public culture. (Not the other way around.) The things that make the British Virgin Islanders express a strong sense of their distinctiveness, pointing to the more serene and rural nature of their island life, their economic well-being, and their independent and friendly character, is the same thing that's makes OTHERS (non-belongers) hate us.

Both of these responses speak of a desire to keep BVI land in BVI hands, and both establish a connection between an essential BVI character and the privileges of BVI citizenship. But they also allude to the dangers inhering in this project, and in particular as it promotes inequality and incites the antagonism of people with whom BVIslanders share a common Caribbean experience and a common African heritage, from whose labor the BVI economy has prospered and with whom many BVIslanders have intermarried. These posts and the commentary to which they responded remind us that, emerging from colonial interactions, ideologies of racial purity that ground modern-day nationalism represent a particularly perilous grounding for conceptualizations of national unity by Europe's "raced, non-nationed Others" (Olwig 1993: 90).

In this respect, finally, it bears noting that even as BVIslanders move to consolidate a sense of themselves as a larger family of distinctively BVI names, linked by common blood and a shared heritage of the spilt blood of their ancestors, these bases of their claims to being a national community are appropriated to another reading. This is a reading, to be found in the seat pockets of every American Eagle airplane carrying passengers to the BVI, that applies the same symbolism and the ideological precepts upon which it is based to a rendering of the BVI as a mythological paradise stopped in colonial time: "As for the residents' attitude toward visitors, no West Indians maintain their dignity better while extending a warm welcome than do the various Penns, Pickerings, Stoutts, and others. The cliché 'salt of the earth' may seem banal, but it applies fittingly to these gentle, helpful souls, as proud of their homeland as any crowned head is of his kingdom" (Harman and Harman 1993: 34). This quote from the *Latitudes* magazine published by American Airlines underscores a problem of nationalist ideologies that base notions of belonging on constructions of racial or ethnic uniqueness. That is, the same ideological move can be and is used to essentialize and exoticize a people. These issues appear again in the next chapter, which takes up issues arising over struggles for control over media representations of the BVI.

CHAPTER 5

Like Looking at
Ourselves in a Mirror

COLLABORATIVE ETHNOGRAPHY IN PARADISE

DISTINCTIONS THAT INFORM INTERACTIONS among British Virgin Islanders and between belongers and nonbelongers are based upon socially constructed categories of race, ethnicity, and nationality, but these categories are experienced as nonetheless real. In this, they operate as *naturalized codes*, that is, as understandings about the world that are "so widely distributed in a specific language community or culture and . . . learned at so early an age, that they appear not to be constructed . . . but to be 'naturally' given" (Hall 1993: 95). Like the stereotypes that are at the base of images of the BVI disseminated by tourist brochures or idealizations of paradise carried in tourists' heads, these distinctions and the meanings that they carry saturate the settings within which people in the BVI work, walk, live, play, and interact. In this chapter, I discuss an ethnographic video that I made in collaboration with BVIslander Kenne Hodge, *Split Screens, Split Subjects* (Cohen and Hodge 1995).

I met Kenne in 1994, when a mutual friend introduced us. We were both interested in how the BVI is represented to the world at large, and this friend thought we might benefit from working together. My interest in the topic was largely academic; Kenne's interest was more deeply personal and political. As a BVIslander who daily had to deal with a tourist gaze that saw him variously as "exotic," "uncivilized," "friendly," or "scary," he was interested in challenging the images of the BVI upon which such gazes were grounded. The video that emerged from our collaboration reflects both of these interests, and the discussion in this chapter demonstrates how we managed to interweave them.

The video *Split Screens, Split Subjects* exposes the naturalized codes in images that market the BVI as "Nature's Little Secrets" and looks at the effect upon the people of the BVI of a marketing strategy that reinstates tired but durable associations of the Caribbean and Caribbean people with a premodern paradise. Focused on representations of the BVI, the video also asks questions about who can or cannot, who is or is not, in a position to represent the BVI to the world at large. In this latter respect, the video also interrogates the ethnographic enterprise, even as our collaboration points to new directions in this enterprise.

I started shooting video as part of my ethnographic research in 1992, and I loved being behind the camera. The camera focused my attention differently from the way watching and taking notes did. As I describe in the field note below, I moved in the observational space in another way when I had a camera on my shoulder. The camera often also gave me access to events and spaces that might otherwise have been closed to me. But as the field note below also indicates, as much as working with a camera might have made me feel like an insider, I was in some respects no different from tourists who pass through and take pictures of the BVI.

[Field note 7.20.1994] Moco Jumbie [stilt dancer] Practice . . . I now drive into the moco jumbie practice yard with the assurance of a regular: past the people gathering outside the high school gates for their nightly volleyball game, through the gate, a wave to the security guard, who no longer even bothers to mouth the words "moco jumbie" with a questioning look on the face. He just hails me, and looks back down to his newspaper. . . . I pull up, and get out of my car slowly, some mumbled greetings to kids putting on their stilts as I amble past toward where Binghy and Trevor are: Trevor sitting in the driver's seat of Binghy's car, doing paperwork, Binghy leaning against the car, handing things into him. Small talk is what we engage in mostly, a few comments about the small improvements we're seeing in some of the first year moco jumbie, the need to bring the radio out into the yard more, so the dancers can hear the music better, insurance coverage for the troupe. I have gotten to the point where my comings and goings, and what I do while I'm here, bear the mark of informality and seeming indifference to routine that characterizes everyone's activities—save, of course, when they are performing or practicing a certain trick or dance. Apart from these moments of concentrated activity—and the demanding scrutiny of the moco jumbie elders as they instruct from the ground or on stilts (it always reminds me of military drill or ski-race coaching)—moco jumbie are striding, dancing, forming small groups, leaning against buildings, adjusting leg wrappings, getting their stilts on, taking them off, in random pattern . . . the activity follows no set pattern; the plan emerges, rather, as the configuration of the practice group on any given day coalesces. Yesterday, for example when a good number of the younger moco jumbie showed up, Skelly and Binghy decided "to take the children out for a stroll." And that's how I came upon them, two orderly lines of 18 moco jumbie, ranging shortest to tallest—with Binghy on the ground between them, and Skelly, ever-present saw clutched in his right hand should someone need their sticks shortened, bringing up the rear—coming through the front school gates, for a practice walk past the basketball courts to the village and back again. Today, not so many youths appeared—those who did were complaining of calf and foot cramps—likely resulting from yesterday's stroll. So today's work was on "the train": the line-up of moco jumbie hopping on one foot, raised foot held from behind by the next moco jumbie. The culminating practice routine tonight was a circle train: 15 moco jumbie in a circle each holding the other's raised foot. I move among moco jumbie, camera on shoulder; my camera, like their stilts, an extension of my body. And so I walk among them, sometimes moving directly into the middle of a practice group, frequently shooting over the shoulder of one of the coaches, today even carrying on a conversation with two young women about jouvert. No apparent problem here. I'm comfortable with my work, and the group is comfortable with me. But when I leave, it is to go to no one waiting for me at home, with no plans to stop off at a friend's for a chat that could easily turn into an all-evening social gathering, no fish to boil up in a pot, no church meeting. My meeting places are still for the most part the same public meeting places of all outsiders: the man not feeling welcome at home by his mother or woman, the tourist looking for a local night spot, the ex-pat seeking out the island's best happy hour. I could go home, I say to myself, bathe my skin, take a few minutes to catch up on some notes. But my empty room, the silent TV that carries no news that I want to hear, the instant soup containers that await only hot water and a five minute wait for a nutritious meal, hold no appeal. I head west anyway, deciding to let the decision wait until the moment I either turn into my road or pass it by. I don't mind being alone tonight, but I don't want the loneliness; I'm just not certain where least loneliness lies: at home, by myself, or in a crowd with some people I know, but who don't really know me?

Working behind a camera also made explicit to me and whomever I happened to be around that there was some sort of documentation going on. In some respects, walking around with a video camera felt more honest than observing and then writing up my observations in field notes; at the very least, it announced my intent to observe and record. But visual representations can also be startlingly dishonest, the more so because of their pretense of indexicality.

The politics of representation is at the heart of contemporary ethnographic inquiry. As we write or make videos about the cultures we study, ethnographers make a great effort to ensure that these representations of other people's lives are as true as possible to what we have come to know about them. Of course, our knowledge is always partial, in both senses of the term. Our knowledge is necessarily incomplete, and although our collaborations with people who live in the place we are writing about surely expands our knowledge, what these people know is also only part of what is to be known. Partial, as I am fond of telling my students, is also a word that implies preference, as in "I am partial to strawberry ice cream." In this sense of the word our knowledge is also incomplete. For our partiality can and does blind us to what Trouillot (1995) terms the "unthinkable," those events, modes of thought, frames of meaning that are literally outside our ken because our own way of seeing the world does not allow us to consider them.

One of my goals as an ethnographer is to identify naturalized codes that are in play in a culture and, through my field notes and ethnography, produce descriptions of them. To paraphrase Clifford Geertz's classic assertion about thick description (1973a), in my work as an ethnographer I seek to know a culture deeply enough to be able to distinguish the difference between a voluntary wink and an involuntary twitch of an eye. But in my effort to provide a sense of what it is like, for example, to live in a place that is marketed and experienced as paradise, I also work to understand how who I am inhibits, allows, or shapes the knowledge that I develop. This is why I find collaboration to be so important to my work. Working across what Faye Ginsburg in thinking about collaboration in ethnographic film refers to as "the boundaries of difference that for better or worse exist" diminishes the realm of the unthinkable. Importantly, Ginsburg points out, working across difference can also subvert hoary myths that persist about difference itself.

> Critiques coming out of some branches of cultural studies, while raising important points about the politics of representation, are so critical of all "gazes" at the so-called other that . . . we would all be paralyzed into an alienated universe, with no engagement across the boundaries of difference that for better or worse exist. . . . Underlying these responses, of course, is the idea that "we" and "they" are separate, which in turn is built on the trope and mystique of the noble savage living in a traditional, bounded world, for whom all knowledge, objects, and values originating elsewhere are polluting of some reified notion of culture and innocence. . . . Questions about the legitimacy of one's presence in a foreign setting (especially in which power relations are unequal) as an outsider with a camera should always be raised. . . . Conversely, the fact that one is an "insider" does not guarantee an untroubled relationship with one's subject. (Ginsburg 1995: 263–264)

The question of who controls the process by which ideas about a place and a people are proliferated is vital for any group, insofar as this process limits or expands the realm of the unthinkable. It is a particularly important question for a country like the BVI that markets itself as a tourist destination.

An anecdote provides an example of how naturalized codes that undergird representations of the BVI can and do shape tourists' experience. In July 1994, fragments from the comet Shoemaker-Levy 9 were colliding with Jupiter. I was invited to view this event at a small observatory that sits on one of the highest peaks of Tortola, with Kenne Hodge and an amateur astronomer from Africa who lives in the BVI and is married to a BVIslander. On my way to the observatory, I stopped by Stanley's Welcome Bar for some dinner. A beach bar famous throughout the bareboating world for its cheeseburgers and its taciturn owner Stanley, the bar was a nightly gathering spot for bareboaters anchored in Cane Garden Bay. As I ate dinner and visited with Stanley, a group of four bareboaters at a nearby table overheard me talking about my trip to the observatory, and asked if they could go along. After dinner, I loaded them into my car and we climbed the steep hill to the observatory. The seven of us—the bareboaters, me, Kenne, and the amateur astronomer—spent two hours in the observatory watching the comets fall on Jupiter, and as we were about to leave, one of the bareboaters asked us, "What is an observatory doing here?" The astronomer and Kenne and I all looked at each other and almost in one voice answered, "Because this is the highest peak on Tortola." The look of confusion on the bareboater's face told us that this was not the answer he was looking for. What his question really meant was, "What is an observatory doing here, in the BVI, the untouched and pristine paradise of tourist ads?" For him, an observatory in the BVI was "unthinkable."

The construction and marketing of images of the BVI that make an observatory "unthinkable" to the tourist was the subject of the first of three videos that I made in collaboration with Kenne Hodge. The video came about because of two related ethnographic events: in the third summer of my fieldwork in the BVI I was asked to join the camera crew of Virgin Islands Television (VITV), the BVI television station, shooting the events of the annual Festival. Through my association with VITV, I began to explore some of the political issues related to the production of local programming. The following year my colleague and sometimes co-author Fran Mascia-Lees asked me to take part in an electronic media poster session for the 1995 meetings of the American Anthropological Association. Entitled "The Anthropology Trade Show," the session focused on the commodification of anthropological knowledge. Both instances presented themselves as ideal opportunities to produce a video about representation, politics, and commodification. What I had not anticipated when I first started to work on the video was the extent to which it would force me to examine my own position and practice as an ethnographer. As the following field note attests, however much I might wish to expose my own partiality, the naturalized codes that inhere to being a white Western scholar are difficult to see and to undo.

[**Field notes 11.8.1995**] The VITV editing and sound studio occupies the first and second floors of a pink triplex apartment sitting on the steep southwestern facing slope of Butu Mountain. To get there, you climb the Fort Hill road almost to the top, turning in to the left at the sign that announces (in the manner, I have come to believe, of a plot foreshadowing) "The Cloud Room." Negotiating a sharp left turn up and against a cliff that bears the clear marks of cars that failed to time the turn in the manner that allows for a smooth transition from the macadam road onto the rough concrete/dirt mix of the road to the studio, you keep driving along steeper and ever more narrow roads until, as you pass the four large satellite dishes that line the road immediately leading to the studio, you nose your car over a sharp dropping off drive and, making a sharp right turn (and braking quickly so as not to go over an embankment), you arrive in the parking area above the apartments housing the studio. . . . As usual, I approached the whole day of editing with great anxiety and nervousness. Convinced that we would not be finished by the 3:00 press conference with the Chief Minister, I saw every step as a delay and potential for disaster. At one point I severely tried Chris's patience by explaining three times to him something that he grasped on the first go-round; in another instance I had to leave the room as Chris worked with a voiceover to shorten it to fit the visuals for which it was intended. This is clearly a control thing, as Kenne pointed out to me continuously throughout this evening. When will I learn to let go? This is obviously a question of more than simply personal import. If indeed I am committed to a new way of doing ethnography, to relinquishing control over the process of ethnographic interpretation and representation, at the very least to the point of constructive dialogue or negotiation (even the terms suggest the retention of control on the part of the anthropologist), then I must be much more aware of both how my very presence (white, Western, woman, professor) structures the terms of engagement, and how my refusal to acknowledge how what I do is ultimately directed toward maintaining my control over things is a willful act—of arrogance, power, vanity, what have you.

NEGOTIATING REPRESENTATIONS OF THE
BRITISH VIRGIN ISLANDS—VITV

The field note above is one of many that I kept, documenting the process that Kenne Hodge and I went through shooting and editing *Split Screens, Split Subjects*. Most of these field notes record the challenges we encountered and the struggles that we engaged in as we brought our different perspectives to the project. Structurally, the video interweaves a critique of the images and narrative of a promotional video produced by the BVI Tourist Board with a documentary on the efforts on the part of VITV to produce and distribute local programming. In a similar juxtaposition, while Kenne approached the question of control over representation from the perspective of someone whose understanding of the BVI was being mis- or un-represented, I was drawn to the question through my work behind the camera at VITV. This work, too, was collaborative and, like my later work on our video, provoked a heightened awareness of the ethnographic enterprise that I was engaged in as I sought to learn about, write about, and make visual representations about the BVI. Thus, I begin this discussion of collaboration, ethnography and representation with some reflections about my work with VITV.

My first encounter with VITV actually took place well before VITV existed. Dave Douglas is the man responsible for bringing local television programming to the BVI through VITV. Dave Douglas also made quite a name for himself in the late 1960s as a young radio DJ broadcasting ska and reggae from ZBVI, an AM radio station that was launched in 1965 and that continues to broadcast to the present day. At that time no one in the eastern Caribbean was broadcasting such programming, and to do so was perceived as a radical cultural act. Dave Douglas recalled these days in his contribution to a booklet commemorating ZBVI's fortieth anniversary.

> I would like to state emphatically that Reggae Music was formally introduced to the Eastern Caribbean by Radio Station ZBVI. I hosted the first Reggae Radio Programme in 1969 called Reggae Party. Fan mail poured in from throughout the region from Trinidad to Puerto Rico. . . . On reflection, I can understand the concern of the authorities back then. It must have been a culture shock hearing Station IDs made up of words such as Jah Rastafari, a Dread at the control in Chocolate City [Tortola] preceded by roaring lion. I must admit, those 30 seconds promos and IDs would have raised a few eyebrows in some quarters, similar to the reactions Elvis Presley received when the cameras picked up his gyrations and delivered sex and rock and roll to Americans back in the 1950s. Yes, ZBVI had a persona that was different, daring if you will, to defy the colonial "Oh Island in the Sun" image replacing it with a hip, pulsating, drums and base rhythm of the new Caribbean sound of reggae. (Douglas 2005: 78)

Subsequent to his work with ZBVI, Dave set up a sound recording studio in Road Town, where he made cassette tapes of local and regional musicians.

The most famous musician to record in his studio at the time was Banky Banx, from Anguilla.

From sound recording, Dave branched out into video, and when I met him in 1990 he was renting out video movies from a small store in the vestibule of his sound recording studio. I was one of his regular customers. In 1991, Dave Douglas secured a pioneer grant from government. This grant gave him the exclusive rights to broadcast television programming in the BVI for a seventeen-year period, and also allowed him to import duty free all the equipment necessary to start up the station. In addition to the grant, Dave Douglas secured a license to produce national television programming and distribute it over cable. Initially, the station broadcast programming and sporting events (mostly cricket) that it downloaded from satellite broadcasts from other stations in the eastern Caribbean. Additionally, VITV recorded numerous official events for BVI Government Information Service (GIS), and on occasion VITV would broadcast these events over the local cable as well. But Dave Douglas's principal goal in starting the station was not unlike his goal as a radio DJ for ZBVI. He wanted to "defy the colonial 'Oh Island in the Sun' image" and develop VITV as a source of local programming that would, as one VITV producer put it, be "like looking at ourselves in a mirror."

In a 1994 interview that Kenne Hodge and I recorded for our video, Dave Douglas elaborated: "We're committed to local TV first, regional TV second. And it stops there. When people come in and ask us when are we going to put on a movie or something on VITV—it ain't gonna happen. You know, if it's going to be a movie, it's going to be a movie that we produce. And it's got to be saying something about the islands we live on. Or the region" (Cohen and Hodge 1995). Some of the first events that Dave Douglas produced for broadcast over local cable were the events associated with the Emancipation Festival that takes place annually in the first week in August. At the time that he started documenting the BVI Festival, Dave was working with Hi-eight video cameras; all of his editing was analogue (from tape to tape), and he had no ability to broadcast live. In fact, I remember being on a sound truck shooting footage of a band that was taking part in an early morning Festival parade, and reaching down from the truck to give my tape to a VITV crew member, who ran it up to the studio so it could be broadcast "as if" live.

Although Dave and I initially knew each other through his video store, when Dave saw me at Festival with my video camera in hand, he recruited me to work as part of the VITV camera crew. It was 1994, the second year that VITV was taping Festival, and my second year using video in my fieldwork. But even at that early stage in the development of personal video recorders, we were not the only people doing visual documentation of the Festival. Indeed, I remember on my first nervous excursion into Festival Village to shoot video the year before, being struck by how many BVIslanders were there doing essentially the same thing. Seeing so many other people with video cameras was reassuring. For one thing, I didn't feel that I stood out any more than I normally did. It was also exciting. Thanks to the accessibility and usability of technologies that only a few years earlier had been entirely out of reach, I was one of many "ethnographers" documenting the events of Festival. Ethnography as a practice was being cracked open; ethnography's conventional subjects were now doing "insider" work.

Faye Ginsburg is in the forefront of anthropologists documenting indigenous media practices, and she sees these practices as "a distinctive form of cultural activism" (Ginsburg et al. 2002: 8), that uses visual representations of indigenous culture to make political statements about history, identity, and cultural autonomy. For example, Ginsburg sees Inuit-produced television programs about Inuit life as an intentional "effort to turn the tables on the historical trajectory of the power relations embedded in research monographs, photography, and ethnographic practice. . . . The *fact* of their appearance on television on *Inuit* terms, inverts the usual hierarchy of values attached to the dominant culture's technology, conferring new prestige to Inuit 'culture-making'" (2002: 45; author's emphasis). Likewise, in his work with Kayapo video makers, Terence Turner notes that indigenous video makers "have been able to employ video representations, *and specifically the processes of producing them*, to strengthen their sense of cultural identity and the continuity of cultural traditions" (2002: 80; author's emphasis). Mokuka, a Kayapo video maker, adds, "Do whites alone have the understanding to be able to operate this equipment? Not at all! We Kayapo, all of us, have the intelligence. We all have the hands, the eyes, the heads that it takes to do this work. I am not doing this work for my own selfish advantage. I have learned this skill to work for our common good. That's what I am doing here. This is what I am doing and telling you about" (quoted in Turner 2002: 81).

As important as the work of Ginsburg, Turner, and others has been to me in thinking about my work in the BVI, I am somewhat discomfited by my comparison here of BVI media users with Inuit and Kayapo video makers. First, to my knowledge only one of the many video makers I saw in Festival Village the first time I walked in with my video camera was intentionally involved in what might be understood to be self-conscious media production, in Ginsburg's terms. And for him, the documentation was more a matter of building a personal collection of images than of engaging a politics of cultural representation. Second, Caribbean people do not have the same history as the Kayapo or the Inuit. While their access to media production technologies has been constrained by the forces and interests that keep all colonized people from the sites where knowledge is produced and legitimated, Caribbean people have a long history of documenting their concerns about issues self-representation. Consider, for example, the work of Derek Wolcott, Aimé Césaire, C.L.R. James, Édouard Glissant, Mutabaruka, Michelle Cliff, Jamaica Kincaid, Paule Marshall, Rex Nettleford, Lord Chalkdust, and George Lamming. In conflating BVIslanders, the Inuit, and the Kayapo without recognizing important historical and cultural distinctions, I simultaneously discount these important Caribbean voices and activate a Western tendency to lump all non-White Others into the same conceptual category.

This sort of self-assessment eluded me that first night of walking with my video camera in Festival Village. To be honest, when I saw so many people with video and still cameras that night, and despite the fact that I was engaged in ethnographic video making of the most traditional sort, all I could think was, "Indigenous media. Here in the BVI. Wow." The following field note conveys the almost breathless enthusiasm with which I "discovered" BVI involvement with technology:

[Field notes 7.8.1995] High Tech. Friends send faxes back and forth to each other, and businesses less than three blocks apart rely on them for smooth operation. The head of BVI finance and planning remarks in passing to his brother that CNN is making things difficult: how can Government keep claiming that its interest rates of 10% are tied to US prime rate when CNN reports the prime rate as 7½%? Even the country people today know about global finance. At Myett's today stopping by after a dip in the sea, I am pulled aside by Karim, to show me his new video mixer; his high eight video camera is far more sophisticated than mine, and I try to contain my excitement when he proposes we do a shoot together at Quito's Saturday night. Forget about the insider perspective; I want to get my hands on his technology.

As partial as my first understanding of BVI video makers in Festival Village may have been, it did stimulate me to look more closely at local media production in the BVI and the people doing it, and to think more deeply and carefully about issues of control over representations of BVI culture. This was surely abetted by my work with VITV, for in my role as part of the camera crew I was able to get into events and to observe them more closely and intensely than would otherwise have been possible. While working the camera for VITV, I was also connected by wireless earphone and microphone to a local television producer who was selecting and switching shots in the mobile studio. I had direct access to an "insider" point of view, as well as to the ideas behind what was being constituted as good or bad, genuine or fake.

Of course, it took only a few interactions with different producers to realize that there was no single "insider" point of view. As notably, the programs that VITV produced for local consumption, while focused on local topics, were edited using an aesthetic that governs conventional TV or documentary editing. For example, in a 1994 program aired by VITV about Virgin Gorda's annual Easter Festival, the events are covered by an anchor who provides a running commentary to the action unfolding around him. In one notable sequence, which we included in *Split Screens, Split Subjects*, the anchor leans in close to a man selling handicrafts and says to the camera, "If you can see these little dolls, they're beautiful," then, holding the microphone to the craftsman, "are these made here in Virgin Gorda?" The man holds up one of the dolls to the camera and says into the microphone, "Yes, they are locally made by one of the ladies who was born here as well." The shot concludes with an interchange between the anchor and the craftsman:

ANCHOR: "OK, so that means you can get locally created products here?"
CRAFTSMAN: "Lots of local crafts. You know, you just got to know where to find it. You see, there's not really the market but there's a lot of skilled people in the BVI, you know."
ANCHOR: "Well hopefully with this little interview, we can point out that we have some talented people here in Virgin Gorda and you can come down and get these products all weekend long."

In thinking about the aesthetics of ethnographic film, David MacDougall suggests that the formal conventions of camerawork and editing in film shape the stories that may be told and how they may be told; certain events and ways of being in the world are simply not compatible with the style of ethnographic film (1998). When I first looked at the above sequence about local crafts, I was stunned by its resemblance to American talk shows and commercials, particularly local used car commercials. But immediately following this initial reaction I thought, "Well, of course. Why not? Whatever made me think that BVI media wouldn't reflect a long-standing interaction with the West?" Surely, this interaction makes the images that are produced no less authentic, but it does signal how encumbered and complicated the project to control representations of the BVI is and can be. Similarly, while I was initially wildly enthusiastic about being behind the camera for VITV, this situation, too, was more fraught than I had thought.

The following three field notes, written days apart during the 1996 Festival season point to a few of the complications I encountered.

[**Field notes 7.27.1996**] I can no longer run about doing taping of things without a clear sense of what it is I want to do with the footage. I can't afford this practice on two counts: one, when I am behind the camera, I am somewhat protected as a participant-observer, but I at the same time miss a lot of stuff. I am seduced by the notion that I am capturing everything to the point that I don't really pay attention to much except the aesthetics of a shot. Secondly, I cannot possibly go through all of the footage that I could take in order to construct a more condensed record or account. So it's back to the basics of field notes, with the addition of focused videotaping for a particular documentary purpose—this year, the purpose of documenting the efforts of VITV to bring festival live to the people of the BVI. Sort of the VITV story. But even this is difficult, as I prefer the anonymity of being behind a VITV camera, being told what to do by the producer, to the sort of ambiguous status of someone wearing a VITV tee-shirt, but not really shooting for the air.

[**Field notes 7.28.1996**] The cold that had started to manifest itself in a sore throat on Saturday morning has worked its way deeper into my head. . . . I am not feeling very perky, emotionally or physically, and wonder all the way over the hill how I will ever get myself through a full night of video work at Festival Village. . . . Every other year I have been caught up in so much work during the day . . . and have been so enraptured with the music and goings on at night, that I was suffused with what I took to be the erotic of Festival. I had no sense of balance or normalcy. The normal is far less engaging than the over-the-top feeling of first discovery. It means going through the day in a small country where you have to work hard to make a living, as well as—from Kenne's perspective at least—to keep from killing any one of the many people who know too much of your business and want too little for your success. The small encounters in the bank, in the street, in the market, are always potentially dangerous in this regard, as they will result in someone carrying some information back to someone else who may or may not have some interest in having it. And what they do with it is always out of your control: they may be pleased to hear that so and so ran into you, or they may be vexed, "Why hasn't she called me?" "What's she doing at the bank that time of day?" etc. I fear that my low profile this summer will have tongues wagging—"What she doing if she not out on the street?" "Who she hanging with?" "How serious was she ever about this if I don't see her like usual?" And yet, I simply cannot drag myself out to do more that I am. . . . I can't deal right now with three different people wanting me in their troupe, and hardly feel the energy to work with VITV on the parade and *jouvert* [early morning pre-parade street dance]. I know that this space that I occupy provides me an important perspective on life here, life in which Festival emerges not as some all-encompassing erotic that takes over people's minds and hearts, but as a series of things to do, some of which provide momentary opportunity for release, some of which for engagement in the passion of politics of a small place.

[**Field notes 8.4.1996**] Dave calls and wants me to shoot the Sunday Morning Well. The rest of the crew is running around setting up feeds for the marathon 24-hour shoot that is coming up, but Inard is pressing Dave for two camera coverage of the Sunday Morning Well. What this means, when only one camera shows up and it's me behind it, is up for grabs. But I wouldn't be surprised if it were taken as an insult to Inard and the event. After all, this is what Festival is about: the celebration of emancipation and the proclamation read on August 1, 1834. The Sunday Morning Well is an explicit celebration of that event, and foregrounds African roots, the emancipation from the oppression of slavery. So Dave is going to send this white camerawoman who, although most people know of me by now, is still outside of the circle of sentiment that this event is about. This is hard.

Split Screens, Split Subjects

Inspired by the insights into the politics of cultural representation my work with VITV allowed me, in 1994 I started to think about a video that would interrogate my position as framer of ethnographic stories while juxtaposing a BVI produced for tourist consumption, a BVI produced for local consumption, and a BVI produced for ethnographic consumption. When I first conceptualized the video, I had no intention of making it collaboratively, apart from the help I would receive from VITV, and the inclusion of nonoriginal video from other sources. But at a BVI Woman's Club luncheon featuring the readings of original works by members of a BVI writer's group, Writers in Progress, I heard Kenne Hodge read his poem "In the News." Kenne and I had run into each other on several occasions in previous years, and that particular summer we seemed constantly to be introduced to each other by mutual friends, who thought that his interests and my work coincided in important ways. It was almost becoming something of a joke. Thus, when I approached Kenne Hodge about reciting the poem for the videotape that I wanted to make, he agreed, but only on condition that he be able to set up the shot. The shot that he had in mind had him reciting his poem silhouetted against a setting sun. The shot took several days to get right and by the time it was finally done to our mutual satisfaction, our hours of debate and argument about what the video might be and whose story it would tell had turned the project into a collaboration. From that point on, we worked on all aspects of the video together. In fact, *Split Screens, Split Subjects* turned out to be the first of three video projects that Kenne Hodge and I did together from 1995 to his death in September 2001. A field note from November 1995, describes one of the many exchanges that took place between Kenne Hodge and me as we worked together making this first of our three videos.

[**Field notes 11.8.1995**] I left here at 8:15 this morning and after dropping off my laundry, headed for the Riteway, where I picked up some orange juice, fruit, and bread—and some beer—for this morning and for later at the studio. I got to Kenne's at 9 a.m., and we headed up Huntum's Ghut to go over to Butu Mountain via the Ridge Road. On my way into town I had seen that there was another cruise ship in town—the third one in three days, fourth in five days. So I wasn't too surprised to encounter safari after safari loaded with tourists, heading west and north on their scenic tours of the island. As we were a bit early for our 9:30 appointment at the studio, Kenne and I stopped on the Ridge Road, overlooking Guana Island, so he could read to me again the interview with Aimé Césaire in the book on Caribbean cinema. He continued reading as I started up again, and was reading aloud still as we squeezed past a line of five safaris that had stopped and partially discharged their passengers so they could take a picture of their cruise ship, docked in the harbor. I thought this was a great scene, and expressed this by saying, "I wish I had tape in my camera." Kenne was silent for a while, and then he turned to me and said, "So what's the difference between the tourists taking pictures of their ship and the anthropologists taking pictures of them taking pictures of their ship?" That's the note on which the editing session started.

Similar questions about the difference between the anthropologist and the tourist were asked of me on several occasions during my work in the BVI, and this question highlights two issues relevant to ethnographic practice. One is the issue of the knowability of the culture within which the ethnographer works, and the extent to which what the ethnographer "knows" is shaped by her own gender-race-culture-class-bound understandings. A second is the issue of who speaks for whom and the implications of *speaking for*, whether it is the ethnographer speaking for an individual or culture or an individual from within the culture speaking for all. This ultimately reframes the question somewhat and asks not "What is the difference between the anthropologist and the tourist?" but rather, "What is the difference between the anthropologist and the people she studies?" This is a question that is also relevant to the people of the BVI, whose lives as parents, husbands, wives, bankers, lawyers, doctors, politicians, entrepreneurs, taxi drivers, waiters, teachers, managers, clerks, TV watchers, and vacationers are more like than unlike the lives of tourists, to whom they are marketed as exotic Other.

The video *Split Screens, Split Subjects* was completed in late 1995, with the assistance of the staff of VITV. In addition to incorporating footage shot expressly for the video, we used material from a video produced by the BVI Tourist Board to market the BVI as a tourist destination, and footage shot by VITV for local broadcast. Thus, the video is collaborative in the sense that all documentary filmmaking is collaborative. As film scholars Ilisa Barbash and Lucien Taylor assert, "collaboration, conscious or not, involves multiple authorship, acknowledged of not" (1997: 74). However, the sort of collaborative relationship that I address here is a highly self-conscious one, marked by a process of constant negotiation in putting together the visual document, negotiation marked by distinct and sometimes conflicting understandings, politics, and power plays. Following MacDougall (1994). I find it useful to frame my discussion of this collaboration with the question "whose story is it?" This question addresses simultaneously the subjectivity of the ethnographer, the subjectivity of the ethnographic subject(s), and the subjectivity of the ethnographic document itself. Of course, the question, "whose story is it?" and what is at stake in being able to tell it also has broad political and material implications in the BVI. As the following field note reveals, the production of this video about struggles over images of the BVI gave rise to questions of control over the visual images that we were producing. Thus, the production process itself also became an object for reflection on questions concerning ethnographic representation and collaboration.

[Field notes 11.11.1995.] Video Negotiations. Kenne and I are spending long days in front of the TV previewing the footage from which we will be making the final cuts. There is a scene in the video when Floyd is doing Festival coverage, in which he is interviewing Uncu from The Burning Flames, a popular soca band from Antigua. He compliments Uncu on their hit song, "Pick Up Rubbish." Uncu explains that it is a song that they wrote to help Antigua out by emphasizing the importance of controlling litter. In the interview Floyd responds that it is good to keep all the islands clean, because the tourists like it. I want to use the shot in the video, because to me it conveys a certain mind set that I feel would be good to expose. Every time I play the shot to get the timing down, however, it makes Kenne cringe. "I don't like it when we can't see we need to do these thing for ourselves. Every time I hear that line it make me sick." The shot stays out. Later, I am previewing the Festival footage to select shots for a sequence in which Floyd keeps appearing on camera with different individuals involved in Festival, saying, "here we are with. . . ," "here we are with. . . ," "here we are with. . . ," and I realize, going through the shots in my mind, that the only women in the entire video are me, a beauty queen, and a doll. I turn to wake up Kenne, who has fallen asleep in his chair during this whole process of timing the shots. "Kenne," I say in a panic, from my seat in front of the TV "I have to put in the shot of last year's interviewer, you know, the woman playing steel pan." He is not drawn into my hysteria. "Uh huh," he mutters. "You know why, don't you?" My rising voice betrays my growing alarm. He has fallen back asleep.

To provide a sense of the shape of the argument that the video makes, we can look at three scenes toward the end of the video: the first of these is a sequence from the promotional video that promotes the BVI as a place that is "good for the soul." This sequence is followed by a scene in which the Kenne and I are discussing, off camera, the difference between our video, which sets up one vision of the BVI, and tourist videos. This scene is followed by one in which a local television producer reflects upon the vision behind the work of the television station. We have seen this man earlier in the video, talking about the long-range objectives of the local TV station, and interviewing people involved in an annual BVI Festival and in other cultural events.

Scene 1

Visual: Quick dissolves of: tourists in the sea; white woman in natural backdrop, staring off into the distance; jellyfish swimming; pelican in natural backdrop; flying pelican silhouetted against sky; white woman in white bathing suit on beach, turns toward camera, smiles, runs in slow motion toward camera; sailboats silhouetted against setting sun; pull back from sailboats silhouetted against setting sun, and overlay of slogan: Discover Nature's Little Secrets: The British Virgin Islands.

Male voiceover: Xeno, a famous Greek philosopher who lived more than two thousand years ago, once said that the goal of life is living in agreement with nature. It may well take us another 2,000 years to realize that goal but isn't it worthwhile to start working on it right now? Come to the BVI. It's time you discovered Nature's Little Secrets for yourself.

Scene 2

VISUAL: Sunset over the island of Jost Van Dyke, with sound of tree frogs and crickets in the background

AUDIO: Tree frogs and crickets. Off-camera voices.

COLLEEN: You know, you can't fault the tourist video makers for making sunset pictures. It's beautiful.

KENNE: Yeah, I ain't faulting (pause) Me ain't faulting them for making sunset pictures. I faulting them for going to go make damn pictures to present to people that's a fake. Like only them is supposed to be.

COLLEEN: And us setting up this poetry reading wasn't fake?

KENNE: Hm? Hm? (pause) Hm?

COLLEEN: And us setting up this poetry reading wasn't fake?

KENNE: What I'm saying in relationship (pause) the fakishness of what I'm talking about is trying to depict a situation where, OK, you take the expatriates that come to a person's country to exploit and set up residence and use them to show as the indigenous people of the country. That's telling a lie to the world.

Scene 3

VISUAL: Pixelated image of producer of Virgin Islands Television, sitting in studio, talking to camera

AUDIO (PRODUCER): So it's a, its a very unique thing we have and we have to treat this thing with kid gloves and we have to nurse it and be tender and gentle to it and not force it into anything that it shouldn't be. And this is island TV. Just like people travel all the way around the world to come to an island, we'd like our people to look at our TV station and feel like they're home, like they're looking at themselves, through a mirror.

In writing about the danger in collaborative filmmaking "that the film-maker may remain the real author, with the participants simply being brought in to legitimate a collaborative rubber stamp," Barbash and Taylor argue for the need for collaborative films that are "a hybrid effort at poly-vocal authorship, in which distinctions between the participants may be visibly (or aurally) retained in the finished film." Ideally, such a collabora-tive film would operate to "acknowledge that the film embodies multiple sources and forms of authorship, each with their own distinct form of authority" (Barbash and Taylor 1997: 89). This is certainly one of the things that we were trying to achieve in *Split Screens, Split Subjects*, as exemplified by these three scenes. For instance, the last of these scenes and the scene immediately before it tell a different story about the BVI from the one the first scene tells. In their conversation the ethnographer and the poet do not challenge claims made in the promotional video about the beauty of the BVI. Rather, I express concern about the ways in which sunset pictures of seemingly uninhabited islands might feed into notions of a premodern paradise that give the promotional video its symbolic punch. And Kenne Hodge challenges the veracity of a video that depicts as BVIslanders people who are actually from other Caribbean countries; the complications of local and regional histories are flattened, if not ignored. The concern to expose and fill in gaps in historical knowledge is central to work being produced about themselves by indigenous people elsewhere (Ginsburg 1995: 265). In this scene the voice that declares, "it's telling a lie to the world" challenges the authority of Xeno, the famous Greek philosopher, to tell the BVI story.

The last scene challenges the authority of Xeno more indirectly, contrasting the people to whom Xeno's story is directed with "our people." In this scene, as well as throughout the video, the television producer speaks about a national television audience and a "we" in ways that suggest that there is a single "insider" perspective or point of view. Making claims for such a perspective is entirely understandable, given the television station's mandate to produce programs that will be universally meaningful to a BVI audience. It also coincides with what we have seen is an emerging nationalist discourse that posits individuals of BVI heritage (regardless of whether they reside in the BVI or even hold BVI citizenship) as people of "own kind" and in opposition to a growing population of nationals from other Caribbean countries. In editing the video, we tried to offset such a homogenizing perspective. In the case of these three scenes, we tried to present a sense of multiple and distinctive BVI voices by contrasting the producer's benign vision of "our people . . . looking at themselves, through a mirror" with Kenne Hodge's description of these same individuals as "expatriates that come to a person's country to exploit and take up residence." I am not certain that we succeeded in this effort. The promotional video images are really slick, and their artificial and constructed quality is actually highlighted in juxtaposition to the *cinéma vérité* quality of much of our footage. As a consequence, the polyvocality of local voices tends to register as one authentic indigenous voice, despite our efforts to represent them otherwise.

This brings me to a second point about this collaborative video project. This is a point about the assumptions that Kenne and I became aware of in the process of collaborating, assumptions that we subsequently found it important to undermine. The first is an assumption about the nature of the relationship between the ethnographic camera lens and the ethnographic subject it frames. In general, this assumption posits a relationship in which the ethnographic subject emerges as the passive object of the ethnographic film's gaze. This is a gaze that is activated and authorized, according to film scholar Bill Nichols, "in the observational stance that puts distance between another culture and the person behind the camera lens," and that has its roots in the narrative tradition of travel writing that actually "underwrites the authority of the ethnographic film" (1994: 64). A second and related assumption is about types of knowledge and the types of subjects who are presumed to possess them. This is the assumption that ethnographic subjects have a uniquely native knowledge, and that this knowledge is of an order different from the theoretical knowledge of the ethnographer. To generalize, ethnographic subjects tell the "what"—indeed, they are frequently represented as embodying the "what"—and ethnographic filmmakers tell the "why." In pragmatic terms, both the assumption about the passivity of the ethnographic subject and the assumption about who can theorize about the ethnographic subject, began to be undermined as soon as Kenne demanded artistic control over the shot that I wanted of him. In fact, his demand was for more than artistic control. It was a demand for entrance into the debate over representation that the video engaged.

This intervention is represented in the shot that opens the video. In this opening shot we see a close up of dreadlocks, silhouetted against the sun setting behind an island in the distance. Off camera, we hear a man's voice, with a Caribbean accent: "O.K., Drop it some more. Drop it, drop it, drop it, *drop* it! No, no, no, no. Drop the, drop the lens. Lift the camera up, let the lens go. No, lift the camera *up*. Lift the *back* of the camera up. O.K. sorry. Let the lens drop toward the horizon. O.K. fine. O.K. Lift it up now, lift it up, no, no. Lift the—let the lens come up some more. Let the lens come up, let the lens come up, let the lens come up." The camera finally shifts up and to the left, so that the dreadlocks are at the far right of the frame, the islands in the background and the setting sun taking up most of the frame. At this point the off-camera voice says, "Hold it right there." The frame freezes, and the title rolls up accompanied by the opening verse to the song "Welcome to the BVI": "Welcome to the BVI / Throw off your frown and put on a smile / Forget Hussein in the Arab land / And try to enjoy my virgin sand." In much the same way that this verse subverts tourist desire for a premodern paradise outside of history, the prolonged monologue that opens the video destabilizes the ethnographic gaze by raising the question, literally, of who is calling the shots.

Similar interventions are made in the scene immediately following the titles. In this scene we see the full body of the dreadlocked man, in shadow and silhouetted against the setting sun. He talks directly into the camera:

AUDIO: [KENNE]: This is not about—this is not a tourist video. This is
a high tech video. So where would the silhouette of a Rasta man,
or somebody with locks, period, on some remo-o-o-te island, you
know (he gestures to the islands in the distance) somewhere too
far up in the sky for you to even see anything but water beyond
where they sit. You know. And maybe the sunset somewhere in the
background. Know about even uh TV (long pause) to be able to talk
about this shit that is aired, aired about ourselves? And the picture
as the silhouette, whatever, identifies that by the subject. You don't
have to see a color in the subject as the silhouette, because the
locks represent immediately so in peoples mind, that have to be "oh,
a Caribbean person." (Leaning into the camera) "Somebody from
Jamaica here" (he laughs, and a person off camera laughs). That's the
only place them know, I mean, fair enough, you know.

Following this scene the video cuts back to a close-up of the dreadlocks that we saw in the opening scene, and Kenne begins to recite his
poem, "In the News." Kenne Hodge wrote "In the News" in March 1995,
in response to television coverage of the O. J. Simpson trial. When he first
told me that he wanted to be on camera reading his poem against a setting
sun, I assumed that it was for the visual affect; as I remark elsewhere in the
video, the sunsets are beautiful. The above scene reveals a very different
reason for his visualizing the scene the way he did. Instead of the disem-
bodied ethnographic voiceover establishing the theoretical terms of what
we are to see, it is the embodied ethnographic subject who does this. Back-
lit, his skin color doesn't register so much as his dreadlocks do and, as he
points out, "you don't have to see a color in the subject as the silhouette,
because the locks represent immediately so in people's mind, that have
to be, 'oh, a Caribbean person.'" When he throws in the line, "Somebody
from Jamaica here," and I laugh, his response simultaneously exposes limitations in the viewers' knowledge and locates their knowledge in a specific
subject position: "that's the only place them know . . . fair enough." If the
message in this scene eludes the viewer, Kenne's reading of the poem in
the next scene makes explicit both who is doing the theorizing and what
is being theorized:

Black folks in the news, white folks present the views
The opinions, the situation.
From their production studios they edit the decisions
Of who is who.
Who is the hoodlum, who is the hero
Which black role model they see as a fake

Who is the martyr for the six o'clock take.
And air it at dinner.
Like ribs, like chitterlings, like souse, like tripe
For black folk to lap up like hogwash.
Our gospel view of ourselves.
Presented by white folks in the news.

VIDEO NEGOTIATIONS

The collaboration that produced *Split Screens, Split Subjects* was marked by contention, debate, laughter, and negotiation. In working together, Kenne Hodge and I confronted our differences in race, in gender, in power, in what's at stake in the story we were telling, and in how we should tell it. For example, where I wanted to use some out-of-focus or under-lit shots to play with aesthetic effects, Kenne often felt constrained from doing so: an Afro-Caribbean man working very much within a postcolonial context, he was all too aware that such shots could be read as a sign of his lack of expertise, professionalism, or artistic sense. The following excerpt from field notes that I kept during editing details another conflict that we had over what material to include in the video. The conflict in turn highlights our different positions as tellers of the story in *Split Screens, Split Subjects*.

[**Field notes 11.8.1995**] I had really fallen in love with a shot from Kenne and my time spent up at Sage Mountain recording "In the News." In the shot, Kenne finishes up the poem by getting up and, as he passes in front of the camera, saying, "Dan Rather couldn't do it no better, Walter Cronkite, go on!" It is a heady moment in which Kenne feels good about the take (it is probably the tenth take of the night), and in which, in my eyes, all of the issues attendant to globalization and the need for local control over media production and images are focused. He has done the job as well as the figures who serve as his major reference for TV interpretation, the media giants sitting in the newsrooms in the states. In Kenne's eyes, however, his enthusiastic pleasure at having gotten the recitation of the poem done to his satisfaction is an unsuitable display of vanity and arrogance, something that he indeed comments on immediately following his exclamation of pleasure, saying, "I don't mean to be arrogant or anything." As soon as I previewed the footage the first time I wanted to figure out a way to work the shot into the final video. Various draft scripts and story boards have the shot appearing in different places in the tape. In one draft, it is the penultimate shot, leading into a shot in which we have a discussion about what constitutes "fakishness" in the media; in another draft, it appears as part of a "list" of images contrasting tourist market images of the BVI as a pristine, untouched paradise with other images revealing it to be a highly developed, cosmopolitan, and self-conscious place. No matter which draft it appeared in, however, Kenne found it objectionable, and just yesterday asked somewhat peevishly whether he still had the right to another veto or not. (This refers to another editorial discussion we had a couple of days ago over whether or not to include a sequence from the VITV Festival coverage in which Floyd suggests that the only reason for the BVI to think about cleaning up rubbish is because "the tourists like it"—see 11.6.95.) In an effort to negotiate this shot, I had written a final script in which just Kenne's voice comes in as a voiceover the final shot in the video. Kenne had stopped saying anything to me about this shot, but as the time came to make the last edits in the video, the tension between us grew. He had seen me transfer the shot to the bump roll, and as the time approached to make the final edit he asked me once again whether I intended to include the sequence. "Only as a voiceover," I remarked curtly over my shoulder, "and only if it works," I added. I instructed Chris (also somewhat curtly I now recollect) to preview the last shot with the added voiceover. As I watched Kenne and Chris pull their chairs close together in front of the monitor, I knew the shot was doomed. I also saw, as soon as it was previewed, that it simply didn't work as I had hoped. Chris's response that he didn't think it added anything was greeted by Kenne with a smug nod. I told Chris to leave the voiceover out. Later tonight, as Kenne and I sat in his yard, he brought the whole issue up again. . . . "Colleen, what would you have done if the shot had worked? Would you have kept it in?" I was tired, and my head hurt from all of the energy I had been putting into putting the video together and from the challenge to acknowledge my intransigence when it came to my reluctance to give up my authority or control. I equivocated, "I saw how much you didn't want it in, and I would have left it out." "You keep forgetting," Kenne replied, "that while you come here and leave, it is I must continue to live here." I thought about other remarks of Kenne's that we kept in the final edit—remarks that I saw as extremely radical and critical of the status quo—in contrast to what I saw as a harmless expression of pleasure, and realized with a shock how very little I have actually learned, or at least how little of what I have learned I have chosen to adopt as part of my worldview. I repeated, hoping it was true, "No, Kenne, I wouldn't have kept it in." "How many times did I tell you I didn't like the shot?" he responded, and without waiting for a reply, "So why didn't you just drop it out?" I turned my face away from his and declared with a mixture of shame and defiance, "I didn't want to hear it." "Well at least you knew enough to say that," he concluded. And the discussion was finished

In working on this and other collaborative video projects, Kenne Hodge and I also encountered our similarities in working styles, in the subjects we wanted to work on, sometimes even in our experiences of otherness (I as a North American woman of Irish-Mexican descent, he as an Afro-Caribbean man; I as a feminist, he as an Africanist). I think, in fact, that a key element contributing to our ability and willingness to work collaboratively was the similarity of our positions vis-à-vis the technologies and networks of ethnographic filmmaking. This is a sphere of knowledge production in which women and black men still have little presence or voice. These encounters with our similarities were in some ways more unsettling than our encounters with our differences. The awareness of such similarities may be the thing that distinguishes the anthropologist from the tourist, but our similarities seldom resulted in a seamless narrative line or ethnographic gaze. For example, we were both highly critical of the images used in depictions of the BVI as a tourist destination. But I tended to focus my critical attention on the eroticization of the BVI through references to conquest and sexual possession; Kenne tended to focus his critical attention on the primitivizing of the black subject, and the consequences of this for BVIslanders.

Of course, these are not mutually exclusive subjects for critical attention, nor did we treat them as such in our selections of or negotiations over content. And both of these critical gazes are incorporated into the video. In one scene, for example, I recount to the camera an incident in which I refused to follow the television producer's directions to get some "crotch shots" of young girls taking part in a late-night Festival dance contest that we were covering live on national television, "I just couldn't put crotch shots of little fourteen-year-old girls out over national television, even though I could say, 'It's just a dance.'" In another scene, Kenne's voiceover a shot of a beautiful BVI beach, overlaid with the slogan "Discover Nature's Little Secrets," asks, "Now who the hell would know about technology, sitting down talking about 'black folks in the news, white folks presents the views?' You know, like, 'Where them gonna know that from when they're supposed to be somewhere about swinging in a tree and (chuckle) maybe in a grass hut somewhere.' You know?"

As I pointed out at the beginning of this discussion, when I first started thinking about this video project, I saw it as a means of interrogating my position as a framer of ethnographic stories, while telling an "inside" story about local efforts to gain control over the images being produced about the BVI. One of the visuals that I thought might accomplish this was from footage one that I shot while hanging out in the VITV studio one day, shortly after it had gone on line with downloaded video programming that it could put out over cable. As three video monitors above a sound board displayed three different programs coming in over satellite, four members of the TV station looked at monitors on an opposite wall, previewing footage that had been taken earlier in the day of a local reggae band. I had my camera trained upon one of the images coming in over satellite, a commercial of a dancing cereal box that purely by coincidence was dancing to the beat of the reggae that was being played over the studio's sound system. As I pull back from the monitor to a wide shot that takes in all of the activities going on in the studio, the producer asks me what I am shooting. When I explain to him that the cereal box on the ad coming in over the satellite is dancing to the beat of the reggae on the other monitor, everyone turns to look for a moment; then they turn back to the local programming. Only the producer makes a comment: "The mind of the anthropologist, ladies and gentlemen."

When I originally conceptualized the video, I saw this as a perfect opening shot: it demonstrated the interpenetration of globally available media into the BVI, it showcased a local arena in which media messages were being manipulated, and it had an ethnographic subject engaged in a critique of the ethnographic gaze. The shot does appear in the video, but not as the opening shot. While I still think the shot highlights multiple subjectivities, it does not subvert the viewer's desire for a single authorial voice nor undercut in any substantial way the authority of the ethnographic gaze. On the contrary, my colleague and ethnographic videographer Jeff Himpele pointed out to me that, much like Geertz's narrative of the Balinese cockfight (1973b), this shot establishes my intimacy with my ethnographic interlocutors, and thereby establishes me as in the know.

As Kenne Hodge and I worked on this particular project, our complicated situations as historical, gendered, and raced subjects became more evident, shaping the project to an extent that the space of our negotiations itself began to emerge as another voice in the dialogue about representation. This is one of the values of collaborative efforts such as ours; as David MacDougall points out, the special value of films that highlight "the simultaneous perception of two frames of reference" is that "they enable us somehow to confront the intersecting worlds they describe" (1994: 28). I think that the video succeeds reasonably well in both respects. But in the process of negotiating its content in the collaborative relationship I have just described, I began to value collaboration differently. Collaboration undoubtedly has the potential to enhance an ethnographic practice by making explicit the intersubjective world in which ethnographic representations are rendered. But I think that its real value lies in its potential to unsettle, to force us to work directly on the issues of power and difference with which so much of our ethnographic thinking is concerned.

In some respects, the getting beyond difference that Kenne and I found happening in our collaboration with each other can also happen in tourism, albeit to a lesser degree. As we have seen, images and narratives that are employed in marketing the BVI as a tourist destination promote it as a premodern paradise inhabited (if at all) by premodern, friendly, and exotic Others. In traveling to the BVI, tourists are invited to enact and perform the binaries upon which such representations are based, experiencing through this travel the seeming naturalness of their own modern subjectivity. In fact, tourism scholar Tim Edensor argues that Western tourism, and the repetitive performance of binaries that it invites, is a major way that arbitrary distinctions are transformed into the "naturalized codes"—subject/object, mind/body, self/other—that are the basis of Western epistemology (2001). And, as tourism scholars Claudio Minca and Tim Oakes suggest, so long as the tourist does not reflect upon the constructed and performed nature of these binaries, "the tourist's sense of relaxation and 'getting away from it all'" is preserved (2006: 10). Returning to terms developed in the early part of this chapter, the tourist's sense of what is "thinkable" or "unthinkable" remains unchallenged. By extension, a large part of servicing tourists who visit a destination has to do with ensuring that tourist settings and encounters accord with tourists' enactments and performances of the binaries on which their sense of themselves as subjects is grounded. However, as the anecdote about the bareboaters who came to the observatory to watch comets fall on Jupiter suggests, there can be moments in travel that force tourists to reflect upon the arbitrariness of the naturalized codes that they are performing. In fact, Minca and Oakes maintain that in tourism "performativity both encrusts hegemonic social conventions *and* creates opportunities for the disruption of those conventions. What we notice about travel is that it often creates exactly those kinds of opportunities for reflexive disruption even while it provides the option of unreflexive bliss on the beach" (2006: 10).

In the next chapter, I show how encounters between tourists and BVI sites and residents of the BVI serve to both fix and challenge the binaries that ground Western subjectivity. I also look at the challenges to BVIslanders' subjectivity that are posed by advertisements promoting the BVI and its residents as premodern and fixed in time and space.

CHAPTER 6

Stanley's Swing
and Other Intimate Encounters

TOURISTS PREPARING FOR A VACATION to the BVI have multiple resources available to assist them in their pretravel speculation and fantasy. Travel guides, Web sites, information from friends who have visited, and tourism brochures put out by the BVI Tourist Board and tourist businesses all help travelers to the BVI create an emotional and psychic template for their vacation. Studies of tourism brochures (Dann 1996; Selwyn 1993, 1996; Wildman 2004) suggest that regardless of what tourist destination they treat, tourism brochures generally can be read from one of two general perspectives. On one hand, they present images and texts that invite travelers to "step back in time into a pre-modern paradise where, free from the pressures of modern life, they can relax, unwind, and rediscover themselves" (Wildman 2004: 3). This is exemplified in a BVI advertisement that, inviting the tourist to "lose yourself," is actually an invitation to self-discovery. As we have seen, depictions of the BVI as a pristine premodern paradise predominate in everything from travel guides to Tourist Board brochures, lending credence to tourism scholar Gavan Titley's claim that the defining role in the global economy of all the islands of the Eastern Caribbean is "that of pre-modern touristic construct" (2001: 80). In either case, the tourist to the BVI travels with precise fantasies and expectations, constructed through travel brochures and travel guides and grounded in a very particular Western episteme.

Tourist brochures can also be read from a more postmodern perspective, presenting the world as a smorgasbord, "the gathering together of everything from sites to emotions to persons, into a cash nexus" (Wildman 2004: 3). This is exemplified in another BVI ad, for a Pusser's restaurant on Virgin Gorda. In contrast to BVI ads depicting a solitary sailboat in a quiet cove or a pristine white-sand beach, this ad pictures a beach on which many people are engaged in many different activities. The narrative that accompanies this picture offers vacationers a range of activities—exploring coral reefs, swimming and picnicking on uninhabited white sand beaches, sailing, water skiing, snorkeling, scuba diving, playing tennis, fishing, playing volleyball, dining, drinking, or just lazing in the sun—in "a millionaire's playground that you can afford." The important point in the case of either reading is that regardless of the approach taken by tourist brochures to sell a destination, "they are increasingly presenting a world that is far removed from the realities of everyday life" (Wildman 2004: 3). And to enter this world is to enter a space, to borrow a phrase that has been used to characterize filmmaker Maya Deren's fascination with possession rituals, of the erotic mystery of the self (Sitney 1979: 11, cited in Russell 1999: 207). In this chapter, I explore the psychic and emotional dimension of BVI tourists' quests, by looking at their practices in specific BVI tourist locales. I pay particular attention to the allure of discovery that BVI tourism publications promote, and argue that as BVI tourists seek to know an undiscovered premodern place, they also seek access to an authentic unmediated self. Simultaneously, I reflect on how tourists' expectations and quests affect the lives of BVIslanders, as they, too, negotiate their identities in a mobile and intricate world. I begin with observations of one of the BVI's most popular tourist spots, Stanley's Welcome Bar in Cane Garden Bay, on the island of Tortola.

[**Field notes 8.18.1997**] Sitting at Cane Garden Bay in the late afternoon I watch as a taxi man brings a white tourist couple out onto the beach. They don't appear to be planning to stay long, for they have no beach towels, no coolers. No bathing suits even; just shorts and sandals and tee-shirts. They walk past a group of local women who are sitting under the shade by Stanley's Welcome Bar watching their children swim. "My God!" the man exclaims, "everything is changed; I can't believe how much has changed in the last 12 years." "O.K.," I say to myself, "he's made the 'I am in the know therefore I control' move." This is such a familiar move on the part of tourists who come to Stanley's that I don't even trouble myself to reach the 10 inches to my bag where my notebook sits. Too hot. The tourists and the taxi man go down to the edge of the bay. I get up and walk slowly into the water. The man is still going on about change when he makes another less typical but still quite common comment, "Last time I was at Cane Garden Bay, there was nothing here."

In the years that I have spent in the BVI, I have heard many people from Cane Garden Bay grumble about comments like this one. What they find so objectionable is the notion that there was nothing here before the tourist arrived. Even before there was a beach bar on the Bay there was something. What does it mean to someone from the BVI to hear that phrase, "Last time I was at Cane Garden Bay there was nothing here"? One answer lies in the response of Kenne Hodge with whom I was discussing the changes that had taken place in Cane Garden Bay since the early 1960s. I document his response in a field note in which I also describe a photograph of Cane Garden Bay taken in the 1960s and in which I erroneously claim that there were two churches in Cane Garden Bay.

[Field notes 11.4.1995] After correcting me, to the effect that there was but one church in Cane Garden Bay in the 1960s, he asks me to clarify what I mean by the bay calling forth images of earlier times. I respond, by saying that perhaps it would be better expressed in terms of a capacity to satisfy a desire for the image of a pristine beach. Perhaps, he nods. "But tell me. Were there Rhymers living in the Bay in the 1960s? Hodges, Henleys, Clynes, Callwoods? And weren't they building then? And what is the difference between them building then and them building now? Why does the white mind insist on seeing blight where it is simply a continuation of what people were doing then? How can one be seen as pristine and one not if there were and still are people living and building in the Bay?"

Of course, what tourists insist on seeing when they come to a place that is marketed as "Nature's Little Secrets" is the pristine and dreamlike experience of tourist brochures. Considering that tourist brochures make the people of the BVI into one kind of person—nurturing and gentle—it is hardly surprising that the tourist whom I observed making these comments about Cane Garden Bay ended his discussion with the taxi-man by saying, "I wonder whatever happened to that young boy who climbed that palm tree to get us coconuts. I'll bet that was you, right?" Although the taxi-man responded that he wasn't even *in* Tortola twelve years ago, the tourist man didn't hear him. For he had already walked away from the edge of the water to get a picture of his wife swinging on Stanley's Swing.

STANLEY'S SWING

Stanley's Swing was an old tire, hung by a rope from a palm tree outside of Stanley's Welcome Bar on the beach of Cane Garden Bay. In pictures of Cane Garden Bay taken in the early 1960s, before the road over the mountain was graded and paved, the only thing you see on the beach is white sand, with palm trees stretching in a perfect crescent shape around turquoise blue waters. The village proper stands back from the sea, with the Methodist church the largest building of note. Boats pulled up along the shore line, and jeeps pulled beside houses are signs of mobility and activity, but when I look at these pictures, I am drawn, as is the tourist, to the palm-fringed crescent beach that so readily invokes for me "pristine paradise." Throughout the 1970s as the BVI yacht chartering industry grew, and before the reefs bordering the narrow channel into Cane Garden Bay were marked by lighted buoys, cruising guides directed yachts through the narrow channel into the bay by advising skippers to line up the boat's stern with the cut between the islands of Jost Van Dyke and Little Jost Van Dyke to the north of Tortola and to point the bow on the turquoise gates of Stanley's Welcome Bar and the swing hanging off a palm tree on the beach in front. At the time, Stanley's was the only beach bar on Cane Garden Bay, and both the bar and Stanley were must-visits for bareboaters.

The special allure of Stanley's was described in a 1988 article in *Yacht Vacations* magazine, which I found tacked to a wall at Stanley's Welcome Bar itself in 2006. Despite being encased in a plastic sleeve, the article was weatherworn; it hung just above a Christmas card picturing two white children in front of a snowman, with the heading, "Snow Bound in Boston." The article is headed with a picture of Stanley, sitting by a refrigerator behind the bar, with tee shirts dangling overhead. Stanley is smiling into the camera.

> Captain Buzzy Macintire has been to Stanley's Welcome Bar before. The red-tiled roof covering the open-air patio sits on a white sandy beach just 30 feet from the Caribbean Sea. It's the kind of place that draws repeat customers.
>
> In fact, it has been five years since Buzz last visited Stanley's in Cane Garden Bay on the island of Tortola. Even so, some of the local islanders are the same—only the people on sailing holidays change. . . . Stanley's T-shirts are imprinted with its most memorable landmark: the precariously leaning tree growing where the sandy beach meets the steps of the bar. An old tire is roped to this palm.
>
> Now, to get the most out of Stanley's "natural high," you have to shinny monkey-style up the tree where the tire is held in place for you to climb into it. As you lean your body weight to the right, hands let go and you swing out across the beach, adding a distinctively new dimension to sailing. Unwary beachcombers and boat people just arriving at Stanley's have been known to pass out before they ever have a drink. It seems, however, that more people swinging from the palm bite the sand than do beachcombers. Locals use the easterly entrance off the street.
>
> You could easily believe that Stanley's Welcome Bar is one of a kind—and one of those moments in time when you had to be there to get the message. (Bowers 1988: 40)

Today there are seven bar/restaurants on the beach in Cane Garden Bay. Guesthouses and villas in the village and on the hillside overlooking the bay provide accommodations for hundreds of vacationers. Fixed mooring buoys can accommodate up to forty yachts; on occasion I have counted more than one hundred yachts moored and anchored in the bay. A large metal storage building sits at the eastern entrance to the village of Cane Garden Bay, and a small auto body repair yard sits at the westernmost point of the village. In early 2008, the first service station on the northern coast of Tortola was built on the end of the spit of land that forms the eastern point of the bay. It is to Cane Garden Bay that taxis carry cruise ship passengers who on their day trip to the island express a desire for a swim at a pristine Caribbean beach. A field note from 1998 provides an idea of what Cane Garden Bay looks like on a day when cruise ships are visiting Tortola.

[**Field notes 4.18.1998**] I write this sitting under one of the new umbrella tables, on the sand, under the palms, at Cane Garden Bay. On our way over, I read in the *Beacon* of the grim problems here at the bay, caused by overuse by tourists (mostly cruise ship day trippers) and of the need for better facilities. Already, construction is almost completed on the sewage treatment plant behind the school, and the bay seemed to clean itself well after Sunday's rain. Stanley's swing moves slowly in the breeze, just next to a yardarm that is nailed to a palm tree and with a sign hanging from it that reads, "Stanley's Welcome Bar A Fun Place-2-B." It features a table set with a glass of wine, a hibiscus, and a lobster. In the background is Stanley's famous swing, silhouetted against a setting tropical sun. This picture, evoking the sense of what Stanley's is supposed to be ("serving mouth watering lunch and dinner in the most friendly and breezy atmosphere") is framed, from where I sit, by a backdrop of lush green tropical foliage: palm trees marching down the white-sand beach, leaning over turquoise blue water, wild and cultivated vegetation covering the steep slopes of the mountains that surround the bay. But when I look away from the sign, down the beach this is what I see: tourists in various styles of swim and resort wear walking the beach, lounging on chaises by the beach bars, or, in the case of the three directly in front of me, lying on their backs in the sand head to head in the shade, their bodies like spokes of a wheel. Unbeknownst to these three, an island dog, her teats swollen with milk, has positioned herself between one of the spokes, and I am reminded of that painting, in which the lion lays down with the lambs (who's the lion, who the lambs?). The smell of a cheap cigar assaults my senses—most likely a bareboater, I think, as I recall the many stories my father has told in which the pleasure of smoking a cigar on a tropic beach figures centrally. Beyond the cigar-smoker, to my right, going toward Quito's, I see lines of white tourists sprawled on their chaises, greased, and sunning themselves. They move at indiscriminate times, to keep their fronts facing the sun's rays, 100%; otherwise, they are entirely still, save for the occasional move to turn a page. Everyone seems to be reading the latest Grisham novel, *The Partner*, and every time I pass yet another one with the paperback in their hands, I mentally kick myself for spending my time on this writing rather than writing the tropical murder mystery I keep promising myself to write, for my retirement fund. . . . Mixed in among the tourists, in the water and on the beach, are a few local children, this being Saturday. Otherwise, the only local people are behind the bar, braiding hair under the shade of a tent, or renting sea kayaks to the kids (among them my son and his friend) for $5 a half hour.

As the article about Stanley's, and even the first part of my field note indicate, to the tourist eye, the one-of-a-kind-ness of Stanley's Welcome Bar makes a visit to it a moment out of time, so much so that while the people on holidays change, in the tourist mind the local people never change. This notion of the timelessness of the place and the people, and especially in

6.1. Sunset from Stanley's Welcome Bar at Cane Garden Bay. Photo by Karen Buckman.

contrast to the changeableness of the tourist population, reminds us that tourist mobilities always secure the immobilities of others, in one way or another (Sheller 2004: 30). It also points to the importance to tourists and local entrepreneurs alike of maintaining a BVI that is stopped in time, outside of history. Thus, for example, although the original palm tree holding Stanley's Swing was destroyed in 1998's Hurricane Georges, a replacement swing marks the spot where the original once hung. I detail this in a field note from 1999.

[Field notes 3.27.1999] When I arrived at Cane Garden Bay today, the first thing I saw was a big telephone pole-sized post in the sand, with a large "arm" bolted onto it out of the top, perpendicular. And off of the arm was the rope holding Stanley's Swing. The swing sat idle, about four inches off the sand. Behind the whole apparatus was what was left of the palm tree that held the original swing: 6 feet of painted stalk, abruptly broken off at the end. I sought out Tony, who currently runs the bar:
  "Why, Tony, did you build the post and put in the new swing?"
  "The people was harassing me so, I had to do it."
  "What people? The locals or the visitors?"
  "The visitors, man. They the ones want it. They the ones pay the money. So I do what they want. They say it wouldn't be Stanley's without the swing."

By 2001, this yardarm too had fallen prey to a tropical storm. A bar down the beach from Stanley's hung a swing from one of its palms, where it remained for a couple of years, but at the time of this writing there are no tire swings on Cane Garden Bay. Nonetheless, as recently as March 2008 I overheard a returning bareboater regaling his newbie crew with stories of Stanley's Swing.

This anecdote about Cane Garden Bay and Stanley's Swing is an apt introduction to the subject of the role of intimacy in the tourist experience in the BVI. By *intimacy* I am referring to the second, more obscure of its two usages. In standard usage, intimacy refers to a state of being personally familiar and is frequently used as a euphemism for sexual relations. As I argued in chapter 3, this notion of intimacy informs to a large degree the way that the BVI is represented to a global tourism market. It also figures centrally in Western conceptualizations of the Caribbean and of tropical locales in general. But another usage of the term is more obscure; in this usage intimacy is understood as an inmost nature, an inward quality or feature (*Oxford English Dictionary*). This distinction between the two usages of the term is important. For while BVI ads reference heterosexual intimacy to sell the BVI, I think that a singular focus on sexual intimacy keeps us from understanding an equally strong desire that the Western traveler to the Caribbean has for authenticity of experience, for unmediated contact with the Other in a hypermediated world. For the tourist man I observed at Cane Garden Bay and for the 1989 visitors to Stanley's Welcome Bar alike, intimacy in this second sense refers to the one-of-a-kind experience of Stanley's Welcome Bar, "one of those moments in time when you had to be there to get the message." In this more obscure sense of the term, Stanley's Swing works much like the souvenir, offering a trace of authentic experience, a partial referent to a world of direct and continual experience of the Other, and through the Other, of the self (Stewart 1993).

In her essay on the souvenir as object of desire, Susan Stewart argues that the power of the souvenir resides in its ability to conjure "a context of perpetual consumption for its context of origin. . . . The souvenir . . . is an allusion and not a model; it comes after the fact and remains both partial to and more expansive than the fact. It will not function without the supplementary narrative discourse that both attaches it to its origins and creates a myth with regard to those origins. What is this narrative of origins? It is a narrative of interiority and authenticity" (Stewart 1993: 135, 136). In no small measure, for the visitor to the BVI a "narrative of interiority and authenticity" is linked to the experience of having found a place that accords with an idealized untouched Caribbean, not unlike the historic "discovery" of the Caribbean and its peoples that marks "the moment when 'the West' became a conceptual entity—for these were the West's first genuine overseas colonies" (Mintz 1989: xxi). To visit the BVI is to summon up that moment when local histories were obliterated, rewritten to stabilize the West as the center of power and knowledge (Hulme 1992). In this sense, the pristine BVI constituted in tourist industry representations is rendered a site where to discover nature's little secrets is to achieve the transcendence of the knowing subject. And for the visitor to the BVI, a site like Stanley's Swing serves as a touchstone for that moment of transcendence. I talked with Stanley about this notion one afternoon in 1998, during a telephone conversation that we were having. I describe the conversation in my field notes.

[Field notes 7.25.1998] I turned our conversation to his beach bar—when did he first start it? He couldn't remember when, exactly, but thinks it was around '70, '71. "So," I asked, "you saw something start to happen and so." "No," he replied, "wasn't anything happening but a few chirren on the beach selling gum and candy. No white people anywhere." It was that his father wanted him to do it, and so he did. I related to him what I had learned from the tourists at Quito's—about the way that the songs written make a visit to the places commemorated in the songs (cheeseburger in paradise, tire swing) special; despite the fact that you are one among a crowd of what is exclusively white tourists, you experience your self as in a very local and exotic local. Stanley's reply: white people are like that. They might even want to sit on a bench where a famous person sat. When I pointed out to him that he was famous, and then joked that it must be his talkativeness (Stanley is known for being taciturn, and he is always riding me for asking so many questions), he said that he stopped talking altogether now, so as to save some for later. We chatted a bit more, and then I rang off, leaving him to his ball game.

While I was correct in thinking that the white tourist man's claim that "everything is changed; I can't believe how much has changed in the last 12 years" was an "I am in the know, therefore I control" move, what I had missed in my initial observation of this moment on Cane Garden Bay was the extent to which something like Stanley's Swing can and does evoke for the BVI tourist a sense of an authentic inmost nature, a promise of access to the unmediated self. In his work on Caribbean tourism, Gavan Titley makes a similar point, identifying the Caribbean as a key site for the "search for authenticity, a projected definition onto the other which details a sense of loss and a timeout from modernity" (2001: 84). Indeed, Titley suggests, in the context of the increasing economic, social, and cultural integration and interdependence that characterize globalization, the economic survival of the Caribbean in a global tourism market "depends on it being the untouched remnant, an unpeopled space organised and framed by outside desire" (2001: 80).

Reverse Souvenirs

As the field note with which I began this chapter implies, a notable aspect of BVI tourism is the fact that many BVI tourists are return visitors. There are no data on return visits to the BVI, but the 1996 *National Tourism Development Plan* identifies return visitors as an important sector of the tourism market; a questionnaire on the back of an immigration form instituted in 2006 elicits information about number of previous visits to the BVI; and in 2009 the BVI Tourist Board initiated a BVI VIP program targeting return tourists. There is a small community of expatriates from the United States and the United Kingdom who winter in the BVI, and anecdotal information from villa rental firms and yacht chartering firms suggests that a healthy portion of their clientele is made up of return visitors. One need simply listen to the chatter on flights or ferries delivering visitors to the BVI, to the conversations in line at grocery stores, to the back-and-forth at beach bars to know that a good number of visitors have been to the BVI before; to wit, "This is my fifth time down here sailing"; "I have been coming here since the mid-eighties"; "I remember when Quito's Gazebo really *was* just a gazebo." In marked contrast to the invitation to *discover* nature's little secrets, return tourists revel both in their intimate knowledge of the place, as in the white tourist's exclamation that "so much has changed," as well as in signs that they *know* and are *known* by locals, as in his claim, "I'll bet that was you, right?" Of course, part of this sense of *knowing* and *being known* is stimulated by the marketing of the BVI as secrets. As a 1998 *BVI Tourism Directory* exclaims: "Secrets may lose their fascination with discovery, but not nature's little secrets. They are more beguiling when you're privy to their special world." People who work in tourism often play to this notion of being privy to a special world by greeting returning tourists with a hearty "welcome home." Likewise, as the following field note illustrates, visitors to the BVI sometimes equate their sense of intimacy with the place and the people with *being home* or *being at home*.

[**Field notes 3.20.2008**] The seas are so rough that waves are breaking in the channel leading into Cane Garden Bay, and the coast patrol has prohibited boats from anchoring or mooring. These "ground swells" are normal occurrences during the winter and early spring, kicked up by storms off the northeast coast of the U.S. Locals I talk with say that these are the biggest ground swells they've seen since 1991's "perfect storm"; Stanley's and Quito's are closed up tight, and mud and sand have washed up on the road in front of the Methodist Church. I go into Myette's for some lunch and to watch the ground swells. A stormy day. An older white man sits at the bar—looks to be in his seventies . . . J. [a BVIslander from Cane Garden Bay] walks in, says hello. Shortly thereafter two middle-aged blond women walk in and sit at the bar, taking the two stools between J. and the white man. It is clear that at least one of the women knows J., as they are chatting, and touching. This woman and the white man start to talk. Here is the story that I overheard her telling: This is her fourth visit to the BVI. She and her friend are entrepreneurs from the States. They have their own business and work very very hard. She made her first trip to the BVI in order to go to one of Bomba's Full Moon Parties, and when the taxi man dropped her off at the Cane Garden Bay guest house where she would be staying, her first thought was, "What am I going to do here for six days?" But then she met J., and he introduced her to some other local people, "and within a couple of days I was trying to figure out how to *extend* my trip. I don't know what it is about this place, but as soon as I get here, I feel like I'm home." Surely, some of this feeling of being at home may relate to the fact that she has been befriended by a local, who, in her words "showed me things, where to go." Later tonight, I brought up this conversation when I was out to dinner with M. [a BVIslander who owns a business in which she deals with tourists on a daily basis]. She had a different take on this question of tourists feeling at home in the BVI: "I think it's because it's so laid back here, they feel like a different person when they're here. And this is the person they want to be all the time."

One aspect of BVI tourism that contributes to tourists' sense that they are privy to the special world of nature's little secrets is the absence in the BVI of large all-inclusive resorts like Atlantis on the aptly named Paradise Island in the Bahamas, or like Sandals in the Bahamas and on the islands of Jamaica, St. Lucia, and Antigua. Even tourists staying at the boutique resorts of Little Dix Bay on Virgin Gorda and the Peter Island Resort on Peter Island have the opportunity to take day trips to places where they can mingle with local people outside of the resort environment. The numerous bars and restaurants spawned by the bareboat charter industry provide ideal opportunities for tourists to know and be known by locals. Providing a social space for visitors and locals to mingle, allowing visitors to run a tab at the bar, encouraging diners to linger indefinitely at their table, creating entertainment in which visitors participate, permitting visitors to decorate the locales with things they leave behind, are just some of the ways that these bars and restaurants encourage camaraderie and create an atmosphere that makes even the first-time visitor feel welcome and "at home." One first-time visitor, reflecting upon his short stay in Cane Garden Bay, provides a sense of this atmosphere: "I hung around Cane Garden for several days. . . . Several times a day, I'd walk down the beach past the selection of small hotels, restaurants, and bars. The music and laughter flowed from one to the other like waves and I'd simply wash ashore wherever the good times seemed to be hitting the high-tide mark. In just a couple of days, I had become a regular and felt quite at home" (Friel 2000: 2).

At Stanley's Welcome Bar throughout the 1980s and the early 1990s, tourists and locals crowded under the covered verandah of Stanley's nightly to dance to steel pan music; a return trip in a subsequent year would likely find many of the same locals there. Although the Stanley after whom Stanley's Welcome Bar is named reports remembering only a few of the thousands of tourists who return to his beach bar year after year, "I does hail all of them 'Hi Doc,' and that make them happy" (field notes, July 31, 1996). Likewise, an ad for Foxy's, a beach bar on the BVI island of Jost Van Dyke and a renowned favorite of bareboaters, exclaims, "where friends are met and memories made" (*British Virgin Islands Welcome Guide* February/March 2008). These sentiments accord with Polly Pattullo's observation of

Caribbean tourists in general that "tourists want locals, whether working in tourism or not, to be friendly" (1996: 145).

What I find most interesting about the sort of narratives of interiority and authenticity that attach to BVI locales like Stanley's Welcome Bar and to objects like Stanley's Swing is that the narratives are not activated just by things or memories that people take away from them but as well by things that people leave behind. Return visitors to the BVI frequently bring something with them or do something notable to make themselves stand out from among other tourists. The bareboaters featured in the 1988 article about Stanley's, for example, brought glow-in the dark jewelry: "Buzz knew that out-of-the-way Stanleys would be a highlight for his bareboat crew from St. Louis. Thinking ahead, he purchased eight pairs of Chem-lite earrings—some pierced, some clip on—all dangling tubes of cold chemical light that glow in the dark for up to 12 hours if shaken.... Stanleys Welcome Bar is atwitter with curiosity" (Bowers 1988: 40). In June 2007, nineteen years after Captain Buzzy's visit to Stanley's Welcome Bar was memorialized in print, I witnessed a bareboating couple greet the bartender at Quito's Gazebo, also on Cane Garden Bay, by putting a necklace with a glow-in-the-dark pendant over his head. When Quito arrived to perform for the evening, he was greeted likewise; Quito wore the pendant throughout his performance, much to the delight of the gifting couple.

Like the occasional lover who signals a desire for a more committed relationship by leaving a toothbrush behind, BVI tourists also regularly leave behind traces of their passing. As is the case of the photograph for Roland Barthes, these traces also ratify what they represent (1980: 85); they are proof that the tourist was there at a given moment in time. When I first visited Stanley's Welcome Bar in 1977, an entire wall was covered with business cards left by visiting bareboaters. By the mid 1980s the business card wall had been replaced by tee shirts hung from fishnets that adorned the ceiling; the tee shirts in turn were eventually replaced by yacht club flags. Two of the most popular and famous BVI tourist hot spots are similarly festooned by what I have come to think of as reverse souvenirs. These hot spots are Bomba's Shack on the island of Tortola and Foxy's Tamarind Bar and Grill in Great Harbor on what is billed in numerous advertisements and travel guides as "the barefoot island" of Jost Van Dyke.

Bomba's Surfside Shack is located on the beach at Capoon's Bay on Tortola's northwest shore and is conventionally referred to as "Bomba's" or "The Shack." Described in a BVI Chamber of Commerce publication as "a boisterous meeting place for the wild and uninhibited, with catchy music and memorable shenanigans" (Munoz 2006), Bomba's is famous for its full moon parties and full moon mushroom tea. On days of Bomba's full moon parties, the ferries from St. Thomas to Tortola are crowded with partiers, and vacationers to the BVI frequently schedule their vacations around the dates of the full moon (BVI tourism director, personal communication). A tourist's post to a BVI vacation Web site attests to the popularity of Bomba's full moon party.

> It's amazing the amount of people that come to the party. I've known many a tourist or visitor who plans part of their vacations around the Full Moon Party. I must admit that my daughter's wedding here on Tortola had the Full Moon Party as part of her and her husband's things to do on their activity list for the over forty friends and relatives that came to Tortola for her wedding. Unbeknownst to me, that particular Full Moon Party was their bachelor/bachelorette party! I've seen as many as eight hundred to a thousand people attend the Full Moon Parties, probably the biggest party on Tortola every month. So if you're into partying hard or just want to come partake in Bomba's Mushroom Tea and people watch and make new friends on Tortola, Bomba's Surfside Shack is the place to be! (http://www.escape-bvi. com/BombaShack.aspx)

The owner of Bomba's Shack, Charles "Bomba" Callwood, built the Shack in 1976 as an informal hang-out and bar for surfers who came to Capoon's Bay when the waves were high. Over the years, it was added onto, and today a sort of Bomba's Shack annex sits directly across the road from the original; Bomba refers to it as "the backyard." Bomba's Shack sits between the road and the sea on a bit of land that is less than twenty feet at its widest point. The Shack is put together from a variety of discarded and found materials, on which visitors have written their names and personalized slogans and on which Bomba has written messages exhorting all visitors to drink his famous Bomba Punch and all women to leave behind their undergarments.

The Bomba Shack Web site highlights the invitation to leave intimate apparel behind, in a questionnaire that asks "Do you have at least one pair of sexy panties? (If you answered yes, you got to give 'em up)" and in a closing statement that reads "Give Bomba Your Panties and be Blessed" (http:// www.bombasurfsideshack.com). A visitor to Bomba's Shack remembered: "Garnishing nearly every bit of available rafter space, were his wall-coverings of choice—women's panties. One of the Shack's traditions is the awarding of a T-shirt to any woman in exchange for donating her unmentionables to the cause of interior decorating. And you can't mail it in. The Donation has to happen in view of Bomba, himself. You've heard of drop ceilings—this is a drop-your-pants ceiling" (Friel 2000: 3). While visitors to Bomba's most

6.2. Bomba's Shack, with undies hanging over bar. Photo by Jeffrey Cohen.

commonly leave behind undergarments, as at Stanley's Welcome Bar visitors also leave behind tee shirts and hats. Despite its ramshackle appearance, Bomba's Surfside Shack has occupied its site on the beach at Capoon's Bay since 1976, and has withstood the winds, sea surges, and rains of numerous hurricanes. Of course, most of the panties that have been left behind over the years have blown away, but when I visited Bomba's Shack for the full moon party of June 30, 2007, I counted over one hundred panties and bras hanging from its rafters.

The island of Jost Van Dyke lies off the northern coast of Tortola and has a resident population of under two hundred people. A Jost Van Dyke souvenir tee-shirt that reads "Jost Van Dyke: A drinking island with an occasional sailing problem" captures the tourist ethos of Jost Van Dyke, for most visitors to the island come by chartered yacht and spend a lot of time in Jost Van Dyke's numerous beach bars. Country singer Kenny Chesney yearns for Jost (pronounced "yost") in his song, "Somewhere in the Sun" (Gross 2006). Indeed, for tourists Jost Van Dyke's charm lies in its relatively uncrowded beaches, its barefoot relaxed style, and, as the an April 2006 post to a travel site attests, the opportunity it provides to know and be known by the local people: "I love JVD! I was there last June and will try to return every year. It is beautiful and the people (local) are great. . . . My favorite thing to do there was get myself (at Ivan's) a cold

drink and relax in a hammock or catch some sun on the beach" (yahoo://
travel.yahoo.com/p-reviews-481778-prod-travelguide-action-read-ratings_
and_reviews-i).

A BVI travel guide is similarly enthusiastic about the opportunity Jost
Van Dyke provides to know local people. In an article entitled "The Nicest
Man in the World," this travel guide asserts that Ivan Chinnery, the owner
of a Jost Van Dyke Beach Bar and Campground, "represents the best of the
BVI. In fact, he may be the human manifestation of what these unique
islands are all about. . . . Everybody loves Ivan. Sure, Mick Jagger and Keith
Richards and Kenny Chesney are fans, but it's not just celebrities . . . if you
ask anyone who has met Ivan, if you even mention his name in a conversation and someone next to you hears it, the response is almost always the
same, almost always something like: 'Ivan, yeah, isn't he the nicest man in
the world!'" (Acheson and Myers 2007: 50).

One of Jost Van Dyke's "people to know" is Phillicianno "Foxy" Callwood, the owner of Foxy's Tamarind Bar and Grill in Great Harbour, a
beach bar that is known simply as "Foxy's." Foxy is famous for the ribald
calypsos that he sings at his visitors' expense, and Foxy's "Old Year's Night"
celebration is reputed to be the third largest New Year's Eve celebration in
the world. Erected in March 1968, this first of Jost Van Dyke's many beach
bars, and its owner, are arguably the most famous bar and proprietor in
the BVI. A posting to a BVI bareboat Web site proclaims, "The BVI and
Jost Van Dyke in particular, would just never be the same without Foxy's
Beach Bar & Restaurant!" (http://www.bareboatsbvi.com/jvd_foxys_
bar_restaurant.html). A 1993 book about Foxy and his beach bar confirms
that "repeat visitors point to the same little island and the same unique
man as the reason for their return. 'We came back to sail to Jost Van Dyke
again, and see Foxy.' Foxy Callwood is a living legend, a real-life Caribbean
myth, a wonderful waterfront wacko. . . . You can mention Foxy's name in
almost any port on the planet . . . just mention the Fox, and you'll soon be
swapping sea stories about the Virgin Islands with a new friend" (Farrell
1993: 1).

Signaling the fame of Foxy's Tamarind Bar and Grill as well as the
meanings that Foxy's holds for tourists, are the objects left behind by visitors. As is the case with Stanley's Welcome Bar, hats and tee-shirts adorn
the rafters of Foxy's; an occasional undergarment echoes the reverse souvenirs found at Bomba's. But in addition one sees at Foxy's license plates
from every state in the United States and from many European countries.
Names, dates of visit, and messages to future visitors are scrawled on much
of Foxy's structure, even the PVC downspout to the cistern. While one can
imagine spontaneously leaving behind a tee-shirt or hat or even a graffito to mark a memorable moment in time, the hundreds of license plates

are evidence of the number of return visitors who come to Foxy's as well as of the forethought and planning that precede their visits. A 2007 video posted on YouTube, "A Visit to Foxy's on Jost Van Dyke," is testimony to the centrality of a visit to Foxy's for many return tourists to the BVI. The video shows a group of bareboat tourists sitting at Foxy's bar while they sign their names to the yacht club flag that they have carried with them to hang in the rafters. The "about this video" section explains, "Foxy's beach bar on Jost Van Dyke is always a favorite stop for sailors. We make our annual pilgrimage to decorate the ceiling" (http://www.youtube.com/watch?v=OlqqsX6rdOc&feature=related).

That this tourist refers to the visit to Foxy's as a pilgrimage is telling, for it points to the transcendent quality of this return visit, and to the spirit of interiority and authenticity with which the reverse souvenir is imbued. As we have seen, one of the allures of this particular site is the promise of knowing and being known by locals, and particularly by Foxy. Foxy plays to this yearning for intimacy, enacting the friendly BVIslander with his good humor and ribald jokes, even making a life-sized replica of himself as a stand-in when he is not around. While one might think that a Foxy substitute would disappoint the tourist on the quest for interiority and authenticity, a post to a BVI bareboat Web site suggests that even this

6.3. Reverse souvenirs: License plates at Foxy's. Photo by author.

action is read as evidence of the extent to which Foxy cares about those who come to visit: "What can be said about Philicianno Callwood? I find myself smiling just thinking about this irrepressible man! Who else would have a life sized, mannequin, known as 'epoxy Foxy' made as a stand in for himself so guests won't feel slighted on his days off?"(http://www.bareboatsbvi.com/jvd_foxy_callwood.html). In speaking of Foxy the entertainer, another post to this same Web site constructs a caricature of an individual whose life centers on his guests: "Foxy Callwood, the barefooted man with the saucer eyes, bowl chest and engaging grin, delights in strumming his guitar and playing amusing songs for his restaurant guests" (http://www.bareboatsbvi.com/jvd_foxys_bar_restaurant.html). Both of these descriptions point to what Ian Strachan notes of tourism throughout the English-speaking Caribbean. That is, although many tourists "are not interested in the cultures or ways of life of Caribbean people as those people may believe them to be," they are eager to experience "the stereotyped snippets that they are already carrying in their heads before they arrived" (2002: 91).

No doubt, Foxy—like Stanley and Bomba—performs for tourists an idealized Caribbean friend. In catering to the desire of tourists for a certain kind of experience, Foxy also performs an idealized Caribbean of laidback lifestyle and of people "so close to nature that their dispositions are derived directly from the climate" (Titley 2001: 84). But while we might be inclined to read this as the internalization of negative stereotypes of subservience, such constructs of identity seem more frequently born of self-assurance and savvy entrepreneurship, and a benevolence on the part of these BVIslanders toward visitors to their establishments. I witnessed the performance of a similar attitude toward tourists in a skit performed by BVI schoolchildren in the Prince and Princess Show put on as part of 1990 Festival celebrations. A pageant for young boys and girls representing their local grammar schools in island-wide competition, the Prince and Princess show—as other beauty and talent shows put on during Festival (see Cohen and Mascia-Lees 1993)—highlights what BVIslanders value. An excerpt from a field note from 1990 elaborates.

[Field notes 7.29.1990] Prince and Princess Show, Cultural Center. Arrive at about 5:30, and place is filling up fairly quickly with adults (mostly women) and children, all in quite dressy dress. Elroy Turnbull opens festivities, with introductory speech which emphasizes culture: "Culture is very important to us and so this show is also intended to stimulate cultural awareness. We feel that by concentrating on young people we can return to our culture. Bring back the old values."

In the Prince and Princess show, the young boy—wearing white dinner jacket and gloves—who can most gallantly escort his poised, formally attired, perfectly coiffed partner around the stage, scores high points toward a final tally that will also include an assessment of his and his partner's presentation of swimwear and casual clothing. The entire pageant emphasizes the importance of elegance and sophistication, reinforcing for children a historical pattern of British civility. Addressing more contemporary self-conceptions, skits showcasing contestants' talents and billed as representing "aspects of BVI culture," focused in 1990 exclusively on tourism.

In each of these skits, one child in the couple played a tourist, inevitably clothed in white shorts, tee shirt, sneakers, neon visor, and fanny-pack, with camera hanging from his or her neck and sunglasses shading his or her eyes, while the other depicted an employee in some sector of the tourist economy servicing the tourist's needs. The scenario enacted by the winning couple of the 1990 Prince and Princess Show revealed what was an underlying theme of the other skits: Here a friendly and helpful stewardess came to the aid of a man incapable of dealing with the demands of airline travel. As he fumbled with flight instruction card, fidgeted in his seat, unable to get comfortable, and ultimately vomited into the small white barf-bag, the flight attendant stood patiently by, helping him solve each dilemma with self assurance and competence. The tourist was represented not as knowledgeable world traveler or cosmopolitan, but as awkward and inept, thus inverting the civilized/primitive, sophisticated/childlike dichotomy underlying tourist promotions. We see a comparable inversion in the stanza of a poem, "We Want Them to Know," written by a BVI primary school teacher and appearing in a 1989 booklet, *Tourism Awareness through Education*:"They come in shorts and mid-rib bare / As though their bodies they want to show; / But mutual respect we should try to share. / That's another thing we want them to know" (Department of Education and Culture 1989).

In one sense, these depictions of tourists as helpless and needing schooling about how to behave can be understood as deriving meaning from the arbitrary inverting of terms, evidence that the use of essentialist categories on which cultural stereotypes are based can be a powerful and disruptive tool when used by the subaltern (Bhabha 1990; Spivak 1987). But we should not think of such inversions in terms only of representational contestation or contrast, for they cleverly and strategically manipulate the West's images of the Other in order to constitute a sense of self-identity grounded in a desire to maintain tourist-based economic prosperity. A connection between BVI identity, the performance of tourism's Other, and economic prosperity was made evident in early 2009 when Foxy Callwood was appointed a Member of the Order of the British Empire (MBE) by Queen Elizabeth II, in recognition of his success as "an unofficial ambassador for the BVI" and for his "exemplary contributions to the Territory's tourism industry and the preservation of its culture" ("'Foxy' Receives MBE Honour").

Likewise, the leaving behind of reverse souvenirs—a tee shirt, yacht club hat, or business card at Stanley's; a license plate, tee shirt, yacht club flag, or graffito at Foxy's; a tee shirt, bra, or pair of underpants at Bomba's— is a material manifestation of tourists' desire for intimacy with the Other and, through the consumption of a precultural BVI outside of global flows of time or money, with an inmost, authentic self. But from the standpoint of the local entrepreneurs who own and run these establishments, catering to tourist desire by encouraging visitors to leave behind their license plates, undergarments, yacht club insignias, and baseball caps is simply good business. From this standpoint, there is little difference between a tourist leaving behind a baseball cap and a tourist leaving behind hard cash. A statement that heads the Bomba Shack official Web site makes this explicit when it urges, "STOP . . . Be a friend, Make a friend, Spend a buck" (http://www.bombasurfsideshack.com/default.asp).

THE EROTIC MYSTERY OF THE SELF

One need not be a return visitor to the BVI to indulge in the erotic of the reverse souvenir. For as tourism scholar Chris Rojek points out, an important aspect in the construction of all travel and tourist sights is the "speculation and fantasy about the nature of what one might find." In this regard, tourism involves not just travel from one point to another, but "mobility through an internal landscape which is sculptured by personal experience and cultural influences" (2000: 53). For the new visitor to the BVI, the promises held out in BVI tourist brochures and travel guides serve as templates for constructing their experience as effectively as do the memories of returning tourists. We see the convergence of tourist expectations and fantasies with the constructed tourist experience, in the recollections of a tourist to the BVI, that appeared in an article in *Sail* magazine.

> what we had was one of the most pleasant cruises I can remember . . . the sea caves on Norman Island, where rumors still persist of buried treasure; the Baths, on Virgin Gorda, where cathedral light and the ocean's swell bounce gently back and forth beneath church-size rocks; Cane Garden Bay, on Tortola, where the evening sun turned the palm trees golden; Sandy Cay, which has a beach as beautifully white as the image its name conjures up; . . . and Foxy's Tamarind Bar, on Jost Van Dyke, where in the afternoon, while we were picking out lobsters for our end-of-the-cruise evening meal ashore, Foxy himself played his guitar for us and told us how he had planned to travel to America and

become a big star—and would have, too, he said, if he hadn't learned at the last moment that in order to board the airplane he would be required to wear shoes. (Payne 1992: 101)

The perfect match in this tourist's recollections between, for example, the fantasized and real sand, reveals the effectiveness of the images disseminated by BVI tourism brochures in playing to Western preconceptions of the Caribbean. Meanwhile, in its references to cathedral-like scenery the narrative's imagery actually supersedes what is offered in tourist ads, turning the special into the sacred. The nineteenth-century-type romanticism revealed in this prose—finding God in nature—is typical of what John Urry asserts is a general upper-middle-class tourist need: to seek in traveling to satisfy the romantic yearning for "solitude, privacy and a personal, semi-spiritual relationship with the object of the gaze" (1990: 45). Although Urry is speaking here of a relationship between the tourist and historic or scenic sites, the stress in the above narrative upon the fact that "Foxy *himself* . . . played for *us*" makes clear that even the barefoot beach bar service satisfies the same yearning for the "personal, semi-spiritual relationship with the object of the gaze." A testament to the iconic status of this narrative is that as recently as 2005, the article from which it is excerpted could be found in *Fodor's U.S. and British Virgin Islands*.

What is perhaps most telling in this narrative is how powerful the desire is on the part of the Western traveler for an Other of extreme dissimilitude. The excessive and almost hysterical production of the mythic Other in this narrative, as in other narratives that we have looked at here, resembles Judith Butler's description of the production of heterosexuality as an "incessant and *panicked* imitation of its own naturalized idealization" (1991: 23). How else to account for a narrative that insists on casting as quaintly ignorant of the ways of the cosmopolitan world a successful entrepreneur whose establishment is in fact showcased in almost every British Virgin Islands Tourist Board publication? In this sense, the tourist subjectivity expressed here is not unlike heterosexuality which, Butler claims, "is always in the act of elaborating itself" because it senses the absence at its center, because "it 'knows' its own possibility of becoming undone" (1991, 23). Likewise, imagined as pristine paradise, the BVI is the stage upon which tourists act out the binaries by which they make sense of the world. As they seek to know and be known by locals, they construct experiences that accord with their idealized notions of the Other. As they make pilgrimages to idealized places and leave behind their reverse souvenirs they create touchstones for this experience. Actively and incessantly producing that which they consume, they seek access to a self that emerges *in opposition to* the other; a self that is the nonmodern self represented *by* the Other.

In her important work on the Caribbean, Mimi Sheller makes a similar point, understanding the consumption of paradise as an "ingestion" of the Other, a form of "consumer cannibalism of Caribbean difference" (2003: 145). Sheller draws upon the work of Sara Ahmed (2000), and both Sheller and Ahmed deal with the literal consumption of items associated with "exotic" and "strange" locales. Looking at the long and enduring Western fascination with Caribbean flora, fauna, and people, for example, Sheller suggests that "Western (or Northern) cultures visually and metaphorically 'eat' or consume racially marked bodies as a kind of spice or condiment to flavour the bland whiteness of mainstream culture or to enact an expansive 'global culture'" (2003: 144). We see this figurative consuming given expression in a Web post by a BVI tourist who was treated to a private concert on his chartered yacht by BVI singer/songwriter, Quito Rymer, as a fiftieth birthday surprise from his family: "We were treated to the incredible experience of hearing & seeing Quito from a few feet away. . . . After the first seven or eight songs, when Quito said, 'Next?,' I said, 'Man, this is like eating too much of a great dessert, I'm not sure I can handle any more.' But I did" (http://www.bvi-sanctuary.com/Tom's%2050th.htm). Likewise, Sara Ahmed demonstrates how, in the context of globalization and the popularity of multiculturalism as an ideology, the consumption of things like "ethnic" foods (what she refers to as "the consumption of strangers") maintains white Western hegemony. In her articulation of this process, Ahmed approximates the point that I am making here, that in seeking intimacy with a premodern Other, tourists seek to stabilize a sense of themselves as active modern agents: "The consumption of strangers allows the redefinition of the consuming subject and an expansion of her or his agency. . . . It is the consuming self who has the agency *to become different*, rather than simply *be different* (the authentic stranger or the authentic spice)" (Ahmed 2000: 118; author's emphasis).

The compulsion to produce materially or symbolically that which they consume points to a central paradox in tourists' quests for intimacy. For the places and people that tourists consume are never fixed in time or space, nor are they made and consumed solely by tourists. Rather, they are constantly being made and remade by the interactions, fantasies, economies, and politics that are activated in the practice of tourism. And, as Sheller and Urry point out, the multiple and contested meanings that places take on in the practice of tourism "often produce disruptions and disjunctures" (2004: 3). In a field note recorded on July 31, 2004, I describe a series of disruptions and disjunctures that occurred when bareboat tourists arrived in Cane Garden Bay, only to find that most of the beach bars and restaurants were closed due to the Festival that commemorates the 1834 emancipation of slaves in the British Caribbean.

[Field notes 7.31.2004] Stanley's Swing, Redux. As I was laying in the hammock outside Stanley's, four people off a charter boat came up and asked if Stanley's was going to open for dinner. I told them that it was closed until October; that yesterday was their last day open. They expressed regret, saying that they had sailed from Anegada today in order to be able to come to Stanley's for dinner and to see Stanley. When I told them that Stanley had turned the business over (they thought to his children, I told them to another person from the Bay), they were very sad—wanted to know where Stanley lived. I pointed his house out to them, and told them that I was sure that Stanley would be sorry he missed them, then, at their request, suggested alternative places for dinner (their response to my telling them about Festival Village as a good place for dinner was decidedly negative, and when I told them that Jesse Jackson would be giving the sermon in the CGB Baptist Church at 10 am tomorrow, they said they would be sure to leave by 9).

When I told Stanley (by phone) this evening about the encounter, he seemed interested to know about them and who they were. I told him they were last here 8 years ago, and 8 years before that. He wouldn't know them, but always made people feel welcome at his bar (hence, The Welcome Bar). As a result, he became a legend among cruisers, and people returned, always expecting a warm welcome, a welcome to make them feel as if they were coming back home. I know how hard Stanley worked all those years to make his business successful; I also know how happy he is to be out of that business—as he has put it to me, he would be happy not to have to talk to anyone again. But tonight I heard in his voice a genuine pleasure at having been remembered, an attachment to that persona and those interactions that made him and his bar so famous. As for the disappointed cruisers: I felt terrible for them. They had anticipated a certain experience (idealized tho it may have been), and they did not have it. On top of this, they had sailed from a lovely anchorage on Anegada, to a Cane Garden Bay that is essentially shut down for Festival. Participating in Festival does not have a place in the mental frame that they have set up for themselves so they are doomed to disappointment. Unfortunately, in reviewing their disappointment they are more likely to attribute it to "things having changed for the worse" than to the limitations in what they allowed themselves to expect. This is the challenge that confronts Janis Braithwaite-Edwards [Tourist Board director], as she works to deliver the BVI product to tourists: she must constantly be vigilant to make sure that what the tourist gets is what the tourist has been led to expect of the BVI. In this case, short of an advertising campaign to charterers that stresses the joys of Festival (and offers shuttles from anchorages to Festival Village and back), Janis cannot succeed. Besides, what the charterers are buying is the pristine BVI with locals who cater to their needs and meet their expectations of the friendly and accommodating Caribbean person, not locals who are celebrating

their emancipation (one of the individuals in the group thought that emancipation meant independence from Great Britain—"so they're not a colony
anymore?") and partying until 3:30 a.m. in large crowds in the Village.

As this field note recounts, a pilgrimage to Stanley's is disrupted when
the real-life Stanley gives up his beach bar and turns its operation over to
someone else, and the fantasy of a Cane Garden Bay that is outside of time
and history is shattered by a visit to one of its churches from a famous
African American politician. Likewise, my mother recalls that on her first
visit to the BVI, she went expecting to find an "authentic" folk culture;
in a twist on Ahmed's understanding of the consumption of strangers, the
Mexican folk art that she accumulates is a major component of her identity
as a Mexican American woman. She was dismayed to find a bustling population and very little in the way of local crafts or folk art. As she recalled to
me while I was in the middle of writing this book, "women were dressed in
business suits and high heels, as if they were in downtown San Francisco."
Similarly, however much the tourist on the beach sought an authentic self
through a visit to Stanley's Swing, the BVI is a place where people go about
lives that deflect this quest. Beaches on which people build storage units,
and speaking subjects who themselves travel beyond the borders of the
BVI, deny the tourist the fantasy of an unchanging place or of an immobile, ahistorical Other.

Travelers and tourists always run the risk of having their expectations
dashed, their fantasies exposed as artifice. In fact, tourism scholars Claudio
Minca and Tim Oakes submit, the possibility of dashed expectations and
exposed fantasies is the essence of the contemporary traveler's experience,
if not subjectivity.

> While we are trying to build our cognitive mapping of modernity and
> to achieve some sort of order within which we can place ourselves as
> relatively stable, immanent, subjects in place, we actually travel ... the
> purpose of our travels is both the definition and the transgression of
> that mapping, of its reassuring stability and the fascination with what
> is not only behind, but also beyond the map. . . . Traveling in places,
> we seek out an object of difference to reconfirm our sense of order,
> while at the same time opening ourselves to the possibility that others
> will not always re-enact their expected roles, and that our order will
> be transgressed and deferred. (Minca and Oakes 2006: 19, 20)

In thinking about travel as an endless deferral of a search for order—what
they refer to as the "paradox of travel"—Minca and Oakes are raising issues
pertinent to what it means to be a postmodern subject, or "the placed nature

of identity and subjectivity in the highly mobile cultures of modernity" (Minca and Oakes 2006: 1). But when the primary role of the place one travels to is to stabilize the agency of the mobile Western subject in opposition to the immobile and premodern non-Western Other, as is arguably the case of travel to the BVI, there can be no pleasure in the disruptions that occur when places and people fail tourists in their search for order. This certainly seems to be borne out in the experience of the tourist visiting Stanley's swing, whose statement that "everything is changed; I can't believe how much has changed in the last 12 years" was a lament, not a celebration, that the BVI had been caught up in the same currents of time as he. And I cannot help imagining the disappointed bareboaters from the above field note raising sail at dawn in order to ensure a timely departure from the sullied Cane Garden Bay of deserted beach bars and Jesse Jackson's sermon.

POSTMODERN SUBJECTS
IN PREMODERN PARADISE

As the field note about the disappointed bareboaters illustrates, one of the major challenges in marketing and delivering the BVI product is to satisfy tourist desire for an uncomplicated Other, even as the BVI involvement in global tourism and international finance makes it a place of multiple and intricate mobilities. Meanwhile, the challenge for BVIslanders is how to perform identities and places that are intelligible to tourists while they themselves are involved in the same "highly mobile cultures of modernity." This is the conundrum that Gavan Titley identifies for all the islands of the Eastern Caribbean, whose residents "cannot, it seems, expect to be recognized as a member of the global community unless they step into the perspectival framework which sees the Caribbean in a very particular way. It seems difficult to sustain the idea that global trajectories of contact increasingly involve the mediation of identities, if a feature of the economic contract which brings people together is the immutability of homogenous Caribbean types" (2001: 85). This conundrum was the subject of a conversation between Kenne Hodge and myself that I describe in fieldnotes from 1997.

[Field notes 9.13.1997] Kenne and I had been at Long Bay for breakfast on Thursday (9.11.97) and had sat on the verandah for two hours talking about tourists and tourist desire. In brief, we had gotten into an argument over the white tourist mind: what does it "see" when it sees someplace like Bomba's Shack, big houses on the hills owned by locals? I argued that Bomba's is a symbol of free sexuality that they associate with a place like this. Kenne countered that there is no way that the tourist even *imagines* people in a place like this, much less what sort of sex life they have. Instead, he says, the tourist carries with him to a place like this a notion that to be away gives him permission to act differently than when he is home—coming from the sexually controlled/repressed environment of white society he would "naturally" break free of this when away. Bomba's Shack, says Kenne, was originally and is today still Bomba's Surfside Shack. Something that Bomba started when he saw that the surfers coming here represented some market that he could tap into. Then he saw that it could be something in addition and started his full moon parties. That people now see Bomba's Shack as someplace where you get stoned on mushroom punch and engage in lascivious sexual behavior doesn't change the fact that it is Bomba's Surfside Shack. In laying out his argument to me, Kenne said that if tourists see this place as having people at all, it's people living in shacks, huts. This is why the houses on the hills become such an important symbol, in his eyes. Consider, he says, the white tourist going on his tour and he asks the taxi driver who owns all those beautiful houses on the hills, and the taxi driver says, "We do." And points out his house to the tourist. Now the question the tourist wants to ask, but doesn't, is, "If that's your house, how come you're driving a taxi for a few pennies?" But when the tourist goes, he walks with the taxi driver's card, and when his friend comes down, he gives him the card and tells him to take the tour (and catch the taxi driver in the lie he told). But when the friend goes down, this time he goes inside the taxi driver's house, and so on and so on, and eventually, the white tourist begins to see something different. To this I counter that even if this were the case, the tourist would still reassert white superiority by saying, in effect, "Well, the BVI people are a different sort of Caribbean person" (something that is, in fact part of both BVI Tourism campaigns and the BVI nationalist movement).

As I pointed out in chapter 4, for BVIslanders, the BVI is a place where the village or island that you come from and the family name that you carry is a crucial marker of your BVI-ness. Considered from the perspective of intimacy as an inmost quality, this understanding of an identity that is linked to the land and to blood is not unlike the sense of an authentic self that the tourist seeks in travel to a place like the BVI. This notion of an authentic national self is reinforced every time a school teacher "recognizes" a child's family background, presumably just by looking at her face, or starts out the school year by asking each child in the class, "Who are you for?" It is a sense of an unmediated self that I witnessed one day in 1993, when I was invited to go along on a high school field trip to a small farming plot, or "ground." The purpose of the trip was to give students a sense of their culture through exposure to the 'traditional' agricultural practices of BVI farmers. The connection between land and an inmost BVI self was provided

by the teacher who, asserting to his students that it was imperative that the
BVI protect the land and support small-scale farming "as a piece of our
culture," gave as an example the sense of spiritual renewal he experiences
upon, "thrusting my hand into the land" (field notes, March 9, 1993).

While this man seeks in the soil an unmediated connection with an
authentic self, like the tourist to the BVI, he is deflected in this search. For
the BVI is a place where the tens of thousands of tourists who come to the
BVI regularly misrecognize as "authentic" BVIslanders the waitress who is
actually from St. Kitts, the yacht skipper who is actually from Grenada, or
even the African American Hollywood actor who is actually in the BVI on
vacation. This last reference is to a story that circulated among BVIslanders
in the late 1990s regarding actor Morgan Freeman. As the story was told
to me, Freeman was sailing in the waters around Virgin Gorda and was
mistaken by another bareboater as a "local" skipper. These misrecognitions
are compounded for BVIslanders by a cultural calculus of citizenship in
which claims to belong to the BVI on the part of individuals who carry
a BVI name but were born in the United States or in Santo Domingo are
countered by claims of individuals born in the BVI of parents from elsewhere that they "born here." In the context of all of these subjectivities,
the BVI is simultaneously the deeply local place of historical experience,
family, memory, and habit and a place that is constantly being made and
remade by the transit of images, economies, tourists, immigrants, expatriates, and of BVIslanders themselves that shape the place and lives in it. For
BVIslanders and tourists alike, this place that is always in play is the shifting
ground on which identities must be negotiated, desire for the stability of
an authentic self notwithstanding.

In this respect, the BVI is like the hypermediated visual space described
by media theorists Jay David Bolter and Richard Grusin (2000). This is
a visual space that satisfies the desire for an authentic experience of the
real not by promoting a sense of a unified point of view or of unmediated
contact with the object of representation, as is the case of virtual reality or
perspective painting. Rather, hypermediated visual space is heterogeneous,
and representation is conceived "not as a window on to the world, but
rather as 'windowed' itself" (2000: 34). Chris Rojek makes a similar observation about how tourists experience tourist sights. Using the computer
concepts of mouse clicks and file dragging, Rojek suggests that the experiences that the tourist has when interacting with a tourist sight or locale are
best understood as a process of dragging elements from different image and
text files, for example, from tourist advertising, cinematic references, traveler's tales, literally to make the physical place (2000: 54). In both cases, place
is made through the practices of its users. Likewise, to the extent that place
is linked to subjectivity—of the authentic Western self or of the autoch-

thonous national self—the experience of authenticity is a factor not of a unified unmediated real, but rather of the heterogeneous windowed real of clicked and dragged images, memories, events, interactions, stories.

Despite the fact that BVIslanders make their lives in a place that is marketed, imagined, and enacted as premodern paradise, and notwithstanding claims to a unique BVI "essence," their understanding of themselves as subjects is informed by the mobilities and changes that characterize their historical and contemporary experience. Just as the computer user interacting with the windowed space of the computer screen "oscillates between manipulating the windows and examining their contents . . . between looking at a hypertext as a texture of links and looking through the links to the textual units as language" (Bolter and Grusin 2000: 33), so BVIslanders move in their world not as "the toured," not as complicit in their own commodification, not as objects of study or of knowledge, but as active subjects, "making the world abstract and knowable, and creating opportunities for the disruption of these binaries and abstractions" (Minca and Oakes 2006: 20). In the rest of this book I look closely at how BVIslanders express and explore their subjectivity, in the context of their lives in tourism's paradise. In particular, I am interested in the ways that popular culture and heritage are used by BVIslanders simultaneously to appeal to tourist desire for a performed Caribbean, to ground expressions of an authentic identity, and to expose these performances and expressions as contingent, fluid, and malleable.

CHAPTER 7

Of Festivals, Calypso Kings, and Beauty Queens

STANLEY'S SWING, BOMBA'S SHACK, AND FOXY'S hold special meaning to visitors to the BVI in large part because they are places where tourists can enact and confirm their identities as modern Western subjects. In like fashion, the annual BVI Festival that commemorates the 1834 emancipation of slaves in the British Caribbean is an occasion that holds special meaning for people residing in the BVI, not least because of the opportunity it affords for enacting their multiple identity positions in the hypermediated space of the contemporary BVI (Cohen 1998). I began to study Festival in summer 1990. At the time I had no sense of how Festival would illuminate questions I was asking about the impacts of tourism development; in fact, there was very little scholarly attention being paid at all to popular cultural events like Festival. Although my six weeks of research overlapped with the weeks of Festival, I went to the BVI in 1990 intending to focus on tourism and its social and economic impacts. But looking back at my notes from that summer, it is clear that Festival insinuated itself early on as the primary focus of my research. The first several days of notes detailing interviews with people involved in tourism also record something that these people brought up about Festival, and by the fourth day most of the interactions that I recorded were concerned almost exclusively with Festival, as in the following field note summarizing an interview that I conducted with the office manager of the BVI Tourist Board.

[Field notes 7.18.1990] Ivy O'Neal, meeting about Festival. Ivy is the administrative assistant at the Tourist Board, and I have contacted her, on advice of Eileene Parsons, "she knows everything about Festival" and right away, she goes over the Festival schedule:

> 7/27 8 pm. Village opens—Miss BVI 89 to cut ribbon and perhaps Chief Minister or maybe Louis Walters, Minister of Education, to give address.

There will be 25 cooking booths and one toy booth. After that, music every night to August 11.

7/29 5 pm. Prince and Princess Show, Cultural Center.

8/4. Queen Contest, Cultural Center: "This is the big event"

8/5. Sunday Night Ft. Burt "New York Group" (I later find out, from BR that this is a group of BVIslanders, living in New York, who come down for festival every year and have a troupe) will have a party (they've hired Caribbean Ecstasy as the band). One Jouvert road march will start from here.

8/6 4:30 am. Jouvert—"Rise and Shine Tramp" starts at Holiday Beach Club (one also to start from Sea Cow's Bay): "It's wild, they love it, everyone goes wild, which is the point." 12 pm. Parade.

8/7. Water Sports at Ferry Dock, Horse Race at Sea Cows Bay.

8/8. East End Parade (Jouvert first).

8/9. Picnic at Cane Garden Bay.

. . . She then starts talking about the specifics of the parade, floats, children involved. She advises that I see the cultural officer in the Ministry of Education, about school children participation. At 5 p.m. today the youth steel band will be practicing, and she urges us to be there to watch the practice (also to find the Chairman of Festival Committee), which is being led by BJ from Trinidad. L. of Roadtown Wholesale, is in charge of floats [phone number], K. of Water and Sewerage is in charge of the Sunday Morning Well Speech [phone number]. In speaking of the Queen contest, Ivy starts to go over the timing of the contest, and mentions the opening number as a "Lambora," in which contestants will be in native dress, what she describes as a red dress with BVI print. Then, the evening gown competition . . . she picks up again on the topic of what I now take to understand is the Lambada competition (without partners)—something that she refers to as "that dance from South America." Practice for this will begin tomorrow night at 5:30 above Bobby's and upon learning that one of my students knows the Lambada, she calls [the woman] who will be training the contestants, and asks her if she'd like an assistant.

This field note is one of the first of hundreds of field notes focused on Festival that I wrote between 1990 and 2007. The note hints at the centrality of Festival to BVI national identity that subsequent notes were to document. Ivy O'Neal's position with the Tourist Board points to the close association between Festival and BVI government, as do the positions of two other people that she suggests I talk to, who work in the civil service. Likewise, her reference to the BVI print of the dresses for the Miss BVI contestants' opening number and to the chief minister's opening address signals a connection between Festival and national identity, even as the choice of the lambada for the opening number points to the implication of the BVI in global flows of taste and fashion. What I learned is that BVI Festival is all of these things: a deeply local event that simultaneously showcases BVI culture and opens up space for multiple interpretations of what BVI culture is; a stage for articulating and negotiating the relation of BVIslanders to people from other Caribbean islands, as well as to the flows of ideas, values, people that shape BVI history and present; a valuable product to be fought over and controlled. What Garth Green and Philip Scher note for the many forms that Trinidad Carnival has taken over the years is true as well for the many BVI Festivals that I have documented on videotape and in my field notes, "Whatever the Carnivals may be in their many incarnations, they are the products of unique histories, manifestations of social tensions, barometers of cultural change, and crucibles for creating, discovering, and asserting identities" (2007b: 9).

BVI FESTIVAL

The British Virgin Islands Festival Committee 1975 was born out of the desire on the part of the young and not so young British Virgin Islanders to actively participate in a community activity with one goal in mind: its continued improvement. And that activity is the annual Festival. Our yearly celebration of our freedom from man's inhumanity to man: slavery. We invite everyone to become a part of the celebrations this year, our fifth anniversary. Come out to the various functions. Join in the laughter at the calypso tent. Relax with friends as you enjoy the gaiety of the Village. Get a group together to attend the Miss BVI Show, or to join in the parade. Set our own pace. But participate. (Festival 1980 Program)

The annual British Virgin Islands Festival is a bellwether of national sentiment and pride, and originated as a small church-based affair commemorating the Sunday, August 1, 1834, emancipation of enslaved Africans in the British Caribbean. According to local accounts, August observances of emancipation have taken place on Tortola since 1835. These days, Festival is an official national holiday, with all schools, government offices, and banks closed on the first Monday, Tuesday, and Wednesday of August. In preparation for Festival, individuals and groups in communities throughout the islands organize parade, dance, and steel band troupes, and plan events such as beauty queen contests, calypso contests, and family reunions. These and other Festival events provide opportunities for public expressions of opinion on issues of general concern by all residents of the BVI. They are also key arenas for demonstrating BVI cultural identity; in the words of the minister of culture and education upon the opening of Festival in 2006, "In essence, [culture] is the fabric of our society that identifies us as a people and therefore worthy of preservation. Remembering our past and providing entertainment and fun for all is what festival is about" (quoted in Trotman 2006: 2).

In its sequence of events, Festival in the BVI is structured much like Trinidad's pre-Lenten Carnival (Green and Scher 2007a; Hill 1972; Miller 1994; Pearse 1988), with a queen contest on Saturday night, music and dances and calypso contests on Sunday night, an early-morning "rise and shine tramp" that opens Festival on Monday morning, and parades through the close of Festival on Wednesday. With its soca music (soca is an acronym for soul calypso, a style of calypso that emerged in the 1970s with the move to electrified instruments and synthesizers) and unrestrained street dancing, its opportunities for drinking and eating to excess, its elaborately costumed parade troupes, and its three days of public holiday, Festival also contains many elements of bacchanal with which pre-Lenten Carnivals like Trinidad's are associated. However, like the festivals documented by Frank Manning in Antigua and Bermuda (1977, 1978), BVI Festival is a self-consciously secular event.

The distinction between Trinidad's pre-Lenten Carnival excess and BVI Festival as a secular event that commemorates emancipation is rigorously maintained by many in the BVI. I have witnessed people who use the term "carnival" being reminded that what the BVI has is a "festival." Such corrections are frequently accompanied by a discourse about people getting too caught up in bacchanal, and about the perils of forgetting BVI Festival's historical roots. Two separate guest editorials written following Festival 1996 noted the "all too ready willingness of Virgin Islanders to allow the customs of others to dominate rather than insist on their own" ("Redesign August Festival"), and that "there is always talk of Festival marking the emancipation from slavery, but apparently some of us are becoming slaves to money and forgetting what we are saying through the other side of our mouths about celebration" ("Festival Needs Cultural, Historical Emphasis"). A decade later, a newspaper article reporting on the opening of Festival 2006 was entitled "BVI Festival Is Not Carnival, Still Have Fun." The opening paragraph of this article began, "Although the BVI festival is a time of national fun and frolic, it is not a carnival," and closed paraphrasing the remarks of a public official, who "stressed that festival is a time of remembrance of emancipation and the journey that has followed that momentous occasion" (Trotman 2006).

A ceremony at the well where the Emancipation Proclamation was reportedly read on Sunday August 1, 1834—the Sunday Morning Well—is the primary event devoted to recognizing Festival's roots in emancipa-

tion. As a flyer from the Sunday Morning Well Emancipation Service from
Festival 1992 indicates (figure 7.1), the Sunday Morning Well ceremony
is religious in tone, although I have also seen it used as an occasion to
celebrate African heritage, with African dances, and speeches exhorting
participants to apply the lessons of their ancestors to present-day affairs. The
Sunday Morning Well Emancipation Service is often the only Festival event
that devout Christians attend; in 2004 the Reverend Jesse Jackson gave
the feature address, to mixed reviews. The slogan on the official tee-shirt
for Festival 2004, which was being celebrated as the fiftieth anniversary of
Festival, highlights the link between Festival and emancipation: "Golden
Like Never Before: Festival the Celebration 1954–2004. Emancipation the
Foundation 1834–2004." In 2008, the BVI Tourist Board Web site made
the link between emancipation and Festival official, heralding Festival as the
"BVI Emancipation Festival" and describing it as "the territory's Premier
Cultural showcase with an array of activities, events, including *the freedom*

Road Town, Tortola, British Virgin Islands
Emancipation Sunday
2nd August 1992 – 4:00 PM

SUNDAY MORNING WELL EMANCIPATION SERVICE

Introduction:	Chairperson Ishmael Scatliffe
Invocation:	Pastor Melvin Turnbull
Hymn:	Now Thank We All Our God
Historical review of August celebration:	Dr. Quincy Lettsome
Musical Selection:	Sparkplugs
Remarks:	Honourable Louis Walters, MHE&W
Feature Address:	Vernon Pickering
Hymn:	Lift Every Voice and Sing
Reading of the Proclamation:	Elton Georges, Deputy Governor
Remarks:	Honourable Omar Hodge
Musical Selection:	Ian Smith
Vote of Thanks:	Lynette Harrigan
Hymn:	Faith of Our Fathers Living Still
Benediction:	Pastor Melvin Turnbull

7.1. Emancipation Proclamation ceremony program

march, emancipation service, Calypso monarch competition, boat races, Rise and Shine tramps, August Monday's Parade, and much more" (http://www. bvitourism.com/WhatToDo/Events/; emphasis added).

Festival begins officially on the first Monday in August, which is known as August Monday. August Monday is given over to the early-morning rise-and-shine tramp and a soca band competition known locally as a *road march*, followed by a late-afternoon parade; Tuesday is given over to water sports and horseracing; and Wednesday to festival activities in the Tortola community of East End/Long Look. Festival time proper begins as early as two weeks prior to August Monday, with the opening of Festival Village. But well before the opening of Festival Village, pennants looped across the streets in Road Town and East End, standards hanging from electricity poles, newspaper contests for the Festival slogan, and radio shows playing soca songs composed for Festival are all indications that Festival time has begun. A field note from July 1994 gives some sense of the activity that precedes the official opening of Festival Village.

[Field notes 7.15.1994] Festival is really heating up. The radio is beginning to get people excited about the soca band road march competition by talking about the new soca bands forming, and playing some of the new music that has been composed for road march. New bands this year: Show-time (Trevor, the moco jumbie, is the singer in this one), EFX (Donel and Dwite Flax of Caribbean Ecstacy back again). The top band, the one to beat by all accounts, is Prime Time (according to Sigrid their road march song is "The Bernie;" taking off on [the movie] *Weekend at Bernie's 2*, it includes The Bernie dance: arched back, arms akimbo, head back and rolling). Then there's System, Emphasis, Latitude Stars (System the only local band with a following close to that of Prime Time); and from St. Thomas, Imagination Brass ("Imagy") and Jam Band. . . . It's Friday, and the opening of Festival Village is just a week away. There's no Coney Island [amusement park] yet, and although in previous years the possibility of no Coney Island has had people up in arms, the widespread "knowledge" (read: speculation) that it's on the dock, awaiting some Government something (with Government in England doing battle over election reform, the sense is that nothing will be done until their return), has tempered this sort of reaction. It'll have to await Monday, and still no sign of Coney Island, before the discontent starts to crescendo. Meanwhile, this Friday afternoon, sparked by radio announcers' reminders that "Festival time is here," there's an excitement in the air. The traffic out of town toward the round about is stopped all the way back to Miracles, the normal Friday afternoon slow passing around the roundabout to check out

what's happening at Market square slowed all the more by a Fish Fry that, at
3:00, is already drawing crowds. Trucks and cars pull haphazardly out of the
slow stream around the round about, cutting through traffic to bounce over
the curb and onto the well-work dirt track that passes for the main road onto
market square. Meanwhile, down by the Pasea RiteWay, another Fish Fry sets
up. Sponsored by Road Town Wholesale, it features Prime Time, and specials
on cases of Heineken beer, that can be bought up to 9 p.m. from the ware-
house that will remain open late for the occasion.

Festival Village is bounded by a circle of upward of twenty-five privately
operated booths selling food and drink. A raised stage is set up in the middle
of the area circumscribed by the booths, for the various musical and cultural
performances that are held nightly Conventionally erected on a piece of
public land near the center of the BVI capital of Road Town, which is also
used for religious revivals and informal cricket matches, from 1998 to 2003
Festival Village was erected on the walled Recreation Grounds across the
street from these public fields. Festival Village also features a small amuse-
ment park, or "Coney Island." Festival Village is the logistic and symbolic
center of Festival: it is the site of most of the major events of Festival and it
is where people congregate after events that are held in other venues. People
come from throughout the BVI to be in Festival Village on its opening night,
in anticipation of meeting up with family and friends. Special events such
as soca band, steel band, fungi band, and folk dance demonstrations; a peas
and rice cooking competition; and a calypso contest are held nightly during
the week prior to August Monday and also draw large crowds of supporters
and participants. Festival Village events are scheduled to begin at around
nine o'clock in the evening, and are usually followed by live soca music.
Combined, the special events and the soca music keep Festival Village open
until two or three o'clock in the morning.
    From early evening to early morning, Festival Village booths provide a
steady supply of drink and typical BVI foods such as goat head soup, bull
foot soup, stewed mutton, stewed conch, stewed welk, salt fish, johnny cake,
barbecued ribs and chicken, as well as foods from other Caribbean islands,
such as roti and curried goat (from Guyana and Trinidad) and patty and
jerk chicken (from Jamaica). Festival Village booths tend to be associated
with the locale of the person or group operating them, and are patronized
accordingly, so that one is likely to find Nevesians congregating around a
booth operated by the Nevis Association, Guyanese around a booth operated by people from Guyana, and so forth. Thus, to walk a circle around
Festival Village is to catch a sense of the communities making up the
BVI. And to circle Festival Village on any given night, or to attend any of

Festival's many events, is to have an open window on the cross-currents of values and interests that dominate BVI social life. In a memoir of his life, BVIslander Joseph Reynold "J. R." O'Neal recalled that the August Festivals of his youth also provided opportunities for catching a sense of the communities making up the BVI.

> The August Monday festivities of 1924 were the biggest I'd seen. Festival really started out as a getting together of family and friends living on Tortola, the sister islands and the neighboring US Virgin Islands. The big event was the August Monday picnic in Road Town, which would be followed by other picnics. One of the favourite sites for the picnics was at Fahie Hill. There would be crowds of folks, lots to eat and drink and music by which to make merry. Folks one had not seen for ages would be there to spin a tale with you and catch up on the year's happenings. We did not call it Festival back then, nor did we have jouvert or "rise and shine" tramps. There were, however, many activities on that one day. There would be a cricket match. Sometimes it was Long Look against Road Town or it might be Tortola against St. Thomas. At the same time, there would be the plait pole in the market with music provided by the Brewley brothers of Free Bottom. The greased pole and boat racing would also be going on, and so would horse racing. (O'Neal 2005: 25)

Festival today is vastly different from the Festival of J. R. O'Neal's recollections and from the church-based commemorations of emancipation from which it derives. Not only does it span several days and have more events, the communities that come together during Festival are composed of individuals from throughout the Caribbean as well as from North America and Europe. Anthropologist Frank Manning noted a similar historical shift "of emancipation commemorations from quiet folk celebrations to centralized, baroque festivals" (1977: 270) in Bermuda and Antigua, and observed that this transition was accompanied on both islands by democratic reform movements and the development of tourism as the foundation of the economy. A similar change in the BVI commemoration of emancipation, from church-based picnics to today's Festival, occurred in the early 1950s. This change coincides with major constitutional reform and the development of a legislative and infrastructural basis for international tourism in the BVI.

Yet BVI histories neglect any such connections. Rather, most local accounts attribute the form and style of today's Festival directly to Queen Elizabeth's coronation, as explained in an article in the program for BVI Festival 1989, "Notes on Festival in the BVI."

The idea of parading with troupes and floats as part of the celebrations on August Monday and Wednesday came from the 1953 celebrations held in honour of HM Queen Elizabeth II. On seeing the gaiety and art that troupes and floats added to the celebrations, citizens thought, why not do this at August festival time too? Government accepted the proposal, and decided to support it by organizing a committee and offering the printing facilities at the Administration Complex. Public spirited citizens worked hard to publicize the new idea and dimension to Festival celebrations and to involve as many British Virgin Islanders as possible.

In my field notes I comment on the irony of Festival, a local cultural activity celebrating emancipation from slavery, taking its contemporary form from an event celebrating the most explicit representation of British colonial power, the English monarchy. But irony is misleading; what is important about this piece of history is its telling. For in conflating a contemporary emancipation commemoration with Elizabeth II's coronation, this account points to the contingency of history and to local efforts to stabilize it, even as it underscores the changing currents of power, affiliation, belief, and affection that did and do shape these efforts and their outcomes.

Likewise, the issues that emerged when I first started my formal research during Festival 1990 differ from the issues that captured people's attention in Festival 1994, Festival 2004, or Festival 2008. For example, Festival 1990 was about celebrating BVI identity, in contrast to St. Thomas on the one hand and residents from other Caribbean islands on the other. By the early part of the twenty-first century, the BVI had experienced the death of the leader known as "the father" of the BVI nation (and whose birthday is now a national holiday), had seen the rise to power of a new political party, and had undergone constitutional reform that changed significantly its relation to the United Kingdom as well as to the non-BVIslanders who made up over half of the national population. And what people concerned themselves with in Festivals during this period reflected these changes. The snapshots of Festival events from various years in the rest of this chapter give a sense of what is at stake in Festival and underscore how Festival provides a key arena for negotiating what I have come to think of as a hypermediated BVI identity.

"THIS IS DE TEST":
PERFORMING INTRICATE IDENTITIES

"This is de test for all de rest. This is de test," is the chorus to "De Test," a song written for BVI Festival 1990. "De Test" refers to a contest between Caribbean Ecstasy, the British Virgin Islands soca band that composed the song, and its rival Jam Band, a soca band from the USVI island of St.

Thomas. The soca contest for which "De Test" was written takes place each year in the predawn hours of August Monday. Referred to locally as a "road march," the contest takes the form of a "tramp" in which crowds dance down the road behind soca bands that are set up on the beds of eighteen-wheel tractor-trailers. The band with the most followers behind it at the end of the tramp is declared the winner. This early-morning "rise and shine tramp," as it is known in the BVI, is a take off on *jouvert*, the street parade that opens Trinidad's pre-Lenten carnival, and whose name comes from the French *jour overt*, or day opening (Nunley and Bettelheim 1988: 212). I have heard the term *jouvert* used in the BVI interchangeably with the term "rise and shine tramp." However, as is the case with the Festival/carnival distinction, people use "rise and shine tramp" in order to distinguish BVI Festival from Trinidad carnival, and to point to its uniqueness as a BVI product. For some individuals, *jouvert* is also negatively associated with excessively sexual or ribald behavior and is thus eschewed in favor of the more benign "rise and shine tramp."

The competition between Caribbean Ecstasy from the BVI and Jam Band from St. Thomas was the major focus of public attention and debate in Festival 1990, and particularly because Caribbean Ecstasy was threatening to boycott the very road march where these two competitors were to face off. The threatened boycott was the result of an incident that had occurred three months earlier in April 1990, when Caribbean Ecstasy was not allowed to clear customs into St. Thomas and was therefore kept from competing in the St. Thomas Spring Carnival road march. In response to this affront, British Virgin Islands government prohibited USVI bands from participating in *its* August Festival. However, as Festival approached, the British Virgin Islands government rescinded its ban. Upon learning of this, Caribbean Ecstasy announced in a letter that was published in a leading BVI newspaper that it and fellow BVI bands would "consider . . . protest by boycotting [Festival] inclusive of 1) Village entertainment, 2) Shows, 3) Jouverts, 4) Parades and tramps" ("Bands Consider Boycotting 1990 Festival").

For BVI bands to *threaten* a boycott of Festival was considered an appropriate response to what was broadly taken as yet a second insult to BVI pride, and this time at the hands of British Virgin Islands government itself. A formal boycott, on the other hand, did not receive widespread support. For example, members of Festival Committee, the formal body responsible for organizing Festival, feared that without live music, the spirit of Festival would be ruined and that revenues would be so low that they would be unable to put on a good Festival the following year. For BVIslanders in general, Festival 1990 provided a means for BVI bands to demonstrate on their own turf their equality with St. Thomas bands, to go "mano a mano with St. Thomas" (field notes, July 17, 1990), as one BVI woman put it to me. A BVI man put it more explicitly, "For years it was Jam Band, Jam Band. Now we have something local that is better. . . . So this year, everyone is waiting to see which band will be better. That's why they had to let Jam Band back in the country. We are waiting to show them what we have. That we don't have to be going to St. Thomas all the time for it" (field notes, July 20, 1990). As this latter quote indicates, while threatening to boycott Festival "until a fair agreement is firmly established" ("Bands Consider Boycotting 1990 Festival"), BVI bands in fact *had to* play at Festival. Other-wise, they would not be able to demonstrate that the BVI was capable of competing in a larger arena.

The song "De Test" speaks expressly to Caribbean Ecstasy's agenda. Referring to the upcoming contest, its opening lyrics name and challenge its rival, Jam Band. In "calling-out" the St. Thomas band to compete, the BVI band leveled a challenge from a position of equivalence. As its letter of protest made clear, after "[having] spent considerable time, energy and money over the years developing the musical product of the BVI to a standard as good or better than foreign groups from the USVI and elsewhere," this band was ready to compete ("Bands Consider Boycot-ting 1990 Festival"). At the same time, songs composed by Caribbean Ecstasy for its Festival cassette evoked a BVI reputation for civility, like that grounding the "Yes We Are Different!" tourism slogan. For example, a song that referred to an increase in violence and racial antagonisms during St. Thomas Carnival claimed, "We want no fighting here." Another song established a distinct contrast between the "Jam Band Style" of dancing—a style so called "because of the song's 'mash dem on their big toe' refrain" (de Albuquerque 1990: 58)—with Caribbean Ecstasy's more civil and egali-tarian sensibility: "Watch how you're jumpin', watch how you're prancin' / Me no want no misbehavin', me no want that kind of nonsense. / If you really want to join the line, watch out for your black brother / If you really want to join the line, watch out for your black sister."

These contradictions between a desire for equivalence and a claim of distinctiveness, between a readiness to spend vast sums of money on developing a musical product and a reluctance to be associated with the derogated practices of St. Thomas bands, are some of the things that made a boycott untenable. In the public letter in which they declared their intent to boycott Festival, Caribbean Ecstasy pointed out that "musical groups from the USVI have traditionally been allowed to perform in the BVI at the disadvantage of local groups, for we are not allowed a recip-rocal allowance to perform in the USVI during their festivals or any other time" ("Bands Consider Boycotting 1990 Festival"). The same letter lumped

St. Thomas bands with groups from "elsewhere" into the same category, "foreign," thus making a claim for a BVI national sovereignty. Yet in a BVI radio broadcast expressing outrage over the original incident in which they had been kept from entering the USVI, Caribbean Ecstasy pointed to a history of unencumbered social and cultural interchange between these two island groups, stressing the redundancy of national borders.

Forces at work in the larger world of Caribbean music were also implicated in the boycott dilemma and soca band controversy. A BVI radio talk show devoted to the boycott alleged that the boycott was actually being orchestrated by a music agent who had been fired by many of the BVI bands in question, when they determined that they could make more money without him. Members of Caribbean Ecstasy claimed that the agent stood ready to book lesser-known BVI bands that were under contract to him, should the boycott result in canceled bookings. I do not present this version of the boycott gratuitously; it circulated widely, in a variety of contexts, and was generally believed. Most important, it appears to have had a significant impact upon the eventual outcome of the road march competition between Jam Band and Caribbean Ecstasy. For the road march was won by Jam Band. In spite of appeals to national sovereignty and pride, by jeopardizing Festival with its threat of a boycott Caribbean Ecstasy had revealed itself to be as driven by financial self-interest as the derogated St. Thomas bands. And in this arena, St. Thomas bands, with their stronger financial backing, more powerful amplifiers, and more extensive music-industry ties were winners hands down. Indeed, by managing to get into the BVI to compete at all, St. Thomas bands had already signaled their superiority in the world of money, manipulation, and influence.

As a piece, the threatened boycott of the road march soca competition provided a context for articulating without resolving the multiple and contradictory positions that BVIslanders occupy in relation to residents from other Caribbean islands, to their U.S. neighbors across the channel, and to the global community in which they are enmeshed. Likewise, the 1990 Festival slogan "Unity in 90" stood as an appeal for unity in a society that had experienced rapid economic, technological, and demographic change. Indeed, the showcase for BVI cultural representations and enactments, the Festival parade, was a prime occasion for political commentary upon and contestation of the Festival theme, "Unity in 90." For example, the parade troupe that won first prize in Festival 1990 was the "New York Posse," a troupe composed almost entirely of BVIslanders residing in New York City. Its first-place award thus served to legitimate a notion of unity that transcended daily, local, shared experience or even national boundaries, while drawing upon the notion of some fundamental tie to a native land. But the "New York Posse" troupe's first-place award was publicly contested by a local troupe leader whose second-place troupe of "Mexican Dancers" was notable for the number of white expatriates marching in its ranks. Arguing that the first-place troupe was composed of "outsiders, from St. Thomas," and thus had no right to compete in—much less win—the parade competition, this troupe leader played upon negative images of United States–British Virgin Islands affiliation while making a unity claim based simultaneously upon local residence and global brother/sisterhood. Meanwhile, the first prize for the best "Floupe" (Combined Troupe and Float) was shared, without protest, by the BVI Heritage Dancers and the BVI Latin Association, the one a group that performs BVI "folk" dances, the other a social club that also served as lobbying group on behalf of Dominican Republic nationals residing in the British Virgin Islands.

CALYPSO KINGS AND BEAUTY QUEENS

[Field notes 7.25.1996] It's another Festival, my seventh summer here in the BVI covering Festival, and the work is now to the point where I don't have to ask the questions. People stop me and say, "I expected to see you earlier, why weren't you at the Queen Show? Do you know what happened . . . ?" This attention to the details that so interest me isn't something that I have fostered with my presence and investigations, rather my investigations were directed there by the sort of intense interest that I noted people paying to the details—of queen show planning and outcomes, of festival events, of the personnel changes of festival committee. For example, while in town yesterday getting my car, I ran into L. and M., who started to go on about the new person in charge of the queen show, and noted with some satisfaction that she had "ousted" [the previous chairperson]. . . . Similarly, while I was on the phone with C., she started to talk about how the person who won the queen show this year shouldn't, because it's just her father who is from here—she has been raised in the States—the *States* States, not the USVI. Although recognizing that the woman had a perfect legal right to compete, C. said that she really shouldn't have and then added somewhat cattily, "I imagine she would do a good job of representing the country—if she knew anything about it."

In BVI Festival, the beauty queen contest shares with the calypso contest the distinction of being the most anticipated of events. For individuals competing in either of these competitions, winning can have important and far-reaching consequences with respect to social status and career. Meanwhile, the payoff for the majority of the public attending these contests is the opportunity to reflect on, comment on, and engage each other over issues of local political and cultural consequence. In this regard especially, calypso and beauty queen contests are key occasions for articulating, expanding, negotiating, and challenging idealizations of BVI nationhood and identity. The commentary in calypso contests is fairly direct and explicit; calypsonians compete against each other with songs that are composed about locally relevant issues and scandals. As is the case of calypso contests throughout the region, it is the content and sentiments of a given calypso, and not the reputation or fame of the singer performing it that most influences what contestant an audience will support.

The winner of the 1991 Festival calypso contest was a St. Kitts national who won with his song, "Where We Born Is Where We From." As its title suggests, this song presents an argument against British Virgin Islands citizenship law, claiming instead that "where a baby first see the sun should be his home." According to its author, Benji V (Vanclaire Benjamin), he wrote the song "to reach the ears of certain people who made the laws" ("Benji V Is Calypso King"). Played on BVI radio weeks preceding the contest, the song articulated the sentiments of many non-BVIslander residents, but its catchy chorus in fact invited all segments of BVI society to sing along. Notably, in setting up the song's argument Benji V assumes the voice of a native-born BVI male. Attacking the cultural logic of "natural" citizenship, the song's lyrics voice a challenge to citizenship's legal basis.

> They say if my girlfriend get her baby in my country
> The baby can't have the same rights like me
> How come when anybody go to Rock City [St. Thomas] to get
>   their baby
> Their baby could have the same right like a Tomi? [St. Thomian]
> Where a baby first see sun, that country must be their own,
> They must have the rights like anybody born in the same region.
> So if mother born in Antigua and she children born in Tortola
> Where we born is where we from.

In the calypso contest of Festival 1993, a Dominican-born calypsonian and twenty-five-year BVI resident signaled *his* sense of cultural citizenship in a song bemoaning the commercialization of Festival. In the same contest, a St. Kitts–born calypsonian acted out the lyrics of a song about his devotion to the BVI by covering over a replica of his Kittitian grandmother with a map of Tortola.

Festival 1999 saw its first white calypsonian compete: Lord Land Crab is a frequent visitor to the BVI from the United States, has a vacation house on the island, and is widely known for his efforts to speak in the local dialect. The MC for the calypso show introduced Lord Land Crab's first song by alluding to his interloper status: "First they steal we from

Africa, then they steal Africa from we, now they stealing our emancipation celebration" (field notes, July 28, 1999). Although many in the audience felt that Lord Land Crab gave a good show, the overall sense of the crowd mirrored the MC's sentiments. In 2000 Land Crab competed again, introducing his first number, "The time has come, Land Crab is here. He isn't white, he's just clear [term denoting light-skinned individual of African descent]. Deep down he want to be black. Ladies and Gentlemen, your Land Crab is back" (field notes, August 1, 2000). This obvious effort at self-critique received loud applause, but Lord Land Crab failed to place in the competition, and in 2001 he stopped competing. The year 2002 saw the first BVI calypso queen crowned, followed in 2003 by the renaming of the winner of the Calypso contest "Calypso Monarch." Meanwhile, in 2004, Festival-goers unanimously condemned a calypsonian whose song viciously attacked Caribbean people from other islands, and first prize was awarded to a song about a local political controversy. The following field note about a 2004 junior calypso contest gives a sense of the range of topics covered in calypsos.

[Field notes 7.26.2004] Cass had come by this morning, after being in town, to tell me that she had seen Algie and that Algie had told her to tell me that his daughter, Channiece, was going to be singing in the village tonight. . . . The show was scheduled for 8, so we arrived at 9, and from the looks of things, we could have gotten there as late as 10 and still been early: the Village was all but deserted and the backup band was just warming up with some pretty tame soca. So we took a seat near the Nevis Association booth and just chilled. About 9:30, after a turn around the village (which was beginning to be more populated) I found Algie and Agnes. The show started around 10:15, with the first two performers, two young boys, the first of whom sang about BVI music and did a very good job of having all the calypso moves. . . . Channiece's song was about children—with a chorus that said, "Children listen to too much music and not enough news, children keep secrets so we don't know who is abused." A great song, and she had the moves down perfectly (even controlling for my bias, for Algie and Kenne were first cousins). After the fourth calypsonian, while the judges were deliberating, Algie came out as Mako [his calypsonian name] and sang his song which was about doing good for the little guy. . . . King Paido also sang his winning calypso "Dolly," that refers to the voodoo doll that had allegedly been brought into the country, by [a well-known person] in order to do obea against [a person who accused a relative of hers of sexual assault]. When Channiece was crowned junior calypso monarch, the crowd was totally behind her—she had done a wonderful job.

Festival Queen Contests

The commentary in queen contests is more symbolic and representational than the commentary in calypso performances. Moreover, while beauty queen contestants do address local interests and values, they as frequently engage the conflicts that arise when local interests, values, and needs intersect with regional and international ones. This is because queen contestants must meet local standards of beauty, social and moral deportment, citizenship, and talent but are also evaluated in terms of an international aesthetic. The tension between the local and the global is particularly salient when the local queen contest is also a venue for selecting a contestant to go on to compete in other contests abroad (Cohen 1996). As the BVI continues in its efforts to articulate and promote a sense of what the BVI is, its beauty contests also emerge as forums for expressing an official BVI identity. In making note of the special character attributes that make them the preferred representative for their country, for example, BVI beauty contestants emphasize personal qualities that accord with advertising images of the BVI as a place of civil and friendly people, and point out physical attributes that made them especially suitable as representatives of the "natural beauty of our islands" (field notes, July 31, 1994). In their fashion demonstrations, contestants highlight the consonance of BVI aesthetics with a global economy of style, but their attention to proper dress and deportment also reflects local ideas of what women BVI citizens literally should look like.

BVI beauty queens' participation in competitions abroad, the details of which are recorded in local newspaper articles, provides another opportunity for beauty queens to make a link between their success and the success of the nation they represent. For example, the comments of Miss BVI 1990 upon her return from the Miss Universe competition underscored the link between BVI national identity and its tourist economy, as well as highlighted features predominating in BVI promotions of itself as a tourist destination: "Although I did not reach the top ten, I am happy to have sold tourism for the BVI. My sash indicated my place of origin and allowed me to explain the Territory's geographical location and the natural beauty it possesses" ("Miss BVI Returns from Las Vegas"). In like manner, the comments of the 1991 winner of a regional Miss Caribbean Talented Teen pageant mirrored the sense of national pride and regional preeminence that has accompanied BVI economic prosperity: "What's so great about [being selected over contestants from nine other Caribbean countries] is that we were the smallest islands there" ("Bisa Smith Wins Crown"). Meanwhile, audience responses to the interviews and performances of beauty contestants are always loud and lively. A key component of the appeal of these competitions, audience responses provide a good indication of trends in public opinion. Thus, a negative or incredulous response by the audience to the representational content of beauty contests registers a challenge to any coherent or singular notion of British Virgin Islands–ness.

Beauty Contests as "Shows"

A beauty contest has been part of Festival since 1952, and from 1952 to 1976 the Festival Queen contest was the central social event of Festival. In 1976, when Festival Committee secured a franchise for a Miss Universe pageant, the Festival Queen pageant was transformed into the Miss BVI Pageant, and up to 1991 the Miss BVI Pageant was the only venue for selecting a national representative to compete at the international level. This changed in 1991 with the introduction into the Festival calendar of the first Miss World BVI contest, which was held to select a candidate to compete in the Miss World Pageant. Promoted as pageants and structured as contests, both these events were referred to in daily conversation as *shows*. Each queen show was broadcast over national radio, but its value as a show was assessed largely in terms of its success as a form of entertainment in which one participated directly: as a member of an audience watching and judging a performance; as a member of an audience making a performance in interaction with formally staged enactments; as on stage oneself, participating in what was considered one of a limited number of occasions annually on which one could really get dressed up.

The use of the term *show* to describe these beauty contests is noteworthy. For in addition to being a place where particular ideals are held up for public scrutiny and challenge, like Festival's soca contests beauty contests are also occasions for *showing up* a competitor or for *showing* who's in charge. In this sense, what's at stake in such shows is more than just a title or a prize, and this is as true for audience members as it is for the contestants themselves. As in Carla Freeman's study of Barbados office worker's consumption practices (2000), BVI queen shows make explicit the connection between conspicuous fashion consumption and social status. In fashion portions of queen shows, contestants are putting on display not just their physical attributes and their taste and sophistication, but also their knowledge of what it takes to be an appropriate BVI woman citizen. Likewise, queen show audience members put on a show for each other, as they arrive with hair elaborately done and in newly purchased outfits.

Because of its central place in the Festival calendar and its longstanding status as the only event to send a BVI representative to an international competition, the Miss BVI contest was considered the sole legitimate forum for the selection of a national beauty queen. In 1991, the Miss World BVI contest posed a challenge to this legitimacy. The admission for the 1991

Miss BVI contest was $15. The admission to the Miss World BVI contest was $20, but the higher ticket price to this show was generally considered to be in keeping with its unique offerings of international judges and entertainers, including top models and soap opera stars from the United States, and prizes that included a modeling contract in New York City. In 1991, the Miss World BVI contest outdrew the Miss BVI contest by a ratio of 2 to 1. This discrepancy in attendance at the two contests was a commentary not just on perceived differences in their quality, but also on the Festival Committee itself: its degree of sophistication, its organizational and leadership ability, its policies and decisions, its right to the control it wielded over Festival events. Mirroring public and political debate about how Festival should be organized, who should be in charge of Festival, and whether or not Festival should be developed as a tourist event, evaluations of the relative merits of the two contests also operated as commentary on the status of the BVI in a larger world, in which the localized content and concerns of a small-island festival could seem awfully parochial.

Festival 1995 saw a continuation of competition between the Miss BVI contest and the Miss World BVI contest. General disarray among the people putting on the Miss World BVI contest, however, and successful efforts on the part of the Miss BVI contest to improve their product, had positioned the Miss BVI contest to regain its place as the premier BVI beauty contest. It was into this competitive milieu that Miss Budweiser stepped. Miss Budweiser was actually a young woman from Dominica who had lived in the BVI since childhood. A BVI resident and a graduate of the BVI high school, she was in important respects a "local" product, her lack of citizenship notwithstanding. She had also attained some local fame as the first Afro-Caribbean woman to appear on the cover of the *Welcome Guide* not in Festival garb, and also as a visible and successful representative for Budweiser beer. An experienced and studied performer with aspirations to a career in modeling, she could be expected to bring to the Miss BVI contest a degree of style and sophistication more usually associated with the Miss World BVI contest.

The Miss World BVI contest had been held several weeks prior to the start of Festival season, but public opinion held that it was not a very good show. The possibility of having as a contestant a woman known for her beauty and modeling abilities thus presented an ideal opportunity for the Miss BVI contest organizers to show up the other contest. However, Miss Universe Pageant franchise rules made it quite clear that as a noncitizen, the woman would not be allowed to represent the British Virgin Islands in the Miss Universe Pageant. Despite this possibility, and despite the fact that any contestant must spend a great deal of time, money, and energy in preparation to compete for the title of Miss BVI, the woman maintained her interest in competing. For their part, the organizers of the Miss BVI contest began to consider how this might be made possible. In the end, the woman did not enter the Miss BVI contest. Nevertheless, her actions and the response to them by the organizers of the Miss BVI contest under-score several salient features of both the contest and the broader context in which it takes place.

While the Miss BVI and Miss World BVI contests play upon and play up notions of national pride and loyalty, in the eyes of many of the contestants what these contests are really about is individual advancement: about winning scholarships and cars, about acquiring sponsorship, about clothes, about local status, about advancing a career. That the noncitizen woman continued to express a desire to enter the Miss BVI contest, even knowing that she would not be able to go on to compete for the Miss Universe crown, brings to light the contest's individualistic and entrepre-neurial aspects. Additionally, that the members of the committee responsible for putting on the Miss BVI contest even entertained the possibility of her competing brings to light its commercial and consumerist aspects, for having her in the contest would have drawn the sorts of crowds that would have made the contest a financial success. Finally, in the context of the ongoing competition between the Miss BVI contest and the Miss World BVI contest (which was even offered that year as a pay-per-view event on the local cable), a successful Miss BVI show would also have elevated its value, and the status of Festival Committee, in a local cultural/political market.

The dilemma of the contestant who never competed is emblematic of the complications of citizenship and allegiance with which many of today's residents of the BVI live. That a resident noncitizen would be allowed to participate in a national beauty contest despite Miss Universe rules that reject the legitimacy of such participation points to the willing-ness at the local level to conceptualize citizenship in a flexible, transnational mode, at least in some circumstances. Actually, I think that complica-tions such as these are why beauty contests assume such importance in BVI life. Beauty contests are important not because they invite demon-strations that stabilize and normalize experience but because, putting into play the complexities and contradictions of BVI experiences and affilia-tions, they foreclose any such possibility. This was borne out in June 2009, when the contestants for the 2009 Miss BVI competition were announced ("Meet the Beauties"). Of the six contestants for the Miss BVI crown, only one had a BVI surname; the rest had surnames associated with Nevis, St. Kitts, Santo Domingo, Antigua, or Grenada. That the crown was in the end won by a contestant who vigorously laid claim to her status as "a BVIslander, just like all of you" despite her European looks and Santo Domingo parentage, suggests that the BVI sense of subjectivity is informed as much by the sort of global cosmopolitism described by tourism scholar Gavan Titley as by "national" imperatives. This is a global cosmopolitanism marked by "the conscious recognition of the hybrid, the actuality of mediation, an increasingly diverse semiotic environment, and, importantly, abundant resources for imagining identity" (2001: 80).

CULTURAL POLITICS OF CULTURAL PRODUCTS

Considering the magnitude of the symbolic burden that Festival bears, it is hardly surprising that Festival and its events are the focus of intense public debate and political jockeying. A good deal of debate over the quality of any Festival event is based on comparisons that are made by nationals from other Caribbean countries residing in the BVI between BVI Festival and their home country festivals. A major concern of organizers of British Virgin Islands Festival is to put on an event that is both distinctive and high quality; a major dilemma is how to do this in a way that will invite the participation of non–British Virgin Islanders while at the same time will produce a distinctive BVI cultural product. The ability of individuals or groups to assume control over any arena or practice that, like Festival, showcases BVI culture is in large part a matter of access to the places where national culture is produced and enacted: educational institutions, government ministries, media outlets, tourist boards. In the BVI, a legal code that gives BVIslanders preference in all hiring, but particularly for jobs in the civil service, assures that this access is granted to BVIslanders before non-BVIslanders.

From 1953 to 1996, Festival was planned, organized, and run by a committee of private citizens. The Festival Committee of 1990 was made up of British Virgin Islanders from the professional and managerial class, most of whom had worked on the committee for over a decade. As a private organization, Festival Committee received a small grant from the government. The government also subsidized Festival by providing printing facilities, free water, and electric service to Festival Village and, in the case of members who also work in government, by providing office space and telephone access. The appearance of highly placed government officials at opening ceremonies, and as MCs of Festival shows, served to endorse Festival as a national event. Nevertheless, the financial operations of Festival Committee remained closed to public view. Public debate about what Festival should be and who should control it was fairly continuous throughout the 1990 Festival season, as well as in subsequent seasons. People favoring greater government involvement argued that it would mean more money up-front for Festival, and that the finances of Festival would be open to public scrutiny. Others argued that increased government involvement would change little in the way of financial oversight and might preclude the participation of all segments of the community in Festival events. Yet others saw government involvement as essential to having a Festival with a single vision, or a Festival capable of drawing tourists to the BVI during the slow summer season.

In 1998, the woman who chaired the Festival Committee from 1975 to 1981 and whose Heritage Dancers Float has taken first prize in every Festival parade became minister of culture and education. The same year, BVI government made Festival part of that ministry's portfolio, and Festival Village was moved from the open field on which it had been held for decades to the walled recreational grounds across the street. This move occasioned widespread criticism, as I record in my field note account of this event.

[Field notes 7.22.1998] Once again it is very clear that Festival is an occasion on which a lot of additional stuff is loaded. When I first arrived here, in my first interaction, I was asked what I thought about the placement of Festival Village in the Recreation Grounds. I had known, from a phone conversation with L. the previous week, that this was a burning issue, if not the burning issue this Festival season. The reasoning behind the placement of Festival Village in the Recreation Grounds isn't clear to me. I would surmise that it has something to do with making a statement about this being a Festival with a difference (i.e., with a new batch of people on board), or with being able to control the flow of people into festival and therefore being able to charge money to get in. . . . The reasoning behind the objections to the placement of Festival Village is that the Recreation Ground is where the youth practice track and field, and it therefore will be unavailable to them for practice for a crucial three weeks during the height of the competitive season. . . . As well, when Village is dismantled there will be left behind nails and glass from broken bottles, making the subsequent use of the field somewhat risky. All of the acrimony and bitterness expressed as people take up sides is fueled by the fact that this is a highly charged political climate: there will be a national election within the next several months (December? February?), and already people are campaigning. No surprise to anyone, it is K. and H. who have been in the forefront of the opposition to the placement of the Village; it is these same men who went into the Recreation Grounds and pulled out the stakes marking the placement of booths. I picked up most of this information from a conversation with R. and N., and both of them told me—independently of each other—to be careful as I go about with my anthropology business. In all the years that I have worked on Festival and with all of the various controversies, this is the first year that I have been warned to be careful, to take care with whom I speak and what I say. . . . Meanwhile, I proceed with my plans to take new footage of this Festival.

By 2002, noting that "Festival is excellent for tourism," the BVI Tourist Board devoted $20,000 to marketing Festival abroad, "especially in the African American market and to BVIslanders overseas" ("BVI Festival 2002—July 14–August 7th"). A 2003 report establishing policy and planning for public investment in all sectors of BVI society and economy singled out Festival as an event in need of greater oversight and management. This report, "The Public Sector Investment Programme 2003–2007," argued that "the festival fairs, cultural, historical and other related events are very important events for the BVI as such events promotes the economy, through the increase in visitors traveling into the BVI during festival celebration. These events also reflect values and traditions of the BVI giving the BVI population an opportunity to celebrate and be proud of their historical accomplishments." In 2005, the Virgin Islands Festival and Fairs Committee Act made the Festival and Fairs Committee an official British Virgin Islands government statutory body, and just prior to Festival 2008 the minister of culture and education announced plans to hire an officer to give Festival year-round attention. In Trinidad, neoliberal conceptions of Carnival as property resulted in the copyrighting of key Carnival performances and events (Ballinger 2007). Although this is not yet the case of BVI Festival, the marketing of Festival as a tourism product, the focus on Festival as part of the Public Sector Investment Programme, and the formal incorporation of Festival planning and management into a statutory body nonetheless suggest that BVI Festival is also seen as a product, the shape and tenor of which is subject to manipulation and control.

As the demand for a unique BVI culture grows among tourists and BVIslanders alike, Festival responds accordingly, as the following field note excerpt suggests. The excerpt begins after a description of the kinds of pageants that were held throughout the year, including a Mr. Millenium Man pageant, a Caribbean Miss Bold and Beautiful pageant, and the Prince and Princess pageant.

[Field notes 8.6.2000] This year saw Danielle Wheatley winning [the Prince and Princess pageant]. Danielle is a second-generation queen now, for her mother was Miss BVI for 1984. According to everyone I talked to, Danielle won primarily because all of her performances were exactly what the judges were looking for: Her sportswear featured Cricket, her talent featured local BVI crafts. In other words, she highlighted local-ness, and downplayed any reference to styles or traditions outside of the BVI. In this same respect, the Miss BVI pageant HAS undergone some change. While the pageant always showcases local talent (with the requisite dance performance by the BVI Heritage Dancers, background music by a local band—in this case Sensations—and performances by talented youth—in this case a brother and sister each of whom was featured in a pan [steel drum] solo), the references of contestants' performances to local culture or history has been sketchy and uneven. Thus, when Ann Lennard won her crown in 1990, her talent was a lip-synced dance performance of "Hey, Big Spender." The opening dance number for the 1990 show was the Lambada. The opening dance number for the 2000 show on the other hand had the contestants in traditional costume, dancing a more "traditional" dance. Similarly, the fashion modeling component of the 1990 show featured the standard swimsuit, sportswear, business wear, evening gown competitions to be found in international pageants. In 1998 this changed. That was the year that saw the addition of the heritage/history component to the show—it was also the year that Government took over the Festival and that Emancipation was showcased explicitly, both in booth decorations and in a highly organized and well-attended Sunday Morning Well Service sponsored by the local churches. In this component in 2000, contestants compete with costumes that depict an aspect of BVI history or culture: Windmill/Cane Factory, Steele Pan (with carnival dress), Fish skirt, Pea Soup, Moco Jumbie [stilt dancer].

In addition to the changed content in the Miss BVI pageant, Festival 2000 also saw Thursday of Festival week devoted to a "Cultural Fiesta" in the rural seaside village of Carrot Bay on Tortola's northwest coast. By 2008, the Carrot Bay Cultural Fiesta—which features local foods and such "traditional" events as donkey races and wooden boat races—was scheduled to take place for three days, beginning the Thursday of Festival week. Finally, in sharp contrast to 1990, when the ability of the BVI to attract international bands to perform was the mark of a "good" Festival, in 2008 the Festival and Fairs Committee announced its intent to beef up the cultural component of Festival, and to showcase local talent. The chair of the Festival and Fairs Committee pointed out in a newspaper interview that "to some extent we will be cutting back on the international artistes, because I personally feel that we have enough local artistes who are capable of putting on exceptional performances . . . these artistes can hold the crowd and we are giving them the chance" (McPherson 2008: 4).

Responding to this announcement on the Web site of *BVINews*, an online newspaper, a reader affirmed, "The lineup this year is a good start we have to get things local back show the ppl [people] BVI culture. I wouldn't mind some more international artist in too but it good. It's time for us as BVI residents to support our home. If u don't like it stay home. It's our culture and we have to embrace it for the better of this country" (http://www. bvinews.com/main.asp?Search=1&ArticleID=643&SectionID=5&Sub SectionID=47&S=1).

Providing an arena for representing BVI experience, for assessing past and current relations of the BVI to other nations, and for airing positions in debates about future relations and developments, Festival is undoubtedly about constituting a sense of BVI identity, autonomy, and sovereignty. Simultaneously, however, Festival's performances and representations of BVI experience necessarily reflect the constant movement and resettlement of people across national and international borders, the conceptual and legal shifting and reconstituting of borders through time, conflicting citizenship claims, the spaces between shared histories and experiences. As Festival participants and audiences alike negotiate their positions in relation to the representational content of Festival's events, they also have to consider their positions in relation to other positions being taken up. Thus, in addition to working to stabilize a complicated British Virgin Islands present by codifying one particular historical and cultural reality, Festival also unlooses a series of contingent histories and realities to be reflected upon, negotiated, challenged, and contained.

The complexities of constituting identity within what Stuart Hall, in referring to the Caribbean experience, has characterized as "this sense of difference which is not pure 'otherness'" (1990: 229) are seldom attenuated, stabilized, or otherwise resolved by Festival performances, soca songs, or queen shows. Neither are they simply put into play, festival dramas of life's dilemmas, to be put aside when the partying is over. Understood as concrete, albeit protean, aspects of life, fixed and entrenched through intertwined discursive, legal, and material practices, they are also continually strategically engaged, challenged, undone, and re-configured within the context of stabilizing notions of unity and difference, and the shifting positions and possibilities of individuals and the groups they are affiliated with. So too, this account of tourism and nationalism in the BVI moves between the stabilizing effects of ethnographic description, and the desire to keep in play and in tension the multiple meanings residing in peoples' representations, enactments, and contestations of events and ideologies, and the connections and contradictions between these representations and ongoing social, political, and economic developments in the BVI today.

Such a rhetorical positioning is crucial, not just in order to construct an account that accords with local understandings of what is going on and what people are doing, but to underscore the dynamism of the complexities that characterize present BVI experiences. In the next chapter I elucidate these complexities by looking at the lives of four individuals who are involved in producing BVI culture.

CHAPTER 8

Performing Paradise
and Making Culture

The thing about culture in relation to tourism is, what can we do different? What are we about as a country, as a nation? What do we have to offer? Tourists come from where they come from, and they're looking for something that's different. And if we have something that's different, then why not promote it?

(Interview, Director of British Virgin Islands
Tourist Board, July 24, 1998)

Culture is an asset of significance and can be marketed as a unique part of the tourism product. The diversity of Caribbean and other world cultures existing in the BVI can be combined to produce something unique to offer the international visitor and add to our tourism product as part of our history, sociology and entertainment. The cultural elements of our music, food, dance and otherwise ways of life can add significantly to tourist expenditure in our country. This extra contribution may be realised via an integrated programme of cultural, entertainment and tourist activities.

("Towards Sustainable Development" 2.2.2)

IN THE LAST CHAPTER I focused on the ways that Festival's cultural events articulate and put on display political and social issues in the BVI, primary among them issues that arise in the context of the demographic changes resulting from tourism development. In this chapter I look at the multiple positions that people in the BVI occupy as they produce and perform a culture that evokes a sense of who they are, where they have been, and where they are going, even as it satisfies tourist desire for Caribbean paradise. In particular, I consider the experiences of four British Virgin Islanders—Quito Rymer, Elmore Stoutt, Eileene Parsons, and

Jennie Wheatley—although I reference the contributions of others as well. These four individuals have been particularly active in BVI cultural production and performance. In addition to illuminating the relation between tourism development and cultural development in the BVI in the past thirty years, their experiences reveal the negotiations and strategies of BVIslanders as they actively make the world in tourism's imagined paradise.

One of the more notable aspects of tourism development world-wide is that the tourist desire to hear, see, taste, and experience local culture engenders a local preoccupation with culture and heritage (Bruner 2005; Kirshenblatt-Gimblett 1998). Festival is a major showcase for BVI culture. But the places where tourists stay, eat, shop, and congregate are also sites for displaying and performing BVI culture. Tourists staying at the Peter Island Yacht Club and Resort, for example, may be treated to twice-weekly steel pan concerts, sometimes featuring performances by the BVI Heritage Dancers; tourists staying at the Long Bay Beach Resort or dining at the Tamarind Beach Club or at Fat Hog Bob's on Tortola can hear local fungi music performed by the Lashing Dogs, the Sparkplugs, or the Lover Boys; visitors to Leverick Bay on Virgin Gorda or cruise ship passengers shopping at the colorful collection of craft and tee-shirt shops located just down from the cruise ship pier might catch performances of the BVI Moco Jumbie [stilt dancers]; and bareboaters anchoring in Great Harbor on Jost Van Dyke or in Cane Garden Bay on Tortola are treated to the musical renditions of local musicians Foxy Callwood and Quito Rymer, respectively.

Cultural performances such as these can also be seen annually on the Festival stage or in the Festival parade, and many of them were historically part of the fabric of BVI cultural life. Well before the BVI began to develop its tourism economy, for example, musicians playing fungi music (a scratch band kind of music said to originate in the Virgin Islands and also known as *quelbe*) serenaded from house to house at Christmas time. As BVIslands educator and fungi musician Elmore Stoutt recalled, "The men would come around with all their instruments. You had two, three bands serenading each house. And as the men serenaded, they would drink your rum, your liqueur. Sometimes you had special liquor for certain men because you knew what they drank over the years. Sometimes the men would also carry a bag and they would collect drinks, cakes, and some people gave money, too" (interview, July 28, 1992). Monthly "tea meetings" held in various villages, and Harvest Cantatas held in churches were occasions for singing, recitations, and dramatic performances. And the calypso form upon which Foxy Call-wood and Quito Rymer draw traces back to the plantation period and to the call-response form of some African song traditions. As the BVI tourism economy developed, BVIslanders began cultivating these and other cultural forms for consumption by tourists, as well. A 1991 newspaper article about Elmore Stoutt's efforts to revive fungi music traditions makes explicit the connection between cultural revival and tourism development: "Mr. Stoutt wants to see tourists and foreigners coming to the BVI and being entertained with Fungi music: the naturalness of the territory [*sic*]. And at the same time 'our people must see what we produce is good for ourselves and others,' he explains" ("Fungi Music: The Melodious Tradition Needs Greater Support").

A short anecdote provides a sense of the context within which BVI culture is being produced as well as the negotiations and strategies that are involved in its production. A decade and a half before he wrote the song "Paradise," Quito Rymer wrote the song "Tortola," a song that also expresses a yearning for an idealized paradise of "snow white sand and blue green sea." Tourists visiting Quito's Gazebo in Cane Garden Bay consistently request "Tortola" more than they request "Paradise" (Quito Rymer, personal communication); meanwhile, "Father's Land," the song in which Quito confronts the West's desire to "take island in the sun," is hardly ever requested, and then only by locals or the resident anthropologist. Yet "Father's Land" was the first of Quito's many songs to secure a strong position on the region's musical charts. Within the BVI, many white expatriates and some British Virgin Islanders were critical of "Father's Land" when it first played on local radio, taking special exception to Quito's assertion about white people that "being the boss is in their blood" (Quito Rymer, personal communication). Although Quito refused to change this verse, he did insert a musical bridge, with the lines, "come walk with me, talk with me / we can get along / walk with me, talk with me / we will get along." The original version of "Father's Land" can still be heard on the cassette on which it was released. But in performance Quito sings only the revised version, with its conciliatory bridge.

The sorts of complications and contradictions that emerge in this anecdote about Quito Rymer and the songs that he writes and performs are not limited to his experience, or even to the BVI tourism context. Nor can Quito's response to criticism of "Father's Land" be read in simple terms of sell-out, submission, or cultural commodification. On the contrary, as Alexis Celeste Bunten submits with regard to the Tlingit Tour leaders she studied in Sitka, Alaska, "the cross-cultural experience mediated through tourism is much more complex," and cultural producers in tourism contexts are far more self-conscious, critically aware, and resistant than tourism scholarship generally allows (2008: 382). As in BVI tourism, tourists to Alaska carry with them stereotypes and expectations that exoticize and homogenize both the place and the Native people living there, and the success of the tourism industry is dependent upon packaging the cultural product "according to consumers' desires, desires that are informed by specific ideas about what constitutes the value of non-Western culture, art, literature, medicine, and bodies" (2008: 386). The Sitka native tour guides that Bunten studied were conscious of the need to present and perform a self that accorded with "what being Native American looks like, sounds, like and means" (2008: 387). But their performances also drew upon a repertoire of identities. So while the Sitka Native tour guides played to the tourist gaze, they also subverted it, for example, by alluding to different interpretations of Tlingit culture from that provided by guide-books, by making jokes at the tourists' expense, by making reference to their own involvement in a modern world. In fact, Bunten asserts, it is acts of subversion or resistance such as these that balance out the acts of self-exoticization that the Native tour guides performed daily (2008: 389).

"Trying a thing" is a strategy that BVI poet and scholar Patricia Turnbull noted among the tourism workers she interviewed for her Ph.D. dissertation on pedagogy and practice in BVI tourism (2002). Referring to the discursive practices of tourism workers as they "interact with tourists, rail against the system, parody their plight, and celebrate their manipulation of extenuating circumstances" (Turnbull 2006: 101), "trying a thing" includes activities undertaken in the broadest context of BVI tourism. This is a context not just of tourists and the expectations and preconceptions they bring with them but also of BVI residents and local structures of sentiment and value. Thus, for example, while tourist demand has moved performances of BVI culture off the Festival stage and into hotel restaurants, shopping areas, and laid-back beach bars, local response to cultural performances in such settings is often negative, conditioned by local understandings of what constitutes "proper" public behavior. As Patricia Turnbull points out, events like Festival are recognized as special occasions for celebrating a collective identity, but performers of culture outside of this sanctioned space are frequently dismissed as "passive agents of commodi-fication, or 'low' culture entertainers who only 'play' culture to feed the locals' occasional nostalgia for a better past, or the tourists' appetites for a present paradise" (2006: 108). Considered in light of "trying a thing," Quito Rymer's including the conciliatory bridge in the song "Father's Land," while retaining the line "being the boss is in their blood," highlights the complexity and intertwining of influences upon BVI culture producers and performers. It also points to the fraught subject positions of these indi-viduals, as they produce and perform culture for tourists, belongers, and nonbelongers alike.

PERFORMING PARADISE

The interactions that visitors to the BVI have with the people they encounter and the experiences they have in the places they visit determine the nature of their vacation experience. In consideration of the fact that the vacation product that visitors to the BVI are buying is marketed as "Nature's Little Secrets," it is important that these places, people, and experiences provide a sense of what the slogan promises. The invitation to "*Discover* Nature's Little Secrets" in particular promotes the possibility of an experience of an uncomplicated lifestyle with friendly people willing to know and be known by visitors. As I pointed out in chapter 6, this promise is realized in many respects through the interactions that tourists have with iconic locales and personages. But it can also be realized through the experience of contact with a "folk" culture. Local handicrafts and local foods are items that enable tourists to experience intimacy with a "folk" culture through the literal consumption of difference (Ahmed 2000; Sheller 2003), but such items are available on a limited basis in the BVI. On the other hand, throughout the BVI, tourists have numerous opportunities to listen, dance to, and purchase recordings of homegrown music. Foxy Callwood on Jost Van Dyke is one performer of such homegrown music, and we have seen how the persona that he performs contributes to tourists' sense of both being special and being in a special place. Quito Rymer is arguably the most well known and successful of the makers of BVI homegrown music. While his music gives tourists access to a local sensibility, his experience as a singer/songwriter and performer sheds light on the complicated position of the artist in the contemporary BVI.

Still Small and Gentle Is the Voice

"Still small and gentle is the voice of authority" is a line from the lyrics of a song "Congratulations NDP," that was written by Quito Rymer to celebrate the 2003 electoral victory of the National Democratic Party (NDP). The NDP is the newest of BVI political parties. Formed in 1998, the NDP claimed to bring a fresh vision to the BVI, and a government capable of competing on an international political and economic stage. Quito Rymer is a member of the same generation as the NDP founders, and was an early supporter of the party and its policies; he also wrote and performed the song that the party used in its successful 2003 electoral campaign. The line "still small and gentle is the voice of authority" is also an apt descriptor of Quito Rymer himself. The biblical reference of the phrase "still small and gentle is the voice" points to Quito's roots in the Methodist Church, even as it conveys a sense of his mission as an artist and of his presence as a performer. Meanwhile the phrase "of authority" points to Quito's use of his music as a form of social and political commentary. While his fellow BVIslanders likely know him in all of these capacities and more, for most tourists Quito is solely a friendly, welcoming troubadour whose music provides the soundtrack for a vacation in paradise.

In a field note from July 1998, I describe Quito Rymer's appeal. The field note also reveals that even as I write about the complicated and vexed position of the performers and producers of BVI culture, I am also a consumer of that culture and, in writing about it in field notes or in this book, a producer of it as well. Mimi Sheller makes a related point regarding her book, *Consuming the Caribbean*. Locating her book within "the circuit of cultural commodities consumed as 'knowledge' about the Caribbean," she sees her work as being "about 'The Caribbean'—the invention, the fantasy, the idea, the context for my writing" (Sheller 2003: 196, 200).

[**Field notes 7.25.1998**] There are a few things that I carry with me in my daily planner, to remind me of the BVI: a dried out rose that my friend Kenne gave me, a soft many times folded up piece of paper that has the phone numbers of my many contacts in the BVI (my friend Catherine says that you could do the archaeology of my fieldwork just from looking at this paper. I started keeping the paper in 1990 and even though the numbers are now all entered in my computer, I still keep the paper and always refer to it first whenever I have to make a phone call, whether from the States or when I am down there), and a picture of Quito. In the picture he sits on a high stool on the stage of his beach club/bar, leaning on his guitar, a picture of Bob Marley behind him. He is wearing what I think of as his trademark black beret and he is smiling directly into the camera. Catherine took the picture in the summer of 1996, during a video taped interview that I was doing of him. I come across the picture regularly, as I am digging through the pile of other pictures that I carry of my kids, my husband, and other BVI friends, and it always makes me feel just terrific. In part this is because over the years Quito has been a special friend to whom I have turned when I have been lonely, homesick, or simply confused. One summer that I would otherwise be happy to forget he was a rock for me as I worked damage control on a student who was part of a larger group I had with me doing research, and whose behavior threatened to sabotage the project. . . . But in another part, the picture makes me feel so good for the same reason that Quito makes all Western visitors feel so good—his music and manner convey all that is so seductive about the tourist paradise that the BVI is to the tourist: romance, music, a friendly face, exotic experiences. He *is* paradise.

Quito Rymer is the owner of the popular and successful beach bar/restaurant, Quito's Gazebo, and of the Ole Works Inn, the guesthouse that sits directly across the road from the Gazebo. I describe Quito's Gazebo in field notes from 1998.

[**Field notes 7.29.1998**] The first beach bar that you come to when you're coming into Cane Garden Bay from the East, down Soldier's Hill, is Quito's Gazebo. You will know that you are there by the jetty that has been built out into the bay from the rock outcropping across from the Ole Works Inn and the Lighthouse Villas, the guest houses owned by Quito and his sister Malcia, respectively. Before you come to the jetty, as you drive into the village of Cane Garden Bay (or just "the Bay"), the sea is directly to your right, separated from the road by a very narrow stretch of beach. Small fishing dinghies rest upside down and close to the road, under the shade of sea grape trees. To the left small houses with low-walled yards and jalousied windows line the road; most of these houses are plastered concrete, with galvanized hip-roofs but some older wooden houses still remain. Quito's Gazebo and the Ole Works Inn sit on a little rise in the road, just as the road curves to the left, to go right again and around the Bay. The Ole Works Inn is the renovated ruins of an old sugar mill, and has eighteen rooms for rental to tourists. It sits on the side of the road across from the sea. Quito's Gazebo, a wooden structure with a large bar and dance area that opens onto a covered deck, is directly on the beach. It is so close to the sea, in fact, that it has gone through several transformations, the result of being washed away by the ground swells that roll in across the Atlantic from the north every Fall. Quito remembers the most major one of these, that washed the Gazebo away in October of 1991. Quito has written a song in which the chorus goes, "Oh those billows, they're mountain high / Oh those billows. . . ." When he rebuilt the Gazebo, after it had been washed away, the chorus to this song served as a caption to the before and after photos that he epoxy-ed onto the surface of the new bar. In the daytime, the deck is where you want to be. Accessible from both the road side (passing through the bar) and the sea side, one usually come up the steps from the beach in order to sit on the deck, with a cool drink, watching the sea, the kids, the boats, the pelicans, or whatever else happens to be framed in the view. It's quiet on this section of the Bay, the only noise during the day usually being that of people playing in the water, or the motor of an occasional dinghy coming into the jetty from one of the charter yachts. When these dinghies come in during the day, it is to discharge passengers to spend a day on the beach, or to drop off garbage, or to visit Stanley's Swing, or to take a walk to a road in the center of the Bay, just past the Baptist Church, that leads to the Callwood Rum Distillery. Some of these tourists find their way to Quito's, where they sit on the deck and drink in its pure Caribbean flavor. *Paradise* is a word that you hear often from these visitors. At night, Quito's Gazebo becomes simply Quito's, where people go to hear Quito play his music.

Quito Rymer, the author of "Tortola," "Paradise," "Father's Land," as well as dozens of other original songs, was born in Cane Garden Bay in the mid 1950s, and witnessed firsthand its transformation from a small isolated agricultural village on Tortola's northwest coast to the tourist hot-spot that it is today. In addition to being a singer/songwriter and entrepreneur, Quito is an artist. His paintings hang in the lobby of the Ole Works Inn, and the beginnings of one of his murals decorate the outside wall of the Gazebo. In fact, Quito claims that painting was his first love, and attributes this to a white American woman artist who used to vacation in Cane Garden Bay and who taught him to paint when he was a young boy, "to see," as Quito put it to me, "light and shadow, to see colors beyond the flat greens and browns" (interview, July 22, 1993). This ability to see "beyond the flat greens and browns" is also characteristic of the lyrics of the songs that Quito writes, and is arguably a contributing factor to his success as a musician and entrepreneur.

Quito's mother was a preacher in the Methodist Church, and his father, an agriculturalist and sailor, played banjo in a fungi band. Like most boys in his village, Quito looked forward to the Christmas season when the local fungi bands serenaded from house to house and island to island. When he was about twelve years old Quito and his friends took up playing the ukulele and joined in the serenading,

> We couldn't wait until Christmas day. All the boys in the village my age would get up and some could play [the ukelele] and some couldn't. We'd always take the fourth string off, it was too much. Three strings, three strings all the way. Of course we always played every song in the same key. And so we would go around at Christmas time, Boxing Day, to all the neighbors, playing the tunes and we'd get eats and drinks and pennies in our pockets. And, you know, after a while I thought, well, why just only Christmas time, because I like it that much . . . let's get good enough so we can start our own band. So a few of us did, some dropped out. And I kept on practicing. (Interview July 22, 1993)

Quito's mother disapproved of Quito's burgeoning interest in music because, as Quito recalled, "a musician was something like a vagabond." Even Quito's peers didn't see his music or his original songs as anything worthwhile.

The friends who played with you didn't think—if you wrote the song it wasn't a song. It had to be something off the radio for it to be a song. So when I went into the hills to look for the goats, I would sing at the top of my lungs. I think it was back in '76, '77 when I started taking a tape recorder and laying down some of the tunes I had written, and I would play them back to myself to work on them. Change this, change that, to make it sound like a finished song. (Interview, July 22, 1993)

The sense that Quito's music is not as valuable or as authentic as the music from the States or the United Kingdom or even from Jamaica lingers today; for example, Quito and his band are frequently passed over in favor of international bands as headliner acts during Festival. This indifference to Quito and his music is attributable in part to the fact that as a performer Quito is associated with tourism. As we have seen, however much the BVI is dependent upon the tourist dollar, work in tourism is accorded lower status than work in the civil service, for example. The indifference may also reflect a concern with respectability character-istic of colonial societies throughout the Caribbean, and particularly in light of the lower social standing of families from Tortola's northwest coast vis-à-vis the elite families from Road Town. As Quito reflected in consid-ering why as a youth he was passed over for a scholarship, "I wanted to go off to art school. I wanted to be an architect and it was always, I always got passed by . . . back in those days, it was who was a big name . . . my family is not a big name" (interview, October 28, 2003).

Quito Rymer opened the Gazebo in 1981, upon his return to the BVI after several years working in St. Thomas and the continental United States. While abroad, he worked mainly as a waiter and bartender for Rockefeller Resorts. This experience, combined with his desire to have a venue to play his music, was the inspiration for the Gazebo. While abroad he even took business courses in anticipation of opening his own place. Having started a couple of musical groups before leaving the BVI, and having played a few concerts in St. Thomas, Quito returned home deter-mined to go it alone, with his own music. Quito recalled this on two different occasions.

It took me going to Jackson Hole, Wyoming—so many thousands of miles away—to gain a confidence to come back and build this bar and play my music. Because at the time here people did not appreciate one, a solo artist. You had to be a band and you had to be with the "in" thing now, and back then I realized there was people who appreciate just someone entertaining. (Interview, October 28, 2003)

I started my business with the idea in mind that this is what I am going to do. I was going to play my guitar. Set up something, a place where I could play. I always thought, "I'll be honest with myself. If I see people keep walking out the door when I start to sing, I'll give it up." So I started up in my little Gazebo with its sand floor and playing my guitar and a couple of guys would come in and beat on the bottle for rhythm. But you know what? They didn't walk out the door, so I kept on, kept on trying. (Interview, July 22, 1993)

Quito opened his Gazebo just as the BVI bareboat business was taking off. Cane Garden Bay offered a protected anchorage, and Stanley's Welcome Bar had been a favorite stop for bareboaters since it opened in 1971. With its sand floor and local musician, Quito's Gazebo became another tourist favorite. Today Quito's Gazebo is a two-storied stucco building with a large dining area taking up the entire second floor, and is packed with tourists during the season, most of whom come to listen to Quito play his music. As a review of Quito's on a popular travel Web site noted, "Quito's is exactly what you imagine a Tortola vacation to be. Sitting at the beachside bar/restaurant and listening to Quito (sometimes solo and sometimes with his band perform) is awesome . . . the drinks are delicious, and the music is great. This is what an island vacation is all about" (http://www.tripadvisor.com/ShowUserReviews-g147354-d147881-r5325125-Quito_s_Gazebo-Tortola_British_Virgin_Islands.html).

Quito's music spans genres that include reggae, soul, gospel, calypso, rock, and soca. While he covers songs by Jimmy Buffet and Bob Marley, for example, most of the songs that Quito performs are his original compositions. Many of Quito's earliest compositions were gospel and praise songs, reflecting his upbringing in the home of a Methodist preacher; today Quito's songs are as likely to praise Jah Rastafari. Others of Quito's early compositions—like "Tortola," "Papa and Me," "Momma Love," "Calloused Hands," "By the Sea"—are ballads and calypsos about experiences or people from his life, that paint a musical picture of an uncomplicated and special island in the sun. Speaking of "Tortola," for example, Quito recalled that "it was my little homecoming, my little welcome back song to myself. For the first time I think I really admired the beauty and all the special things about the island." But Quito Rymer also acknowledges the appeal of "Tortola" for tourists, "I realize, it's not just my song. It's everybody's song and that's cool. That's really cool because, you know, Tortola's a beautiful place. I know there are other people, other beautiful parts of the world and those who have come here and found peace within themselves and found this to be a home away from home, I'm happy to have them" (interview, October 28, 2003).

Quito recorded these and others of his songs onto cassette tapes—later CDs—and sold them out of his Gazebo. As tourists to the BVI took his music home with them, Quito's fame among BVI visitors spread, and he achieved a degree of celebrity. Many visitors to Quito's Gazebo come already having heard his music; for some of these visitors, "Tortola," "Caribbean Run" (and more recently, "Paradise") serve as what Quito calls "packing songs . . . they pack to them" (interview, October 28, 2003). With their references to local people, places, and events, they also contribute to tourists' sense of being part of a local experience, as illustrated in the following note recording my conversation with some bare boaters at Quito's Gazebo.

[Field notes 7. 21.1998] The people turn out to be from Atlanta, here on a yacht charter vacation. This is the second visit to the BVI for the "captain" and his wife, who had been on a sailing vacation here several years ago; this is the first time in the BVI for the other two couples with them, but already they are making plans for a return visit. The "captain" and his wife tell me that weeks before leaving for their vacation they listened to Quito's *Caribbean Run* CD, "you know, the one with 'Tortola' on it." When they listen to the music at home, it puts them in the Caribbean mood, but "when you're here" (returning to my question about what makes Quito's feel "local") "you're actually in the song." It is this sense of being part of the place, the man concludes, "that makes it so special."

Quito started out playing in the Gazebo every night, but he now limits his solo performances to two nights midweek; on Friday and Saturday nights he plays with his reggae band, The Edge. Likewise, while Quito began as a solo performer singing songs with an island-in-the-sun sensibility, today most of Quito's efforts as an artist are devoted to the music that he plays with The Edge, and many of the songs that he now writes are more political in orientation, influenced by the tenets of Rastafarianism as well as by his involvement in BVI politics. "Iron Strong," for example, is a song that he wrote in the late 1990s. The chorus of "Iron Strong," "I'm iron strong, I'm iron strong / I keep Jah in my vessel, that's why I smile at any storm / you can't keep me down / because I am iron strong" speaks to Quito's experience when he stood for his district's legislative seat in the 1999 elections. As he recalled,

I felt it was time for some change in our country because we have to think about the future and it's not just today and today's dollar, but our children and their future and their children's future and I really could not see any light at the end of the tunnel . . . I was just, you were looking down danger zone, you know, and therefore it didn't matter whether you like it of not, it was the person that did something that changed the course and so I had to rise to the occasion. . . . And so that's where the song "Iron Strong" came of. I just sat and I thought about it and I said, "You know what? I'm gonna be strong, and not just strong. I'm going to be iron strong." (Interview, Quito Rymer, October 28, 2003)

Although Quito Rymer was not successful in his bid for elective office, he remains active in local politics. He was a member of the BVI Tourist Board, he lobbies in behalf of small business owners, he is an advocate for an easier route to BVI citizenship for Caribbean immigrants to the BVI, and he is a long-time supporter of the NDP. Indeed, many attribute the NDP electoral victory in 2003 to the campaign song, a traditional calypso, that Quito Rymer wrote and performed. Speaking about a verse in the song concerning excess government spending—"They spend and they spend like their money couldn't done. / Now they're dipping in the reserves, all fall down"—Quito reflected on the song's impact on older voters in particular.

You know, I've heard from quite a few of the older folks and they have also said to me that, you know, "we heard off and on on the radio what was happening with the money and all that was being spent [by the government of the other party], but we paid no heed to it until we get the CD in our hands and we listen to it and then we started checking out, is this really true?" And so I've had some, quite a few, older people come up to me and say, "You know, that song opened up our eyes," and I'm so glad I could open up some eyes. (Interview, Quito Rymer, October 28, 2003)

Also deeply spiritual, Quito is, much like his preacher mother, someone who seeks to heal and uplift peoples' spirits. As he says of his performances in the Gazebo, "lots of nights I come in to play and my spirit's down, but I can't let anybody see that. My spirit is down . . . that don't mean that yours have to come down. I'm here to lift yours up and you know what the main thing that happens in the process of you trying to lift somebody's spirit? You lift yourself right up" (interview, October 28, 2003). Referring to lyrics from his song "Even," which claim that "we are all flowers in Jah's beautiful garden," Quito elaborates, "it's very simple how we are expected to live . . . I liken us to flowers in a garden, God's garden on earth and we are all His children and we are here for a purpose, to beautify His garden in many different ways. Some of us in our songs, some in our education, some in our art, some in our work, some in just being good inspiration to others" (interview, October 28, 2003). Conceding that "every artist has dreams about selling his songs and hitting the big stage at some time," by his own account, Quito realized "a long time ago, not everybody's gonna be a superstar, not everyone's gonna make millions of dollars." While this means that Quito might never get from his fellow BVIslanders the sort of recognition for his music that he receives from tourists, Quito contends that making money or achieving fame are not the reasons he has kept on singing and performing: "It was for me. I made my music for me and then I realized that it touches other people and it brought comfort to other people. It brought smiles to other people and that was like fuel in my tank. And it still is" (interview, October 28, 2003).

The Virgin Isle Is a Garden

The voice that tourists hear when they listen to Quito Rymer entertain them is the voice of paradise; likewise, when I think of Quito's singing style and demeanor, the phrase "still small and gentle is the voice" seems to fit. Yet as Quito draws his inspiration from multiple life experiences and musical genres, so Quito's voice is a multiplicity of voices. Patricia Turnbull reflected on this in an interview I conducted with her in 2003.

> Quito makes this thing of paradise a much more complex thing than we take it for granted to be . . . [with] the voice of the artist, the voice of the local boy growing up in Cane Garden Bay, the voice of folk, the voice of compassion in a life lived spiritually, the voice of creativity, and most importantly, I think, the voice of a kind of wisdom—a kind of knowledge that unfortunately in this small island we don't often connect to ourselves. (Interview, October 30, 2003)

This paradise that is a "much more complicated thing than we take it for granted to be" is the context within which producers and performers of BVI culture operate, tourists' expectations notwithstanding. Moreover, as Patricia Turnbull intimates in the above interview and as my discussion of Quito's life experiences suggests, while tourists may desire a vocal expression of uncomplicated paradise, local response to the contributions of artists like Quito Rymer is likewise shaped by what people expect or what they want to hear or to know.

Elmore Stoutt is another notable BVI songwriter and performer who for over thirty years performed with his fungi band, The Sparkplugs, for tourists staying at the upscale Long Bay Beach Resort, or dining at Sebastian's Restaurant in Capoon's Bay. The BVI Calypso King in 1966 and 1978, Elmore Stoutt is widely known as "the fungi master" and as the man who reinvigorated the fungi music tradition in the BVI. He is also an educator with forty-six years of experience in schools throughout the BVI, and was the principal of the BVI High School from 1987 to 2005. Upon his retirement from education in 2005, the BVI High School was renamed the Elmore Stoutt High School. Elmore Stoutt was a member of the BVI Legislative Council from 2005 to 2007, and from 2006 to 2007 he served as minister of communications and public works in the NDP government. Elmore Stoutt was born in the Cottage Hospital in Road Town in 1945, and was raised in the village of Long Bay on Tortola by his grandmother, who was also the mother of the late chief minister Hon. H. Lavity Stoutt.

Like Quito Rymer, Elmore Stoutt was drawn as a young boy to the fungi music that he heard being played at weddings, house blessings, and during the Christmas season, and his first instrument was the ukulele. In a 2007 article that he wrote for *Business BVI*, Elmore Stoutt recalled that "when I was a child, the adult men of my community gathered every afternoon under the shade of a tree to play music. They played for leisure; they played as a way to relax. We didn't have television, and there were only a few radios around, so the music had a special flavour that attracted us, the young boys of the village. I spent many afternoons listening to these men play." He went on to say, "I wrote my first fungi songs when I was in primary school, and by the time I was a young man I had joined a fungi band. At that time, fungi music gave you a kind of recognition. It was a way for you to create an identity for yourself, and it caused the older people in the community to know you. On top of that, it gave me a sense of satisfaction and happiness that I could not find anywhere else" (Stoutt 2007: 83–84).

Because fungi music was associated with "dancing, with good times, and with rum" (Stoutt 2007: 84), Elmore Stoutt's involvement with fungi, like Quito Rymer's involvement with calypso and reggae, was not always well received by his fellow BVIslanders. Speaking of a 1962 fungi performance that he organized for his local church, for example, Stoutt recalled that "a lot of people frowned up their faces. Play a ukulele in church? Because ukulele and those instruments are associated with dirty music" (interview, July 28, 1992). In a 2008 interview, he elaborated, "during a Christmas program we had rearranged the church to put the stage across from the altar, and it wasn't anything vulgar. But it was the association of fungi music and fungi players at that time that had a negative implication on your character, and so on, because it seemed that fungi players were looked upon with distaste. So any association with fungi music was hitting the lower class" (interview, October 23, 2008). As a young teacher "moving up the ladder," Elmore Stoutt stopped singing calypso and fungi for several years, because of the negative associations they held, as he explained.

> If you rhyme something on the spot now, people think that's crazy; you know, they laugh, but still they feel that you're idiot, you know, you're a stupid fellow. Not in the way that you're stupid, but in like you're just like comic. They don't see the work and this is why in those years after '66, '67 I didn't compete. . . . It was my time of moving up the ladder as a teacher. You didn't want to be associated with something which people thought was very negative because they didn't like their culture, they saw, they looked back and they see, they saw their culture as something which was degrading. Well, why as a young teacher would I want to be associated with something which was, which other people see as degrading? Especially calypso. (Interview, July 28, 1992)

Even thirty years after his bringing a ukulele into the church, and long after he had resumed performing, Elmore Stoutt's involvement with calypso and fungi music was seen by some BVIslanders as lowering his status as an educator.

> Remember, in this small community, there are a number of people who feel that a teacher—there's still some of them still feels—that a teacher should not be singing calypso, should not be involved in anything like that kind of culture which they look down on. A remark was passed a few weeks ago by a teacher who said she saw me with my school band performing during Spring Concert, and I "even don't feel shame or anything to sing about some of the songs," and so on. So that's the way some people still think. That culture has something which is shamefully attached. (Interview, July 28, 1992)

Fungi bands like the Sparkplugs are conventionally made up of ukuleles, guitars, and small four-string banjos, with a washtub base, a grooved squash (calabash), a conga drum, maracas, and a triangle keeping the rhythm. The name *fungi* comes from a West African word describing a dish made of a mixture of okra, beans, and cornmeal; the fungi music played in the BVI has its roots in the work songs sung by enslaved Africans, but combines rhythms as diverse as the European waltz and two-step and the meringue and mambo from the Spanish-speaking Caribbean (Stoutt 2007: 83). Fungi songs typically take as their topic historic events or people, folk tales, and the like. As Elmore Stoutt characterizes it, fungi music "truly brings out the color, the feeling. It captures the atmosphere around a situation. It's calypso, but fungi is supposed to tell a story, it's supposed to be something extracted from the daily happenings of society" (interview, October 23, 2008). Thus, like the early compositions of Quito Rymer, fungi songs can and do convey a sense of a folk Caribbean from the past. One of Elmore Stoutt's most famous compositions is "Fungi and Fish," a song that extols the virtue of a favorite local food in contrast to "two chicken wing and some greenish thing:"

> One day I came home hungry, guess what me momma left for me.
> One day I came home hungry, guess what me momma left for me.
> Two chicken wing and some greenish thing, a corn beef patty.
> I took up the dish and dash it away.
>
> Come hear me bawlin', fungi and fish (momma bring), fungi and
> fish.
> Fungi and fish, lord, that's my favorite dish.
>
> Mommy I don't want no chicken wing, I tell you I disgust and sick
> o' dem things
> I really don't want no meat, I say the strands they stick in my teeth
> Momma say I gettin' rude just because I wouldn't eat she food
> She complain me to me dad, Daddy came home going on bad
> He said give the boy as he wish, give the young fella fungi and fish
>
> Come hear me bawling, fungi and fish (momma bring), fungi and
> fish
> Fungi and fish, lord, that's my favorite dish.

Elmore Stoutt won the 1966 BVI Calypso King title with "Fungi and Fish," and the song was a crowd favorite when Elmore Stoutt and the Sparkplugs performed it at the regionwide Carifesta exposition in Trinidad and Tobago in 1992. Especially in light of the song's local and regional allure, it is notable that "Fungi and Fish" was composed in response to a tourist's desire for "something local, real local," as Elmore Stoutt recalled.

> Once the project [Long Bay Hotel] got going there was a little fungi band that my cousin Zephaniah Stoutt had and we got playing at the hotel at the dining room. There was a lady [from America] who was one of the first guests and she used to pay me to sing for her. She was

at one of the cottages—Long Bay Hotel was like a family setting. There were many, many things Caribbean, but they wanted something local, real local. That is when I composed "Fungi and Fish," on the spot. I went later to the calypso competition that year and won the contest. (Interview, October 23, 2008)

Many of the other songs that Elmore Stoutt performs are, like "Fungi and Fish," "real local," taking as their topics events and people from BVI history. For example, "Ella Gift" recounts the story of the woman who during Prohibition smuggled rum from the BVI to St. Thomas in her pantalettes; "Louie Louie Loose Yo Mule" is about the young man who traveled to St. Thomas in the 1930s for work and the ill effect this had on his courting of a young BVI woman; "Captain What's Your Cargo" recreates the work songs that accompanied the cutting of a foundation, when "we would bring together all the strong bodied men with their hand tools to dig down a foundation . . . during a moonlit night" (Stoutt 2000). While these songs take visitors on a musical excursion of a pretourism BVI, others of the songs that Elmore Stoutt writes and performs take as their topic the beauty of the BVI, and center on the tourist experience. Demonstrating a knowledge of modern life and tourist expectations, such fungi songs tend to complicate images of the BVI as untouched, premodern paradise. "Welcome to the BVI," for example, enjoins tourists to "forget Hussein in the Arab Land / And try to enjoy my virgin sand." The chorus to "The Virgin Isles Is a Garden" extols the beauty of "the views from the hilltop, the white sands down on the shore" that "invite the tourist to stay here forevermore." Meanwhile the verses to "The Virgin Isles Is a Garden" demonstrate a keen eye for tourist desire and behavior.

> A lady from America, she came to reside right on Tortola
> She say America is too cold and how it makes she feel so old
> But as she reached my island of sun, she say "Oh mi boy, I feeling
>   so young."

> A couple came for the Festival, they say they ain't going back at all
> They say they done with them kind of place where everybody has
>   a long sulky face
> And they stayed in the Virgin Isles, where everybody wearing a
>   smile.

Indeed, in speaking about his song "The Virgin Isles Is a Garden," Elmore Stoutt acknowledged its self-conscious construction of an island that would satisfy tourist desire: "my song really portrays that we want to have the island in a way where when you come you want to be enticed to come again and again and again. . . . Tourists want to see things cultural, they want to see things natural, they want to see things, you know, which is traditional. . . . I think those are elements that would cause people to want to come back" (interview, July 29, 1993).

When I first saw Elmore Stoutt and the Sparkplugs perform in 1990, I was aware that Elmore Stoutt was the principal of the BVI High School, having met with him in his office there. When I watched him perform, I was captivated by what I took to be an "authentic" bit of BVI culture, but I was also struck by what I thought of as an incongruity between the man performing a stereotypically friendly and "folk" Caribbean, and the man who was charged with educating youth for a future in a global economy. In hindsight, my sense of a disjunction between his two roles seems little different than the teacher's response to Elmore Stoutt's performance in the 1992 Spring Concert that saw culture as having "something which is shamefully attached." In fact, Elmore Stoutt sees a direct connection between his role as a teacher and his role as an entertainer, using fungi music to teach tourists about the BVI and using performance in the class-room to get a point across.

> When people come here they look for something typical of the community and that is what fungi music is. That's how I got into entertaining. I wanted people to come here and experience something cultural from here. As a young teacher it was important that what I put forward or put forth had a lasting effect on people. And you got to be able to switch. There is the formal you and the informal. As an enter-tainer you got to bring people into you. Entertaining is like teaching, you know. As a teacher you got to bring people along with you. If you lose the class, the teaching is over. (Interview, October 23, 2008)

Due largely to the efforts of Elmore Stoutt, fungi music is today esteemed as a uniquely Virgin Islands cultural form. Fungi music is a co-curricular activity in the high school, the annual high school Spring Concert regularly includes fungi music selections, and children throughout the BVI learn fungi in primary school summer programs. These develop-ments are in keeping with Elmore Stoutt's overarching commitment to pass cultural practices "from long time" on to subsequent generations, to "show the children that a certain people at a certain time did it this way. What caused us to move. We have developed financially, technologically. We have been able to purchase things that are more modern. But this doesn't mean that we forget our culture or despise our culture, but you expose the children from here, and from other islands to the ways people did things a long time ago, so they could see how much time it took" (interview, October 23, 2008).

Since retiring from teaching and politics, Elmore Stoutt has stopped performing with The Sparkplugs, save at local weddings or small concerts. But he continues to develop ideas for projects that will bring young people together with older people, believing that "someone needs to harness the youth from each village and bring them in with the older people and the older people could tell their story. If it is a fishing man, he could tell how he did it. If it is a country woman who would bake bread and carry it to market on her head, she would tell her story" (interview, October 23, 2008). When I asked him how he defined culture, Elmore Stoutt replied that "culture is actually the way you are taught to think. It has to do with your belief, with what you do and how you do it" (field video, July 23, 1995). Elmore Stoutt also contends that "culture is not static, it is only relevant to the people and the time of that era. People who have come to this country and have contributed much to our growth—whether it is economically, socially, educationally, spiritually—so I come to love your [pointing to me] corn chowder, and I learn to cook it" (interview, October 23, 2008).

In fact, Elmore Stoutt sees fungi music as incarnating his vision of culture as something that is "always moving, a little integration here, a little integration there" (interview, July 28, 1992). A posting about Elmore Stoutt on the Elmore Stoutt High School Web site reiterates, "Stoutt, who plays guitar, ukulele, and sings . . . cites the dominant African influence in the drums, and the BVI's 300 years of British and European engagement evidenced in the waltz and swing two-step. Then there is input from Santo Domingo and Puerto Rico, which add elements of merenge and mambo to the music. 'It's people in progress. Nothing is static,' Stoutt observes with joy, breaking into song to illustrate this massive cultural cook-up" (http://elmorestoutthighschoolparentsblog.blogspot.com/2008_10_01_archive.html).

Performing and Producing Heritage

As I pointed out in chapter 3, the BVI that tourists travel to today is a mapped and historical place. Upon arriving at the airport in Beef Island, tourists are greeted by dozens of brochures inviting them to visit sites such as the Old Government House and Museum, the Church of the African Location, the Sugar Mill Ruins at Mount Healthy, the Copper Mine in Virgin Gorda, the Callwood Rum Distillery in Cane Garden Bay. Meanwhile, cruise-ship visitors on a tour of the island are taken past the Great Wall, where they see murals painted by local artists that depict key events, activities, and personages from the BVI past. Among the activities and events pictured on the Great Wall are: cane cutting, loading sand, walking to market, boiling sugar, making coal, feeding the fowls, terracing land, preparing crabs and rice, racing donkeys, and fungi musicians going from house to house on Boxing Day. An article on BVI culture that appears in a book put out by the BVI Chamber of Commerce and Hotel Association explains that "The Great Wall, or wall mirror, seeks to summarize some of the cultural history of the BVI. Perched on the Ridge Road in the Fahie Hill area, the traveler comes face to face with aspects of life in the Virgin Islands as early as the 1950s" (Wheatley 2004: 52).

Taking center stage on The Great Wall is a large mural captioned "Bamboshay Time" that shows a group of dancers, the men in white pants and shirts with red sashes, and the women in white skirts and ruffled petticoats, with red peasant-style blouses, trimmed in white ruffles. One of the women wears a kerchief, two wear hats, and one has a flower tucked behind her ear; all the dancers are framed by palm trees, with islands and the sea in the background. In the context of the other murals on the Great Wall, which depict practices, clothing, house styles, and even transportation systems from earlier times, "Bamboshay Time" seems to be yet one more graphical depiction of a recovered memory from long ago. In fact, "Bamboshay Time" is a fairly indexical representation of a contemporary dance troupe, the BVI Heritage Dancers. The mural even showcases its founding member, Eileene Parsons, whose likeness appears in the foreground at the far left of the mural, wearing the hat and sunglasses that anyone familiar with the Heritage Dancers or with Eileene Parsons would recognize as her signature look. Painted by the same Quito Rymer who wrote "Paradise," "Tortola," and "Father's Land," this mural that is a rendering of a contemporary dance troupe but appears in the middle of a historical panorama painted for tourists points to a sense of culture that is simultaneously celebratory and tactical. As the note below illustrates, the production of this particular piece of BVI cultural history culture is a process informed by contemporary desire and historical memory, and supported by individual commitment and creativity, and the resources of the BVI state.

[Field notes 6.13.2008]. Ms. P. was . . . the motivation behind the Great Wall, which was painted in 2001–2002. "Legislator Ethlyn Smith had the wall put up, and I don't like to see bare walls. As a child in St. Thomas I would go to the Post Office at Emancipation Gardens and they had two murals there, one of them was of Tortola sloops offloading livestock and provisions. And I used to go in as a child of ten, twelve years of age, and just stare at the murals. So when the government put up this wall on the Ridge Road, all along where the safaris take tourists to see the vistas, I started pushing for a mural wall." She contacted then Speaker of the House Reuben Vanterpool, who is also a

8.1. The Great Wall mural of Bamboshay time. Note artist rendition of Eileene Parsons in foreground. Photo by author.

well-known artist, and in a short while they had worked out what the panels should be. They then contacted some other artists: Quito Rymer, Cecil Turnbull, Thor Downing, Garth Hewlett, Pearl Friday. And the wall was painted. Now she has set her sights on the wall that surrounds the A. O. Shirley Recreation Grounds. "Only this wall would commemorate all the great BVI athletes."

BVI Heritage Dancers

Asked to name the person whom they associate with BVI culture, many British Virgin Islanders "call the name" of Eileene Parsons, or "Ms. P.," as she is also known. The impetus behind the painting of the Great Wall, Ms. P. has been the driving force behind everything from the Miss BVI Beauty Pageant to the BVI Softball League. One of the first two women to be elected to the BVI Legislative Council (in 1995), the first woman to be a minister of government, the first woman to hold the position of deputy chief minister, a former minister of health, education, and welfare, a former director of tourism (and originator of the "Yes We Are Different!" slogan), a former chairperson of the BVI Festival Committee, and a former secretary general of the BVI Olympic Committee (O'Neal 2001: 128), by her own account, the accomplishment of which Eileene Parsons is most proud is the BVI Heritage Dancers. This dance troupe, which she founded in 1979, performs at many official events, from Festival to the opening of new government buildings. The Heritage Dancers are also regularly called upon to represent the BVI at regional cultural competitions as well as at its tourist boards in the United States and Europe. In a 2008 conversation with me at her home on Tortola, Eileene Parsons remembered how the Heritage Dancers came into being.

[Field notes 6.13.2008] "I returned home in 1974, to accept a job with the Tourist Board, and it bothered me that there was nothing cultural here; it was a cultural desert. So in 1975, not being able even to carry a tune, I founded a group called the community singers. We met in my house around my little piano, and then Mr. Wheatley got us the school band room for our rehearsals. After this, in 1979, I said to myself, 'I believe I could form a dance group.' I sent out 50 letters, 25 to men and 25 to women. Elihu Rymer gave us permission to use Prospect [Reef Hotel], and we met there on March 17, 1979." She had a record player, and a record of the music of Jamsie and the Happy Seven, a fungi band from St. Croix. She winnowed the group down to 17 couples, and she would bring Mongo Niles from St. Thomas over to help them learn dances. "He came with Alicia Saddler, and I would pay his way, put him up at Sea View [Hotel], where Maria gave me a reasonable rate. By 1984, I became Cultural Officer, and Mr. Wheatley, who was the Chief Educational Officer, sent me to the Jamaica School of Dance for six weeks in the summer of 1984, and for six weeks again the next summer, too."

In 1986, the manager of the Peter Island Resort approached Ms. P. about having the troupe come over to Peter Island Resort once a week to perform. She demurred, saying they weren't a professional group. But he offered to pay them $450 a performance, to feed them and give them whatever they wanted to drink. "So we would go over there, and he would have a wonderful meal for us, and anything we wanted to drink, and then at 8:30 we would go in and perform for an hour, and then afterwards, have more to drink." Every year after that, the Heritage Dancers would "keep a concert." "We've been very fortunate that they [government] have used us as tourism ambassadors. We have danced in San Francisco, New York, Germany, and also at Carifesta. I have had more enjoyment out of all the things we do—from sewing the costumes to making up the dances. The years of enjoyment! I've had a ball. And you know, every church in this place has a dance group. Sometimes its just little children throwing their hands around so, but it is a dance group. They should give me a knighthood for it!" (I couldn't agree more).

I asked her about the music, recalling that when she and I first met in 1990, she told me they would take some music from somewhere else, choreograph a quadrille to it, call it something like Night at Peter Island, "and it would be ours." She concurred, and elaborated: "We had a dance called

Bellvue Mamselle that we put to some music from St Thomas. Some times we would take music we learned as children, like Brown Girl in the Ring, and make it a dance. But our crowning piece is our Festival float. I like to say we have had 18 years of Festival floats and 18 first prizes, not just for float but for best cultural as well."

The BVI Heritage Dancers perform in costumes sewn by Eileene Parsons and meant to represent traditional dress. Likewise, the float on which the BVI Heritage Dancers perform during Festival parade always has plenty of salt fish, red peas soup "with a lot of pig tail," and *ground provisions*—sweet potato, tania, green bananas—to serve up and hand out to Festival goers, in keeping with the troupe's role of keeping "tradition" alive. But, as we see in Eileene Parson's descriptions of her creative process, the dances performed by the BVI Heritage Dancers tend to be an ad hoc mixture: of European, Cuban, Dominican, and Jamaican dances and regional music with "local" names attached. As is the case of the life experience of Eileene Parsons herself, the culture performed by the BVI Heritage Dancers is forged in the context of the particularities of BVI historical experience, tourism development, and growing nationalist sentiment.

Eileene Parsons was born Eileen Lucia Stevens in the early 1930s in Cooten Bay, an agricultural village in the hills above and to the east of Road Town, on Tortola. Her mother and grandmother were both agriculturalists, and "at the age of one year and one day" she was fostered to an aunt. Eileene Parson's early years were spent in the circle of family and village. In an interview with British Virgin Islander and scholar Eugenia O'Neal, Eileene Parsons recalled her experience as a flower girl at a wedding in the early 1940s as a series of visits and feasts between villages and families, giving special attention to the renown of the women who prepared the wedding feast.

> People would give things like flour and family would save your goat and pigs and calf because it was days of feasting. . . . In those days the top-level cooks were this lady at Fort Hill, Miss Emma Fahie, my great-aunt Mamselle, Catherine Malone, my grandmother, a lady who was living by the burial ground, Miss Kate. They were the top-notch cooks of the day and the cake-makers. They would go from village to village. They would be there with their big aprons, they cooked in kerosene tins. The cakes were baked in brick ovens. This cooking would happen in the different villages and people would send the stuff to the family. (Eileene Parsons, quoted in O'Neal 2001: 70)

As this interview makes clear, Eileene Parsons has a prodigious memory, and in particular for the names and families of individuals who were particularly good at, for example, cooking cakes, making fishnets, singing songs, telling stories, healing wounds, plaiting straw—all activities that she associates with the BVI heritage and tradition from which she comes and which she is actively engaged in preserving. Moreover, as Eugenia O'Neal aptly points out, during the period that Eileene Parsons recalls in this interview, events such as weddings were important occasions for reaffirming ties and encouraging social homogeneity but also "for reinforcing family pride and family identity . . . [and] family pride translated into community pride" (2001: 70). Particularly in light of the connection between cultural performance and community recognition that O'Neal documents, it is hardly surprising that Eileene Parsons, and indeed many other BVIslanders, make a connection between the practices of "long time" (long ago) and national pride. Elmore Stoutt made a similar connection between cultural practices and national pride in an interview that I conducted with him in 1993.

> Through culture, you develop a sense of pride for nation. What is culture is what we actually are. The way we do a particular thing makes us a particular type of people. The Caribs and the Arawaks, they were known for the type of huts they built, the type of canoes and other art that they did, and they were identified by these artifacts. The way we bake a coconut bread or we cook a man soup is typical to the Virgin Islands, and these are what make you a Virgin Islander as a matter of fact. Not just Tortola being a Virgin Island or Anegada, but the norms, the morals, the values, everything which were traditional to the indigenous set of people. (Interview July 29, 1993)

When she was between nine and ten years old, Eileene Parsons left Tortola for St. Thomas, where her aunt had secured steady employment. While the move to St. Thomas also afforded greater educational opportunities, Eileene Parsons recalls that although she "left in second standard, because of the grounding I received here [Tortola] in the Methodist school, I was put into the fourth grade, which is a testimony to the solid grounding we got from teachers who were all but children themselves" (interview, June 13, 2008). Throughout her childhood and teen years, Ms. Parsons lived in St. Thomas, returning to Tortola during the summer months. As an adult, Eileene Parsons also spent time at school in Puerto Rico, learning sewing, and at Oswego State Teacher's College in New York, for teacher training. Undoubtedly these experiences broadened her perspective and gave her the skills and knowledge that enabled her to contribute as she has.

We see the influence of Eileene Parsons's time away from the BVI on the development of the BVI Heritage Dancers when she prefaces her discussion of the origins of the dance troupe with the observation that "there was nothing cultural here; it was a cultural desert." Eileene Parsons recalls her years away from Tortola with some ambivalence. In St. Thomas she was always the "Tolian, from the country," and in the States an outsider, as well. Even when she returned to Tortola for visits she was out of place, a country girl with education and experiences that exceeded her family's social position as agriculturalists. She recalled, for example, being more outgoing and having more formal education than her peers, and "when I was placed on the Library Services Committee, people thought that Norwell Harrigan had lost his marbles. But he knew what I could do" (interview, June 13, 2008). I made note of this ambivalence, following an interview with Eileene Parsons in 1992.

[Field notes 7.15.1992] As usual, Ms. Parsons is completely voluble and forthcoming. What I had not realized, and did from the interview, is that she had been director of tourism from 1974 to 1981 and that it was she who originated the slogan, "Yes We Are Different." Of course, this is not surprising, given her centrality to so much that has gone on in the past fifteen years, as well as given the beauty of the BVI. But when one considers especially the fact that as a young girl from the country she was fostered to her aunt, who then took her to live in St. Thomas, and that she was educated in St. Thomas but always experienced a pull toward home, the romanticization of the BVI as different from the place where she never felt at home is even more interesting. Also interesting in another regard is the way she casts her initial move into the position [director of tourism] that enabled her to be the framer and articulator of a national image. In speaking of that moment, she recounted it with great excitement, and talked about being stopped on the street all the time and congratulated—"the girl from up country who received an education." She contrasts this exceptional fact with the accepted practice of the elite families from Road Town sending their children to Antigua for education—something that was possible because of their superior social and economic standing. In contrast, her feat assumes something of the miraculous about it. Although the scholarship that first enabled her to go to school in Puerto Rico and later in the States was every much a part of the colonial structure as the entrenched local social structure into which she was unable to break, in speaking of herself as "from the country" (in contrast to the Road Town elite) her ascendancy assumes the quality of an origin tale, her authenticity grounded in the countryside and traditions of the country people.

Virgin Islands Studies

In his discussion of the link between folk culture and national identity, Robert Foster notes that "folklore often conjures up images of rural life and the peasantry to evoke a timeless and natural connection of 'the people' to the land," and in this way naturalizes citizenship in the nation (1991: 241). The tourism development that propelled the BVI economy toward a 2008 Gross Domestic Product of one billion dollars also contributed toward a sense of nation of "own kind" by providing Western consumers eager for local cultural products. Likewise, the burgeoning of the BVI population by nationals from other Caribbean countries, drawn to work in the tourism economy, induced a protectionist response and abetted efforts to identify and preserve practices, histories, foods, and forms considered unique to the BVI experience. We see this response in a speech delivered by Eileene Parsons on the anniversary of the reading of the Emancipation Proclamation of August 1, 1834: "We have to know and respect our traditions. We have to be willing to stand up and speak out for those traditions that we inherited. We have to be willing to make efforts to preserve those traditions wherever possible and be willing to defend our way of life against the daily onslaught of outside influences" (Parsons 2008). In this latter respect in particular, cultural productions like the BVI Heritage Dancers or BVI Festival are like the Jamaican national cultures described by Deborah Thomas (2004, 2002). Sites of anticolonial struggle and emerging "hand in hand with the development of political nationalisms," they are "simultaneously processes of celebration and containment" (Thomas 2002: 512).

In her capacity as a director of tourism, culture officer, minister of health, education, and welfare, and chairperson of the Festival Committee, Eileene Parsons was undoubtedly positioned to influence the way in which BVI national culture developed. But she was not alone or unique in her sentiments and efforts. Countless British Virgin Islanders have had a hand in producing BVI culture through their poetry, art, music, crafts, and vision and are part of a long-standing tradition of creative expression in the Caribbean. Like the original musical compositions of Quito Rymer and Elmore Stoutt, many of the creative expressions of British Virgin Islanders take the form of tributes to BVI nature, practices, or people. We see this in the poem "Virgin Beauty," written by British Virgin Islander Jennie Wheatley. Calling out the names of all the islands making up the BVI as the rising sun strikes them, the poem expresses a sense of awe similar to that found in many tourism publications. But the last stanza, which has Norman Island whispering to neighboring islands, moderates the awe and situates the appreciation of the beauty that it extols within a local gaze:

It softly whispers
To Deadman's chest
"Are St. John and the rest
up and around?"
What of Tortola? Anegada?
Jost Van Dyke?
They are awake;
Their people ready to face
The grim realities of the day
Yet conscious ever of the beauties
And every morning since,
When turtle doves call
From east to west
Along the mountain range,
Echoing to town and village—
A new day has begun.
Rise and Shine.
—Jennie Wheatley 1982

Jennie Wheatley is a writer, collector, storyteller, and retired teacher who in 1993 was awarded the Most Excellent Order of the British Empire (M.B.E.), in recognition of her contribution to the education and culture of the BVI. Born in the East End of Tortola and with family ties to Anegada, she did her early training at Teacher's College in Antigua, received her bachelor's degrees in English and education from Mount Allison University in Brunswick, Canada, and did advanced training at the University of Leeds in Britain. During her career as an educator, Jennie Wheatley taught in most of the primary schools on Tortola, and taught English and was an assistant principal at the BVI High School. She counts among her former students taxi drivers, teachers, surgeons, songwriters, poets, lawyers, politicians, and scholars, and wherever she goes in the BVI, and even in St. Thomas, she is likely to be hailed as "Teacher Jennie."

It is Jennie Wheatley who is most commonly called upon to give a historical or cultural overview at ceremonies commemorating BVI individuals or events, as in the remarks that she delivered at the Sunday Morning Well Emancipation Ceremony in 1998 that Kenne Hodge and I documented in our second ethnographic video, *Big Festival in a Small Place* (Cohen and Hodge 1998).

What we remember most about slavery are its cruelty and its inhuman acts. People of this generation now sit in the shade of a great tree. They can own their land, get their deeds, go to the bank, and build their houses. On this, our celebration time, let us share with each other the gifts that *we* have. And above all, let us be grateful to almighty God for the freedom which we have to worship Him. And to build up a home that our ancestors have passed on to us.

Jennie Wheatley is also a regular visitor in the homes of older BVIslanders, listening to their stories, encouraging them in handicrafts such as straw plaiting or securing details on traditional practices such as baking bread in a charcoal fire. As she put it to me in an interview on June 16, 2008, "I like to discover how things were done earlier on." It is in combining her dedication to education with her interest in "how things were done earlier on" that Jennie Wheatley makes her singular contribution to BVI culture.

While at the BVI High School, Jennie Wheatley worked with its staff and students gathering Virgin Islands proverbs, sayings, and bits of wisdom; these were published in 1974 as the collection *Bohog Put in Gol' Teet'* (Wheatley 1974). In the mid 1970s, inspired by the proverb project and looking for something that would capture the interest of her more recalcitrant readers, Jennie Wheatley wrote a series of stories about the adventures of a young Caribbean boy, Boysie. Gathered into the collection *Boysie and the Genips* (Wheatley 1984) these stories were published by UNESCO in 1984. *Boysie and the Genips* was followed in 1991 by more Boysie stories, in the collection *Pass It On!: A Treasury of Virgin Islands Tales* (Wheatley 1991). Subsequent to the publication of *Boysie and the Genips* and *Pass It On!* Jenny Wheatley published four children's books, *Timmy Turtle Runs Away* (2005a), *Danielle's Trunk* (2005b), *Arianna Likes to Read* (2005c), and *Who Is the Best in the Garden?* (2006). All of the stories in these books are based in the Virgin Islands, and all of them are written with the intention of encouraging young children to read. In 2009 Jennie Wheatley published a collection of her poetry, *Along the Road*; ever the educator, she published this book with the hope that her readers "may feel challenged to write down their own thoughts" (2009: xii).

One of Jennie Wheatley's most recent projects is the Virgin Islands Studies Program, which was established in 1999 as one of the academic divisions of the H. Lavity Stoutt Community College (HLSCC). HLSCC course offerings tend to concentrate on skill and knowledge areas that will enable students to go on to careers in business, tourism, education, marine studies, or to transfer to a four-year BA program at another institution. The Virgin Islands Studies Program augments a largely preprofessional curriculum with courses in anthropology, field research methods, and Virgin Islands history and culture. Archaeological excavations carried out under the auspices of the Virgin Islands Studies Program enabled the development of historical sites that are featured in tourism brochures, and it is the Virgin Islands Studies Program course on Virgin Islands history that people wishing to become belongers must take, as a requirement for BVI citizenship. The HLSCC itself was founded in 1989, the inspiration of the late chief minister H. Lavity Stoutt. Lavity Stoutt's motto was "A country without vision will perish," and he saw the founding of an institution of tertiary education in the BVI as crucial to the development of the BVI people, as a 2008 online news article reported.

> Stoutt will be remembered for much, but his one quote from the Bible has become a mainstay of Virgin Islands politics and local community development: "A country without vision will perish. I have a vision for my country and people. And I thank God I live to see my vision, large schools, a college, boats and large buildings," the late Stoutt had said. "Best of all a college that my people will meet world wide standards for education, because we are in a competition education-wise on that level. I hope someday my people will enjoy the benefits I have provided for them. I love my people, and my country I have at heart." (Wilkins 2008)

All of Jennie Wheatley's projects reflect her commitment to local education and to encouraging in young Virgin Islanders a passion similar to the one she has for history and culture. She spoke to this commitment in the preface to *Pass It On!*

> *Pass It On!* consists of incidents that took place during my early years and stories that were handed down to me via the Oral Tradition. I have tried to trim, reshape, and decorate them in such a way that they would appeal to young readers.... Above all, the writings set out to prove that in the Virgin Islands there are subjects to write about. To a great extent the inspiration for this first series came after reading some long hidden poems by Alphaeus Osario Norman (1885–1942) of Anegada.... I felt that if Norman (writing in the Victorian age when Thomas Hardy was still alive) could produce such outstanding poetry, then every present-day Virgin Islander blessed with a wider formal education, more resource material and a recognized body of Caribbean literature, ought to make some literary contribution, no matter how small. (Wheatley 1991)

The link that Jennie Wheatley makes in this preface between Alphaeus Osario Norman *writing in the Victorian age* and the potential for "any present-day Virgin Islander . . . to make some literary contribution, no matter how small," points to the complicated positions of BVIslanders from the generation of which Jennie Wheatley, Eileene Parsons, and H. Lavity Stoutt in particular are representative. Born in a colonial BVI, they came of age during the period that the BVI was establishing the political and economic bases for its emergence as an independent nation. While steeped in the manners, laws, and education that are the legacy of British colonial rule (every British Virgin Islander over the age of sixty whom I know can recite Wordsworth's poem, "Daffodils," and H. Lavity Stoutt was an avid student of Winston Churchill's diction), their adult lives are marked by activities that eschew the colonial experience by establishing the BVI as a sovereign national and cultural entity. For Eileene Parsons, Elmore Stoutt, and Jennie Wheatley, this is a process that entails the recuperation of a BVI "folk" culture; for H. Lavity Stoutt it was a process that entailed building an educational institution that would legitimate the BVI as fully modern and "capable of meeting worldwide standards."

In either case, much like the development of the creole nationalism of preindependence Jamaica that Deborah Thomas documents, the songs, dances, and stories that establish a BVI people with a shared and unique folk tradition and the institution of higher learning that points to a future of unlimited potential stand as proof of the BVI's cultural and political maturity, and model "a particular vision of their own cultural distinctiveness" (Thomas 2002: 534). Additionally, to the extent that fungi songs, Quito's compositions, and the collected stories of Jennie Wheatley also evoke a moral ethos or essence, this period of cultural production in the BVI is analogous to the period of Jamaican creole multiracial nationalism that Deborah Thomas claims was characterized by an "emphasis on the 'folk,' on defining what was indigenous," and by the hope that "this reconstituted past, in publicly recognizing the contributions of Africans and their descendants to the historical and cultural development of the Jamaican nation, would provide moral codes for its future" (2002: 534).

Of course, in addition to their similarities, the individuals treated here bring to the project of cultural production life experiences that are different in important respects. For example, the association of Eileene Parsons and Quito Rymer with "the country," and all that this association meant with regard to their social standing, is a common thread between them, as are their experiences living and working away from Tortola. Meanwhile, Eileene Parsons, H. Lavity Stoutt, and Jennie Wheatley, being fairly close generationally, have historical experiences of the BVI different from those of Quito Rymer, or even those of Elmore Stoutt, who stands somewhat between, generationally. Likewise, while Elmore Stoutt and Quito Rymer endured similar negative responses to their association with tourism and

as performers, the trajectories of their lives as an educator and an entrepreneur, respectively, have given them different perspectives, their shared
involvement with the National Democratic Party notwithstanding. These
differences and similarities among British Virgin Islanders are seldom seen
by or revealed to BVI tourists, although they, like the multiple and varied
experiences of people living and working in the BVI, animate life in the
"paradise" that tourists visit. Likewise, tourism has transformed the BVI
socially and economically, and continues to shape the way that British
Virgin Islanders understand themselves and their place in a larger world.
Even as the BVI moves closer toward political independence, its sense of
itself as a nation is difficult to separate from its sense of itself as a prime
tourist destination. I thus turn, finally, to the relation between tourism
development and the forging of an identity as an independent nation.

Conclusion

Technically, It's a Country

In this conclusion I consider what is in store for the British Virgin Islands as a tourist destination, as a major center for international financial services, and as a country. As I complete this book, the BVI is experiencing the impact of a global economic downturn in both its tourism and its financial services sectors. A 2008 first quarter increase in visitors by 14.6 percent over 2007 numbers was heralded in a Tourist Board press release, "British Virgin Islands Tourism Sector Starts 2008 on Positive Note"; but by the first quarter of 2009, the BVI Tourist Board chairman reported that "while most of the Caribbean reported 30–50 percent decreases in their tourism sectors, the VI only took a 15–30 percent hit" (quoted in O'Connor 2009a: 20). While the BVI may take some comfort from this comparison with other Caribbean countries, as the political relationship between the United States and Cuba thaws, the terrain on which the BVI competes for tourists to the Caribbean can be expected to change (Henthorne and Miller 2003; Miller et al. 2008). Additionally, the BVI Tourist Board chairman noted that a decline in the number of people traveling and the growth of tourism to destinations such as Dubai, China, and the Seychelles, "some of which offer a higher quality product, higher level of service, better cuisine and lower prices," also pose challenges to the BVI tourism sector ("Tourist Board Chairman Addresses New Rotary Club" 2009).

The BVI financial services sector sustained correspondingly great losses. Although there are more companies registered in the BVI than in any other offshore domicile (Robert Mathavious, personal communication), by the first quarter of 2009, the BVI financial services sector that in 2008 contributed to over 65 percent of the GDP had seen a 40 percent drop in company registrations. Rathbone Brothers Plc—"a financial trust powerhouse" whose BVI branch manages about $1.2 billion in assets— was putting its BVI branch on the market (O'Connor 2009b: 5), and the BVI was anxiously awaiting the results of the G-20 summit, where strict financial services regulations were being drafted in an effort to capture tax revenues from money held in offshore jurisdictions ("VI Readies for Likely G-20 Storm"). By September 2009, the BVI government had signed more than the twelve Tax Information Exchange Agreements (TIEAs) the G-20 required for the BVI to be placed on the Organisation for Economic Cooperation and Development (OECD) white list of compliant offshore jurisdictions. But the ongoing global economic crisis continued to have a negative impact upon the revenues generated by the BVI financial services sector (O'Connor 2009c), and BVI government predicted a 5 percent budgetary shortfall in projected revenues for 2009 (French 2009).

As revenues in the BVI financial services sector declined and the BVI considered the possibility of losing its financial services industry altogether, its tourism industry emerged as an ever more vital resource. At a Tourism Industry Action Plan meeting in February 2009, the BVI Tourist Board chairman pointed out that "we have to protect tourism at all costs . . . tourism may very well become the financial backbone of this country" (quoted in O'Connor 2009a: 20). The fallback on tourism under-scores BVI dependence on outside economies and events. And while it is difficult to predict what strategies the BVI will implement to meet the challenge of global recession, it is precisely the relations that the BVI has with forces, values, people, events, and economies outside its borders that have shaped the BVI experience from the inception of the BVI tourism industry. These relations influence profoundly the way that BVIslanders think about themselves and about people living among them. They also engender a sense of the BVI as a nation that of necessity takes into account its status as a commodity in a global marketplace. By looking at the BVI as a commodity in relation BVI nation building, we get a sense of what I refer to as corporate nationalism, and this in turn provides a framework for considering the BVI future.

COMMODIFICATION AND CORPORATE NATIONALISM

I take the title of this chapter, "Technically It's a Country," from a television commercial that was aired early in 1999 by the online brokerage firm, Discovery Brokerage. In the commercial, a grungy tow truck driver named Bob gives a ride to a man in a suit and tie whose car broke down. As Bob drives along in his junky tow truck he tells his passenger that he only drives his truck to keep busy, that through his online trading he has made enough money to buy his own tropical island. Bob shows his passenger a photograph of his island paradise and muses aloud about what to name it. Perhaps he'll name it Bob, after himself. The commercial concludes with Bob returning the photo to its place in the sun visor and ending the conversation by explaining, "technically, it's a country."

When we consider the joke of the technicality of the island's sovereignty, the allure in Bob's being able to name the island after himself, and
the fact that the conversation about the island takes place between two
white men, we can read this ad as telling an old and reassuring story about
tropical regions up for grabs, the stability of white male privilege, and
the endurance of colonial imperative. This is a familiar story to islands of
tropical regions, and especially so the British Virgin Islands, whose tourism
industry was launched when Laurance Rockefeller purchased land on Virgin
Gorda in the early 1950s to build the Little Dix Bay resort. In fact, the
story of Bob and his island is a lot like other stories that are told about
people buying pieces of the BVI, and these stories themselves point to the
entwining of geography, mobile capital, and ambivalent sovereignty that
conditions the BVI contemporary experience.

One of these stories appeared in a January 1974 issue of *The British
Virgin Islands Welcome Guide*, and recounts the purchase in 1970 of a large
tract of land on Virgin Gorda by a Norwegian investor, Mr. Engelsen, and
two of his friends. According to the story, the three Norwegians had spent
all of one day walking the hills of Virgin Gorda above North Sound, a large
sheltered body of water that is today a favored anchorage of bareboaters.
In the late afternoon they came upon Biras Creek, "a truly beautiful bay"
at the southeastern end of North Sound on Virgin Gorda, and "by the end
of that day the three Norwegian visitors had decided that the site must be
theirs and negotiations for its purchase were quickly concluded. One of
them was reported as saying, 'it was a beautiful jewel which just couldn't
be resisted.'" The article concludes pointing out that on the same visit "Mr.
Engelsen's Company also made a very substantial investment in the Territory through the purchase of some 750 acres of prime development land at
Beef Island" (Smith 1974: 3–4), thereby neatly transforming acquisitiveness
into benevolence. This textual transformation is mirrored in many BVIslanders' own renderings of the relation between outside investors and the
tourism industry as, for example, when a British Virgin Islands director of
tourism conflated investment with philanthropy: "Tourism in the British
Virgin Islands was significantly influenced by wealthy investors, who may
accurately be called philanthropists, who visited the islands in the late
fifties and early sixties, fell in love with the islands' beauty and people, and
decided that the leisure business was a natural area for investment in these
islands" (Harrigan 1992: 79).

The other story is a short piece that appears in the 1999 *Sports Illustrated* swimsuit issue as part of a longer article on Richard Branson, CEO
of Virgin Atlantic Airlines. Entitled "An Island of One's Own," this piece
describes Branson's purchase of Necker Island, an island located just outside
of North Sound (Nack 1999). As in the stories about Bob's purchase of his

island and Mr. Engelsen's purchase of Biras Creek, the story about Branson's purchase of Necker Island makes island buying sound easy, stating, "As fast as Branson could make out a check, Necker Island was his." To make buying a piece of the BVI plausible, the article also purges Necker Island of any meaning apart from its existence as a commodity. "Never heard of them," Branson is reported to have said when first told about the British Virgin Islands. Like the textual strategies of eighteenth-century travelers into the "unmapped" and "unnamed" interiors of South America (Pratt 1992), Branson's "never heard of them" opens Necker Island for whatever meaning we wish to inscribe on it. In this case, what is depicted as "a mostly barren shank of rock" is transformed "into what [Branson] now calls 'my private island paradise'" (Nack 1999: 196).

A similar erasure and transformation was the basis of an advertising campaign that commodified the concept of nation itself, using a British Virgin Islands island to create The Republic of Cuervo Gold. The Republic of Cuervo Gold campaign was launched in 1995 to commemorate the 200th birthday of Cuervo Gold Tequila, and included activities at bars and sports venues throughout the United States and that were organized around the "Republic" theme. Among the planned activities were "on-premise citizenship drives and asylum nights in bars, some of them designated official 'Republic of Gold' embassies" (Khermouch 1996: 18). A major feature of the Cuervo Gold campaign was and continues to be an annual two-week-long party held on Marina Cay, which is located in Trellis Bay on Beef Island, off the eastern tip of Tortola. During the two weeks of revelry, Marina Cay becomes the Republic of Cuervo Gold; an Associated Press news release elaborated: "Attention tequila-swilling party animals: Your dreams are about to come true. The marketer of Jose Cuervo Gold has crafted an elaborate promotion to declare the tequila *its own nation* in the British Virgin Islands. . . . The Republic of Cuervo Gold" ("Tequila Gives Birth to a New Country"; emphasis added). During the two weeks that Marina Cay is the Republic of Cuervo Gold, bands are flown in from the United States, stages are built, video crews are readied, and Cuervo Gold "citizens" are flown in to populate the Republic. In October 1997, twenty tons of artificial snow was imported, and a snowboard free-style exhibition was put on at Marina Cay/The Republic of Cuervo Gold for its "citizens'" pleasure.

What makes the representation of Marina Cay as the Republic of Cuervo Gold plausible is the same process that makes it possible to transform a piece of the sovereign territory of the British Virgin Islands into Engelsen's "beautiful jewel" or Branson's "private island paradise." In all instances an object is taken out of its cultural and historical context and recontextualized in terms of its logic as a commodity. As Stephen Fjellman's study of Walt Disney World illustrates, by uncoupling objects from their originating context and then recontextualizing them in neatly packaged bundles of signs, objects can be presented for consumption in a way that negates any sense that they are out of place. In the case of Walt Disney World's Epcot Center, for example, recontextualizing the signs for Mexico and Japan enables the Epcot tourist to move easily through these spaces with no sense that Mexico is out of place next to Japan, or that either is out of place next to Adventureland (Fjellman 1992). Whether it is a snowboarder doing freestyle jumps on the snowy slopes of a tropical island, a passport from the Republic of Cuervo that allows its holder entrance into any party in the world, or a tropical island named Bob, because these objects and events are understood as and interacted with as commodities, the sense that they do not go together or cannot happen is neutralized.

Such recontextualizing is particularly explicit in the use of the concept of *nation* in the Republic of Cuervo Gold campaign. For example, in speaking of the decision to locate the Republic of Cuervo Gold on an actual island, one of the executives of the advertising agency that developed the campaign asked, "Isn't it time we had our own homeland?" Speaking of the combined efforts of merchandising agencies, public relations agencies, and advertising agencies that went into the campaign, the executive elaborated, "Nation-building requires a big team" (Khermouch 1996: 19); and an October 1999 visit to the Republic of Cuervo Gold Web site informed me that the Republic of Cuervo Gold was "now officially registered as the 192nd nation in the world" (http://www.onboardent.com/pages/cuervo.html). By 2002, the original Republic of Cuervo Gold campaign had spawned so many different activities by local distributors that, as an article on the campaign put it, "instead of one nation indivisible, Cuervo Republic's ad campaign in its initial version was more akin to a mélange of disparate tribes" (Leggiere 2004: 1). In response to this promotional tribalism, the Republic of Cuervo Gold concept was revamped and a new Web site, Cuervonation.com, was launched. And, as if mirroring the trajectory of the development of BVI national consciousness, a company spokesperson characterized the 2002 revamping as tapping "the tantalizing concept of an island nation-state in a truly global way" (quoted in Leggiere 2004: 1).

An advertising initiative that uses a British Virgin Islands cay for two weeks each year as the site for its own theme nation would seem to present a direct challenge to what we have seen are profound concerns with British Virgin Islands identity and sovereignty. However, using a BVI cay two weeks a year for the purpose of constructing a promotional theme Republic is not very different from marketing the BVI as an idealized Caribbean paradise. In fact, lyrics from the "Cuervo Nation Anthem" that refer to the Republic of Cuervo Gold as "an escape from the rat race," "a paradise of sun and waves," "the island of your dreams" (*Cuervo Nation*) differ little from tourist brochure descriptions of the British Virgin Islands; in 2008 I saw a Cuervo Nation flag wrapped around a palm tree at Foxy's Tamarind Bar and Grill on the island of Jost Van Dyke. In consideration of these similarities, it is hardly surprising that those BVIslanders who concern themselves at all with the goings-on at Marina Cay treat them as just one more tourism-oriented event. Then again, even as multinational corporations and media conglomerates deploy the imagined space of the nation

9.1. Cuervo Nation flag at Foxy's on Jost Van Dyke. Photo by author.

to sell their products to consumers for whom the nation is as reasonable a commodity as anything else, so the BVI government looks to corporate structure and rationality to model its practices. This is particularly the case of the government of the National Democratic Party that was elected to power in 2003.

Organized around the slogan, "Time for *The* Change" (National Democratic Party 1998), the National Democratic Party (NDP) was founded in late 1997 by a group of young BVI men and women, many of whom originally came together as members of a private investment club. At the time of its founding, most of the members of the NDP were in their mid-thirties to mid-forties, most had received college educations in the United States or the United Kingdom, and most had risen to key posts in BVI government under the sponsorship of the mainstream Virgin Islands Party (VIP), and in particular its long-standing leader, H. Lavity Stoutt. Notably, it was not until after Soutt's death in 1995 that his protégés undertook to form their new party. In its statement of principles, the NDP presents itself as bringing a more rational and modern approach to government than the VIP, one characterized by a deep commitment to building the BVI as an international presence. For example, I was told by two NDP members who are central players in the international tourism and financial services sectors, respectively, that in the national elections scheduled for 1999 they would be looking to support for chief minister a person who could "play in Hong Kong" (field notes, September 14, 1997).

The NDP emphasis upon establishing an international presence was contrasted in their campaign rhetoric with the more parochial and paternalistic politics of the VIP. Among the twenty objectives that introduce the official NDP statement of principles are objectives that call for the "*prudent management* of the territory's financial resources"; that seek the creation of "*an investment and business friendly* environment" and "the establishment of a *knowledge-based culture* "; and to "*position the BVI* in the regional and international communities" (National Democratic Party 1998, emphasis added). Not surprisingly, in light of the corporate management style of its language, the NDP statement of principles also "seeks to establish an 'investment fund' coupled with a strategy to assist BVIslanders interested in investing in the tourism and financial services sectors of [the BVI] economy." Indeed, the NDP envisages the people of the BVI "not only as employees but most importantly as *equity stakeholders* in [its] developing economy" (National Democratic Party 1997; emphasis added). Although the NDP did not secure a majority in the 1999 national elections, they did win a majority in the 2003 elections, and from 2003 to 2007 BVI government was an NDP government.

The sort of corporate nationalism exemplified in the NDP statement of principles reflects the history of BVI government's involvement in developing the BVI as a tourism and financial services product, but is not limited to the NDP understanding of governance. For example, a National Integrated Development Strategy (NIDS) that was crafted in 1996 to establish "the broad strategies, policies, and implementation framework" for BVI government for the five-year period from 1999 to 2003, characterized the role of the state as that of manager of economic resources and partner of the private sector: "the state has an important, if not decisive, role in the development process even in a market economy, and more so for one at our stage of development. . . . We recognize, also, that development progresses fastest when the public and private sectors work in a complementary manner. A high performing public sector not only provides quality services to citizens, but also provides a faciliatory and enabling environment for private sector development" (*National Integrated Development Strategy* 1996: 4.9).

Both the NDP statement of principles and the NIDS document highlight the powerful role that global economic forces play in BVI conceptualizations of the nation as a political entity. Likewise, a foremost British Virgin Islander who is an esteemed international lawyer argued in a 2007 *Business BVI* interview that "the Virgin Islands has never really been a political country. It is an economic country. . . . Economics is the prevailing accent in public life in the BVI and it has been so for a long time" (quoted in "The Evolution of the Legal Framework in the British Virgin Islands" 2007). Reflecting upon the nature of his NDP government, Chief Minister Dr. Orlando Smith expressed a similar understanding when he reiterated that "the National Democratic party had a simple philosophy for the continued development of this country, 'grow the economy'" (Smith 2009). The corporate nationalism encapsulated in these remarks and documents emerged in the context of the neoliberal economic policies of the latter part of the twentieth century. Like the neoliberal governmentality that Aihwa Ong details in sectors of Southeast Asia and East Asia, this approach to government reconceptualizes governing activities as "nonpolitical and nonideological problems that need technical solutions" (2006: 3). Importantly, it is also a governmentality that partially embeds "the national space of the homeland . . . in the territoriality of global capitalism" (2006: 7), and this has radical implications for conventional conceptualizations of sovereignty and citizenship.

DEVELOPING NATURE'S LITTLE SECRETS

The global outlook of the NDP and the NDP emphasis on growing the economy figured centrally in the national elections of 2007. In these elections, the NDP was defeated by the VIP, which took charge of the government in August 2007. Meanwhile, the question of the relation of the BVI to the rest of the world continued to dominate debate over the direction that the economic development of the BVI should take. The BVI is acutely aware of both the natural beauty of the islands and the value of that beauty as a commodity in a global tourism market. As a 1994 government position paper on BVI sustainable development noted, "our environments, both land and marine are our most valuable assets (along with our human resources). . . . Our tourists must choose us as a destination because of the way we are able to maintain our natural serene beauty, protect our marine life and assets and integrate our tourism product with the environment" ("Towards Sustainable Development" 1994: 2.2.2). The 1961 founding of the BVI National Parks Trust, which was inspired and supported by Laurance Rockefeller, was followed in 1979 by a Marine Parks and Protected Areas Ordinance, in 1984 by the establishment of a Conservation Office within the Ministry of National Resources and Labor, in 1985 with a Beach Protection Ordinance, and in 2008 with a *British Virgin Islands Protected Areas System Plan 2007–2017* (2008).

All of these initiatives point to a long-standing concern in the BVI with its natural and cultural resources. But it was the National Integrated Development Strategy (NIDS) identifying the BVI marine and coastal environment as "of strategic importance" to the tourism industry (*National Integrated Development Strategy* 1996: 2.5) that impelled widespread efforts to protect the resources upon which BVI tourism depends. Following up on recommendations in the NIDS document and in a position paper prepared for a 1994 United Nations Global Conference on Sustainable Development for Small Island Developing States, the BVI government built sewage treatment plants in several beach villages to alleviate the problem of pollution of marine resources, installed a system of mooring buoys to protect coral reefs from damage by anchors, and planted new mangrove seedlings to restore wetlands ravaged by land reclamation. These efforts coincided with the development of a robust marine studies program at the H. Lavity Stoutt Community College, and with the addition of environmental studies to the primary school curriculum.

Such environmental initiatives are intended to ensure that the product marketed to the elite tourists who rent private villas, stay in boutique resorts, or sail BVI waters on chartered yachts remains the pristine paradise evoked in the "Nature's Little Secrets" slogan. But as the following 2006 State of the Territory Address by the chief minister of the NDP government, Dr. Orlando Smith, indicates, the BVI is also challenged to consider its position in a highly competitive global tourism market.

No challenge is greater than the reality that the BVI today is part of an ever more connected global marketplace. That means we have access to customers and markets a world away. But it also means that we must compete with every country on earth. In this highly connected and highly competitive global marketplace, we must constantly push ourselves to strive for excellence. We cannot allow ourselves to rest on past successes or content ourselves with our current well-being. If we hope to compete and win in the global market of 2010 and beyond, then we must find new ways to grow those areas in which we already excel, while at the same time making a serious and sustained commitment to expanding our economic base. (Smith 2006b)

At the time of the chief minister's address, the BVI had not seen any new large-scale tourism development since the early 1990s. By 2007, the BVI tourism product was looking a bit shabby, causing the chairman of the BVI Tourist Board to declare that "The BVI has lost its competitive edge and we need to regain that" (quoted in Bakewell 2007a: 63).

A concern to regain the BVI competitive edge was the impetus for a Hospitality/Tourism Seminar that I attended in July 2007. Sponsored by *Business BVI* magazine and with presentations from tourism industry professionals and members of government, the seminar addressed the need for the BVI tourist industry to cater to what was characterized variously as the *ultra affluent* and the *luxury* traveler. According to a seminar presenter, the ultra affluent market is made up of people who make over $10 million a year, whose choices are controlled by exclusivity and uniqueness, and who are interested in travel that includes mega-yachts and private jets. According to this presenter, "It is important to take into consideration the growth in the use of private jets. If you make it easy for jets to land here then you will be attracting these people" (field notes, July 11, 2007). Other seminar presenters pointed out that it is the luxury resorts of Barbados, Anguilla, and the Turks and Caicos, and not quaint guesthouses and private villas of uneven quality that luxury tourists seek. While the economic downturn of 2008–2009 undoubtedly diminished the number of private jet and mega yacht–owning millionaires, in 2007 it was through the development of its upscale tourism industry that the BVI was looking to bolster its position in the Caribbean tourism market.

Between 2003 and 2007, the BVI government of the NDP launched several initiatives to build up the BVI upscale tourism sector, among them a one-million-dollar training program for tourism industry personnel that stressed "servitude in the past, service in the future" (field notes, July 11, 2007). During this period, government also signed development agreements with three "major players in the upscale tourism industry" (Bakewell 2007a: 63), one of which planned a $60 million dollar development of Smuggler's Cove on the northwestern tip of Tortola, and two of which proposed five-star resort developments on Scrub Island and Beef Island, off the eastern tip of Tortola. Scrub Island lies just across from Marina Cay, Cuervo Tequila's newly named Cuervo Nation. The $65 million development plans for Scrub Island include "a boutique hotel, spa, 100-slip marina and luxury residences and estates" ("Caribbean and Bahamas: Hotel Growth Continues"), as well as eight swimming pools with waterfalls, three restaurants, a shopping village, and an observatory. That Scrub Island is intended for the ultra affluent traveler was made clear by a vice president of the Scrub Island development company when he explained, "The trend is that those individuals that can afford to own a yacht want a place to keep it" (quoted in Bareuther 2008: 40). An article in *Elite Traveler: The Private Jet Lifestyle Magazine* was also explicit about the clients Scrub Island was hoping to attract. Detailing the advantages of a vacation home on Scrub Island, the article elaborated, "Easily accessible for a private jet traveler, yet secluded enough to grant real privacy, each of these new island homes is a true, tropical dream house" ("Owning a Caribbean Paradise").

The proposed Beef Island resort project is even grander than the Scrub Island project. According to the Beef Island Development prospectus, the Beef Island Resort project includes a luxury resort hotel and spa, an eighteen-hole Jack Nicklaus Signature Golf Course, a fractional ownership units club, 663 custom-built residential units, a mega-yacht marina, and over 100,000 square feet of retail and commercial space (www.bvihcg.com/ paper/beef_island_project.pdf). The Development Order of Agreement to purchase 640 acres of land at Beef Island was signed with BVI government in December 2005, and in August 2006 a joint venture agreement was signed, clearing the way for the Beef Island Project to begin.

The revenues from these developments were estimated to be over $440 million for a twenty-year period, with annual spin-off revenues in excess of $30 million annually ("Land of Plenty": 32). Nevertheless, public response to them was for the most part negative. People with homes near Smuggler's Cove, many of whom are white expatriates, regarded the proposed development as a threat to the natural and cultural environment alike. Residents in Tortola's East End, near the Scrub Island and Beef Island projects, were apprehensive about the impact that the addition of over 1,600 construction workers would have on their already crowded communities. And people throughout the BVI joined environmental groups in expressing concern about the impact of golf course construction and fertilizer run-off on Beef Island's fragile marine environments ("Land of Plenty"). The sentiments of one BVIslander summarized these concerns: "the continued functioning of the Beef Island ecosystem is equally as important to economic prosperity as a viable development project" (Georges 2009).

While the proposed development projects stimulated concern about environmental and social impacts, they also made explicit the NDP government's commitment to engagement with outside economic interests on a global scale. And in the local political arena this commitment was read by many as the NDP selling out to outside interests while forgetting local needs. The leader of the NDP government acknowledged that "the VIP did a good job in communicating what they wanted the people to hear. . . . They were saying that because we were pursuing developments we were selling out to foreign interests" ("Why They Won, Lost"). Nevertheless, the NDP support of development projects like Beef Island was in keeping with its commitment to economic growth and to enhancing the BVI's competitive edge in a global market place. Additionally, the former chief minister of the NDP government argued, revenues from development were "the only way that the social needs of the people of the BVI could be met, and schools and hospitals and airports built. . . . All of these social developmental projects must be financed, they need money to make them happen, and that money can only come from building a strong economy. . . . And that is the reason that the past administration pursued new developments in tourism, and made every effort to promote our financial services" (Smith 2009). An NDP supporter also stressed what he saw as the pragmatism of the NDP, in contrast to BVIslanders who would rather not acknowledge a world outside their doors: "BVIslanders, they want to keep the world small. . . . They don't want to see the world. But the world is here. It is all around, and no amount of closing doors or closing minds going to make it any different. It's the same with money. No way that we—this small country—could do what we done without outside money" (field notes, June 20, 2007).

The 2007 electoral victory of the VIP over the NDP reflected the widespread opposition to the development policies of the NDP government, and in particular to the impact these policies would have on the marine resources on which BVI yacht-charter tourism has been built. Also underlying this opposition was a sense that in looking beyond the boundaries of the BVI, the NDP was neglecting its local constituents. Nonetheless, the present VIP government faces the same challenges that confronted the NDP government, exacerbated by a global recession. These challenges were aptly summarized in an April 2009 online response to Orlando Smith's reflections about the successes of his NDP government from 2003 to 2007, and his defense of his support of the Beef Island project (Smith 2009). The online post simultaneously evokes the natural beauty of the BVI, argues for the need to enhance the tourism product, and references BVIslanders' involvement in a world beyond their borders.

I completely identify with our need to preserve our natural surroundings, however, our way of life is governed by the financial sector and
tourism. Many people may come and say that they love the island
untouched the way it is, but what does a golf course on BEEF ISLAND
have to do with changing the landscape from East End to West End, or
even the more natural feel of Virgin Gorda and Jost Van Dyke? We can
give the paying Markets the best of both worlds. We need to realize
that yes, we love our country the way it is, but every time we leave
Tortola and go to Europe or the United States, we don't want to stay
in a Motel 6.

While offering an insight into public opinion about large-scale development in the BVI, these remarks also reflect the complex circumstances
in which the BVI finds itself. Geographically less than fifty-nine square
miles, with a population of under 25,000, in 2007 the BVI was host to over
a million visitors and generated close to one billion dollars in revenues.
Its BVIslander and non-BVIslander residents alike are dependent upon the
dollars that tourism brings in and have grown accustomed to the lifestyle
those dollars allow. If the trust companies that service off-shore accounts
close their doors, their largely British expatriate workers will leave; if the
tourism industry tightens its belt, the non-BVI Caribbean nationals who
constitute a majority of its workers will also have to seek work elsewhere
in the BVI or return to their native islands. And the diminishing work force
in both sectors will have spin-off effects throughout the BVI economy and
society. Importantly, the remarks also gesture toward the ambivalent sovereignty of a country that is as much about economics as politics.
        Issues that arose in the wake of the development agreements signed by
the NDP government were aired throughout the campaigning for the 2007
national elections. Prior to these elections, in late 2005, the Scrub Island
Resort project broke ground and construction was begun on the main
resort and several private homes. But by the summer of 2008 the project
was on hold and its contractors were left unpaid while its developers sought
refinancing in the amount of an additional $99 million ("Mainsail Refi-
nancing Scrub Loan"). The Beef Island project was also on hold pending
a court decision on a lawsuit brought by the Virgin Islands Environmental
Council against Hon. Dr. Orlando Smith and his NDP government, and an
October 2009 finding in favor of the Virgin Islands Environmental Council
is likely to have scuttled the project altogether. In May 2008, the project
slated for Smuggler's Cove on Tortola's western tip was terminated, "after
two years of planning and more than $1 million spent in environmental
studies, public meetings and architectural renderings" ("2008: The Year in
Review"). According to the developer of the project, "I had no choice but

to not go through with the purchase.... The government changed and didn't seem to be interested with us going with the project" (quoted in "Would-be Smugglers Developer Pulls Out").

Also in May 2008, the estate of Laurance Rockefeller transferred a small island off of Jost Van Dyke to the ownership of BVI government, making it the twenty-first BVI national park. In March 2009, another park, this one on Wickham's Cay in Road Town, was renamed The Noel Lloyd/Positive Movement Park in honor of one of the BVIslanders who successfully stopped the sell-off of large tracts of BVI land in the celebrated Wickham's Cay affair of 1964. A local newspaper account of this event left little doubt of its historic and symbolic import, when it extolled the "personal sacrifice in the preservation of the VI freedom of life and culture [that] has enabled a liberty and hope that could not have been enjoyed today" (Needham 2009: 9). Yet even as the renamed park underscored the VIP government's commitment to keep BVI land in BVI hands, an April 2009 *Wall Street Journal* article praised the BVI for easing restrictions on foreign real estate buyers, so that a luxury development on Virgin Gorda (with house lots ranging in price from $1.9 million to $25 million) could proceed apace. Referring to the decision to allow foreigner buyers to secure landholding licenses in under ninety days, the permanent secretary for the BVI Ministry of Natural Resources and Labor of the VIP government acknowledged that "the government realized, given the current economic climate and given that we live by tourism, that we want to have these investors come in" (quoted in Lewis 2009: C6).

TREASURE STORIES AND
AMBIVALENT SOVEREIGNTY

Among the stories that I have heard over the years of my research in the BVI, I have found some of the most intriguing to be about how luck changed the course of the life of a BVI family. For example, one very well-respected Road Town family is said to have achieved its elevated status when a man working on a plot of land the family owned found buried treasure. And, as the story was told to me, "being a simple chap, not too smart, he came right to [the man whose land it was] and told him 'I find something you left behind.' [The man who owned the land] was smarter, and he said to the fellow, 'You workin hard all day, why don't you take the rest of the day and rest.' And that is how [that family] came up: they were smiled upon by fate with the finding of the treasure" (field notes, March 17, 1993). This story of luck and treasure is like the story of the Stoutt family, from which H. Lavity Stoutt, the first chief minister of the BVI, comes. As this story goes, the patriarch of the Stoutt family was able to quit work as a cane cutter in Santo Domingo and return home when he won the lottery.

H. Lavity Stoutt is memorialized as the father of the modern BVI nation, and whenever I heard this story it was told with an ominous undertone, the implication being that if the Stoutt patriarch had not won the lottery, the BVI would be a far different place from what it is today. When I told a BVI friend about my excitement at discovering two such similar stories, he paid little attention to my claim that it hardly matters whether or not they are true, that what matters is that—and how and when—they are told. Instead, he said that there are several families in the BVI whose rise can be attributed to the discovery of treasure, taking care to point out that his family was not one of them.

These stories that attribute success to luck and treasure are very much like the way that the history of BVI tourism development is rendered in official publications and popular discourse alike. Casting as philanthropic the purchase and development of BVI land by wealthy U.S. entrepreneurs is one instance of such rendition. But the earliest BVI tourism slogan, "Yes We Are Different!" also alludes to fortuitous historical circumstances that enabled the BVI to avoid the scourge of urbanization and mass tourism that marks its St. Thomas cousin. Likewise, the "Nature's Little Secret" campaign that plays up the natural gifts of the BVI and hints at hidden treasure implies that BVIslanders are similarly blessed, are also hidden treasures. This sentiment is given expression by a BVI writer in a tourist publication put out by the BVI Chamber of Commerce when she starts out an article on the BVI, "When God wanted to give us a glimpse of paradise, he caused the waters to rise over much of that island plain in the Caribbean, which extended 60 miles to the North, 40 miles to the East and 190 miles to the West, leaving only its Peaks, which Columbus named the Virgin Islands" (Moll 2004: 13). Even the preamble to the 2007 constitution alludes to the good fortune of good character that is at the base of BVI economic prosperity when it claims that "the people of the Virgin Islands have a free and independent spirit, and have developed themselves and their country based on qualities of honesty, integrity, mutual respect, self-reliance and the ownership of the land engendering a strong sense of belonging to and kinship with those Islands" (*The Virgin Islands [British] Constitution Order 2007*). Notably, this section from the preamble also specifies an active BVI people, who "have developed themselves and their country." In this, it gainsays stories of good fortune. Rather, like the "sweat and tears/blood, sweat, and tears" verse of "Father's Land," it points to the effort and resolve at the base of BVI economic success.

The ambivalence signaled in the preamble's commingling of providence and purposive action is, I think, what accounts for stories that attribute success to luck. For a small country that is rooted in a sense of people of "own kind" and yet is the home to people of many kinds, this ambivalence maintains egalitarian values while absolving BVIslanders of the self-interest attributed to outsiders. Likewise, it enables dependence on outside workers, investors, NGOs, and even former colonial authorities while maintaining a sense of primordial rights to the profits of prosperity. We see a similar ambivalence in BVIslanders' attitudes toward non-BVIslanders with whom they live, work, and have children. The see-sawing between the NDP and VIP governments suggests that BVI politics are also characterized by a tension between acquiescence and autonomy, between local paternalism and global vision, between protectionism and a notion of belonging that increasingly takes into account the labor and contributions of noncitizens.

A similar political ambivalence is articulated in the vision statement of the National Integrated Development Strategy (NIDS). The NIDS document identifies four main principles for future development—inclusion of all social partners, environmental sustainability, social acceptance and responsibility, and maintenance of an internationally competitive society—and envisions "a society that is globally competitive and socially cohesive; that is able to satisfy the basic needs of its people; that upholds the principles of equity, human rights, and good governance; that manages the natural resources of the territory in a sustained and integrated way; that generates self-confidence among the people; and that maintains the unique cultural identity of the territory" (*National Integrated Development Strategy* 1996: 1.8)). The friction in this vision statement between globalism and localism, between a universal humanism and a sense of a unique cultural identity suggests an ambivalent sovereignty. This is a sovereignty that grants the existence of a material and bounded geographical territory and at the same recognizes the flows of capital, people, values, and institutions through a place that came about as a national entity as much through its life as a commodity as through political development and constitutional reform. But conditioned as it is by multiple sources of power that are unpredictable and globally dispersed, it is also a perilous and contingent sovereignty.

The global forces that give rise to the ambivalent sovereignty that we see in the BVI are also shaping new forms of governmentality elsewhere, and particularly in regions and territories whose political and economic development is linked to the neoliberal policies of the last decades of the twentieth century. Aiwah Ong cautions that these new forms have "disquieting ethicopolitical implications for those who are included as well as those who are excluded in shifting technologies of governing and demarcation" (2006: 5). But Ong also points out—as I suggest in this discussion of BVI ambivalent sovereignty—that the same forms that align people, capital, commodities, and governance in new ways also challenge in significant and far-reaching ways traditional conceptions of the nation-state as something that merges identity, belonging, and privilege with territoriality. In this respect, the conditions that shape these new forms of governmentality—as they shape the space of the contemporary BVI—also open opportunities for new ways of conceptualizing what it means to belong, what obligations attend to belonging, and what forms of governance will legislate and adjudicate these obligations.

The 2009 BVI is undoubtedly a different place from the 1960 BVI that was just beginning to develop the tourism economy that so transformed the space in which its residents live and work, interact and play, vote and govern. And while the telling of treasure stories may be one way to account for both economic bounty and the many intertwinings and complexities that such bounty brings about, the way that residents of the BVI understand themselves and the conditions in which they make their lives are far more intricate than treasure stories allow. Everything from the National Integrated Development Strategy vision statement to the way BVIslanders negotiate the shifting meanings of cultural performances and beauty contests suggests compound and fluid subjectivities that, to borrow from Stuart Hall's insights into diasporic Caribbean identities in general, are "defined not by essence or purity, but by the recognition of a necessary heterogeneity," and that "are constantly producing and reproducing themselves anew . . . allowing [people] to see and recognize different parts and histories of [them]selves . . . to constitute [themselves] as new kinds of subjects" (Hall 1992: 234–236). To the extent that these subjectivities emerge hand in hand with an acceptance of and familiarity with ambiguous, contingent, and untidy structures and relations, the BVI and its people are as well positioned as any other place or people to imagine and forge new ways of being in the world.

REFERENCES

About Our Country. Road Town: Development Planning Unit, Government of the British Virgin Islands. http://dpu.gov.vg/AboutOurCountry/AboutOurCountry.htm.

Acheson, Pamela, and Richard B. Myers. 2007. *The Best of the British Virgin Islands*. 4th ed. Smyrna Beach, Fla.: Two Thousand Three Associates.

Ahmed, Sara. 2000. *Strange Encounters: Embodied Others in Post-Coloniality*. New York: Routledge.

Alexander, M. Jacqui. 1996. "Erotic Autonomy as a Politics of Feminist and State Practice in the Bahamas Tourist Economy." In *Feminist Genealogies, Colonial Legacies, Democratic Futures*, edited by M. Jacqui Alexander and Chandra Talpade Mohanty, 63–100. New York: Routledge.

Bakewell, Jane. 2007a. "Branding the BVI." *Business BVI 2007 Edition*, 63–65. Road Town: Oyster Publications.

———. 2007b. "Designed in the BVI." *The British Virgin Islands Welcome Guide*. 7 (2): 12–16. Road Town: Island Publishing Services.

Ball, Russell. 2008. "Cruise Ship Debate Continues." *BVI Beacon*, June 5, 2–3.

Ballinger, Robin. 2007. "The Politics of Cultural Value and the Value of Cultural Politics: International Intellectual Property Legislation in Trinidad." In *Trinidad Carnival: The Cultural Politics of a Transnational Festival*, edited by Garth L. Green and Philip W. Scher, 198–215. Bloomington: Indiana University Press.

"Bands Consider Boycotting 1990 Festival." 1990. *BVI Beacon*, July 26, 3.

Barbash, Ilisa, and Lucien Taylor. 1997. *Cross-Cultural Filmmaking: A Handbook for Making Documentary and Ethnographic Films and Videos*. Berkeley: University of California Press.

Bareuther, Carol. 2008. "Buying a Home for Both You and Your Boat: Upscale Developments on the Rise in the Caribbean." *All at Sea*, June, 40–41.

Barthes, Roland. 1980. *Camera Lucida: Reflections on Photography*. New York: Hill and Wang.

"Beauty and the Beaches." 2007. In *Experience the British Virgin Islands*, edited by BVI Chamber of Commerce and Hotel Association, 40–45. Miami: HCP/Aboard Publishing.

"Benji V is Calypso King." 1991. *Island Sun*, August 17, 2, 23.

Bhabha, Homi. 1990. *Nation and Narration*. New York: Routledge.

"Bisa Smith Wins Crown." 1991. *BVI Beacon*, August 29, 1, 4.

Bolter, Jay David, and Richard Grusin. 2000. *Remediation: Understanding New Media*. Cambridge: MIT Press.

Bowen, W. Errol. 1976. "Development, Immigration and Politics in a Pre-industrial Society: A Study of Social Change in the British Virgin Islands in the 1960's." *Caribbean Studies* 16 (1): 67–85.

247

Bowers, Barbara. 1988. "What a Night at Stanley's, Mon." *Yacht Vacations*, September/ October, 40.

British Virgin Islands: A Guide to Crewed Charter Yachts. 1989. Road Town: Charter Yacht Society.

The British Virgin Islands: Nature's Little Secrets. 1994. Video. Road Town: British Virgin Islands Tourist Board. 22 minutes. http://dpu.gov.vg/Plans/NIDS/PresentSituation.htm.

British Virgin Islands Protected Areas System Plan 2007–2017. 2008. Road Town: National Parks Trust. www.bviddm.com/. . ./System%20Plan%202008%20- %20Approved%20Version.pdf.

"The British Virgin Islands Today." 1996. In *National Tourism Development Plan*. Road Town: Development Planning Unit, Government of the British Virgin Islands.

"British Virgin Islands Tourism Sector Starts 2008 on Positive Note." 2008. *V. I. Standpoint Online*. July 4. http://www.vistandpoint.com/content/view/1754/29/.

British Virgin Islands Tourist Board and Management Development Resources. 1996. *Eighth Annual Summer Tourism and Awareness Workshop*. Road Town: British Virgin Islands Tourist Board.

Bruner, Edward. 2005. *Culture on Tour: Ethnographies of Travel*. Chicago: University of Chicago Press.

Bunten, Alexis Celeste. 2008. "Sharing Culture or Selling Out?: Developing the Commodified Persona in the Heritage Industry." *American Ethnologist* 35 (3): 380–395.

Butler, Judith. 1991. "Imitation and Gender Insubordination." In *Inside/Out: Lesbian Theories, Gay Theories*, edited by Diana Fuss, 13–31. New York: Routledge.

"BVI Festival 2002—July 14th–August 7th." 2002. *Island Sun*, June 28, 1.

"B.V. Islanders Outnumbered: Socio-economic Horizon Cloudy." 1993. *Island Sun*. December 25, 1.

"The BVI Scene." 1972. *The BVI Welcome Guide* 2 (1): 8–9.

BVI Tourist Board Statistical Report. 2003. Road Town: Development Planning Unit, Government of the British Virgin Islands.

Campbell, Shirley, Althea Perkins, and Patricia Mohammed. 1999. "'Come to Jamaica and Feel All Right': Tourism and the Sex Trade" In *Sun, Sex, and Gold: Tourism and Sex Work in the Caribbean*, edited by Kamala Kempadoo, 125–156. Lanham, Md.: Rowman and Littlefield.

Cantet, Laurent. 2005. *Heading South* (Vers le sud). Film. Shadow Distribution. 105 minutes.

"Caribbean and Bahamas: Hotel Growth Continues." 2005. *Travel Agent Magazine*, August 1, 14.

Cavaletti, Carla. 1997. "Heading Offshore? . . . Look before You Leap." *Futures* 26: 66–68.

Chambers, Erve. 2000. *Native Tours: The Anthropology of Travel and Tourism*. Prospect Heights, Ill.: Waveland Press.

Cohen, Colleen Ballerino. 1995. "Marketing Paradise, Making Nation." *Annals of Tourism Research* 22 (2): 404–421.

———. 1996. "Contestants in a Contested Domain: Staging Identities in the British Virgin Islands." In *Beauty Queens on the Global Stage: Gender, Contests, and Power*, edited by Colleen Ballerino Cohen, Richard Wilk, and Beverly Stoltje, 125–146. New York: Routledge.

———. 1998. "'This Is De Test': Festival and the Cultural Politics of Nation Building in the British Virgin Islands." *American Ethnologist* 25 (2): 189–214.

———. 2001. "Island Is a Woman: Women as Producers and Products in British Virgin

Islands Tourism." In *Women as Producers and Consumers of Tourism in Developing Regions*, edited by Yorghos Apostolopoulos, Sevil Sonmez, and Dallen J. Timothy, 47–72. Westport, Conn.: Praeger.

Cohen, Colleen, and Kenne Hodge. 1995. *Split Screens, Split Subjects: Subjectivities in the Age of Oprah and CNN*. Video. VITV Studio. 18 minutes.

Cohen, Colleen Ballerino, and Frances E. Mascia-Lees. 1993. "The British Virgin Islands as Nation and Desti-Nation: Representing and Siting Identity in a Post-colonial Caribbean." *Social Analysis* 33 (September): 130–152.

Cohen, Colleen, and Charles Wheatley. 1994. "Transforming Affiliations: Decolonization, Nationality, Bloodlines, Ethnicity, and Color." Paper presented at the 1994 annual meeting of the American Ethnological Society. Los Angeles, California, April 14–17.

Colli, Claudia. 2006. *British Virgin Islands: Sheltered Isles of Sea and Sun*. Oxford: Macmillan.

Cooper, Carolyn. 1993. *Noises in the Blood: Orality, Gender and the "Vulgar" Body of Jamaican Popular Culture*. Durham: Duke University Press.

Coopers and Lybrand Consultants. 1996. *National Tourism Development Strategy 1996–2005*. Road Town: Government of the British Virgin Islands.

Crystal, Eric. 1989. "Tourism in Toraja." In *Hosts and Guests: The Anthropology of Tourism*. 2nd ed., edited by Valene Smith, 139–169. Philadelphia: University of Pennsylvania Press.

Cuervo Nation. "Chamber of Cuervo: Quick Facts." http://www.cuervonation.com/main.aspx?key=104|24064|800|6656|1504|12800|192|12288|114|256|800|7424|416|208|116|27136|800|4096|2560|19712.

Cullimore, Jim. 2008." Cruise Ships Are Beneficial to Territory." *V.I. Standpoint*, June 4, 11.

"Cultural Factors and Attitudes Play a Part." 1996. *National Tourism Development Plan*. Road Town: Development Planning Unit, Government of the British Virgin Islands. http://dpu.gov.vg/Plans/NIDS/Humanresources.htm.

Dann, Graham. 1996. "The People from Tourist Brochures." In *The Tourist Image: Myths and Myth Making in Tourism*, edited by Tom Selwyn, 61–81. Chichester: John Wiley and Sons.

Davidson, Julia O'Connell, and Jacqueline Sanchez Taylor. 1999. "Fantasy Islands: Exploring the Demand for Sex Tourism." In *Sun, Sex, and Gold: Tourism and Sex Work in the Caribbean*, edited by Kamala Kempadoo, 37–54. Lanham, Md.: Rowman and Littlefield.

De Albuquerque, Klaus. 1990. "'Is We Carnival': Cultural Traditions under Stress in the U.S. Virgin Islands." In *Caribbean Popular Culture*, edited by John Lent, 49–63. Bowling Green: Bowling Green State University Popular Press.

Department of Education and Culture. 1989. *Tourism Awareness through Education: Education Week March 12–19, 1989*. Road Town: Government of the British Virgin Islands.

Dirlik, Arif. 1996. "The Global in the Local." In *Global/Local: Cultural Production and the Transnational Imaginary*, edited by Rob Wilson and Wimal Dissanayake, 21–45 Durham: Duke University Press.

Dookhan, Isaac. 1975. *A History of the British Virgin Islands, 1672–1970*. Great Britain: Caribbean Universities Press/ Bowker.

Douglas, Dave. 2005. "Big Daddy O Daveyo, The Master Blaster in the Kitchen Cookin', the Chocolate Syrup of Chocolate City and the Third World Man." In *40th Anniversary 1965–2005 ZBVI*. Road Town: ZBVI Radio.

Edensor, Tim. 2001. "Performing Tourism, Staging Tourism: (Re)Producing Tourist Space and Practice." *Tourist Studies* 1 (1): 59–81.

Encontre, Pierre. 1989. *Why Does the Tourist Dollar Matter? An Introduction to the Economics of Tourism in the British Virgin Islands.* Road Town: British Virgin Islands Tourist Board.

Enloe, Cynthia. 1990. *Bananas, Beaches, and Bases: Making Feminist Sense of International Politics.* Berkeley: University of California Press.

Escure, Crystele. 2009. "Introduction: The British Virgin Islands." In *The Islands' Dream Travel Road Book.* Basse-Terre, Guadaloupe: SARL The Islands' Dream.

Euromoney. 1989. "British Virgin Islands: A New Force Emerges." Euromoney special supplement, May 1989.

"The Evolution of the Legal Framework in the British Virgin Islands: An Interview with Dr. J. S. Archibald QC." 2007. *Business BVI 2007 Edition,* 36–41. Road Town: Oyster Publications.

"FAC Publishes Report on BVI and Other British Overseas Territories." 2008. *British Virgin Islands Business News,* July 13. http://bvioffshoreibc.blogspot.com/search/label/Financial%20Services.

Farrell, Peter. 1993. *Foxy and Jost Van Dyke.* St. John, USVI: American Paradise Publishing.

FCB/Intermarketing. 1989. Press Releases: *Discover Nature's Little Secrets.* New York.

"Festival Needs Cultural, Historical Emphasis." 1996. *BVI Beacon,* August 22, 2.

Festival 1980 Program. 1980. Road Town: Festival Committee of 1975.

Fjellman, Stephen. 1992. *Vinyl Leaves: Walt Disney World and America.* Boulder, Col.: Westview.

Fodor's Caribbean. 1993. *The British Virgin Islands* (updated by Jordan Simon). New York: Fodor Publishing.

Fodor's U.S. & British Virgin Islands. Rev. ed. 2005. New York: Fodor Publishing.

Fodor's U.S. & British Virgin Islands 2007. 2007. New York: Fodor's Travel/Random House.

Foster, Robert J. 1991. "Making National Cultures in the Global Ecumene." *Reviews in Anthropology* 20: 235–260.

"'Foxy' Receives MBE Honour." 2009. *The V.I. Standpoint Online,* February 10. http://www.vistandpoint.com/content/view/2209/33/.

Freeman, Carla. 2000. *High Tech and High Heels in the Global Economy: Women, Work, and Pink Collar Identities in the Caribbean.* Durham: Duke University Press.

French, Gordon. 2009. "Premier Offers Assurances about VI Economy." *The VI Standpoint On-Line,* September 19. http://www.vistandpoint.com/news/local/3319-premier-offers-assurances-about-vi-economy.

Friel, Bob. 2000. "Tortola: Bay-Hopping on the Big Island." *Caribbean Travel and Life,* December, 1–4.

"Fungi Music: The Melodious Tradition Needs Greater Support." *Island Sun,* August 3, 1–2.

"GDP Statistics." In *About Our Country.* Road Town: Development Planning Unit, Government of the British Virgin Islands. http://dpu.gov.vg/AboutOurCountry/GDPStats.htm.

Geertz, Clifford. 1973a. "Thick Description: Toward an Interpretive Theory of Culture." In *The Interpretation of Cultures: Selected Essays by Clifford Geertz,* edited by Clifford Geertz, 3–30. New York: Basic Books.

———. 1973b. "Deep Play: Notes on a Balinese Cockfight." In *The Interpretation of*

Cultures: Selected Essays by Clifford Geertz, edited by Clifford Geertz, 412–453. New York: Basic Books.

Georges, Noni. 2009. "In Defense of Beef Island." *BVI News*, April 22. http://www.bvinews.com/main.asp?Search=1&ArticleID=3014&SectionID=5&SubSection ID=87&S=1.

Gilman, Sander. 1985. *Difference and Pathology: Stereotypes of Sexuality, Race, and Madness*. Ithaca: Cornell University Press.

———. 1991. *Inscribing the Other*. Lincoln: University of Nebraska Press.

Ginsburg, Faye. 1995. "Mediating Culture: Indigenous Media, Ethnographic Film, and the Production of Identity." In *Fields of Vision: Essays in Film Studies, Visual Anthropology, and Photography*, edited by Leslie Devereaux and Roger Hillman, 256–291. Berkeley: University of California Press.

———. 1999. "The Parallax Effect: The Impact of Indigenous Media on Ethnographic Film." In *Collecting Visible Evidence*, edited by Jane M. Gaines and Michael Renov, 156–175. Minneapolis : University of Minnesota Press.

———. 2002. "Screen Memories: Resignifying the Traditional in Indigenous Media." In *Media Worlds: Anthropology on New Terrain*, edited by Faye Ginsburg, Lila Abu-Lughod, and Brian Larkin, 39–57. Berkeley: University of California Press.

Ginsburg, Faye, Lila Abu-Lughod, and Brian Larkin. 2002. "Introduction." In *Media Worlds: Anthropology on New Terrain*, edited by Faye Ginsburg, Lila Abu-Lughod, and Brian Larkin, 1–37. Berkeley: University of California Press.

"Gov't Working with Cruise Lines." 2008. *BVI Beacon*, June 5, 25.

Graburn, Nelson H. H. 1989. "Tourism: The Sacred Journey." In *Hosts and Guests: The Anthropology of Tourism*, 2nd ed., edited by Valene Smith, 1–36. Philadelphia: University of Pennsylvania Press.

Green, Garth L., and Philip W. Scher. 2007a *Trinidad Carnival: The Cultural Politics of a Transnational Festival*. Bloomington and Indianapolis: Indiana University Press.

———. 2007b. "Introduction: Trinidad Carnival in Global Context." In *Trinidad Carnival: The Cultural Politics of a Transnational Festival*, edited by Garth L. Green and Philip W. Scher, 1–24. Bloomington: Indiana University Press.

Greenwood, Davydd J. 1989. "Culture by the Pound." In *Hosts and Guests: The Anthropology of Tourism*, 2nd ed., edited by Valene Smith, 171–186. Philadelphia: University of Pennsylvania Press.

Gregory, Steven. 2006. *The Devil behind the Mirror: Globalization and Politics in the Dominican Republic*. Berkeley: University of California Press.

Gross, Matt. 2006. "Frugal Traveler Goes to Jost Van Dyke." *NY Times Online*, October 29. http://travel.nytimes.com/2006/10/29/travel/29Frugal.html.

Hall, Stuart. 1990. "Cultural Identity and Diaspora." In *Identity: Community and Cultural Difference*, edited by Jonathan Rutherford, 222–237. London: Lawrence and Wishart.

———. 1992. "Cultural Identity and Cinematic Representation." In *Ex-Iles: Essays on Caribbean Cinema*, edited by Mbye Cham, 220–236. Trenton, N.J.: Africa World Press.

———. 1993. "Encoding, Decoding." In *The Cultural Studies Reader*, edited by Simon During, 90–103. New York: Routledge.

Handler, Richard. 1984. "On Sociocultural Discontinuity: Nationalism and Cultural Objectification in Quebec." *Current Anthropology* 25 (1): 55–71.

———. 1988. *Nationalism and the Politics of Culture in Quebec*. Madison: University of Wisconsin Press.

Handler, Richard, and Jocelyn Linnekin. 1984. "Tradition, Genuine or Spurious." *Journal of American Folklore* 97 (385): 273–290.

Harman, Jeanne, and Harry Harman. 1993. "The Breezy British Virgins." *Latitudes: American Airlines Inflight Magazine,* Winter, 32–36.

Harrigan, Norwell, and Pearl Varlack. 1975. *The Virgin Islands Story.* Epping, Essex, England: Caribbean Universities Press.

———. 1988. *Ye Islands of Enchantment: A Profile of the British Virgins.* St. Thomas: Research and Consulting Services.

Harrigan, Russell. 1992. "General Review of the Various Socio-Economic Sectors of Tourism." In *1967–1992 Challenge and Change: A Glimpse at the Past and a Look towards the Future,* edited by Office of the Chief Minister, 77–83. Road Town: Government of the British Virgin Islands.

Henthorne, Tony, and Mark Miller. 2003. "Cuban Tourism in the Caribbean Context: A Regional Impact Assessment." *Journal of Travel Research* (42): 84–93.

Hill, Errol. 1972. *The Trinidad Carnival: Mandate for a National Theater.* Austin: University of Texas Press.

Hulme, Peter. 1992. *Colonial Encounters: Europe and the Native Caribbean, 1492–1797.* New York : Routledge.

"Island of Plenty." 1999. *Sports Illustrated,* Winter, 158.

"Islands as Aphrodisiacs." 1994. *Condé Nast Traveler,* March, 134–135, 165.

Kempadoo, Kamala. 1999. *Sun, Sex, and Gold: Tourism and Sex Work in the Caribbean.* Lanham, Md.: Rowman and Littlefield.

———. 2004. *Sexing the Caribbean: Gender, Race, and Sexual Labor.* London: Routledge.

Khermouch, Gerry. 1996. "An Isle of Their Own." *Brandweek* 37 (5): 18–19.

Kirby, Kathleen. 1996. *Indifferent Boundaries: Spatial Concepts of Human Subjectivity.* New York: Guilford.

Kirshenblatt-Gimblett, Barbara. 1998. *Destination Culture: Tourism, Museums, and Heritage.* Berkeley: University of California Press.

"Land of Plenty: Tortola's East End." 2007. *British Virgin Islands Property Guide,* March, 30–33.

Lamming, George. 1995. *Coming, Coming Home, Conversations II: Western Education and the Caribbean Intellectual.* St. Martin: House of Nehesi Publishers.

"Laurance Rockefeller." 2007. *Business BVI 2007 Edition,* 70–73. Road Town: Oyster Publications.

"Lawmakers Worried about Undocumented Children." *BVI News,* May 11. http://www.bvinews.com/main.asp?SectionID=5&SubSectionID=48&ArticleID=3272.

Leggiere, Phil. 2004. "Cuervo Goes Nation Building." *Online Media, Marketing and Advertising,* January 1. http://www.mediapost.com/publications/index.cfm?fa=Articles.showArticle&art_aid=6497.

Leibing, Annette, and Athena McLean. 2007. "Learn to Value Your Shadow!: An Introduction to the Margins of Fieldwork." In *The Shadow Side of Fieldwork,* edited by Athena McLean and Annette Leibing, 1–28. Malden, Mass.: Blackwell.

Lettsome, Quincy. 1976. *Virgin Verses: Selected Poems and Lyrics.* Road Town: Caribbean Printing.

Lewis, Christina S. N. 2009. "Some Nations Make It Easier for Nonresidents to Buy Property." *Wall Street Journal,* April 29, C6.

Lewisohn, Florence. 1966. *Tales of Tortola and the British Virgin Islands.* St. Croix, USVI: Florence Lewisohn.

Lidz, Franz. 1999. "Dissipation Row." *Sports Illustrated,* Winter, 130–139.

Lovell, Anne. 2003. "When Things Get Personal: Secrecy, Intimacy and the Production of Experience in Fieldwork." Paper presented at the Annual Meeting of the American Anthropological Association, Chicago, November 22.

MacCannell, Dean. 1976. *The Tourist: A New Theory of the Leisure Class*. New York: Schocken Books.

———. 1992. *Empty Meeting Grounds: The Tourist Papers*. New York: Routledge.

MacDougall, David. 1994. "Whose Story Is It?" In *Visualizing Theory*, edited by Lucien Taylor, 27–36. New York: Routledge.

———. 1998. "Complicities of Style." In *Transcultural Cinema*, edited by David Mac-Dougall, 140–149. Princeton: Princeton University Press.

"Mainsail Refinancing Scrub Loan." 2008. *BVI Beacon on Line*. September 10. http://bvibeacon.com/main/index.php?option=com_content&task=view&id=1669&Itemid=5.

Manning, Frank E. 1977. "Cup Match and Carnival: Secular Rites of Revitalization in Decolonizing, Tourist-Oriented Societies." In *Secular Ritual*, edited by Sally Falk Moore and Barbara Myerhoff, 265–281. Amsterdam: Van Gorcum, Assen.

———. 1978. "Carnival in Antigua (Caribbean Sea): Indigenous Festival in a Tourist Economy." *Anthropos* 73 (1/2): 191–204.

Massey, Doreen. 2005. *For Space*. London: Sage.

Maurer, Bill. 1997. *Recharting the Caribbean: Land, Law, and Citizenship in the British Virgin Islands*. Ann Arbor: University of Michigan Press.

McClintock, Anne. 1993. "Family Feuds: Gender, Nationalism and the Family." *Feminist Review* 44 (Summer): 61–80.

McGlynn, Frank S. 1981. "Marginality and Flux: An Afro-Caribbean Community through Two Centuries." Ph.D. dissertation, University of Pittsburgh.

McPherson, Mellica. 2008. "Festival to Showcase Local Artists." *Island Sun*, June 14, 4.

"Meet the Beauties." 2009. *BVI News*, June 9, 2009. http://www.bvinews.com/main.asp?SectionID=5&SubSectionID=47&ArticleID=3635.

Miller, Daniel. 1994. *Modernity, An Ethnographic Approach: Dualism and Mass Consumption in Trinidad*. Oxford: Berg.

Miller, Mark, Tony Henthorne, and Bapu George. 2008. "The Competitiveness of the Cuban Tourism Industry in the Twenty-first Century: A Strategic Re-evaluation." *Journal of Travel Research* 46: 268–278.

Minca, Claudio, and Tim Oakes. 2006. "Introduction: Traveling Paradoxes." In *Travels in Paradox: Remapping Tourism*, edited by Claudio Minca and Tim Oakes, 1–21. Lanham, Md.: Rowman and Littlefield.

Ministry of Education. 1983. *Preservation of Our Culture through Education*. Road Town: Government of the British Virgin Islands.

Ministry of Finance. 1992. *Ministry of Finance Report*. Road Town: Government of the British Virgin Islands.

Mintz, Sidney. 1989. *Caribbean Transformations*. New York: Columbia University.

"Miss BVI Returns from Las Vegas." 1991. *Island Sun*, June 1, 1.

Moll, Verna Penn. 2004. "Welcome to the British Virgin Islands." In *Experience the British Virgin Islands 2004*, edited by BVI Chamber of Commerce and Hotel Association, 12–18. Miami: HCP/Aboard Publishing.

Momsen, Janet Henshall. 1994. "Tourism, Gender, and Development in the Caribbean." In *Tourism: A Gender Analysis*, edited by Vivian Kinnaird and Derek Hall, 106–119. New York: John Wiley and Sons.

Munoz, Saran. 2006. "Night Moves." *Experience the British Virgin Islands, 2007*, edited by BVI Chamber of Commerce and Hotel Association, 4. Miami: HCP/Aboard Publishing.

Nack, William. 1999. "An Island of One's Own." *Sports Illustrated*, Winter, 196.

National Democratic Party. 1998. *The National Democratic Party Broad Principles*. Road Town: Bolo's Hi Tech Printery.

"The National Economy." In *About Our Country*. Road Town: Development Planning Unit, Government of the British Virgin Islands. http://dpu.gov.vg/AboutOurCountry/Economy.htm.

National Integrated Development Strategy. 1996. Road Town: Development Planning Unit, Government of the British Virgin Islands. http://dpu.gov.vg/Plans/NIDS/NIDS.htm.

National Population Report for the International Conference on Population and Development. 1994. Road Town: Development Planning Unit, Government of the British Virgin Islands. http://www.dpu.gov.vg/AboutOurCountry/NationalPopRepICPD/full.htm.

National Tourism Development Plan. 1996. Road Town: Development Planning Unit, Government of the British Virgin Islands. http://dpu.gov.vg/Plans/NationalTourism.htm.

Needham, Cadesha. 2009. "Palm Grove Park Renamed in Noel Lloyd's Honour." *VI Standpoint*, March 4, 8–9.

"New Belongers Must Take Local History and Culture Course." 2008. *BVI News*, July 16, http://www.bvinews.com/main.asp?Search=1&ArticleID=644&SectionID=5&SubSectionID=30&S=1.

Newell, Richard. 1996. "A Hard Life in Paradise." *British Virgin Islands Financial Services (International Money Marketing Special Report)*. Road Town: Government of the British Virgin Islands.

Nichols, Bill. 1994. "The Ethnographer's Tale." In *Visualizing Theory*, edited by Lucien Taylor, 60–83. New York: Routledge.

"Notes on Festival in the BVI." 1989. Road Town: Festival Committee of 1975.

Nunley, John W., and Judith Bettelheim, eds. 1988. *Caribbean Festival Arts*. Seattle: University of Washington Press.

O'Connor, Dan. 2009a. "Tourist Board Lays Out New Plans." *BVI Beacon*, March 5, 3, 20.

———. 2009b. "Rathbone's VI Branch for Sale." *BVI Beacon*, March 12, 5.

———. 2009c. "OFCs May Fare Better This G-20." *BVI Beacon*, September 24, 14.

Olwig, Karen Fog. 1993. *Global Culture, Island Identity*. Philadelphia: Harwood Academic Publishers.

O'Neal, Eugenia. 2001. *From the Field to the Legislature: A History of Women in the Virgin Islands*. Westport, Conn.: Greenwood.

O'Neal, Joseph Reynold. 2005. *Life Notes: Reflections of a British Virgin Islander*. Xlibris.

O'Neal, Michael E. 1983. "British Virgin Islands Transformations: Anthropological Perspectives." Ph.D. dissertation, Union Graduate School, Cincinnati, Ohio.

O'Neal, Ralph T. 2008. "Protecting Our Future." 2008 Budget Address by the Honorable Ralph T. O'Neal. June 3. Road Town: Government of the British Virgin Islands.

Ong, Aihwa. 2006. *Neoliberalism as Exception: Mutations in Citizenship and Sovereignty*. Durham: Duke University Press.

"Owning a Caribbean Paradise." 2008. *Elite Traveler: The Private Jet Lifestyle Magazine*. May/June, 128.

Papanek, Hanna. 1994. "The Ideal Woman and the Ideal Society: Control and Autonomy in the Construction of Identity." In *Identity Politics and Women: Cultural Reassertions and Feminisms in International Perspective*, edited by Valentine M. Moghadam, 42–75. Boulder, Col.: Westview.

Parker, Andrew, Mary Russo, Doris Sommer, and Patricia Yaeger. 1992. "Introduction." In *Nationalisms and Sexualities*, edited by Parker, Russo, Sommer, and Yaeger, 1–18. New York: Routledge.

Parsons, Eileene. 2008. "Speech Delivered at St. Georges Church on August 1, 2008 by Eileene L. Parsons for the Norwell Harrigan Emancipation Lecture Series." Road Town, Tortola.

Pattullo, Polly. 1996. *Last Resorts: The Cost of Tourism in the Caribbean*. London: Cassell.

———. 2005. *Last Resorts: The Cost of Tourism in the Caribbean*. 2nd ed. New York: Monthly Review Press/Latin American Bureau.

Payne, Bob. 1992. "Chartering the Virgins: Me? Dad? On a Spring Break Cruise?" *Sail*, March, 98–101.

Pearse, Andrew, ed. 1988. *Trinidad Carnival*. Port of Spain: Paria.

Penn, Ermin. 2007. "A Modern Day BVI." *Business BVI 2007 Edition*, 32–35. Road Town: Oyster Publications.

Penn, Howard R. 1990. *Memoirs of H. R. Penn: A Personal Account of the Politics and History of the British Virgin Islands in the 20th Century*. Road Town: Caribbean Printing Company.

Perimutter, David. 1978–1979. "Tortola's Tourism Strides Are Measured." *The British Virgin Islands Welcome Guide* 8 (1): 4–6.

Petrovic, Clive, and Everett O'Neal. 2001. "Ecotourism, Yachting and Local Entrepreneurs: A Case Study of the British Virgin Islands." Paper presented at Conference on Sustainable Development of Ecotourism in Small Islands Developing States (SIDS) and Other Small Islands. Mahé, Seychelles, 8–10 December.

Pickering, Vernon W. 1987. *A Concise History of the British Virgin Islands*. New York: Falcon Publications International.

PKF Consulting. 1992. *The British Virgin Islands Tourism and Cruiseship Study*. Prepared for the Office of the Chief Minister, British Virgin Islands. Miami, Florida.

"The Population Situation." In *About Our Country*. Road Town: Development Planning Unit, Government of the British Virgin Islands. http://dpu.gov.vg/AboutOurCountry/PopulationSituation.htm.

Potter, Marcia. 2006. "Los Cocolos y Los Cocolits—Finding a Place in the British Virgin Islands Dominican Republic Exchange." In *Beyond Walls: Multidisciplinary Perspectives*, Vol. 2, *British Virgin Islands Conference, May 26–28 2005*, edited by Simone Augier and Marcia Potter, 56–63. Trinidad and Tobago: University of the West Indies School of Continuing Studies.

Pratt, Mary Louise. 1992. *Imperial Eyes: Travel Writing and Transculturation*. New York: Routledge.

"PRC Remains Most Attractive Destination of FDI, BVI Ranks 2nd among FDI Sources." 2008. *British Virgin Islands Business News*. June 17. http://bvioffshoreibc.blogspot.com/2008/06/prc-remains-most-attractive-destination.html#links.

"The Present Situation Has Implications for Tourism Development." 1996. In *National Integrated Development Strategy*. Road Town: Development Planning Unit, Government of the British Virgin Islands. http://dpu.gov.vg/Plans/NIDS/PresentSituation.htm.

Pruitt, Deborah, and Suzanne LaFont. 1995. "For Love and Money: Romance Tourism in Jamaica." *Annals of Tourism Research* 22 (2): 422–440.

"Public Sector Investment Programme 2003–2007." 2003. Road Town: Development Planning Unit, Government of the British Virgin Islands. http://dpu.gov.vg/Public-Investment/PublicInvestment/GovernmentAgenda/50.htm.

Putley, Julian. 2007. "A Glimpse into the Past: History of the BVI." In *Experience the British Virgin Islands 2007*, edited by BVI Chamber of Commerce and Hotel Association, 14–17. Miami: HCP/Aboard Publishing.

Raas, Lex. 2007. "The World's Premiere Sailing Destination." *Business BVI 2007 Edition*, 67–69, 94. Road Town: Oyster Publications.

"Redesign August Festival." 1996. *BVI Beacon*, August 15, 3.

Report of the Virgin Islands Constitutional Commissioners. 2005. Road Town: Development Planning Unit, Government of the British Virgin Islands.

Rhymer, Elihu. 1992. "Political Development of the British Virgin Islands over the Past 25 Years." In *1967–1992 Challenge and Change: A Glimpse at the Past and a Look towards the Future*, edited by Office of the Chief Minister, 42–45. Road Town: Government of the British Virgin Islands.

Rojek, Chris. [1997] 2000. "Indexing, Dragging and the Social Construction of Tourist Sights." In *Touring Cultures: Transformations of Travel and Theory*, edited by Chris Rojek and John Urry, 52–74. New York: Routledge.

Rosaldo, Renato. 1989. *Culture and Truth*. Boston: Beacon Press.

Russell, Catherine. 1999. *Experimental Ethnography: The Work of Film in the Age of Video*. Durham: Duke University Press.

Said, Edward W. 1994. *Culture and Imperialism*. New York: Vintage.

Scott, Nancy, and Simon Scott. 1993. *Cruising Guide to the Virgin Islands*. Dunedin, Fla.: Cruising Guide Publications.

Secretary of State for Foreign and Commonwealth Affairs. 1994. *British Virgin Islands: Report of the Constitutional Commissioners 1993*. London: HMSO.

Segal, Daniel A. 1991. "'The European': Allegories of Racial Purity." *Anthropology Today* 7 (5): 7–9.

———. 1993. "'Race' and 'Colour' in Pre-Independence Trinidad and Tobago." In *Trinidad Ethnicity*, edited by Kevin Yelvington, 81–115. New York: Macmillan.

———. 1994. "Living Ancestors: Nationalism and the Past in Post-Colonial Trinidad and Tobago." In *Remapping Memory: The Politics of TimeSpace*, edited by J. Boyarin, 221–240. Minneapolis: University of Minnesota Press.

Segal, Daniel, and Richard Handler. 1992. "How European Is Nationalism?" *Social Analysis* 32: 1–15.

Selwyn, Tom. 1993. "Peter Pan in South East Asia: Views from the Brochures." In *Tourism in South East Asia*, edited by Michael Hitchcock, Victor T. King, and Michael Parnwell, 117–138. New York and London: Routledge.

———, ed. 1996. *The Tourist Image: Myths and Myth Making in Tourism*. Chichester: John Wiley and Sons.

Shacochis, Bob. 1993. "The Tropics." *Outside Magazine*, March, 74–75.

Sheller, Mimi. 2003. *Consuming the Caribbean: From Arawaks to Zombies*. New York: Routledge.

———. 2004. "Demobilizing and Remobilizing Caribbean Paradise." In *Tourism Mobilities*, edited by Mimi Sheller and John Urry, 13–21. New York: Routledge.

Sheller, Mimi, and John Urry. 2004. "Places to Play, Places in Play." In *Tourism Mobilities*, edited by Mimi Sheller and John Urry, 1–10. New York: Routledge

Sitney, P. Adams. 1979. *Visionary Film: The American Avant-Garde, 1943–1978*. 2nd ed. New York: Oxford University Press.

Smith, Chris. 2007. "Own a Piece of Paradise" In *Experience the British Virgin Islands 2007*, edited by BVI Chamber of Commerce and Hotel Association, 86–89. Miami: HCP/Aboard Publishing.

Smith, Henry. 1974. "Introducing . . . Biras Creek." *BVI Welcome Guide* 3 (4): 2–4.

Smith, Ian. n.d. "The British Virgin Islands MacroEconomy." *About Our Country*. Road Town: Development Planning Unit, Government of the British Virgin Islands. http://dpu.gov.vg/AboutOurCountry/MacroEconomy.htm.

Smith, Orlando. 2006a. "Constitutional Advancement Fundamental to Territory's Development." Speech by Chief Minister Hon. Dr. D. Orlando Smith. Road Town: Chief Minister's Office, Government of the British Virgin Islands.

———. 2006b. "State of the Territory." Address by Chief Minister Honourable Dr. D. Orlando Smith. Road Town: Office of the Chief Minister, Government of the British Virgin Islands.

———. 2007a. "A New Day in the BVI." Address by Chief Minister Honourable Dr. D. Orlando Smith, OBE. Ceremony to Celebrate the Virgin Islands Constitution Order 2007. Central Administration Complex, July 3, 2007.

———. 2007b. "Chief Minister's Letter." In *Experience the British Virgin Islands*, edited by BVI Chamber of Commerce and Hotel Association, 2. Miami: HCP/Aboard Publishing.

———. 2009. "Statement from the Leader of the Opposition Hon. Dr. Orlando Smith." *BVI News*, April 9. http://www.bvinews.com/main.asp?Search=1&ArticleID=29 20&SectionID=5&SubSectionID=36&S=1.

Smith, Valene L. 1989a. *Hosts and Guests: The Anthropology of Tourism*. 2nd ed. Philadelphia: University of Pennsylvania Press.

———. 1989b. "Introduction." In *Hosts and Guests: The Anthropology of Tourism*. 2nd ed., edited by Valene L. Smith, 1–19. Philadelphia: University of Pennsylvania Press.

"Social Issues: Immigration." 1996. In *National Tourism Development Plan*. Road Town: Development Planning Unit, Government of the British Virgin Islands. http://dpu. gov.vg/Plans/NIDS/NIDSPOPULATION.htm#Immigration.

Spivak, Gayatri. 1987. *In Other Worlds: Essays in Cultural Politics*. New York: Methuen.

Stewart, Susan. 1993. *On Longing: Narratives of the Miniature, the Gigantic, the Souvenir, the Collection*. Durham: Duke University Press.

Stoutt, Elmore. 2000. "Captain What's Your Cargo? (narration)." *Elmore Stoutt, The Fungi Master: Welcome to the BVI*. CD. Jacksonville, Fla.: Anvil Studios.

———. 2007. "Fungi Music: A BVI Cultural Expression." *Business BVI 2007 Edition*, 80–85. Road Town: Oyster Publications.

Strachan, Ian Gregory. 2002. *Paradise and Plantation: Tourism and Culture in the Anglophone Caribbean*. Charlottesville: University of Virginia Press.

"Tequila Gives Birth to a New Country." 1995. *San Bernardino Sun*. August 19, B12.

Thomas, Deborah. 2002. "Democratizing Dance: Institutional Transformation and Hegemonic Re-ordering in Postcolonial Jamaica." *Cultural Anthropology* 17 (4): 512–550.

———. 2004. *Modern Blackness: Nationalism, Globalization, and the Politics of Culture in Jamaica*. Durham: Duke University Press.

Thompson, Krista A. 2006. *An Eye for the Tropics: Tourism, Photography, and Framing the Caribbean Picturesque*. Durham: Duke University Press.

Titley, Gavan. 2001. "Global Theory and Touristic Encounters." *Irish Communications Review* 8: 79–87.

Todman, McWelling. 1992. "Foreword." In *1967–1992 Challenge and Change: A Glimpse at the Past and a Look towards the Future*, edited by Chief Minister's Office, 5–6. Road Town: Government of the British Virgin Islands.

Torgovnick, Marianna. 1990.*Gone Primitive: Savage Intellects, Modern Lives*. Chicago: University of Chicago Press.

"Tourism Creates Both Positive and Negative Impacts." 1996. *National Tourism Development Plan*. Road Town: Development Planning Unit, Government of the British Virgin Islands. http://dpu.gov.vg/Plans/NIDS/TourismStrategy.htm.

"Tourism Product and Infrastructure Strategy." 1996. *National Tourism Development Plan*. Road Town: Development Planning Unit, Government of the British Virgin Islands. http://dpu.gov.vg/Plans/NIDS/TourismProduct.htm.

"Tourism Summary." Road Town: Development Planning Unit, Government of the British Virgin Islands. http://dpu.gov.vg/Indicators/tourism/TourismSummary. html.

"Tourist Board Chairman Addresses New Rotary Club on Impact of Global Economic Crisis on BVI Tourism." 2009. *BVI News*. April 7, 2009. http://www.bvinews.com/main.asp?Search=1&ArticleID=2909&SectionID=5&SubSectionID=30&S=1.

"Towards Sustainable Development." 1994. *Sustainable Development for Small Island Developing States*. Road Town: Development Planning Unit, Government of the British Virgin Islands. http://dpu.gov.vg/Publications/sustainDev/2.htm.

Trotman, Jeff. 2006. "BVI Festival Is Not Carnival, Still Have Fun." *BVI Standpoint*, August 1, 1.

Trouillot, Michel-Rolph. 1992. "The Caribbean Region: An Open Frontier in Anthropological Theory." *Annual Reviews in Anthropology* 21: 19–42.

———. 1995. *Silencing the Past: Power and the Production of History*. Boston: Beacon.

Turnbull, Patricia. 1992. *Rugged Vessels: Poems by Patricia Turnbull*. Road Town: Archipelago Press.

———. 2002. "Hustling to Host: Everyday Practice, Pedagogy and Participation in British Virgin Islands Tourism." PhD dissertation, University of Toronto.

———. 2006. "Everyday Practice, Pedagogy and Participation in Virgin Islands Tourism: An Interdisciplinary Perspective." In *Beyond Walls: Multidisciplinary Perspectives*, Vol. 2, *British Virgin Islands Conference, May 26–28 2005*, edited by Simone Augier and Marcia Potter, 100–112. Trinidad and Tobago: University of the West Indies School of Continuing Studies.

Turner, Terrence. 2002. "Representation, Politics, and Cultural Imagination in Indigenous Video: General Points and Kayapo Examples." In *Media Worlds: Anthropology on New Terrain*, edited by Faye Ginsburg, Lila Abu-Lughod, and Brian Larkin, 75–89. Berkeley: University of California Press.

2007 British Virgin Islands Tourism Directory. 2007. Road Town: British Virgin Islands Tourist Board.

"2008: The Year in Review." 2008. *BVI Beacon On Line*. December 16, 2008. http://bvibeacon.com/main/index.php?option=com_content&task=view&id=1835&Itemid=5.

Uhuru, Sowande. 2008. "Does the BVI Have an Immigration Crisis?" *BVI News*. September. http://www.bvinews.com/main.asp?SectionID=21&SubSectionID=39&ArticleID=516&TM=65108.55.

Urry, John. 1990. *The Tourist Gaze*. London: Sage.

Vanterpool, Hugo F. 1995. *Dusk to Dawn: Herald of the Virgin Islands*. Kingston, Jamaica: Kingston Publishers.

Vanterpool, Judith. 2004. "Hidden Treasures: Accommodations in the BVI." In *Experience the British Virgin Islands*, edited by BVI Chamber of Commerce and Hotel Association, 82–84. Miami: HCP/Aboard Publishing.

Varlack, Pearl I. 1992. Address Delivered at the Recognition Ceremony in Celebration of Twenty-Five Years of Ministerial Government in the (British) Virgin Islands. Road Town: British Virgin Islands Government.

Varlack, Pearl, and Norwell Harrigan. 1977. *The Virgins: A Descriptive and Historical Profile*. St. Thomas: Caribbean Research Institute, College of the Virgin Islands.

Verdery, Katherine. 1996. "Whither 'Nation' and 'Nationalism'?" In *Mapping the Nation*, edited by Gopal Balakrishnan, 226–234. London: Verso.

"VI Readies for Likely G-20 Storm." 2009. *BVI Beacon Online*, March 25, 2009. http://bvibeacon.com/main/index.php?option=com_content&task=view&id=1974&Itemid=5.

The Virgin Islands (British) Constitution Order 2007. Statutory Instrument 2007 No. 1678, Caribbean and North Atlantic Territories. Road Town: Government of the British Virgin Islands. http://www.bvi.gov.vg/products.asp?iProd=129&iCat=15&hierarchy=0.

Waterston, Alisse, and Barbara Rylko-Baurer. 2007. "Out of the Shadows of History and Memory: Personal Family Narratives as Intimate Ethnography." In *The Shadow Side of Fieldwork*, edited by Athena McLean and Annette Leibing, 31–55. Malden, Mass.: Blackwell.

Wheatley, Jennie N. 1974. *Bohog Put in Gol' Teet'*. Cane Garden Bay, Tortola: Compu Rich Printing Services.

———. 1984. *Boysie and the Genips and Other Stories*. UNDP/UNESCO/AGFUND Multi-Island Project.

———. 1991. *Pass It On!: A Treasury of Virgin Islands Tales*. St. Martin, Caribbean: House of Nehesi Publishers.

———. 2004. "Cultural Inspirations." In *Experience the British Virgin Islands*, edited by BVI Chamber of Commerce and Hotel Association, 52–55. Miami: HCP/Aboard Publishing.

———. 2005a. *Timmy Turtle Runs Away*. Road Town: WSTD Publishing.

———. 2005b. *Danielle's Trunk*. Cane Garden Bay, Tortola: Compu Rich Printing Services.

———. 2005c. *Arianna Likes to Read*. Road Town: WSTD Publishing.

———. 2006. *Who Is the Best in the Garden?* Cane Garden Bay, Tortola: Compu Rich Printing Services.

———. 2009. *Along the Road*. East End, Tortola: BookSurge.

"Why I'd Visit the B.V.I." 1989. In *Tourism Awareness through Education: Education Week March 12–19 1989*, edited by Department of Education and Culture. Road Town: Government of the British Virgin Islands.

"Why They Won, Lost." *BVI Beacon On Line*. August 23. http://bvibeacon.com/main/index.php?option=com_content&task=view&id=968&Itemid=5.

Wildman, Kim. 2004. "Picturing Coffee Bay: The Visual Politics of Tourist Representations." *Postamble* 1 (1): 2–10.

Wilkins, Andrew. 2008. "H. Lavity Stoutt Honoured by His Beloved Country." *British Virgin Islands Standpoint On Line*. March 8. http://www.vistandpoint.com/content/view/1022/29/.

Wilkinson, P. F. 1989. "Strategies for Tourism in Island Microstates." *Annals of Tourism Research* 16: 153–177.

Williams, Brackette F. 1989. "A Class Act: Anthropology and the Race to Nation across Ethnic Terrain." *Annual Review of Anthropology* 18: 401–444.

———. 1991. *Stains on My Name, War in My Veins: Guyana and the Politics of Cultural Struggle*. Durham: Duke University Press.

————. 1993. "The Impact of the Precepts of Nationalism on the Concept of Culture: Making Grasshoppers of Naked Apes." *Cultural Critique* (Spring): 143–191.

Williamson, Judith. 1986. "Woman Is an Island: Femininity and Colonization." In *Studies in Entertainment: Critical Approaches to Mass Culture*, edited by Tania Modleski, 99–144. Bloomington: Indiana University Press.

"Would-be Smugglers Developer Pulls Out" 2008. *BVI Beacon on Line*, May 7. http://bvibeacon.com/main/index.php?option=com_content&task=view&id=1437&Itemid=5.

Index

ABOUT THE AUTHOR

COLLEEN BALLERINO COHEN is a professor of anthropology and women's studies at Vassar College. She has conducted research in the British Virgin Islands (BVI) for over twenty years, on the affect of tourism upon national development and identity and on Festival as a site for expressing national identity. Her articles on these topics have appeared in *Social Analysis*, *American Ethnologist*, and *Annals of Tourism Research*, as well as in book that she coedited with Richard Wilk and Beverly Stoltje, *Beauty Queens on the Global Stage* (1996). In addition, Cohen has produced three ethnographic videos in collaboration with native British Virgin Islander Kenne Hodge, on BVI tourism, on BVI Festival, and on BVI musical culture.